TH

Critical Global Health

Evidence, Efficacy, Ethnography

A SERIES EDITED BY VINCANNE ADAMS AND JOÃO BIEHL

The Impotence Epidemic

MEN'S MEDICINE AND SEXUAL DESIRE

IN CONTEMPORARY CHINA

Everett Yuehong Zhang

DUKE UNIVERSITY PRESS *Durham and London* 2015

© 2015 Duke University Press
Printed in the United States of America on acid-free paper ∞
Typeset in Carter & Cone Galliard by Tseng Information Systems, Inc.

Library of Congress Cataloging-in-Publication Data
Zhang, Everett.
The impotence epidemic : men's medicine and sexual desire in
contemporary China / Everett Yuehong Zhang.
pages cm—(Critical global health)
Includes bibliographical references and index.
ISBN 978-0-8223-5844-2 (hardcover : alk. paper)
ISBN 978-0-8223-5856-5 (pbk. : alk. paper)
ISBN 978-0-8223-7574-6 (e-book)
1. Impotence—Treatment—China. 2. Men—Sexual behavior—China.
3. Medicine, Chinese. I. Title. II. Series: Critical global health.
RC889.Z48 2015
616.6′92200951—dc23
2014025037

Cover design by Natalie F. Smith

To Arthur Kleinman

CONTENTS

ACKNOWLEDGMENTS

This book is a result of working with many, many people in various ways. My authorship of this book is the materialization of inspirations, collaborations, conversations, and help I have received in a period of more than a decade.

I am very grateful to the people for telling me about their bodily experiences and their struggles in life. Many encouraged me to probe into the pain and joy in their private lives that shed light on the changing China. In order to protect their privacy, I could not list their names here. But, my deep thanks go to every one of them.

From the very beginning of this project to its publication, I have been very fortunate to receive encouragement. Without the encouragement, this project would not have been brought to fruition. My proposal for this project was first greeted with enthusiasm and firm support from my advisers and teachers at Berkeley. Lawrence Cohen passionately encouraged me to explore in an open-minded way the topic that sounded much odder and therefore much more difficult than it does today. He made me realize that any marginal or tabooed topic can become an exciting and precious anthropological opportunity. Aihwa Ong provided sound analytical and emotional support that, among other uplifting implications, helped solidly define this project from the perspective of gender politics. Lydia Liu offered comments on the issues of the Chinese body and deserves my thanks. I want to thank Paul Rabinow for stimulating me to learn theories and be concerned about the issue of modernity.

Arthur Kleinman's timely and farsighted guidance on conducting research has become an integral part of this book. His studies of neurasthenia in China in the aftermath of the Cultural Revolution were an immediate inspiration for me to think about the rise of impotence as a new epidemic in the reform China. His vision and moral support have sustained me throughout the crucial times when I experienced ups and downs with my efforts to tell the story of China through the body. I am also indebted to James (Woody) L. Watson, Rubie Watson, Byron Good, and Mary-Jo Good for kindly offering a wide range of advice and support.

This project opened up a horizon for intellectual exploration. Just as I was compelled to engage with the social and biological body, so was I lured into the learning of traditional Chinese medicine (TCM). Many doctors— of both Chinese medicine and biomedicine—have stirred up my passion about every detail of medical practices. Among them, Ma Xiaonian, Zhang Shuwu, Wang Jiuyuan, Wang Qi, Cao Kaiyong, Qin Guozheng, Chang Degui, and Wang Zhitian made my fieldwork a rewarding process of learning, both about the practice and about the textual tradition. Zheng Jingsheng and Zhu Jianping in the Chinese Academy of TCM (now the Chinese Academy of Chinese Medical Science) shared with me their conceptual and historical insights.

In the traditions of social, historical, and anthropological studies of Chinese medicine in English, I have benefited greatly from having conversations with Charlotte Furth and Judith Farquhar and engaging with their works.

I benefited from conversations with Pan Suiming, along with Ma Xiaonian, both having played an important role in promoting the studies of sexuality in China.

I am indebted to Robert Weller for my early education in anthropology and for his continuous support for my projects. My development of the topic was due in part to Mayfair Yang's suggestion on studying Chinese masculinity. Her help with my writing of early drafts is appreciated as well.

My research received encouragement and moral support from many teachers, colleagues, and friends on various occasions. Some of them read the drafts, some of them discussed ideas with me and made suggestions, some of them invited me to give a talk on behalf of their institutions, some of them shared their experience of teaching part of the book manuscript that was either published or not, and some of them offered moral support. I thank them all. They are Vincanne Adams, Stephen Bokenkamp, Stanley Brandes, Pheng Cheah, Chen Bo, Nancy Chen, Thomas Csordas, Dai Jinhua, Virginia Dominguez, Wilt Edema, Fan Lizhu, Didier Fassin, Michael Fischer, Sara Friedman, Duana Fullwiley, Merle Goldman, Susan Green-

halgh, Matthew Gutmann, Marta Hanson, Gail Hershatter, Michael Herz-
feld, Sandra Hyde, Michael Kimmel, Matthew Kohrman, Shigehisa Kuriyama, Jender Lee, Li Dahua, Liang Xiaoyan, Sean Lei, Liu Xin, Liu Xun,
Margaret Lock, Richard Madsen, Keith McMahon, Pan Tianshu, Elizabeth
Perry, Louisa Schein, Nancy Scheper-Hughes, Shu-mei Shih, Kaja Silver-
man, Anna Sun, Giovanni Vitiello, the late Frederic Wakeman, Wang Ming-
ming, Jung-Kwang Wen, Ara Wilson, Wu Fei, Xiao Yang, Xu Xinjian, Yunxiang Yan, Yang Yusheng, Paola Zamperini, Zhang Lan, Zhao Xudong, and
Xueping Zhong.

At different institutions, I was fortunate to be with groups of colleagues
and friends during my writing. At Berkeley, conversations with Damani
Partridge and Alberto Sanchez were helpful. In the writing group, I bene-
fited from communication with Angela Beattie, Nana Yaw Boailtey, Karen
Greene, Uriel Grazenkovsky, Anand Pandian, and Rashimi Sadana. I thank
Berkeley's Center for Studies of Sexual Culture for offering the writing fel-
lowship. At Harvard, conversations with postdoctoral fellows Sarah Pinto,
Sarah Horton, Chris Dole, Erica James, Carlos Rojas, Shelley Hawks, Eileen
Otis, Hsiu-hua Shen, and Dan Shao contributed to the development of this
project. I was fortunate to develop friendships with Yao Guizhong, Chen
Jue, Cheng Wenhong, Albert S. Yeung, and Lawrence Park. Shared inter-
ests in traditional Chinese medicine resulted in productive communications
with T. J. Hinrichs, Bridie Andrews, and Ted Kaptchuck. For my time at
SUNY Buffalo, I want to thank Donald Pollock, Barbara Tedlock, Dennis
Tedlock, Roger des Forges, Yu Jiyuan, and Vasiliki Neofotistos for their
support.

At Princeton, I have been very fortunate to be part of the vibrant intellectual community. I am particularly indebted to Benjamin Elman and Susan
Naquin for kindly offering intellectual and moral support. Ben has offered
guidance and encouragement for my development. Sue has been very kind
to offer advice in many aspects. João Biehl has offered great help in refining
the manuscript with his intellectual spirit, his keen attention to critical
issues, and his kindness. His suggestion about the book title is appreciated.
Dave Leheny kindly offered meticulous comments on a part of the manuscript and important support. Carol Greenhouse has paid attention to my
development and always kindly offers encouragement. I want to thank Amy
Borovoy and Steven Chung for sharing the experience of teaching a chapter of this book in the published form and their support. I want to thank
my colleagues in EAS — Janet Chen, Martin Collcutt, Thomas Conlan, Shel-

don Garon, David Howell, Martin Kern, Seiichi Makino, Willard Peterson, and Atsuko Ueda for conversations and support. I thank Chih-p'ing Chou for expressing his encouragement about the progress of the book and his support. I also thank John Borneman, Thomas Christensen, Angela Creager, Janet Currie, Lisa Davis, Jill Dolan, William Jordan, Stanley Katz, Jerome Silbergeld, Stephen Teiser, Keith Wailoo, and Lynn White for various support.

I am indebted to Didier Fassin for his generous efforts to support my development while I was a member of the Institute for Advanced Study. I also thank Joan Scott, Michael Walzer, Nicola de Cosmo, and Danielle Allen for conversations and support.

The three anonymous reviewers at Duke University Press offered very perceptive, meticulous, and sharp comments on the manuscript, and generated inspiring insights that helped strengthen this book.

Many, many of my schoolmates and friends in China deserve my special thanks for all kinds of support they offered when I was conducting fieldwork, particularly in some of the difficult times. I very much depended on the networks of many of my friends to extend my contact with people and approach such a difficult topic. But the list is too long to be included here in full. My wholehearted thanks go to everyone.

Ken Wissoker at Duke University Press has demonstrated intellectual passion and professional acumen that helped me turn the manuscript into what he would call "a smart book." I hope this result measures up to his appraisal and his expectation. I also want to thank Jade Brooks for all the assistance she has offered.

My son Kai's (Keyang in Chinese) birth and growing-up have offered much joy and inspiration for my intellectual development. My parents deserve thanks for being always concerned about my work, even though they never expected me to say so.

I am indebted to Linda Forman for her fine copyediting of the manuscript.

An early version of chapter 1 was published in *American Ethnologist*, a part of chapter 2 was published in *Body and Society*, and a part of chapter 6 was published in *Medical Anthropology*.

The Impotence Epidemic in China

In both Beijing and Chengdu in the late 1990s, concern about *yangwei* (陽痿, the shrinking of *yang*, i.e., male sexual impotence) was more visible and "contagious" than it had been during the Maoist period more than twenty years earlier. Flyers on lampposts along city streets advertised clinics that specialized in curing sexually transmitted diseases and male sexual dysfunction, and commercials appeared in the media touting *zhuangyang*, herbal tonics to cure impotence. Discussions of impotence in the media and on the Internet had become common. In the early 2000s, on a television program showcasing useful gadgets, the inventor of a new type of bicycle seat with a hole in its center boasted that the design would help reduce the risk of male impotence and make a huge contribution to Chinese people's sex lives, given that China is such a bicycle-oriented country.[1]

One Sunday afternoon in late 1999, I observed an especially vivid illustration of this "contagion" in public spaces, when *Television Clinic*, a call-in show on Beijing Television (BTV), aired a special program on erectile dysfunction (ED). The program was sponsored primarily by Pfizer, the pharmaceutical company. Three nationally known urologists answered callers' questions on two hotlines. During the one-hour program, they were inundated with calls and, unable to respond to all of the questions being raised, could only direct many callers to hospitals in Beijing where they could seek consultation or medical treatment for impotence. I observed the live broadcast from inside the TV studio. Four male assistants took the phone calls, jotting down callers' questions and then passing them on to an employee of Pfizer's Beijing office. He selected questions for the three urologists to answer. The four assistants later chatted with each other about their brief conversations with callers who had sounded especially eager for advice. One imitated a

Figure 1.1: Three nationally known sexual education experts or urologists answering questions about male sexual dysfunction through a hotline on the program "Television Clinic" of Beijing Television Station (BTV). The anchor person is on the far left and the two persons on the far right are taking phone calls.

caller who lamented, "My situation is bad . . . I can't do it, however pretty she is!" Another assistant said, "Many women called in, asking about their husbands' problems!" As the phone calls had poured into the studio, one of the three camera operators, a middle-aged man, exclaimed to me, "ED is becoming an epidemic!"

Various lines of evidence confirm the growing prominence of male impotence in post-Mao China. First, although they appeared as far back as the 1970s, the clinic flyers mentioned above had, by the 1990s, become common sights in the urban landscape. The clinics advertised by the flyers were often back-alley operations. Those who ran them were uncertified doctors, considered by many as, at best, *jiming goudao zhi tu* (those who crow like a cock or snatch like a dog, i.e., get up to petty tricks) or, at worst, *jianghu pianzi* (charlatans fooling round). A strong stigma was attached to such clinics.

They were not impotent men's only recourse, however. Since the 1980s, *nanke* (men's medicine), a new division of Chinese medicine that specialized in treating impotence and other male sexual problems, had emerged in hospitals throughout the country. By the end of the 1990s, nanke had become

Figure 1.2:
An advertisement for a zhuangyang patent capsule. The central lines read: "Taking only three pills, you could get it up."

Figure 1.3:
An advertisement for a clinic on a lamppost in a back alley in Beijing, touting rapid efficacy of curing impotence, premature ejaculation, and sexually transmitted diseases.

Figure 1.4: An advertisement for a clinic in Beijing.

a widely established specialty, bringing the concern about impotence out of back alleys and into mainstream hospitals.

A second line of evidence involves literary representations of impotence. In the early 1980s, the well-known novel *Half a Man Is Woman*, by Zhang Xianliang, portrayed a political prisoner's experience of impotence in the Maoist period. Since then, such portrayals have proliferated. In movies such as *Furongzhen*, *Qiuju daguansi*, and *Ermo* and in novels such as *The Rabbit in the Grassy Ground of de Gaulle International Airport*, *The Defunct Capital*, and *Shanghai Baby*, impotence is evoked as a symbol not only of damaged masculine capacity but also of the crises experienced by different groups of people during the post-Mao reform, indexing the shifting social context in which impotence has occurred.

A third line of evidence is the marked increase in sexual joking, or *kouyin xianxiang* (the phenomenon of the lustful mouth, i.e., intensely erotic conversations). The sharing of erotic jokes has in recent years become a veritable fad thanks to cell phone text messaging. The joking often focuses on impotence. For example, one private entrepreneur joked, "Xianzai shi wanshang ying bushui, zaoshang ying buqi" (Nowadays, men just do not want to go to bed in the evening and have difficulty getting up in the morning). "Getting up" is a pun referring to involuntary nocturnal erections (not experiencing them is considered a sign of the decline of potency or of impotence). This man was describing the lifestyle of entrepreneurs and businessmen, who spend much of their time *gouduing* ("thickening" relationships with) state officials or business partners, attending banquets, and seeing prostitutes in the evening. Another businessman joked, "Jiating zuoye kao chiyao; kewai zuoye kao ganjue" (Nowadays, a man relies on drugs to do "homework"— i.e., have sex with his wife—and he relies on feelings or sensations to do "outside work"—i.e., have affairs or see prostitutes).

What is one to make of this "epidemic"? Have more Chinese men suffered from impotence over the past 20 years than in previous years? These two questions call our attention to the close relationship between the rise of the epidemic and the tremendous changes that Chinese society has undergone in the postsocialist era. In this book, I address that relationship, asking whether massive socioeconomic changes account for the epidemic.

Countering the "Biological Turn"

Impotence has historically aroused public concerns in various parts of the world. For example, in seventeenth- and eighteenth-century France as well as in other parts of Catholic Europe, the clergy would grant a divorce to a married couple when presented with evidence that the husband was impotent. This rather public show of investigation and trial was intended to ensure reproduction and thus protect the "sacred nature" of the family (Darmon 1986; McLaren 2007). In the eighteenth century, impotence also became a public issue in Europe partly because of rising concern about masturbation, which was perceived to cause all kinds of problems (including impotence) that led to degeneracy and depopulation (McLaren 2007; Laqueur 2003). More recently, in the early 1970s, a wave of discussion about impotence washed through the media in the United States, the cover story of one issue of *Esquire* magazine asking, "The Impotence Boom: Has It Hit You Yet?" (Nobile 1972). In this case, concern allegedly reflected the increasing pressure on men's potency due to women's empowerment through the sexual revolution and the feminist movement. Historical concerns—about the weakening of the family and the "degeneracy" of the population—did not strike me as particularly relevant for understanding the impotence epidemic in China. Women's demand for sexual fulfillment, the putative reason for the "impotence boom" in the United States, offered suggestive interpretive clues but fell far short of accounting for China's epidemic, which was unprecedented in scale.

At first glance, the epidemic suggested that more Chinese men were suffering from impotence in the 1990s than had been the case two decades earlier. If true, how do we explain such an increase? I turned to existing studies for explanations. However, when I began my fieldwork in the late 1990s, I found that studies of impotence outside the fields of biology and psychology were rare and that there had been no ethnographies of impotence. Impotence was mentioned only in passing or euphemistically in a number of anthropological studies (e.g., Gregor 1977; Gilmore 1990; Herdt 1994; Parker 2009; Godelier 1986; Allison 1994; Cohen 1998), or it was presented as a consequence of undergoing special ritualistic bodily alterations, as in the case of India's third sex (Nanda 1998; Cohen 1995), a phenomenon limited to small groups of men. It was not until the 2000s that ethnographic presentations of impotence began to go beyond anecdotes and become a small but integral part of anthropological studies of masculinity, sexuality, and HIV/AIDS (e.g., Gutmann 2007; Frank 2002). Even in "masculinity studies," one could find few examples that explored the experiences of impotent men.[2] The invention of Viagra in the late 1990s spurred studies of impotence in many fields of the social sciences and the humanities—among them, anthropology, sociology, gender studies, cultural studies, public health, history of science and medicine, philosophy, and communication (e.g., McLaren 2007; Potts and Tiefer 2006; Fishman 2006; Loe 2004; Botz-Bornstein 2011). However, those studies focused more on symbolic representations of the social and cultural effects of anti-impotence technologies than on the bodily experiences of impotent men, with the exception of scattered journal articles (e.g., Potts 2004; Potts et al. 2003).

While psychology and biology have contributed a great deal to our understanding of impotence, their limitations are obvious. The disciplines with the *psy* prefix, for example—psychoanalysis, psychology, psychotherapy, psychiatry, psychological counseling, and so on—tend to lose sight of social context in their etiological analyses of impotence. Below, I provide a brief review of the contributions and shortcomings of psychological and biological approaches to impotence and of the shifting dominance between them.

In his clinical practice in the early twentieth century, Sigmund Freud observed what he called "psychic impotence," which he believed to be "much more widespread than is supposed" (1989b:398). Psychic impotence occurred, he believed, because "the affectionate and sensual currents in love" failed to coincide (398). Male adult sexuality was overshadowed by the Oedipus complex developed in childhood, when the son's sensuality became incestuously fixed on the mother. The result was that, later in life, affection and sensual desire could not merge to enable a man to complete sexual intercourse, or affection was rendered precarious and was disrupted by a lack of sensuality, leading to impotence. Those who suffered from psychic impotence were caught in an impossible situation: "Where they love they do not desire and where they desire they cannot love" (397). Despite Freud's very perceptive insight that family life was the social matrix for the formation of sexual habit, he interpreted impotence as "a universal affliction under civilization" rather than "a disorder confined to some individuals" (398) and as a predominantly psychic abnormality. Thus, his insight was stripped of its power by his presumptions of the essential nature of the Oedipus complex and of increasing repression under civilization and by his dismissal of the rich variety of social forces that might contribute to the condition but that did not fit his thesis of civilization's sexually repressive effect.

Wilhelm Stekel, an Austrian psychoanalyst and onetime collaborator of Freud, wrote a two-volume book on male impotence based on over 120 clinical cases. While he provided a wealth of detail, he did not go beyond the Freudian tradition (Stekel 1959 [1927]; see chapter 3, this volume). Psychoanalytical and psychological approaches continued to develop in the decades after Stekel, culminating in William H. Masters and Virginia E. Johnson's (1970) sensitization therapy in the 1950s and 1960s with its emphasis on strengthening interpersonal relationships to cure impotence (see chapter 4). By and large, for most of the twentieth century, the psychological view dominated the study and treatment of impotence (e.g., Rosen and Leiblum 1992; Kaplan 1974). Sexual therapists did pay attention to more immediate social conditions (e.g., the influence of family background and religious beliefs) but seldom related impotence to broader social and cultural conditions and changes.

Psychology's dominance began to wane in the 1970s, undermined by rapid biomedical development (see chapter 7) that spurred widespread medicalization or, more specifically, biomedicalization of human conditions and problems (Lock and Nguyen 2010; Clarke, Mamo, Fosket, Fishman, and Shim 2010). Tom Lue, a renowned U.S. urologist, pointed out in 2000 that the medical field of impotence had taken "a biological turn": "The past three decades have witnessed a dramatic change in the treatment of men with erectile dysfunction. Treatment options have progressed from psychosexual therapy and penile prostheses (1970s), through revascularization, vacuum constriction devices, and intracavernous injection therapy (1980s), to transurethral and oral drug therapy (1990s)" (2000:1812).

The pendulum thus swung to the biological side in diagnosis and treatment of impotence, reaching its peak when Viagra, an anti-impotence drug, was invented in the late 1990s in the United States. It was introduced into the Chinese market in 2000. Reflecting this new development, one of the most prominent statements about the etiology of impotence asserted that "the penis [in the context of] a rigid erection is the equivalent of a hydraulic system" (Goldstein 1998). Curing impotence, from the biological perspective, requires solving problems related to the blood dynamic system in the human male—ensuring blood's unimpeded delivery to the penis at the proper pressure—just like fixing a hydraulic system for irrigating crops. With the invention of Viagra, then, the pendulum swinging between psychology and biology seemed finally to stop on the side of biology. Human potency was now largely understood as "penile erection," which "is a *neurovascular event* modulated by psychological factors and hormonal status" (Lue 2000:1802, emphasis added).[3]

With this biological turn, two views dominated interpretation of the impotence epidemic in China. Urologists argued that, because the standard of living had risen, people's intake of fat and sugar had increased, potentially increasing the risk of cardiovascular diseases and diabetes, which are closely associated with impotence. The psychological explanation, represented in the country by newly emerging professionals in psychotherapy and related fields, maintained that as the pressure increased to make money in the consumer society created by post-Mao economic reform, male potency fluctuated. While the two perspectives touched on the change that was taking place in Chinese society, they nonetheless were problematic. First, they assumed an increase in the incidence of impotence in the population, which had not been proven. Second, they treated impotence primarily as a neurovascular event with a psychological layer attached to it.

Traditional Chinese medicine (TCM) had managed impotence for more than 2,000 years and had developed a systematic set of diagnostics and treatment long before the ideas of Western medicine (e.g., urology) and psychotherapy were introduced into China. TCM did not, however, develop a formal specialty focused on impotence until nanke (men's medicine) came into being in the 1980s, a symbol of the epidemic (see chapter 1). Nanke offered its own explanations for the epidemic. Two perspectives dominated—one focused on *shen* (the kidney) and the other on *gan* (the liver)—though both paid attention to the adverse impact of changing lifestyles on the male body, in accordance with Chinese bodily cosmology (see chapters 5 and 6). But, under the pressure of biomedicalization, TCM's concern about the impact of social context on impotence tended to be muted.

My anthropological training pushed me to see the impotence epidemic as more than a biological phenomenon and impotence itself as more than a neurovascular event. First, I drew on the trademark contribution of anthropology to studies of diseases and illnesses—understanding the social and cultural contexts and conditions in which diseases occur (e.g., Lock and Nguyen 2010; Kleinman, Das, and Lock 1997; Good 1994; Good et al. 2010; Scheper-Hughes and Lock 1987; Turner 2008). Arthur Kleinman's (1986) demonstration that widespread neurasthenia in China had been associated with political and social conditions in the aftermath of the Cultural Revolution offered an immediate inspiration for exploring the impotence epidemic beyond the "neurovascular event" thesis. Judith Farquhar (2002) pointed to impotence as a symptom of China's transformation, calling for a close examination of how the impotence epidemic had accompanied profound changes—such as decollectivization, privatization, individualization, and commercialization (see, e.g., Kleinman et al. 2011; Yan 2010; Zhang and Ong 2008; Hansen and Svarverud 2010; Liu 2009; Rofel 2007)—that might have had an impact on people's sexual lives.

Second, unlike those who view impotence as a specifically male neurovascular event, I explored both men's and women's experiences with the condition. Experience (*tiyan* in Chinese) is not simply a combination of the biological and the psychological but also includes forces that the body incorporates and feels (Heidegger 1962; Merleau-Ponty 1962; Bourdieu 1977; Csordas 1993; Kleinman 1999).

The English phrase *bodily experience* is similar in meaning to the Chinese term *tiyan* (體驗, to feel with the body).[4] *Ti* (體) means "body," and *yan* (驗) connotes "proving," "examining," and "testing." But the English term *body* does not capture the full connotation of the word *ti*, nor does the double-syllable phrase *shenti* (身體) in Chinese have the same general referent as the English term "the body."[5] A number of studies have pointed out such a gap between shen, ti, or shenti in classical Chinese and the "body." Shen, ti or shenti tend to be open to connotations such as the personhood, the whole person, and even the "being" as seen in the phrases such as shenshi (personal history), shenfen (status), zhongshen (the whole life), and so on (Elvin 1993;

Ames 1993; Brownell 1995; Kohrman 2005; Jullien 2007; Y. Zhang 2007). This linguistic openness of shen, ti, or shenti embodies Chinese philosophical understanding of the integration of human and the universe on the one hand and the practical existence of human beings within the world on the other hand, which is lost in their translation into the body. The whole genre of the anthropological studies of Chinese medicine testifies to just that. In contrast, the term *body* commonly refers to "a discrete given, an independent and isolated object" (Kuriyama 1999:262) and is more a definition of the post-Enlightenment entity than of the ancient Greek. There was no "shenti" in ancient China in the sense of "the body" today.

However, perhaps as the result of the vernacular revolution in the early twentieth century in which double-syllable phrases tended to replace their single-syllable classical Chinese antecedents, the popular usage of shenti in modern Chinese coincided with the increasing influence of the Western anatomy-based notion of the "body" and replaced the meanings of *shen, ti,* or *shenti* in the bodily cosmology of Chinese medicine, Chinese philosophy, and Daoism. As a result, shenti today on many occasions refers to the body. In this book, for the sake of convenience, I use the body to refer to shenti in general but remind the reader from time to time of the gap between the body and shenti, however narrowed it has become.

Since no epidemiological study of impotence in China was available, we are not sure that many more men suffered from impotence in the post-Mao era than in previous periods. Yet the impossibility of confirming an increase in incidence of male impotence in the population, instead of mystifying the epidemic, only opened up a new horizon for exploration of lived experience; the increasing visibility of impotence in and of itself pointed to a new way for me to think about the epidemic. I began to ask whether this increasing visibility had been driven by society's desire—men's as well as women's—to face it and seek its treatment. If so, how?

Recognizing Desire

In inquiring into what compelled men to seek medication for impotence, I was immediately drawn into the traumatic nature of their experience, because impotence was so commonly perceived as a death knell for masculinity. It was not unusual to hear an impotence patient say that he would rather die than continue to live with the condition. According to a survey I conducted, 66.9 percent of patients in Beijing and 57.4 percent of patients in Chengdu would choose to remain potent and die at 65 rather than live to 80 after suffering from impotence for decades.[6] Not surprisingly, many patients looked depressed (see chapters 1, 3, 4, and 7).

The shame associated with impotence derived from the thesis that impotence is a universally acknowledged, timeless, and context-free threat to essential masculinity. Because this essentialist view is hegemonic, the issue is singularly resistant to questioning and reflection. With few exceptions (e.g., Candib and Schmitt 1996 in the humanities and the anthropological studies cited in chapter 1), the literature on how impotence damages masculinity and thus generates unspeakable shame for a man is based more on assumptions than on careful inquiries. The stark contrast between the presumed centrality of potency to masculinity and the lack of empirical social scientific studies of men's experience of loss of potency (outside of clinical psychology) makes a study of impotence experience critically important. To demystify and destigmatize impotence and to question the perception that impotence spells death for one's masculinity, it is necessary to break through the "concerted euphemism" attached to it.

My sample of interviewees showed that impotence in China was not correlated with class, education, profession, or geographic region. Factoring out age, it seemed that, statistically, any man could become impotent.[7] Notably, however, the impotence epidemic appeared to be associated with drastic changes in the social world, revealing that the traumatic nature of impotence including the extreme shame associated with it could be socially and culturally produced.

Many impotence patients reported that they experienced disturbances and instability in their immediate lifeworlds at the time of symptom onset. For example, being laid off from state-owned enterprises during the restructuring of the economy from centralized to market-oriented was a painful experience for many men partly because they had never imagined such a thing, with its attendant decline in social status, could happen. Some men complained that they had been indoctrinated to serve under socialism and then been left behind by postsocialism. But their bodily experience of impotence was often a more powerful articulation than their verbal complaints of the unfairness of their loss of employment during the transition (see chapter 3).

Even those who seemed to benefit from the post-Mao transformation were not immune to the epidemic. For example, in the new consumer culture, business was conducted in the context of abundant and easily accessible food, tobacco, alcohol, and sex. When a businessman felt obligated to constantly engage in a nightlife of banqueting, binge drinking, and seeing prostitutes, the bodily consequences—including impotence—could be traumatic (see chapter 5).

It gradually became clear to me that impotence in post-Mao China was experienced as a disturbance resulting from multiple forces of social transformation that were, to quote Freud, "too powerful to be dealt with or worked off in the normal way" by the body (1964:275). Impotence became a way for the body to respond to this disturbance. But, departing from the Freudian thesis of universal pressure to which men were subjected under civilization, I focused on the specific impact of the post-Mao transformation.

Anthropology has developed powerful conceptual tools for examining how social injustice is inscribed on the body and causes suffering: "structural violence" (Farmer 2004), "the violence of everyday life" (Scheper-Hughes 1992, "social suffering" (Kleinman, Das, and Lock 1997), and "social abandonment" (Biehl 2005). Those frameworks serve as powerful inspirations for interpreting many cases of impotence.

At the same time, anthropology has also produced compelling ethnographic accounts of people's amazing resilience and capacity for desire despite the social injustice they are forced to endure (Biehl 2005, 2010; Scheper-Hughes 1992). I had expected my study of impotence to be about suffering, but I was surprised to find that a unique characteristic of the impotence epidemic had been buried in the narratives of traumatic experience: the articulation of unsatisfied desire and the longing to enjoy sex.

For example, some older people were encouraged by discourse extolling the positive impact of sexual gratification on the well-being of the elderly and by the establishment of nanke, and they challenged the popular view that just because one's potency declines as one ages, one should give up on sex. More and more older men began to seek medical help for impotence, and doctors I interviewed indicated the maximum age among patients seeking treatment was being pushed higher and higher. The ages of the patients I talked to ranged from 18 to 81.[8] Also, the increasing eagerness with which men sought medication for impotence often reflected the urging of women—after couples had had a child under China's one-child policy. Reproduction, then, was not a major reason to seek medical intervention for impotence.

The reason for the suffering associated with impotence—the frustration of sexual pleasure—was recognized and legitimated by nanke and brought out into the open. The impotence epidemic in post-Mao China became a positive sign of what Gilles Deleuze and Félix Guattari called "desiring production" (1983, 1987).

"Wait a minute," the reader might ask, "are you saying that the impotence epidemic might be understood as something other than suffering, a masculine crisis, or an ominous sign of social woes?" My answer is that an individual case of impotence might be experienced negatively in terms of suffering and crisis, but the willingness and urge to seek medical help to satisfy sexual desire represented a positive orientation. Therefore, I view the impotence epidemic in general terms as a positive event of "desiring production" in post-Mao China.

IMPOTENCE AS "DESIRING PRODUCTION"

The idea of "desiring production" was a unique contribution Deleuze and Guattari made to our understanding of capitalism, particularly by enriching the Marxist view of capitalist production of capital and labor while critiquing the psychoanalytical tradition of conceptualizing desire negatively confined in the Oedipus complex.[9] Referring to the mode of capitalism based on creating motivations (investing, gaining ownership of property, consuming goods, etc.), "desiring production" described the force of capitalism in terms of generating flows and producing desire. "Capitalism is in fact born of the encounter of two sorts of flows: the decoded flows of production in the form of money-capital, and the decoded flows of labor in the form of the 'free worker' . . . Capitalism tends toward a threshold of decoding . . . and unleash[es] the flows of desire" (Deleuze and Guattari 1983: 33). If precapitalist society tended to code desire, that is, to place restrictions on the desire, capitalist production tended to decode desire, that is, to unleash the flows of desire. Therefore, an analysis of capitalist production is nothing other than a combination of an analysis of political economy and the economy of desire.

Collapsing the line between desiring production and social production, "desiring production" sheds light on "the intrinsic power of desire to create its own objects" and "the objective being of man, for whom to desire is to produce" (Deleuze and Guattari 1983: 25, 27). Therefore, "social production is purely and simply desiring production itself under determinate conditions" (29).

Many anthropological studies of the post-Mao reform have been anchored in the issue of soaring individual aspirations. Those individual aspirations moved away from the collective passion in the Maoist period, under the determinate conditions of the rise of market economy, individual desire, increasing private ownership, and so on. For example, why did children in Dalian in Liaoning Province desire to migrate to Western countries (Fong 2011), and why did villagers in Longyan in Fujian Province aspire resolutely to such migration (Chu 2010)? Why did people in Zouping in Shandong Province desire more education (Kipnis 2011)? Why were members of the emerging middle class in Kunming in Yunnan Province so eager to own apartments (L. Zhang 2010)? Why did people in Wenzhou in Zhejiang Province want to build so many Christian churches (Cao 2010)? And why did villagers in Mengzhou in Hebei Province aspire to commit suicide (Wu 2010)? Notably, the rise of sexual desire, an exemplification of desire, has been explored extensively (e.g., Yan 2003; Farquhar 2002; Rofel 2010; Zheng 2009; Osburg 2013; Friedman 2006; Farrer 2002; Jeffreys 2006; Ho 2011; Schein 1997; Jankowiak 1993).

Most of the studies cited above focus not only on people aspiring to achieve specific goals in life but also on the making of those aspirants into certain types of persons, selves, or subjectivities—described, for example, in terms of "individualization" (Yan 2010), "the divided self" (Kleinman et al. 2011), "personal voice" (Honig and Hershatter 1988), the "desiring subject" (Rofel 2007), and the "subject of desire" (E. Zhang 2007).

The impotence epidemic provided a perfect opportunity to demonstrate how the subject of desire was produced. For example, the birth of nanke (men's medicine) emerged to encourage impotent men to come forward and seek treatment. Men as well as women now dared to articulate their desire for sexual enjoyment, because the moral nature of sexual desire was altered and the shame associated with impotence downgraded (see chapter 1).

On a more "meta" level, desiring production not only has incited desire for specific objects—for "this or that"—but also has produced the tendency to desire—the desire to desire. I am making a Deleuzian reversal here of the Lacanian notion of desire as "lack in being." According to Jacques Lacan, "Desire is a relation of being to lack. It is the lack of being properly speaking. It isn't a lack of this or that, but lack in being whereby being exists" (1991:223). Deleuze and Guattari refuse to see desire as lack but as often impeded, particularly in precapitalist structures. Therefore, the production of desire in capitalist society not only allows for its fulfillment through satisfaction of specific needs but also promotes the overall tendency to desire in itself. In practice, in the recent past under Maoist socialism, collective passion instead of individual desire was promoted, and more often than not, sexual desire was discouraged or even repressed (chapter 2). The rise of individual desire in post-Mao China has greatly changed the Chinese society and the subjectivities of the Chinese.

Therefore, disagreeing with the common assessment that the impotence epidemic is a negative event, I consider it a positive one, because it signifies the ontological shift in human existence in China from downplaying desire to promoting the desire to desire. We could even call the impotence epidemic "a contagion of desire." It is one of the most profound changes in recent Chinese history. Answering the question of how "the contagion" happened requires turning to ethnography.

Entering the Field of Impotence

I conducted fieldwork in clinics in the city of Beijing, in the north, and Chengdu, in the southwest, focusing on one clinic as a primary research site in each city. The two-site choice acknowledged the traditional sensitivity in Chinese studies to differences between northerners and southerners in styles of living, as reflected in cuisine and cultural habitus, as well as in physical type. Even though the common distinction between "robust northerners" and "delicate southerners" has been subject to revision (Hanson 1998), north–south differences remained a legitimate concern in traditional Chinese medicine (Wang 1995; Feng and Cheng 1997). This distinction was reflected in the etiology of impotence, according to some doctors of TCM. For example, many southerners suffered from impotence because of heavy dampness and heat in the body resulting from the humid climate, whereas northerners often suffered from impotence because of *yin* deficiency caused by the dry climate.

Another important reason for my selection of sites is that I had developed social networks in the two cities. I spent four years attending college in Chengdu and six years in Beijing attending graduate school and working for the Chinese Academy of Social Sciences. My networks not only integrated me into local social fabrics but also generated direct contact with impotent men and others relevant to my research. For example, a friend of mine arranged a dinner so that I could meet and chat with a cohort of *laosanjie* (graduates of high or junior-high schools in the first three years of the Cultural Revolution [1966–1968] who went down to the countryside in 1969). These conversations not only provided invaluable source material for my understanding of the ups and downs of this group of people but also eventually led to a number of individual in-depth interviews. Two of the men at the dinner and the husband of one of the women had suffered from impotence. My conversations with people in their homes, in offices after hours, and in restaurants opened up a rare horizon for me to enter into deep experiential predicaments and the human efforts to cope with them.

Complementing the geographical balance, I also pursued a balance between biomedicine and TCM. In general, an impotent man in a Western country has two treatment choices—he can see a urologist or a psychotherapist. At the time of my study, an impotent man in China also had two choices—to see a doctor of Chinese medicine or a doctor of biomedicine. Psychotherapy was just beginning to attract patients. The global biological turn in the medical treatment of impotence was, thus, juxtaposed to a "local" cultural practice that included techniques such as herbal decoctions and acupuncture and that generated distinctive expectations and demands in and interactions with patients (e.g., Kleinman 1980; Farquhar 1994; Hsu 1999; Scheid 2002; Barnes 2005; Zhan 2009). It became necessary for me to travel between the two medicines to understand not only the strengths and weaknesses of each but also the shifting dynamic between them.

Beijing and Chengdu were two of the four cities in which, in the 1950s, colleges of TCM had been established; they became major bases for the preservation and development of TCM under the Maoist state and remained so in post-Mao China. In Beijing, I chose a hospital of biomedicine (Yuquan Hospital) as a major research site, and I visited a number of hospitals of TCM there, including hospitals affiliated with Beijing University of Chinese Medicine. In Chengdu, I chose the Hospital of Chengdu University of Traditional Chinese Medicine (CUHTCM) as my primary research site, and I also visited a hospital of biomedicine there. When Viagra was introduced into the Chinese market in 2000, I had a front-row seat to observe how it was received. Contrary to biomedical expectations, the response was disappointing. Investigating this surprise led me to discover a lively medical pluralism in the field of impotence, reflected in multiple diagnoses and treatments and in "body multiple" (Mol 2002) that counter the hegemonic reduction of impotence to a neurovascular event.

In my two major field sites—the Department of Sexual Medicine in Yuquan Hospital in Beijing and of Nanke in CUHTCM—I conducted observations and interacted with patients and doctors as a research intern, joining other interns, most of whom were graduate students. Yuquan Hospital, located in Haidian District in Beijing, was formerly owned by the Ministry of Electronic Industry and was eventually commercialized to manage its own revenue. The Department of Sexual Medicine was one of the most popular departments in the hospital, primarily because it was headed by Ma Xiaonian, a well-known sexologist in the 1990s, who advocated sexual openness both in his medical practice and publications and on his talk show on Beijing People's Radio Station (Zhang 2013). CUHTCM is located next to the university campus in Jinniu District in Chengdu. Its nanke specialty was established in 1994. Because Dr. Zhang, its head, was also head of the urology department (located in a separate space), the commingling of TCM and biomedicine was a prominent feature of nanke at that hospital (see chapter 6). Some interns at the Beijing site were conducting research. One, for example, a graduate student of education from a normal university in a southern province, was working on her thesis, which involved measuring sexual dysfunction; interns at the Chengdu site, by contrast, were learning diagnosis and treatment.

While regularly visiting my primary field sites, I also talked to people in various walks of life in different locations—in parks, restaurants, and night-clubs; at social gatherings; in their apartments; in teahouses, coffee shops, or bars; and so on. In addition, I followed doctors to observe them as they engaged in activities outside the hospital, for instance, participating in radio talk shows and visiting sex shops, and I joined them in special sessions of collective diagnosis and treatment in other hospitals. I visited pharmacies, university student dormitories, private clinics, and other pertinent sites. Altogether, I observed and interviewed about 350 patients diagnosed with impotence or related problems and/or their spouses or sexual partners (predominantly Han Chinese). I also observed and interviewed two dozen doctors (half of whom were doctors of biomedicine and half doctors of TCM).

Inspired by Margaret Lock's (1995) studies of menopause in Japan, I combined qualitative and quantitative studies, administering two surveys to two different groups. One survey investigated the socioeconomic status of patients and self-perceptions of impotence and included questions about etiology, definition, preferences for treatment, and ways to cope with impotence and gain sexual pleasure. The second survey investigated perceptions of the male sexual organ, which yielded insights useful for understanding the experience of sexual satisfaction and frustration. I administered the surveys to about two-thirds of the patients I talked with and to about six hundred college students. My sample student population had relatively equal numbers of males and females and science and nonscience majors and included participants from five universities. These two surveys greatly contribute to the ethnographic insights of this book.

YANGSHENG (THE CULTIVATION OF LIFE): ETHICAL REGULATION OF DESIRE

Having recognized that "the impotence epidemic" was a result of desiring production, my daily contact with patients and practitioners of TCM made me aware of the ethical limits of such production of desire. Desiring production in the Deleuzian sense has its own limits. One of the limits consists of "decoding" flows (lessening restrictions to create deterritorialized flows) and its countering tendency—"coding" flows (imposing restrictions on them). To extend Deleuze and Guattari's insights, I found it illuminating to consider the "recoding" of flows of desire a manifestation of the counter-tendency to and the ethical limits of "the contagion of desire." The rise of yangsheng (the cultivation of life) was an example of such recoding.

I had already encountered yangsheng from routinely chatting with people doing exercises or practicing *qigong* in parks near a university campus where I was staying in Beijing. What prompted me to pay more attention to it was the introduction of Viagra into the Chinese market in 2000. Viagra obviously incited expectations among patients and doctors that impotence could be quickly fixed. An impotence-free era seemed to have finally arrived. Pfizer estimated that China had the largest population of impotent men globally, reaching more than 102 million, and the company felt sure that Chinese men and women would embrace Viagra.

Despite the media sensation surrounding the introduction of this "magic pill," I observed a less than enthusiastic response, both in Beijing and in Chengdu. The reluctance of many Chinese men to accept Viagra was due to multiple concerns but definitely involved an understanding of potency that went beyond the simple ability to achieve an erection. Patients perceived potency in terms of one's overall vitality, something that has to be cultivated methodically over the long run and should not be suddenly induced when it is "needed." The story of Viagra in China was a surprise in the context of the biological turn in the medical field of impotence but also an encouraging revelation of the resilience of TCM informed by the ancient Chinese wisdom of "cultivating life" (see chapters 5, 6, and 7).

Yangsheng, a systematic set of tenets and practices for maintaining health, including sexual health, to gain longevity is documented in the literature of

Chinese medicine and Daoist scriptures and has long been a part of everyday life (e.g., through bodily regimens; adapting the use of the body to changes in weather, season, and location; the practice of qigong; preserving seminal essence; etc.). Farquhar and Qicheng Zhang (2012) present yangsheng both as regimented bodily practices and as a strategy for achieving health and enjoyment in the public spaces opened up in post-Mao China—in short, as the pursuit of a good life through self-governed harmonious activities. Drawing on their insights into yangsheng as manifesting "contemporary" Chineseness, I emphasize that, unlike the general tendency of Maoist socialism to deny individual desire and individual cultivation, the revival of yangsheng since the 1990s reveals both the opening up of space for such cultivation and the reemergence of xing yangsheng (sexual cultivation) as the recoding of desire. For example, doctors of nanke not only encouraged sexual desire but also offered caveats against the "loss of seminal essence" (a trend deemphasizing the importance of *jing*, seminal essence) resulting from an excess of desire in consumer culture. But those caveats differed qualitatively from the "coding" of desire by the Maoist state, as they represented a moderate attitude toward sex, one resonating with the ancient Greek ethics of "care of the self." Therefore, xing yangsheng balanced sexual desire with active cultivation of the body to achieve an ethics of being.

THE RISE OF WOMEN'S DESIRE: A MASCULINE CRISIS?

This book is about male impotence. But women played such an important role in the experience of impotence and the production of desire that this book is surely about women as well. One day in early 2000, I was chatting in a teahouse with a group of friends about commercials for yang-strengthening herbal tonics. One woman said, "It is obvious that all the commercials are making fun of men: you are impotent!" This woman presented a gendered voice of desiring production: women were demanding more sexual satisfaction than men could offer, echoing the voice of "the impotence boom" in the United States in the 1970s. I was aware that impotence could also affect homosexual men, but no ethnographic evidence I had gathered made me confident about extending my research to cover such men.

Several years back, an article titled "Who Makes Men Unable to Get 'Hard-on'?" published in *Shishang Xiansheng Ban* (*Mr.'s Edition of Trend*; Xiaoren 1998) claimed that a "new type of impotence" had emerged in China, resulting from women's increasing sexual demands. It argued that

Figure 1.5: Male customers in a sex store in Beijing.

for several thousand years women had been sexually passive but that this situation had begun to change rapidly. A new type of woman had appeared who was more sexually informed and experienced, demanded more opportunities for sex, and was more focused on orgasm. The demand for more and better sex resulted in anxiety for men, leading to impotence. The conversation in the teahouse and the article in a fashionable magazine seemed to converge in assessing the impotence epidemic as a crisis of masculinity. The gender balance seemed to be tilting toward women as male potency weakened.

Since the post-Mao reform began, such "crises" had periodically attracted public attention and comment in China. I single out four examples here. First, in the late 1980s, discussion focused on the idea of "looking for real men" (*xunzhao nanzihan*), as exemplified by the female protagonist's search in Sha Yexin's (1986) drama of that title. Second, in the 1990s and 2000s, women athletes drew attention for outperforming men athletes in international tournaments, a phenomenon known as *yin sheng yang shuai* (yin waxes and yang wanes; see Chen 1996; Brownell 1999; H. Li 2009). Third, in the late 1990s, debate centered on the merits and shortcomings of "Shanghai nanren" (Shanghai men, who reputedly made "superb" husbands; see Long 1998). Fourth, also in the late 1990s, popular books calling for "men's liberation" generated widespread public comment (Fang 1999).

However, a close look at those noisy public debates does not lead to the conclusion that the "manliness" of Chinese men was in decline. In the reform period, two transformations—decollectivization and gender redifferentiation—went hand in hand. If the former rejected Maoist selfless identity, reflecting a change from downplaying the individual self to concern for the individual self,[10] the latter rejected Maoist "genderless" identity, reflecting a change, in somewhat simplified terms, from "gender erasure" to "gender difference."[11] The female protagonist's search for "real men" now fed on a concrete ideal, and women were offered a contrast between two types of masculine figures—the impotent male protagonists of a number of literary works and the masculine figures in foreign movies, like those portrayed by Sylvester Stallone and Ken Takakura (Zhong 2000), rendering clear what "real men" should look like today. However, the call for "real men" was ironic in that the logic of the emergent individual self was inevitably gendered, and the two gendered selves were "naturally" formed into a hierarchy that subjected women to men's power, as reflected in the "entrepreneurial masculinity" of business culture.[12]

In fact, none of the discussion surrounding Chinese masculine crises was either soundly conceptualized or empirically supported.[13] Instead, it was more revealing of the confusion society as a whole was facing in redefining masculinity than of a sharp decline of men's power and privilege in public and private spheres. The confusion concerned what kind of masculinity "real men" represent: a "hard," tough, but dominating masculinity or a caring, sensitive, but "soft" masculinity. More accurately, many men and women seemed to be struggling with the challenge of combining the two into a new type of masculinity, still featuring strength but not at the expense of women's well-being. This kind of confusion is, in my view, what Xueping Zhong's (2000) phrase "masculinity besieged" refers to.[14]

Having cautioned against taking the discourse of masculine crises at face value, I nevertheless stress the necessity of dealing with the impotence epidemic seriously as a gendered moment.[15] My fieldwork confirmed the rise of women's desire but did not go so far as to testify to a "new type of impotence." Instead, all kinds of social forces affect male potency and eventually impinge on the intertwining of male and female bodies and the gendered nature of that intertwining. I call this bodily, gendered relationship "sexual intercorporeality." Success in building and maintaining the bodily skills to engage in sexual intercorporeality enhances male potency, whereas failure to do so contributes to male impotence (see chapter 4).

The Structure of This Book

When I began my fieldwork, I expected its boundaries to be clearly defined for three reasons. First, as I intended to do fieldwork in urban areas, my interviews would be primarily with urbanites. Second, in focusing on nanke and urology departments, I could easily observe how the local, endemic tradition of TCM interacts with biomedicine. Third, in linking patients in hospitals to their residential areas, I could trace their emotional worlds of traumatic experience back to their local social worlds. Yet no sooner had I entered the field than I discovered how difficult it would be to maintain the boundaries I had set.

First, the boundaries between the urban and the rural were blurred. Not only did patients come from different social and geographic locations but they also traveled extensively. As it turned out, the patients I interviewed came from more than fifteen provinces. About 30 percent of them were from rural areas, having migrated to Chengdu and Beijing for economic reasons. I thus gained the advantage of encountering people from places I would never have imagined visiting. Second, patients traveled through the Chinese medical system in its entirety, presenting a more complex picture of the medical body than the one defined by a clear-cut TCM–biomedicine dichotomy. Most patients switched between the two types of medicine, sometimes even within the same hospitals, where divisions of Chinese medicine and biomedicine coexisted. Biomedicine and Chinese medicine became intermingled in diagnoses and treatment. That commingling made unstable and contingent the observations of how impotence was managed and diagnosed and therefore how it helped define the ethics of potency, sexuality, and life. Third, tracing the linkage between clinics and communities was complicated by the existence of "virtual" or "semivirtual" communities. One such community comprised migrant workers brought together temporarily at specific construction sites and their associated dormitories. Another virtual community included patients who tuned into the same radio talk show on sexual health and then found themselves seeing the very doctors in the clinic they had listened to on the air (Zhang 2013).

Realizing that the boundaries in my own mind had been shaken loose, I made my ethnographic moves along what I now conceptualize as "lines," to borrow Deleuze and Guattari's (1987) notion. Lines "have nothing to do with a structure" (Deleuze and Guattari 1987:203). Rather, a structure is occupied by points and positions and always forms a closed system for containment, whereas lines always coincide with escape and opening up, materializing the "decoding of desire" and "deterritorialization." In following the thematics surrounding impotence, I found myself following different lines. I came to envision impotence as an effect of a historical "line of flight" out of the closed system of restricted sexuality in the Maoist period, as men were no longer fixed at discrete points but were moving along various trajectories: between nanke in hospitals and clinics, urology departments, shops selling sex devices and lubricants, pharmacies selling zhuangyang herbal tonics, radio and TV shows, Internet cafés, representatives of international biomedical pharmacies, night clubs, and so on.[16]

I paid special attention to four groups of patients who, loosely speaking, represented "winners," "losers," and those "in between" in the post-Mao transformation.[17] The four groups were the "old three classes" (老三届, laosanjie), migrant workers (民工潮, mingongchao, waves of workers migrating from rural to urban areas), entrepreneurs, and laid-off workers. The latter three groups emerged in the 1980s and 1990s, the numbers of mingongchao, especially, soaring with urban growth and the advent of consumer society. In simple terms, laid-off workers were obvious losers and entrepreneurs were winners. The laosanjie and the mingongchao, the groups "in between," represented temporally distant, spatially reversed, and differentially motivated flows between the urban and the rural. By no means did I select these cohorts or social groups as representative of Chinese society as a whole. They simply emerged from the sample of patients I observed and interviewed. Members of each group shared dramatic ups and downs in their lives. Each cohort or group formed a continuous line of points that stretched across a single community. Putting these lines together led to the breaking open of clinic and community boundaries and to the manifestation of a dynamic social matrix within which the experience of impotence was situated.

Part 1 of this book deals with the social context of the impotence epidemic as desiring production and focuses on the state, society, family, and women. Chapter 1 de-essentializes the shame associated with impotence by locating it in the historical context of China's post-Mao transformation. Through the contrast between declining clinic visits by patients seeking medication for *yijing* (nocturnal emission) and the increase in patient visits for impotence, I discovered that yijing was a symptom of Maoist socialism, when sexual desire was discouraged, whereas impotence became a symptom of the post-Mao reform, as public perception of sexual desire had changed from negative to positive. In the Maoist period (particularly in the Cultural Revolution), one felt ashamed to seek treatment for impotence because it revealed one's desire for sexual pleasure, whereas in post-Mao China, seeking medication for purposes of sexual enjoyment was encouraged. In doing so, men and women were shaped into the subjectivity of desire.

Chapter 2 begins with the discussion of a popular thesis that sexual repression resulted in impotence in the Maoist period. Leaving aside the relationship between impotence and sexual repression, this thesis led me to consider whether and why sexual desire was repressed under the socialist state. I discovered that the structural limitations of Maoist collectivism—the impact of the danwei and hukou systems—led to sexual repression, a point no previous study has made. This point is critical for understanding the rise of the impotence epidemic (the rise of desire) in post-Mao China.

Chapter 3 presents a wide range of social contexts and related personal experiences in which impotence occurs—the changing political class system, increasing inequality, the rural–urban divide, *xiagang* (layoffs from state-owned enterprises), the loss of filial piety, memories of socialist-era starvation, and so on. The wide range of detailed bodily experiences I collected constitutes what I call "one thousand bodies of impotence." Through bodily experience, some historical processes emerge in a new light. For example, one man's story of having difficulty finding a girlfriend under the Maoist political class system reveals that system as a biopolitical invention.

Chapter 4 focuses on impotent men's social relationships in two specific contexts: with natal families and with women. In the former context, I examine the phenomenon of "imagined impotence," in which men who had little sexual experience with women considered themselves impotent. Two cases of imagined impotence suggest that the intervention of a father in a son's romance and marriage had a negative impact on the son's potency.

In the latter context, I explore a number of cases showing a wide range of women's feelings, attitudes, and coping strategies when living with impotent men. I pay attention to bodily details, or "small bodily things" of consequence to sexual intercorporeality.[18] Those small bodily things add up to big changes in the subjectivity of men and women—as fathers, sons, lovers, wives, and husbands. Particularly revealing is the emergence of a new type of masculinity that allows men and women to find sexual fulfillment in non-phallocentric ways.[19]

Part 2 deals with ethical limits to desiring production, in a theoretically incremental way moving from Part 1 of the book to Part 2. That is, Part 1 is about production of desire, whereas Part 2 is about the limits of such production; Part 1 is about decoding desire, whereas Part 2 is about recoding desire; Part 1 is about moral justification of sexual desire and enjoyment, whereas Part 2 is about ethical self-regulation of sexual desire and the ethical goal of sexual enjoyment.

Making this theoretical shift, chapter 5 discusses the relationship between two opposing trends—the loss of jing (seminal essence) and the revival of yangsheng (the cultivation of life). Having been discouraged in the Maoist period, yangsheng regained legitimacy in post-Mao China. In a countertendency to the rise of sexual desire, many men chose to regulate that desire by preserving seminal essence and adopting a moderate attitude toward sex. Instead of repressing sexual desire, then, yangsheng can be seen as a practice of its ethical regulation. It is therefore a technique of self-mastery, a way to form an ethical self.

Chapter 6 deals with the repositioning of TCM in response to the biological turn. In it, I first introduce the debate between two schools of impotence diagnoses and treatment in TCM—the kidney-centered perspective and the liver-centered perspective—revealing the pressure to reposition TCM vis-à-vis biomedicine because of the latter's ascendance. The entry of Viagra into the Chinese market intensified the pressure. Faced with the choice between Chinese medicine and Viagra, men did not completely abandon TCM for biomedicine. Instead, many patients switched between the two, taking both Viagra and herbal remedies. In doing so, they both satisfied sexual desire and cultivated potency, embodying two types of ethical regimes, showing the resilience of TCM on the one hand and growing cosmopolitanism on the other hand.

Drawing on ancient Chinese thought and Western thought as they weave through narratives of cases, stories, and personal encounters, chapter 7 redefines potency as life's fullness. *Potency* refers, first, to the Chinese notion of the fullness of seminal essence, and, second, to the Western idea of "being in the world" through the body. Together, the capacity to maintain the fullness of seminal essence and the capacity to open up to the world constitute life's fullness. Under this understanding, men can remain potent even when impotent, because potency is more than the ability to achieve erection.

Use of the Term *Impotence*

As a final note, I comment on my use of the term *impotence*. In clinical settings, the trend—which started in the United States and has spread to China—is to use the term *erectile dysfunction* (ED). In the United States, the National Institutes of Health (NIH) announced a consensus statement on the terminology in 1992, preferring ED to *impotence* because use of the latter term often led to "confusing and uninterpretable results in clinical and scientific investigations" and also had "pejorative implications" (NIH 1992). As a result, ED and its Chinese translation (勃起障礙, *boqi zhangai*) are gaining popularity in Chinese clinical settings, particularly among younger doctors and urologists. Also, according to my survey, the majority of patients prefer ED to *yangwei* (the Chinese translation of *impotence*).[20] According to some doctors, ED does not sound as morally devastating as *impotence*. A doctor in his early forties commented, "[ED] sounds like there is some obstacle to erections. We can remove it. In contrast, impotence sounds like a death penalty to one's masculinity." Cognizant of these arguments and of the positive psychological connotations of ED, I nevertheless use *impotence* as a primary term throughout this book because *yangwei*, the Chinese equivalent, denotes an etiology of impotence that is historically unique to Chinese medicine. Also, the term helps me inquire into the severe social and cultural implications of impotence and its psychological damage to masculinity and gender equality, which the biomedicalization of impotence might conceal. Yet my goals here are precisely to deconstruct the implications of impotence by demonstrating the forces that can reverse its devastating effect and to delink impotence from the perception that it sounds a death knell for masculinity. In the future, I expect, the term *impotence* to be largely of historical interest.

Throughout the book, I have changed the names of all impotent men and their partners or spouses, as well as any identifying information, to protect their privacy. In some cases, I have also changed doctors' names.

PART I

Society and the State

CHAPTER 1

The Birth of *Nanke*

(Men's Medicine)

The growing impotence epidemic was reflected in the birth and development of *nanke* (men's medicine). How widespread was this medical specialty? I did a telephone survey in Beijing one morning in July 2001, calling sixty-nine hospitals to gather information on their treatment of impotence patients. I found, first, that the majority of the hospitals (sixty-one) welcomed such patients and had at least one doctor on staff, and sometimes an entire department, that specialized in treating impotence. Second, I learned that hospitals of Chinese medicine tended to refer impotence patients to practitioners of nanke, whereas general hospitals tended to refer them to urology departments for treatment.

Third, I discovered that the division between nanke and urology was not always clear-cut. Whereas most of the large-scale hospitals of Chinese medicine had both a nanke department and a department of urology, some general hospitals of biomedicine integrated nanke into their list of specialties within the urology department. In yet other hospitals, nanke and urology were considered separate divisions but shared the same space. At the Hospital of Chengdu University of Traditional Chinese Medicine (CUHTCM), the name on the door of this shared space actually read "Miniao Nanke" (Urology and Nanke).[1]

Amid the "contagiousness" of impotence, nanke exerted a symbolic power that drew people into clinics for a cure. How did it acquire this power? Paula Treichler (1999) coined the phrase "an epidemic of signification" to conceptualize the symbolic politics of AIDS. Borrowing this idea and applying it to the Chinese context, Judith Farquhar (2002:269) emphasizes the significant implications of impotence for social life in the post-Mao era. Through her interpretation of the movie *Ermo* (1994), Farquhar links impotence to the emasculation of the social body in China's dramatic post-Mao transformation. Ermo, a female laborer, is trapped between an impotent old husband and a profligate young lover. The predicament she finds herself in, according to Farquhar, is a "national allegory." "Impotence" represents the "denunciation of the failures of the past and the banality of the future for a China that has committed itself at every level, even the most domestic, to millennial capitalist relations of production" (Farquhar 2002:274). In other words, impotence characterizes the social body, and neither the failed Maoist past nor the increasingly consumption-oriented future seems to offer a cure.

I agree that the impotence epidemic symbolically conveyed a denunciation of the failures of the past. But I am convinced that some of its implications for social life today are positive. That seeking medical treatment for impotence became contagious after the 1980s implies that people had been discouraged during the Maoist period from seeing doctors about the condition. Focusing on this contrast, I ask two sets of questions—one empirical and the other theoretical. The empirical questions are: What medical treatment, if any, was available to impotent men prior to the establishment of nanke? Did they see doctors at all? Were impotent men really discouraged from seeking medical treatment? If so, what was at stake in discouraging such treatment? The theoretical questions are: How, as a society changes, do the social and moral implications of specific diseases change? How do the changing implications of certain diseases contribute to making different kinds of persons and subjects than were produced under previous social conditions?

In addressing these questions, I argue that "impotence as an epidemic" was a force that helped shape the man experiencing erectile failure into a new type of subject—the subject of desire—by encouraging him to seek medical treatment. This chapter tells the story of how that force came to be.

Nanke: A Brief History

The first nanke facility in China—at Yuanling County Hospital in Hunan Province—was established in 1983. The first book on diseases classified as nanke diseases was published in the same year (Li and Pang 1983). For the roughly two millennia during which traditional Chinese medicine (TCM) had been practiced, then, there was no nanke. In contrast, *fuke* (婦科, gynecology) had developed during the first millennium of Chinese medical practice.[2] This contrast initially puzzled me, given the historically male-centered orientation of many aspects of Chinese society. Yet the main function of fuke was, first and foremost, to ensure reproduction and, therefore, the continuation of the familial (i.e., male) line, a pivotal principle of Confucian ethics. As Charlotte Furth (1999) points out, even though fuke benefited women, the concern with the female gestational body, even in the androgynous bodily cosmology of Chinese medicine, was male centered.

Male impotence had been recognized as a medical problem since ancient times. The scriptures of Mawangdui, which are believed to have been produced in the pre-Qin period (before 221 B.C.E.), refer to impotence as "buqi" (不起, not up) and include prescriptions for impotence under the subheading "Yangshengfang" (Formulas for Nurturing Life). *Yinwei* (陰痿, the shrinking of yin), however, was the first recorded Chinese term that specifically denoted impotence (e.g., in the *Inner Canon*) and was in use long before *yangwei* (陽痿, the shrinking of *yang*) appeared in physician Zhou Zhigan's book in the Ming period (1368–1644).[3] In exploring how nanke came into being in the 1980s, I found myself addressing the much broader changes occurring in Chinese society at the time.

The nanke department at CUHTCM, where I did my fieldwork, was first open to the public in 1994. In general, the number of patient visits to nanke at CUHTCM had been steadily increasing up to the time of my study. In May of 1995, the department treated about twelve outpatients per day (306 for the whole month); in May of 2001, it treated about twenty-two outpatients per day (672 for the whole month).

Nanke deals primarily with four types of problems: (1) sexual dysfunction and related problems, such as impotence (erectile dysfunction), premature ejaculation, *yijing* (spermatorrhea, including nocturnal emission), and anejaculation;[4] (2) infertility; (3) prostate diseases such as prostate gland proliferation and prostatitis; and (4) venereal diseases. At the time of my study, impotence was the second most common reason for outpatient visits, showing it to be a prominent concern among patients. Even though prostatitis has topped the list of reasons for outpatient visits since 1995 and accounts for a growing percentage of all problems treated by nanke, impotence is a more visible sign of nanke's work to many Chinese people, primarily because of advertising. Treating impotence is the hallmark of nanke.

Why did nanke not emerge until the 1980s? One cannot simply assume that it was a response to the increasing incidence of impotence.[5] Rather, one must also take into consideration the effect of medicalization on the "production" of certain diseases. A particular illness experience may not become a disease medicine is concerned about until social forces institutionalize it

Figure 1.1: A clinic of men's medicine in Beijing.

as such, as in the case of illnesses resulting from exposure to radiation from the Chernobyl disaster (Petryna 2002).[6]

The birth of nanke was a particularly clear example of such medicalization. As a matter of fact, impotence had been treated before the inception of nanke but for a different purpose than it is today. In other words, impotence was medicalized by nanke: treatment was sanctioned for a purpose that had previously been rendered illegitimate. This medicalization through inclusion is bound up with profound changes in post-Mao China, including a change in "moral symptomatology."

By *moral symptomatology*, I refer to the decisions and judgments of the medical establishment and, ultimately, the state in rendering certain symptoms legitimate for medical attention. Medicine had become an important way for the Chinese state to manage diseases and living conditions that could severely damage the productive force of the population. But, historically, impotence does not seem to have been perceived by the state as having a significant effect on productivity. Impotence can impede productivity at an individual level in the sense that it prevents women from getting pregnant. But its impact on population growth is largely insignificant.

In my fieldwork, I found that male reproductive problems were seen as having more to do with the quality of semen than with the ability to penetrate the vagina. In some cases, the reproductive failure of a married couple prompted their parents to inquire into the couple's life and led to a finding that impotence might be the problem. But, overall, patients were seeking treatment for reasons other than reproduction. The one-child policy enforced by the post-Mao Chinese state in the early 1980s reengineered Chinese sexuality in such a way that concern had shifted away from reproduction. The state was calculating life to suppress rather than increase population growth (Greenhalgh 2008; Greenhalgh and Winckler 2005).

Therefore, the way impotence became a great enough concern to justify the establishment of a new medical specialty had to do with its characterization as a legitimate "disease" warranting medical attention. In general, such characterizations are greatly constrained by a systematic concern about the moral nature of diseases, that is, by the moral symptomatology in place at a particular time. This concern can be expressed indirectly, for example, in the absence of a recognized specialty to deal with certain diseases, through communicative codes in interactions among patients or between patients and doctors that encourage or discourage the medical treatment of certain diseases, and in public discourses concerning the implications of certain diseases for the moral status of patients.

During most of the Maoist era, impotence appears to have been a disease for which medical institutions did not encourage treatment, this institutionalized dismissal deriving from the prevailing moral symptomatology. Moral symptomatology was therefore responsible for the invisibility of impotence in that context. Only when the moral symptomatology changed, when perceptions of men's reasons for seeking medical help for impotence were significantly altered, could patient visits increase. How did this happen? Below I take a close look at the processes involved.

Historicizing the Shame of Impotence

Mainstream medical institutions (primarily biomedicine and TCM in state-run hospitals) in the Maoist period treated impotence very differently from the way it is treated today. Both senior doctors and older patients pointed out the difference to me. In the Maoist period, impotent men sought help from TCM doctors of *neike* (internal medicine). According to Chinese medicine, potency is not only the ability to get an erection but also an index of a man's general health and of the fullness of his vitality. Certain locales in the body (e.g., 腎, *shen*, the kidney) are held to be more responsible than others for a man's ability to get an erection and for maintaining potency and ensuring vitality (see chapter 6). In general, impotence is attributed to deficiencies in general vitality, such as a decrease in the fullness of *qi* (vital energy) and an imbalance between *yin* and *yang* in the body as a whole. It makes sense, then, that a general medical division, such as neike, the TCM division of internal medicine, would treat impotence. This was very much the situation before the 1980s. The biomedical specialty of urology also treated impotence, but, in general, it had very little to offer. Seeing a TCM doctor of internal medicine for impotence was different from seeing a doctor of nanke today. One physician recalled, "Impotence patients tended to *rao wanzi* (繞彎子, take a detour) when they described their impotence in neike. They would start to tell about their illness in the head, the chest, the back, and the stomach. They would tell you their loss of sleep and appetite. It was not unusual for a patient not to tell you their intention to seek medication for impotence until you were about to write a prescription to cure something else. But when a patient comes to nanke, they are normally quite direct and explicit about their problem of impotence."

Nanke created a space in which impotence patients could be more forthcoming in revealing their illness. What prevented patients from admitting their impotence to medical professionals in divisions other than nanke?

A common explanation for this reticence was grounded in the shame and stigma attached to impotence. The shame derived primarily from the perceived loss of masculinity—*yangwei de nenren bu shi nanren le* (阳痿的男人不是男人了, impotent men are not men). When I asked patients why impotence meant the demise of masculinity, puzzlement or annoyance often appeared on their faces, as though I were asking why human beings had to eat to survive. For them, the connection was obvious. One patient said, "Of course, impotent men are not real men. It is pointless to ask such a question! This is the most shameful thing a man can experience." This kind of taken-for-granted perception of maleness—what Matthew Gutmann (2007:187) calls the "totemization of male sexuality"—certainly encompasses expected and acceptable attributes and behaviors (e.g., male adolescent masturbation, men's extramarital affairs and reluctance to use contraception, etc.) as well as unexpected, shameful aspects such as impotence.

But this essentialist view of impotence as shameful privileges male suffering at the cost of refashioning a gender-sensitive masculinity. Moreover, this view is not sustainable, as one can easily point to social and cultural conditions to account for such stigma and shame. In reviewing reactions of men in a variety of societies to their impotence or weak sexual performance, David Gilmore identifies specific recurring concerns about the loss of masculinity that may give rise to a sense of shame. The most prominent have to do with reproduction. For example, in southern Europe, a man is expected not just to make endless sexual conquests but also to spread his seed (Gilmore 1990:41). The shame associated with sexual inadequacy, however, may also extend to other dimensions: in central Brazil, for example, it attaches to a man's inability to satisfy his wife or lover and bring her to orgasm and to whether his failure in this regard is public knowledge, for, as Thomas Gregor notes, a man's "reputation as a lover rides precariously on the shifting currents of community gossip" (1977:137).

Some of Gilmore's observations resonate with the Chinese case. For example, reproductive failure caused by impotence has historically been a concern. In the sixteenth century, Li Shizhen (2005), considered one of the great pharmacologists in the history of Chinese medicine, enumerated *wu bu nan* (五不男, five "un-malenesses," or five inadequacies in a man that result in his inability to impregnate a woman):[7] *tian* (天, primordial), impotence since birth; *jian* (犍, a castrated bull), castration; *lou* (漏, leak), uncontrolled emission of seminal essence; *qie* (怯, trepidation), weak or unsustainable erections; and *bian* (變, lack of consistence), bisexual organs. Among the five bu nan, two are specifically related to impotence. The inability to produce male descendants was a serious flaw according to Confucian ethics, even though women were more likely to be blamed than men for reproductive failure. Mencius's well-known teaching "Buxiao yousan, wuhou weida" (不孝有三, 無後為大, not having descendants is the worst violation of filial piety among the three violations)[8] showed that the moral disgrace associated with impotence was overwhelmingly tied to concern about continuing familial lines. Throughout Chinese history, especially in premodern China, failure to reproduce was far more serious than failure to satisfy women's sexual desire.[9]

Impotence was much more hidden in the Maoist period than it is today, except when it impeded reproduction, which, for a long period of time, the socialist state generally encouraged; even when the state started to restrict reproduction, it took a relatively limited approach.[10] Maoist moral symptomatology, then, justified seeking medical treatment for impotence but primarily for reproductive reasons. This is substantiated by the medical cases published in journals of Chinese medicine in the 1960s and 1970s. As described in these journals, men who had not yet fathered children constituted the majority of impotence patients. For example, an article published in the journal *Jiangsu* TCM in June 1964 cited twenty-three cases of impotence, for which the patients received special acupuncture therapy. Seventy percent of the patients (sixteen) had not yet had a child and wanted one (Lou and Wang 1964). In contrast, only about 20 percent of patients I interviewed between 1999 and 2001 sought treatment for impotence exclusively for reproductive reasons.[11]

Being able to have a child after receiving therapy for impotence was often cited in the 1960s as evidence of a treatment's effectiveness (Li 1955; Lou and Wang 1964; Yang 1962; Yang 1977).[12] In contrast, the effectiveness of therapies for impotence in the 1990s was expressed more often in terms of patients' "satisfaction in their sexual life," indicating that the reason for seeing a doctor for impotence had largely shifted from reproduction to sexual pleasure.

Desire was gradually coming to the fore. Another phenomenon that confirmed its increasing importance is reflected in data relating to clinic visits. In contrast to the increase in impotence patient visits, the number of patient visits for treatment of yijing steadily declined after the beginning of the reform period in the early 1980s. The two trends turned out to be related to each other.

The Shift from *Yijing* (Spermatorrhea) to *Yangwei* (Impotence)

Yijing refers primarily to nocturnal emission (遺精, losing seminal essence, in the form of losing semen), which often occurs during erotic dreams.[13] It also covers the situation of *huajing* (滑精, leaking or dripping of *jing*, semen), which occurs when one is not dreaming and even when one is not asleep. Unlike biomedicine, Chinese medicine has treated it as a disease. But a significant decline in its incidence has occurred since the 1980s. Cao Kaiyong, director of Tianjin Heping Nanke Hospital, said, "We receive a lot fewer patients with yijing in the clinic nowadays. It has almost disappeared." Chen Heliang, a doctor of nanke at Zhuhai Hospital of Chinese Medicine in Guangdong Province, confirmed the trend there. And, although 15 percent of the impotence patients I talked with in nanke at CUHTCM also mentioned nocturnal emission, yijing was not a chief complaint. Table 1.1 shows that nanke at CUHTCM, in fact, received significantly fewer yijing patients than impotence patients in the late 1990s. A decline in interest in yijing relative to impotence is also reflected in the medical literature. Table 1.2 shows a greater increase since the early 1980s in TCM journal articles on the topic of impotence than in articles on the topic of yijing.

Table 1.1 Comparison of Impotence and Yijing Outpatient Visits at
Nanke of CUHTCM

	YIJING		IMPOTENCE	
	VISITS	PERCENTAGE	VISITS	PERCENTAGE
June 19–July 18, 1995	5	1.3	64	17.3
September 1996	8	2.0	48	12.4
October 1996	7	1.5	44	9.0
November 1996	4	1.0	59	14.3
March 2000	7	1.1	98	16.0
March 2001	12	1.9	70	11.1
June 19–July 18, 2001	5	0.8	52	8.2

Source: Registration Books of Nanke of CUHTCM.

Table 1.2 Growth in the Number of TCM Publications on Yijing vs.
Impotence in China

	1949–1983	1984–2000	GROWTH
Yijing	83	643	775%
Impotence	102	1,729	1,695%

Source: Data Bank of Literature of Chinese Medicine of Chinese Academy of
Traditional Chinese Medicine.

The data show, then, that in clinics a significantly higher number of men
had been concerned about impotence than about yijing since the early 1980s
and that impotence was drawing increasingly more attention than yijing
from researchers in Chinese medicine in the same period. How does the
changing moral symptomatology account for the waxing of impotence and
the waning of yijing as related phenomena? Below, I examine this relationship historically.

Yijing under Socialism

Yijing was, historically, a serious disease in Chinese medicine because of the
importance of jing (seminal essence) to life, particularly for men. In the Republican period (1911–1949), yijing was a serious public concern.[14] My im-

pression from reading medical magazines and books from the Republican period is that yijing was taken more seriously than impotence partly because it was often considered a result of indulging in lust and a cause of impotence. Moreover, the loss of jing in the individual body, in the form of yijing, was often related to the perceived weakening of the racialized Han body during China's forced encounters with Western industrial countries since the nineteenth century (Shapiro 1998; Wu 1932). The sensational reference in 1930s advertising to the death of Guangxu, an emperor in the pre-Republican Qing period, having been caused by yijing exemplifies this racialized concern about the condition's consequences (see Shapiro 1998).

This pattern persisted into the socialist period after 1949. Popular medical books continued to address yijing but not impotence. One well-known book of Chinese medical knowledge about the kidney, published in 1956, discussed yijing but not impotence, despite the kidney's importance as an etiological locale for impotence. The author of this book chose to discuss topics on the basis of the letters he had received "from a lot of medical practitioners and comrades around the country" (Zou 1956:1). Obviously, the writers of those letters were concerned more about yijing than about other conditions.

In addition, the assertion that yijing is etiologically responsible for impotence continued to appear in many journals of Chinese medicine. One published case described Mr. Gao, a forty-two-year-old man who had suffered from impotence for half a year. He had suffered from yijing as well. Citing the *Inner Canon*, Dr. Jiang Yubo, author of the case report and a renowned doctor of Chinese medicine, concluded that Mr. Gao's impotence was caused by an excess of sexual activity accompanied by yijing, which had depleted his jing and his blood. The tonic he prescribed contained herbs to condense jing and solidify the renal qi. With this therapy, jing and blood would be replenished without overflowing. The shrinking of yang would thereby be reversed, and yang would automatically be strengthened (Jiang 1965:38). In this case, Dr. Jiang paid considerable attention to yijing because he considered it partly responsible for the man's impotence. In the 1970s, including the latter half of the Cultural Revolution period, yijing was consistently given the same priority as, if not higher priority than, impotence in Chinese medicine.

As biomedicine developed under socialism as part of the modernization project, its increasing influence seriously undermined the privileging of yijing in medical practice. In a popular book of medical advice published in the mid-1950s, the authors—all of whom were doctors of biomedicine—clearly stated, "Yijing is an often seen, normal physiological phenomenon among young men. It is not a disease" (Wang et al. 1956:28). This book also discussed impotence. But, as Maoist socialism underwent intensification through political campaigns, beginning in the mid-1950s and reaching a peak in the Cultural Revolution in the late 1960s and early 1970s, the emergent discussion of impotence disappeared in the wave of struggle against individualism and class enemies (Wuzhou 1977). Its disappearance clearly illustrates that medical attention to a disease is not "natural" but an effect of moral symptomatology. Mr. Cao's experience, related below, shows how the moral symptomatology of the time operated.

Mr. Cao first decided to become a doctor specializing in impotence treatment when he worked as a medical assistant in the army in the late 1960s, during the Cultural Revolution. Mr. Hou, Mr. Cao's superior officer as well as his friend, suffered from impotence. He had had difficulty getting an erection after coming back from a military mission in a border area that had lasted half a year. He was in agony.

Feeling guilty that he could not provide his friend with any relief, Mr. Cao went to Tianjin, the third largest city in China, to look for a hospital where he could learn how to treat impotence. He asked a renowned doctor of Chinese medicine to teach him how to cure the condition. Pointing to the slogan "Never Forget Class Struggle" on the wall of his consulting room, the doctor said with a bitter smile on his face, "Is this the right time to inquire about this kind of disease? Be careful not to do it, otherwise you will be accused of spreading lustful ideas!" Mr. Cao later found out that the doctor had previously gotten into trouble for prescribing zhuangyang herbal tonics for one of his acquaintances. Later, the acquaintance also got into trouble, accused of pursuing the decadent lifestyle of the bourgeois class, which, according to the anticapitalist rhetoric of the time, featured indulgence in sex. Other doctors warned Mr. Cao that trying to learn how to cure impotence would be a mistake that he would regret for the rest of his life. Disappointed, he returned to the army camp. As many of my interviewees liked to recall, "That was an era of tanxing sebian (談性色變, the talk of sex causes the color of the face to change; i.e., talk about sex frightens people)."[15] Just broaching the subject of medical treatment for impotence frightened people because of its negative political implications.

Half a year later, scandal engulfed Mr. Hou. His wife, a beautiful woman more than ten years his junior, got pregnant while he was still impotent.

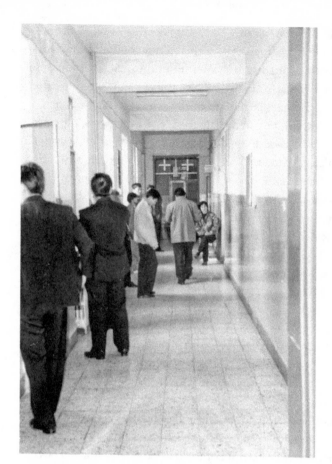

Figure 1.2: A clinic of sexual medicine in Beijing.

Although Mr. Hou screamed at her and wanted her to reveal who had impregnated her, she resisted, for the man would have been severely punished (possibly receiving the death penalty) for destroying the marriage of a military officer. Finally, his wife could no longer stand the pressure and public censure and committed suicide by taking sleeping pills.

Mr. Cao—now a doctor—argued that, if nanke had existed at the time, this tragedy would have been avoided. Dr. Liu, a psychiatrist in Huaxi Mental Health Center in Chengdu, offered the following observations on that time: "In the 1970s most patients came to see me for neurosis, sleep disorder, and insomnia. A common diagnosis then was *xingshenjingshuairuo* (sexual neurasthenia). Sexual neurasthenia was a combination of neurasthenia and sexual obstacles. Yijing was a common complaint of the syndrome of sexual neurasthenia. In almost the whole of the 1970s not even a single patient came to see me overtly for impotence. Not until the end of the 1970s were there patients who came to see me for impotence."

In Dr. Liu's retrospection, a significant shift occurred at the end of the 1970s and in the early 1980s. Instead of complaining of sexual neurasthenia, sometimes a euphemism for impotence, patients started to explicitly complain about impotence. Impotence became, for the first time, one of the primary diseases Dr. Liu treated in his outpatient clinic. More attention, in clinical encounters as well as in research, started to be given to impotence than to yijing. This trend continued into the 1990s and intensified to the point that Dr. Cao had the impression that yijing had almost disappeared from clinical encounters (Cao 1989, 1997). On the basis of the statistics I collected from nanke at CUHTCM, outpatients complaining of yijing made up only a very small percentage of all patients (around 1 percent), and yijing had almost disappeared as a chief complaint of nanke outpatients. In other words, a patient who mentioned nocturnal emissions in a clinical visit was more likely to be seeking treatment for something else. Since the 1980s, then, yijing had become a secondary symptom in the Chinese body, whereas the number of impotence patients had increased significantly.

Moral Symptomatology in Maoist Socialism: Desire Is the Enemy

What was problematic about seeking medical attention for impotence in the Maoist period, particularly at the peak of the Cultural Revolution? Answering this question requires further examination of the moral symptomatology of the period. The following two cases help shed light on what was at stake then.

THE DANGER: THE REVELATION OF DESIRE

In 1999, Mr. Jia, a sixty-six-year-old retired cadre, recalled that he became impotent in the early 1970s, when he was sent down to the countryside for reeducation. He had been criticized for being loyal to the "revisionist ideas" of Liu Shaoqi, the former president of the People's Republic of China and the number-one enemy of the Cultural Revolution. Mr. Jia said he did not do anything directly to address his impotence but had engaged in exercises aimed at strengthening the kidney. It did not even occur to him that he could see a doctor for treatment given the precarious political climate of the time.[16]

Mr. Gao, a sixty-three-year-old cadre, said that in 1999 he had taken Chi-

Figure 1.3: The front window of a sex store in Beijing that was named Eden Health Center touting zhuangyang tonics and other medicines or appliances, with a banner indicating "the three emphases campaign"—the emphases on study, politics, and uprightness.

nese patent medicine for his impotence but that he had hidden the pills even from his family members, locking them up in his office because, he said, *sanjiang* (three emphases)—a new political campaign—was then underway in his work unit. The three-emphases campaign of the late 1990s was far less severe than many political campaigns in the Maoist period. But Mr. Gao's impulse to avoid being spotted taking medicine for impotence, even at home, during the campaign, spoke of a habitus opposed to satisfying individual desire.

The moral symptomatology of Maoist socialism, however it differed from that of previous periods, perpetuated earlier concerns about, and vigilance toward, lust or improper desire, if for different reasons. Concern about lust or lewdness was so extreme then, particularly during the Cultural Revolution, that the bodily function of erection was politicized and moralized, and the effort to recover potency became problematic. Whether a man was impotent or not, the desire for individual sexual pleasure was regarded as antithetical to the collectivistic ethos of revolution. For patients, the shame of seeking to recover potency for sexual pleasure outweighed the shame of impotence itself. Thus, revealing one's intention to recover potency, even to doctors, was discouraged. That no institutional space existed for treating impotence is not surprising. Seen through the lens of Maoist moral symptomatology, sexual desire was anathema.

Why did seeing a doctor for yijing not pose the same political risk as seeking treatment for impotence? It was easier for a yijing patient to present his symptoms to a doctor because nocturnal emission was involuntary, and, therefore, the patient could not be held fully responsible for it.

Yet the patient could not totally shrug off his responsibility. As a Chinese saying goes, "Ri you suo si, ye you suo meng" (日有所思,夜有所夢, one sees in dreams during the night what he or she longs for in the day).[17] The authors of *Knowledge about Sex* (Wang et al. 1956), the sex-education book mentioned above, assigned agency to the individual who suffered from yijing, attributing it either to a lack of knowledge about sex, a long-time masturbation habit, or indulgence in erotic novels. *Knowledge about Sex* was a contradictory book. On the one hand, it sought to assuage anxiety about yijing by saying that it was normal, and, on the other hand, it sought to persuade patients to focus on the collective cause of revolution to reduce the incidence of yijing.

In principle, the patient did not have much responsibility for nocturnal emission, because what one longed for during the day was mediated by many factors. Perhaps most importantly, one who sought medical treatment for nocturnal emission aimed to get rid of "uncontrollable desire," whereas one who sought treatment for impotence aimed to regain the ability to "indulge" in sex. In seeking treatment for impotence, one manifested his will and his aspiration to indulge in sex. Therefore, when sexual desire was defined as serving individual interests incompatible with the sentiment of collectivism, it was morally as well as politically safer for one to suffer from yijing than from impotence. More patients of yijing than of impotence were "produced" by the moral symptomatology of Maoist China. People "chose" to suffer from yijing rather than from impotence.

SEXUAL DESIRE WAS THE ENEMY: SELF-CASTRATION

To illuminate how sexual desire was antithetical to collectivism, Dr. Liu described a case of uncontrollable desire that led a man to request castration. In the early 1970s (the latter part of the Cultural Revolution), he received a patient in his forties who indulged in *mocayin* (摩擦霪, a type of frotteurism: gaining sexual pleasure by pressing the erect penis against the bodies, most often the buttocks, of females in public, e.g., on a bus). The patient was an engineer. According to the authorities of his work unit, he was a good person in every sense except for this terrible behavior. He had been sent to a correctional center three times but could not break his habit. The first time he saw Dr. Liu, he knelt down as soon as he walked into the consultation room and requested that his scrotum be removed. In other words, he asked to be castrated to permanently terminate his terrible habit and eliminate the source of his crime.

The kind of castration requested by this engineer had actually occurred before in Dr. Liu's hospital—performed not by medical professionals, however, but by patients themselves. According to Dr. Liu, several self-castrations had occurred right outside the emergency room. "They chose to cut their scrotums off or injure them right outside the emergency room, so they could have their lives immediately saved," he recalled. "They cut themselves but didn't want to die. They were single, in their twenties. They prepared their knives. The pain must be extremely excruciating, because that part of the body is very sensitive. It happened in the 1970s. Such a thing also happened in the 1960s, but not anymore in the 1980s."[18]

In the 1980s and 1990s, frotteurism continued to be treated, but castration was no longer considered a solution to this form of aberrant sexual behavior. What is one to make of this kind of castration? Castration as a form of self-mutilation is carried out in many places in the world for various reasons. Anthropological discussions of specific instances of castration in India read against its having a universal meaning. There, self-castrated hijras are considered "neither men nor women" but assume a status of thirdness in the sense that their gendered identity lies beyond not only the male–female binary but also male-to-female transexualism (Nanda 1998; Cohen 1995). Hijras reach toward a unique gendered space, a space of "embodied terrain of pleasure and affliction" (Cohen 1995:293). They choose castration as a means of gender transgression rather than as a solution to a moral and political danger.

In the context of China in the early 1970s, however, self-castration had a direct relationship to sexual moralism and the state's tight control of sexuality, reflecting the negative terms in which desire was interpreted. In Western psychoanalysis, castration as a symbolic state is inherent in the complex relationship between the dominant father and the incestuous son. It may also symbolize feelings associated with sexual repression. However, the self-castrations that occurred outside the emergency room of Dr. Liu's hospital were *real* physical acts and recalled castrations in earlier Chinese history. In imperial China and earlier times, for example, many young men conducted *zigong* (自宫, self-castration) to become eunuchs, moving up the social ladder through this bloody means of bodily self-transformation. In contrast, the men who castrated themselves in the 1970s at the doors of modern medical institutions aspired to flee an uncontrollable, demonic desire in their bodies. In socialist China, sexual crimes were treated as among the most vicious sins in an age consumed with the struggle for moral purity, an aspired-to selfless state. No one knows whether the self-castrating men of that era would have chosen other ways to deal with their desire had there been outlets available, as there are in China today (e.g., premarital sex and erotic VCDs and DVDs). But they surely would have had a different imaginary field for dealing with their obsessions.

Under such conditions, the modern and the archaic intersected in the self-castrators' imagination. The repression of sexual desire enticed their imagination and drove them toward a historically known practice. When the clash between their own bodies and society culminated in sexual crimes, self-castration surfaced as a solution, however extreme. By cutting the alleged source of crime from their bodies and altering their sexual capacity, they sought a practical solution. Self-castration in imperial China was, for some, a way to gain status and entrée into the imperial court. In socialist China, self-castration prevented loss of status. According to psychoanalytical theories, symbolic castration plays a role in normalizing the subject by making him identify with the father, after which he progresses beyond the Oedipus complex and becomes harmless to the social order in the name of the father. By internalizing the threat of the socialist state's power, self-castrators identified with the state as the moral authority, becoming harmless to the social order in its name.

Despite its symbolic aspects, self-castration in this context absolutely distinguished itself from the symbolic construction of the subject, through the actual transformation of the self-castrators' bodies, through enacting a reality that was unsymbolizably "real." Lacanian psychoanalysis defines the "real" as the prelinguistic, the inarticulate fleshy being (Fink 1995).[19] The "real" forever lurks behind the symbolic and the imaginary as an undifferentiated fabric that "resists symbolization absolutely" (Lacan 1991:66). It was through the prelinguistic nature of the body (e.g., the image of actual blood shed) that the pain resulting from self-castration was evoked and its bearing on the symbolic order made clear. Castration forcefully transformed a presubject into a subject of socialism, but the pain embedded in the unsymbolizable flesh could not be fully absorbed into the meaning of the subject proper. In other words, the socialist system of morality, law, and medicine transformed the castrated body into a subject of collectivism but left the pain of the lived body behind as a lurking ghost. Although self-castration was integrated into the symbolic order, as it was under the sovereignty of imperial China, the fleshly remnant of the self-castrated man, and his pain, was a reminder of the continuity and corporeality of history in the bloody construction of the order of the sovereign.

Resonating with the pain that resisted symbolization but haunted the present, the change in the symbolic order, including the moral symptomatology, prompted the emergence of nanke after Maoist socialism. It was precisely this pain, the real, which refused to go away and which surfaced in Dr. Liu's narrative, that explains how the same evil—sexual desire—lurked behind both frotteurism and impotence and behind sexuality more broadly. The pain also accounts for the change from a moral symptomatology that withheld medical attention from impotence in the Maoist period to one that has enabled the flourishing of nanke around the country today.

When nanke emerged in the new era, it medicalized impotence and justified individual desire. Medicine participated in the making of the subject of desire in the new era.

The Birth of the Subject of Desire

Shifts in moral symptomatology reflect profound changes in society, more generally. Changes over time in Western understandings of the etiology of impotence clearly illustrate this point (Hammond 1974). The naturalist view of impotence among the ancient Greeks was replaced in medieval times by a Christian view in which impotence was considered a punishment inflicted by God on the man who committed immoral acts (McLaren 2007). The moralistic etiology of Christianity gave way to a scientific view after the Enlightenment, when the underlying physical determinants of impotence were identified (Rosen and Leiblum 1992). Max Weber neatly summarizes the historical transformation, pointing out that, in dealing with problems such as sexuality, "for the Puritan the expert was the moral theorist, now he is the medical man" (1976:264). The location of illness changed from religiously defined sin to scientifically defined disease. Normality rather than morality became the major concern both in etiology and medical treatment and in the politics concerning the control as well as the governing of society.

Figure 1.4: A department of men's medicine in a hospital in Chengdu.

The shift in medical focus from yijing to impotence in China's transformation resembles the change in the West from viewing sexual illnesses as the products of sin to their acceptance as diseases, a de-moralization of the shame of impotence.[20] Commenting on this shift, Dr. Chen noted, "Nowadays, we receive a lot fewer yijing patients, because there are outlets for them to *xuanxie* (get it off one's body, excrete). Nocturnal emission due to *chunmeng* (erotic dreams) is a bad thing to people with less education, whereas it is a good thing to well-educated people, because erotic dreams confirm the existence of sexual fantasy and sexual desire."

Seeking medical treatment for impotence was no longer seen as negative or harmful but became a positive action. The consciousness of desire as a positive pursuit became the celebratory sign of an emergent scientific-minded and consumer-oriented citizenship. In contrast, the fear of sexual desire and fantasy became problematic and a sign of low education as well as of a person's incompatibility with the new era. With desire thus encouraged and valued, it is not surprising that fewer patients were seeing doctors about nocturnal emission and that more people experiencing difficulty with erection felt encouraged to seek medical help. Impotence had been purged of its dense moral implications under Maoism to become de-moralized.

This de-moralization can be seen in the following ditty told by a cadre in the late 1990s:

過去是有賊心沒有賊膽
後來是有賊心有賊膽沒有賊錢
現在是有賊心有賊膽有賊錢,但是 "賊" 不行了

In the past, I had the lustful heart [to indulge in sex]
But, I did not have the evil guts to do it.
Later, I had both the lustful heart and the evil guts,
But, I did not have the dirty money and couldn't afford it.
Now, I have everything: a lustful heart, the evil guts, and the dirty
    money,
But, I can't do it because the thief himself [my penis] does not work
    anymore.

A nanke doctor told me a similar ditty:

票子有了 (*Piaozi youle*)	Now I have money
車子有了 (*Chezi youle*)	I have my own car
房子有了 (*Fangzi youle*)	I have my own apartment
婊子有了 (*Biaozi youle*)	Prostitutes are available now
命沒有了 (*Ming meiyoule*)	My "life" [potency] is gone

Both of these ditties represent the perspective of a middle-aged man,
who expresses feelings of amusement as well as self-pity with regard to the
impotent body in today's consumer society. The feeling of self-pity revolves
around the tension between *yu* (慾, desire), presented as primordial lust, and
the obstacles preventing the satisfaction of such desire. This tension is his-
toricized in the three periods referenced in the two ditties.

The "past" refers to the pre-1980s Maoist period, when the man was
tempted to have illicit sex but did not have the nerve to do it because the
punishment would have been severe. "Later" refers to the first one and a half
decades of the post-Mao reform, the 1980s, when the man had the courage
to engage in illicit sex because the moral consequence for doing so had become less severe and more people were actually doing it, but he did not have
the money and could not afford it (e.g., could not pay prostitutes). "Now"
refers to the period of the full rise of consumer culture in the late 1990s,
when circumstances had changed sufficiently to allow the man to do whatever he wanted to. The control on sexuality had been loosened even more,[21]
and immorality was far less an issue than it had been. Prostitution had become rampant throughout the country. The man had made enough money
to see women (prostitutes or others). He had, however, become impotent.

Under Maoist socialism, particularly in the Cultural Revolution, yu (desire) was perceived so negatively that not only was sexual pleasure always associated with illicit sex but the male sexual organ itself was also called "the thief." Questions arise: Why was sexual desire repressed in the Maoist period? How did it change? This chapter has partially answered these questions, and I explore them more fully in the next chapter. The rise of impotence did not occur overnight. It took more than a decade after the first nanke clinic appeared in 1983 for that medical practice to flourish countrywide. Public perception of sexual desire likewise changed gradually, from negative to positive, between the early 1980s and late 1990s. Certainly, the birth of nanke contributed to this transformation—to the rise of sexual desire, in particular, and the rise of individual desire, in general, that led to de-moralization of impotence.

Today, despite the shift and the decline of moral vigilance, a strong sense of shame still surrounds impotence in China. Its de-moralization did not eliminate the shame associated with the condition altogether but only reconfigured it. This reconfiguration reflects a remoralization of, or, more accurately, the rise of an "ethicalism" with respect to, impotence. That is, the moral stigma attached to the tendency to indulge in sexual desire, a moral flaw, was replaced by an ethical stigma attached to the inability to realize one's capacity as a modern subject, an ethical inadequacy. Nanke came into being to fix this ethical deficiency in male subjectivity.

Many of those I interviewed were convinced that *manzu xingyu* (滿足性慾, satisfying sexual desire) was a *tianjingdiyi zhi shi* (天經地義之事, a matter of the principle of heaven and earth, i.e., perfectly justified), an attitude that has become the norm in recent years. Taking the initiative themselves in most cases (or, in some cases, under pressure from sexual partners), impotent men are now turning to nanke for treatment. Responding to advertisements for nanke, making inquiries about nanke, becoming determined to see doctors, making trips to the hospital, reporting impotence and the desire to alleviate it, and getting prescriptions (e.g., for herbs, Viagra) are all part of a trajectory of remaking one's self. This trajectory consists of repeated actions and feelings, including spending money on medication for impotence and habituating oneself to feeling comfortable with one's desire. It has taken time for many to build up this sense of comfort with desire—to reveal it, seek its satisfaction, and feel good about doing so. The days of feeling like a thief when pursuing sexual desire are over, and openly desiring has become a new habitus and a new orientation in life.

Elaborating on her argument that, in post-Mao China, sexuality is entangled with the issue of modernity, or being modern, Gail Hershatter writes, "In reform-era China, talking about sex is modern. Looking at particular kinds of sexual images is modern. Worrying about scientifically measured standards of sexual performance is modern. Making sex as audible and visible as possible is modern" (1996:93). What makes those sexual actions, activities, experiences, and works "modern" is the justification of individual sexual desire. Going to nanke to seek treatment for impotence today is qualitatively different from seeing doctors about impotence in the Maoist era, because it indicates the rise of a distinctive mode of subjectification revolving around individual desire. In today's China, sexual desire not only "exists" but it is also constructed as central to the subject of modernity.

_____

The story of the birth of nanke throws into stark relief the contrast between discouraging sexual desire in the Maoist period (especially during the Cultural Revolution) and encouraging sexual desire in the post-Mao reform years (particularly since the 1990s). This analytical contrast resonates with a popular contrast between the two eras in terms of the etiology of impotence. "Men suffered from impotence in the Cultural Revolution because of repression, whereas today impotence results from tense competition in the market economy," a male journalist in his late thirties said to me in Chengdu in the late 1990s.

In Chongqing, a urologist in his sixties confirmed this comparison: "I have seen some patients who were classified as rightists, landlords, or rich peasants in the past. They were often struggled against in public denunciation meetings during the day, and they were having difficulty getting it up in the evening. They did not dare to complain about it at that time. They came to see me only now to reveal the situation in the Cultural Revolution."

These assessments echoed the story Zhang Xianliang told in his novel *Half a Man Is Woman*, set in the Maoist period. The male protagonist, a rightist, is a prisoner on the rehabilitation farm in Ningxia Hui Ethnicity Autonomous Region. He suffers from impotence for a long time before he overcomes it with the help of a female prisoner. I interviewed Zhang Xianliang in the early 2000s. He himself had been classified as a rightist, but he stopped short of confirming that his novel is based on his own experience. Instead, he said, "The protagonist represents that era. Fear and depression surely affected one's sexual potency. A French friend told me some men who survived the Auschwitz concentration camp suffered from impotence for the rest of their lives. They could not have sex without taking some drugs. In the *laogaidui* [the 'team of reform through laboring,' an official designation for detention centers, prisons, or camps], impotence was common."

According to some clinical cases as well, sexual deprivation or repression bears on male potency. There is no doubt that the sexual desire of class enemies and their children tended to be more repressed in the Maoist period (as I show in two extended cases in chapters 3 and 7). Class enemies and their children accounted for a lot of Chinese people. According to one study, about twenty million people were classified in the 1950s as belonging to one or another of four black categories—landlords, rich peasants, counter-revolutionaries, and bad elements (this total does not include half a million rightists, a fifth black category). Counting the children and grandchildren of those so classified, about 100 million people were affected, or roughly 15 percent of the population (Li 2009:252). Their experience of suffering was a daunting fact. But what about those who were not assigned to the five black categories? Was the experience of impotence among the revolutionary classes also related to sexual repression? Was the sexual desire of the majority of the population also discouraged or repressed?

As I discuss in chapter 1, sexual desire was discouraged within the moral symptomatology of the Maoist period, reflecting the overall tendency in the general population. But the last question above reflects the skepticism in contemporary Chinese studies about the argument that the Maoist state repressed sexual desire. The current scholarly skepticism is a response to early studies of sexuality in that period (particularly the Cultural Revolution years) that essentialized sexual repression and failed to explain why repression of premarital sex, extramarital sex, homoeroticism, and so forth, was necessary (Ruan 1991; Ruan and Bullough 1989). For example, Fang Fu Ruan and Vern Bullough argued, "Chinese officials discouraged intimacy among married couples by assigning husbands and wives to different parts of the country and allowing them to meet only for brief vacation periods during the year" (1989:199). *Liangdi fenju* (两地分居, physical separation of married couples) was common in the Maoist period, but explaining it in terms of officials' deliberate efforts to prevent intimacy is not convincing. Ellen Jeffreys argues, on the basis of Emily Honig's studies, that reality contradicted the "claim that the communist repression of sex reached its zenith during the Cultural Revolution" (2006:3). Honig conducted a thorough investigation of sexual behaviors during the Cultural Revolution and found that sexual repression coexisted with sexual transgression. She was skeptical that the state ever overtly promoted sexual repression, given that the central government never issued laws prohibiting sex. Instead, she concludes, the state was silent on the issue (Honig 2003).

Overlooked by both sides of the debate is how the Maoist state, instead of intentionally working to repress sex in marriage, achieved that effect through the *danwei* (work unit) and *hukou* (household registration) systems—two cornerstone systems of collectivist society that limited the flows of people, labor, and money and, in that way, impeded the flow of sexual desire, particularly after the hukou system was consolidated in the late 1950s and early 1960s.[1] Existing studies of the danwei and hukou systems have not explored their impact on sexual life. I therefore examine how the structural limitations imposed by these systems shaped people into *danwei ren* (danwei personhood) by constraining their sexual desire.[2]

At first glance, the study of sexual repression in the mid-twentieth century might seem like an academic concern, as Chinese society has moved far beyond Maoist socialism and has allegedly undergone a sexual revolution (Pan 2006; Zhang 2011c). Yet the post-Mao transformation has brought about problems that never could have been imagined in the Maoist period, such as rampant corruption and alarming inequality, and the urge to seek solutions to those problems may tempt some to turn to Maoism for inspiration. Thus, whether sexual repression existed under Maoism bears on how people judge Maoism, a crucial issue in today's politics of public culture. In short, debating sexual repression in the Maoist period is writing a "history of the present."

The first step in examining this debate is to define what is meant by "sexual repression." The phrase does not refer to prohibiting sex within marriage. Rather, it refers to a strong hostility toward and vigilance against premarital sex, extramarital sex, homoeroticism, and other forms of sexual activity outside the context of institutionally sanctioned heterosexual unions. It also refers to discouragement of sex for pleasure and of articulation of sexual desire in public discourse and to the institutionalization of practices that affect dating and even the sexual life of married couples. Pan Suiming (2006) characterizes what I call "sexual repression" as "desexualization."[3] Reexamining "sexual repression" from the perspective of structural limitations, I argue against the essentialist view of sexual repression mentioned above.

In this chapter, I illuminate sexual repression by examining two events. One derives from a long journalistic report, the other from my own experience and fieldwork.

Structural Limitations on Sexual Desire

How did the systems of danwei and hukou restrain sexual desire? This is both a structural question and a question concerning historical evidence.

PHYSICAL SEPARATION UNDER THE
DANWEI AND *HUKOU* SYSTEMS

In the early 1990s, Mai Tianshu, a thirty-something journalist with *China Youth Daily*, published a book based on an investigation he carried out entitled *Xing wangguo de yinmi shijie* (A Secret World in the Kingdom of Sexuality). One chapter, entitled "Social Journey of Impotent Men," is particularly relevant for this discussion.

Mai related the stories of four impotent men (based on cases obtained from psychotherapists) that revealed the kind of "social journey" each man had taken. Here I introduce one of those stories, that of Lao Gao (Old Gao), a forty-seven-year-old man. During the Great Leap Forward, in 1958, at age eighteen, he was recruited from a village to work in a famous steel factory in Beijing. He got married at age twenty-two to a girl from his home county. They lived together for half a year, until 1962, when the failure of the Great Leap Forward resulted in a large-scale downsizing of the workforce that sent migrant workers back to their rural homes. His wife became one of the twenty million workers sent back. Lao Gao continued to live in a danwei (work unit) with a city hukou (household registration), whereas his wife had a rural hukou, living as she did in a village about a hundred *li* (50 kilometers) away. He was allowed a one-month leave of absence a year to live with his wife. But, because of intensified class struggle and political campaigns, the couple's one-month reunion was often disrupted. In other cases with which I am familiar, married couples were given only fourteen days to spend together (this included travel time).

In the third autumn after their separation, Lao Gao found himself impotent. He was devastated by the condition, lost interest in his hobbies, and became introverted. He lived with the condition for thirteen years, from 1965 to 1978.

During those difficult years, he realized that he was not the only one among his coworkers who suffered from impotence. In his factory, 5,734 workers were *laodanshen* (old bachelors), who were in fact married but had been physically separated from their spouses for more than twenty years.

Among them, 638 had, by the mid-1980s, been separated for more than thirty years!

Among urologists, the general consensus was "use it or lose it," meaning that long-term sexual abstinence could result in the loss of the ability to get an erection. Whether or not long physical separation results in impotence, men like Gao as well as their wives were forced to suppress their sexual desire.

Mai expressed sympathy toward Lao Gao and many like him. He attributed their suffering to "the disaster bestowed by history" (Mai 1996:66). But simply condemning history does little to illuminate this disaster. To fully understand it, one must examine how the socialist danwei (work unit) and hukou (household registration) systems gave rise to physical separation of families.

The danwei system was implemented in the 1950s and had become the dominant way to organize the life of urbanites (Walder 1988; Lu and Perry 1997; Bray 2005). The hukou system, also implemented in the 1950s and consolidated in the early 1960s, separated urban residents from rural residents (Wang 2005; Cheng and Selden 1994). It aimed to ensure industrialization underpinned by the forced procurement of grain from rural areas, and it deprived peasants of the right to live the kind of life available to urban residents. Without a city hukou, a peasant could not find a job and live in the city. The danwei system operated to support the centralized economy in the absence of a free market for products, capital, and labor. Both systems limited people's mobility, but peasants were restricted more severely than urban residents.

Under the hukou system, Lao Gao's wife, a peasant, could only dream of changing her hukou from an agricultural one to an urban one, as the institutionalized urban–rural divide deemed peasants second-class citizens. She did agricultural work in a people's commune to earn her subsistence and did not receive any benefits. In contrast, working in a large state-owned enterprise, Lao Gao enjoyed a stable wage and social benefits, including housing, medical care, and accident insurance. On the one hand, it was inconceivable to Lao Gao that he give up his job to return to village life. On the other hand, it was impossible for his wife to relocate to the city because of the hukou restriction. Their physical separation was a consequence of structure.

The hukou limitation in Lao Gao's case was extreme, because his factory was a large state-owned enterprise located in Beijing, the capital of China, and, hence, an impossible destination for a rural hukou holder. Under the centralized economy, it was difficult even to change one's urban hukou from a small city to a medium-size city, it was more difficult to transfer from a medium-size city to the provincial capital, and it was nearly impossible to change one's hukou from provincial capital to Beijing. *Jinjing zhibiao* (quotas for change of hukou from other places to Beijing) were tightly controlled by the central government and city governments. In other words, even if one held an urban hukou, it was very difficult to change it to a Beijing hukou. Switching jobs was made even more difficult by the danwei system. In the absence of a free job market, a danwei (e.g., a factory) recruited new employees through hiring quotas set by the labor bureau of the city in which it was located. Then the quota had to be approved by the relevant supervising administration (e.g., a bureau of mechanical industry overseeing a number of mechanical factories). Once an employee was hired, it was not unusual for that person to spend the rest of his or her life in the same danwei. Just as the danwei had little power to decide the issue of hiring, it did not have the power to lay off employees, because the centralized economy, in the form of a state-owned enterprise, guaranteed the existence of the danwei through subsidies from above, regardless of its profitability. We need to keep in mind that there was also no free market for products. All production and sales were planned and did not reflect consumer demand, as in a free-market economy. A danwei might expel employees who committed crimes, but this occurred only rarely. This rigid personnel management made switching jobs difficult, if not impossible. One could not simply quit one's job to take a job in another danwei, because quitting meant giving up danwei membership, which would undermine one's credentials for getting a new job. A person without a danwei was close to unemployable. Furthermore, no danwei could hire a person unless there was a quota to be filled.

Andrew Walder (1988) points out that job switching did happen, but only under certain conditions. It was a little easier for employees to switch jobs between two collectively owned danwei than to switch from a danwei of collective ownership to a danwei of a state-owned enterprise, because the former was inferior to the latter in wages, benefits, and social welfare. A worker might switch to an inferior danwei to secure a more convenient location, but he or she did so at the expense of benefits, a big loss. When job switching happened, it was almost always instigated by the state in the name of "the needs of the revolutionary cause" or "the demand of the party and the people." Those who were empowered in the structure (e.g., children of high-ranking officials) could switch work units to meet their personal needs. For the majority of the danwei members, however, family concerns could in no way override "revolutionary needs." It is not a surprise that almost every danwei had married but separated couples on its rolls.

One case I knew illuminates the difficulty especially well. It took eight years in the 1970s for one man, then in his late twenties, to switch from a state-owned farm to a state-owned institute of fruit research to be close to his wife's work unit, even though the two work units were located only about ten miles apart, were under the jurisdiction of the same city government bureau, and both husband and wife had city hukou.

Overall, the hukou system limited flows, especially from rural areas to urban areas, and the danwei system limited mobility between work units. Together, by minimizing flows of personnel and the mobility of the population, the two systems provided the structure for the centralized economy and the unity of Maoist collectivism. These structural limitations were reflected in large numbers of physical separations, which, for ordinary people, translated into the repression of sexual desire. Instead of being silent on issues of sexuality, the state articulated its position unambiguously, stifling sexual desire through institutional constraints and structural limitations, notwithstanding the fact that desire transgressed the boundaries it imposed from time to time.

I turn now to an experience of my own to further illustrate the relationship between structural limitations and sexual repression. My story involves a prohibition on dating and unfolded in 1978 (a time still largely influenced by Maoism, though after Mao's death in 1976) in the May First Technical School in Chongqing, then in Sichuan Province. I was a student in the school at the time.

THE NO DATING RULE
When I last visited the school in 2006, I found the whole campus had changed beyond recognition. All but one of the buildings I had known some twenty years before had disappeared; the surviving structure was abandoned and waiting to be torn down. It was as if a whole new world had arisen out of the ruin of the old. I got together with seven of my former classmates, and we talked about how the school had prohibited dating in the late 1970s. We all remembered the "no dating rule" so well that it might have been enacted only yesterday.

Even though no written rule specified *buzhun tanlianai* (dating is not allowed), school administrators made it clear verbally that dating was unacceptable. Anyone caught violating this rule would receive a warning, and the dating relationship had to stop. The warning might cite the dating student for not observing discipline—for example, for missing classes—but the clear message was that dating was to blame for corrupting school discipline.

Ms. Li, twenty years old, and Mr. Gu, twenty-one years old, were caught violating this rule. They received a warning from the school administration and were asked to discontinue their relationship. They refused. Because of their unyielding attitude, school administrators put the two students on probation for a year. The general branch of the Chinese Communist Youth League in the school also punished the two, who were league members, with probation.[4] Even though the probations were temporary and the two students were allowed to keep their membership in the Youth League, they paid a price for their romance—they were the targets of moral accusations and were punished when they received their job assignments at graduation. There was no free job market at that time, and almost every graduate was assigned to a job by the school administration. These two students were deliberately assigned jobs that separated them as far apart as possible in the district.

More than twenty years later, during my fieldwork in 2000, I found Mr. Gu living in the same city to which he had been assigned decades before. He was then the vice head of a state-owned factory, which was facing bankruptcy. He had a daughter who was attending junior high. I joined him for a meal, and we had a long talk. Afraid of offending him, I avoided asking about his wife. Slowly sipping a glass of beer and sticking his chopsticks into the spicy, oily juice of the "fire pot" (or "hot pot," food cooked in and eaten from a boiling soup), he said that his wife still remembered me as her schoolmate—this was his way of telling me that his current wife was Ms. Li, his lover of some twenty years earlier.

This couple's story has long been a great puzzle to me in my effort to understand sexuality and the state in the Maoist period. On the one hand, few events are more eloquent than this story of love and punishment in speaking to the sexual repression of that era.[5] On the other hand, I have encountered no convincing explanations for the stringent regulation of sexual relationships under the socialist state.

Attributing this type of state repression to what Herbert Marcuse termed "surplus repression" of sexual desire is essentialist and simplistic. Marcuse drew a distinction between basic repression, "the 'modifications' of the instincts necessary for the perpetuation of the human race in civilization," and surplus repression, "the restrictions necessitated by social domination" (1966:35). He emphasized the exploitative nature of surplus repression and disagreed with Freud that sexual repression is an inherent characteristic of civilization, but he failed to explain why, historically, sexual repression is often part of social domination. For example, why, in this instance, did dating pose a threat to the sociopolitical order and, so, have to be stopped?

Dennis Altman (2001:130–37) summarized three views on the relationship between sexual repression and the state apparatus (primarily in authoritarian regimes).[6] All three basically argue that because the repression of libidinal energy produces human beings who prefer authoritarianism, sexual repression is necessary. Again, these views are not substantiated by historically specific accounts that explain sexual repression as an essential part of the state apparatus. In the May First Technical School in Chongqing, a collective ethos was promoted, but it was not sufficient to account for measures such as the prohibition of dating.

Anthropologist Bronislaw Malinowski interpreted sexual repression as "a mental 'by-product' of the creation of culture" (1927:x), functioning to promote the coherence of society. He failed to engage with sexual repression historically and could not offer any insight into the role the state might play. It is clear that the administration of the school represented state power at the microlevel. Since the government did not issue orders to prohibit dating, why did the school administrators adamantly object to students dating?

The inability of current theories to explain sexual repression in this case does not justify denying that sexual repression occurred in the Maoist period.[7] How did the prohibition against dating, in this case, serve to maintain the coherence of society and culture, to take Malinowski's view? My study addresses, to quote Foucault, not "simply a question of repression" (1997:126) but the issue of how the social structure of Maoist socialism shaped sexuality in particular and subjectivity in general. I found myself returning to discussion of the danwei and hukou systems for an explanation.

THE INFLUENCE OF THE *DANWEI* SYSTEM
IN SCHOOL: JOB ASSIGNMENT

In the May First Technical School, the practice of *biye fenpei* (job assignment) at graduation marked one's entry into the work-unit system. Everyone knew that once one's job was assigned, it would be very difficult to switch work units.

Even though, at graduation, the school administrators had the power to decide which student was assigned to which job in which danwei, decisions were rarely based on factors other than the "need of the revolutionary cause." Personal reasons, such as dating, could not override that need. Knowing how insignificant personal factors would be when it came to making job assignments at graduation and the difficulty of switching work units afterward, school administrators discouraged students from dating, because it led to the demand from those who did so for *zhaogu* (照顧, special care), for assignment to the same danwei or to danwei not located too far apart. More students dating meant more demand for special care, which the administrators wanted to avoid.

At the time, dating was considered a serious step toward marriage, unlike dating now, which is based on romantic feelings or sexual pleasure and may not be associated with the motivation to get married at all. There would have been a tension, therefore, between administrators' sympathy toward couples who were romantically involved and the room available for them to accommodate "special" requests in work assignments. Out of this tension came the tendency to impose strong regulations on dating and sexual life in the school.

Although the system affected the students in May First Technical School differently than it had Lao Gao in the steel factory—the former suffered from the prohibition against dating, whereas the latter suffered from physical separation after marriage—the grievances of the individuals in both cases derived from structural limitations.

This order, however, was often put to the test in the school in confrontations between the administration and students. Surprisingly, behind some administrators' apparently rigid commitment to stop dating was concern about being put in a position in which they would have to *bangda yuanyang* (棒打鴛鴦, beat apart "the couple of mandarin ducks," a metaphor for an affectionate couple), an immoral thing to do according to many local folk traditions. In other words, the administrators might have seen themselves as doing the students a "favor" by stopping them from dating, helping them avoid difficulties later in life, when they had to face physical separation.

IDEOLOGY: THE COLLECTIVE OWNERSHIP OF THE BODY
Alongside the structure of the danwei, the rationale of collectivism was also seen in the promotion of sacrifice of the individual body for the larger good. Ownership of one's body is a rather modern notion that falls under

the bourgeois discourse of individual rights and autonomy (Tierney 1999).[8] Under Maoist socialism, however, the ethos of sacrifice and the structure of collectivism problematized the notion of one's body as one's property.

In the everyday language of socialist sacrifice, unconditional dedication of the individual body to the party and to Mao was explicitly and repeatedly emphasized. For example, two common slogans, "My life belongs to the party" (我的生命是属于党的) and "My mother only gives my body, but the glory of the party shines through my heart" (母親只生了我的身,黨的光輝照我心), encapsulated the dominant discourse of sacrificing one's life for the revolutionary cause: the body of a revolutionary, ultimately, belonged to the party.

The ethos of sacrifice was exemplified by individuals like Lei Feng, a soldier of the People's Liberation Army, who was well-known for his selfless behavior in performing his duty and helping others. An important aspect of his selfless dedication to the revolutionary cause was his purported asceticism. In his diary, the only reference to a possible romantic liaison with a "female comrade" consisted of his denial of it. Even this lone reference was deleted from the edition of *Lei Feng's Diary* published in 1968, at the peak of the Cultural Revolution, because, as Tian points out, at that time, "any mention of romance, even in the form of negation, was considered a moral stain in a Communist hero" (2011:302). Lei Feng's loving feelings, as expressed in dreams and recorded in his diaries, focused on Chairman Mao.[9]

Prohibiting dating could incite imagination, but only as a side effect, in the overall ethos of sacrifice and asceticism. I remember that, on at least two occasions, one of the technical school administrators emphasized revolutionary morality and cautioned against any "indecent physical contact" between male and female students. He said, "Now we should be more vigilant, because it is already near summer time and the weather is warm, and the female students' summer clothing is thin and transparent. The possibility for indecent behavior and even rape increases." I remember him saying this several times and with passion. In retrospect, his rhetoric produced the same effect each time—it stimulated the sexual imagination of those listening to him. At the time, however, this "enticement" could not alter the reality that very few girls actually wore skirts, let alone transparent attire, even in the summer.

HOW SEXUAL REPRESSION CHANGED

The repressive mechanism constituted through the hukou and danwei systems did not prevent surprises, nor did it remain unchanged. Mr. Gu and

Ms. Li started dating in 1978, a year of many significant events in both the city and the countryside. Nationwide, the momentum in the political struggle between those who stuck to Maoist socialism and those who wanted to reform, particularly in the economic domain, began to shift in favor of the reformers. Officially, the post-Mao reform began in late 1978, when the Third Plenum of the Eleventh Congress of the Central Committee of the Chinese Communist Party announced the state's shift of focus from class struggle to economic development. Deng Xiaoping, who had been vindicated a year before, became the general architect of the reform.

A strong mood of reflection on the ten years of the Cultural Revolution reached new heights when some radicals started openly to criticize Mao, an action that would have gotten them imprisonment or even a death sentence a couple of years earlier. A *dazibao* (大字報, big character poster) was posted in a downtown street in Chongqing, publicly voicing criticism of Mao for the first time. Prohibitions put in place during the Cultural Revolution against old movies and foreign movies were lifted. In this context, in late 1978, many students in the technical school had their ears glued to radios as they listened to a reading of *The Place of Romantic Love* (*Aiqing de weizhi*, 爱情的位置), a novel by Liu Xinwu that justified individual love. Most students did not have their own radios and listened to the program through the loudspeaker of the school's broadcasting station at lunchtime, when it aired.

The story's appeal was enormous. According to one commentary, "When the first novel touching on love — *The Place of Romantic Love* by Liu Xinwu — was published, the readers competed with each other in reading, recommending and passing it on to others. The extent of excitement and joy — because the Chinese could face love — was beyond the imagination of those youths today who wander about in the wood showered in moonlight after just coming off the disco dancing hall" (Chen 1990:24). The author of this commentary is a Sichuan native and was attending Southwest Normal College in Chongqing when Liu's novel was published.

A publisher recalled the era as one when few books were available. He said, "That year [1978], we were listening to radio which was broadcasting Liu Xinwu's *The Place in Romantic Love*, while lining up in the dining hall to get our meals. Everyone was familiar with it. No other books were available, people throughout the nation were reading the same book and listening to the same story" (Hou 2003). Some exaggeration aside, this man's memory of the sensation caused by the novel resonated with many people's recollections. In the first month after its publication, Liu Xinwu received about seven thousand letters from readers (Liu 2008)! Literary critics later found fault with the novel's lack of sophisticated aesthetic taste, comparing it, for instance, to Zhang Jie's *Love Must Never Be Forgotten*, which came out later. In retrospect, author Liu Xinwu agreed:

> *The Place of Romantic Love* is very much a *gainianhua* (概念化, centered around concepts with little skill of literary representation) and unnatural work. The only significance of this work is to print out the phrase *aiqing* (爱情, romantic love) in open publications. When *October* [a literary magazine] was first published, we had a consensus that we must have a work dealing with love in our first issue and the phrase *aiqing* must appear in the title. It would be extremely difficult for today's young people to understand our eagerness then. That was because during the Cultural Revolution all literary representations were without anything on aiqing, and even the normal relationship between husband and wife could not be presented! . . . A sent-down youth in a rural area wrote to me after he had listened to the broadcasting of the novel. He said that one day while walking back home after hours, he suddenly heard the phrase *aiqing* from the loudspeaker of the commune's broadcasting station. What immediately came to mind was: A coup is happening in China! [Deng 1998:4]

The word *coup* here reflects commonsense understandings at that time of how a group of rebels normally initiated an attempt to overthrow an incumbent government in a third-world country: Often, the rebels first took over the government radio station, among other key buildings, to announce their (sometimes exaggerated or fictitious) victory. What a shock this novel was!

The novel aired for half an hour at noon every day for less than a week. The freshness of the theme—the place of romantic love in life—in the aftermath of the Cultural Revolution immediately excited students on campus such that many could not wait for the next installment. In the story, Meng Xiaoyu, a twenty-five-year-old female worker, falls in love with Lu Lichun, a chef in a Beijing restaurant. They meet by accident. Good feelings develop between them to the point at which Meng Xiaoyu feels compelled to justify her special feeling—romantic love—toward Lu Lichun as appropriate, even for revolutionaries. The need to justify this feeling as proper reveals how serious the constraints on romantic sentiment had been.

Three types of constraint are revealed in the novel. The first is a young woman's "self-censorship" with respect to falling in love. Meng recalls how she felt her heart race and her cheeks heat up when she read descriptions of the romantic relationship between two revolutionaries in the novel *How the Steel Was Tempered*, by the Soviet author Nicolai Ostrovsky. Reading about the love between the two revolutionaries, Meng felt that she was "committing a crime," articulating a feeling common to her generation. *How the Steel Was Tempered* was one of the few works I read during the Cultural Revolution that included romantic relationships and an implicit description of sex. I remember feeling, as Meng Xiaoyu did, that I was "committing a crime" when reading the romantic passages. Where did this feeling of criminality come from?

Here, the second constraint on feelings of love becomes relevant. Meng Xiaoyu attributes her own self-censorship to the lack of any language of romantic love in Chinese revolutionary discourse, a discourse of asceticism in the early and mid-1970s. She cites a 1974 movie, *The Heated Era* (*Huohong de niandai*, 火紅的年代), as exemplifying this discourse. In that movie, the heroine is not married and has no romantic life. She exclaims, "Romantic love does not seem to have a place in the lives of revolutionaries!"

The third constraint emerges from a constellation of soft regulations through which the discourse of revolutionary asceticism operated. For example, Wei Shifu, the manager of Meng's workshop, not only oversees his subordinates' work but also is responsible for their proper behavior in dating and reproduction. He monitors Meng Xiaoyu, including curious mail she receives and subsequent changes in her behavior. His agenda is to enforce late marriage and late reproduction. At twenty-five, under the unofficial regulatory norm, Meng is still too young to date, whereas Yamei, another female worker overseen by Wei Shifu, is twenty-eight and therefore eligible to date. Playing the role of go-between is another way for Wei Shifu to monitor his subordinates' behaviors and relationships to ensure moral order. As a representative of state authority and factory management, he is senior in rank and a skilled master in the workshop, exemplifying how well the administrative regulation of marriage and dating is integrated into the workshop's personal, generational, and professional hierarchy.

The radio program appealed to the technical school students as a point of departure for forming a subjectivity of "romantic love," a feeling and sentiment affirming the individual instead of the collective cause. This was a moment of emergence of what Judith Farquhar, in her reading of *Love Must Never Be Forgotten*, called "private selves—emotional, memorious, possessed of needs and idiosyncratic experiences . . . as the demands of the collective began to recede" (2002:190). When fiction and reality intersected—when the listeners of Meng Xiaoyu's story witnessed the unfolding of Mr. Gu and Ms. Li's saga of love and punishment—the notion of sexual desire and pleasure had not yet attained a central position in emerging post-Mao subjectivity. Instead, romantic love was given a central place, as sexual desire is now.

However, a discourse of desire was emerging. Mr. Gu's story seems to confirm the rising interest in bringing desire into the realm otherwise dominated by the discourse of aiqing (romantic love). Mr. Gu had been exposed to human biology, having grown up in a family of teachers at a professional pharmaceutical school. He was comfortable in the dormitory room talking about the human body. He complained that the school's dating regulation went against "normal physiological needs," a phrase that implied more than biology: it expressed a strong political implication, justifying xingyu (sexual desire), an element that gradually started to be included in the discourse of aiqing.[10]

Mr. Gu recalled that he fell in love with Ms. Li during a school sporting event. Both he and Ms. Li were track runners. In one race, Mr. Gu was *daipao* (帶跑, running outside the track parallel to the runner inside) to cheer on Ms. Li, who was racing hard toward the finish line. During a break between races, she bought him an ice bar. They had not really talked to each other before that. A *haogan* (好感, good feeling) toward her, a feeling Mr. Gu considered love, emerged from this encounter. He recalled that during evening studies, he would defy the punishment imposed by the administration and deliberately go to Ms. Li's classroom. The woman who sat next to Ms. Li would leave her seat so that Mr. Gu could occupy it. For Mr. Gu and Ms. Li, normal physiological needs did not mean sexual intercourse. Instead, it meant proximity and restrained physical contact: touching hands or kissing. Many men his age recalled how, in the late 1970s and early 1980s, touching a girl's body or kissing a girl was a thrilling experience.

Mr. Gu and Ms. Li's "love and punishment" was a topic of much discussion on campus. But the talk was more about their dating than about possible sexual intercourse between them, because sex was unthinkable in a context in which six to eight students shared four bunk beds in one room. Mr. Gu and Ms. Li often went out on dates and returned late to campus. Nowadays, people would assume they were having sex, but the gossip about them then was not centered on sex. When I talked with Mr. Gu during my 2000 fieldwork, he told me that he had defied school regulations and continued to date Ms. Li even after he had been put on probation. Yet, he said, they did not have sex until after they graduated. However, another classmate I spoke with in 2000 said that he thought they had been having sex. According to this classmate, one night one of them could not get into the dormitory room when they came back late after a date, so the two went to a cave on a nearby hill and spent the night there.

Looking back, what seems to me to matter most is not the "truth" of their sexual relationship but the informal discourse (rumors, hints, allegations, etc.) built around their intimacy. The lack of talk about sex, even at the peak of their relationship, indicated that "sexual desire" is, indeed, a historically specific phenomenon whose articulation varies from context to context. What was repressed then might not have been what is defined as "sexual desire" according to today's understandings and behaviors but a historically specific pleasure or desire for closeness.

EMERGING SUBJECTIVITY IN DESIRING

Repression not only encountered resistance but also stimulated "sexual curiosity," as in the following case. One night in 1978, around the time Mr. Gu and Ms. Li were put on probation, I walked into a bedroom in the men's dormitory building at the technical school, looking for someone to chat with. I was shocked by what I saw: with the light off, the eight men who lived in the room were lying on their stomachs on their beds, looking out the window. Following their gazes, I saw female students, visible through the windows of their dormitory, undressing. The exposed parts of their bodies could barely be seen in the dimness before the lights went off, but the curiosity among the men in the dark was overwhelming. Peeping also allegedly occurred in the women's shower room. Rumor had it that one peeping tom was caught there when, exhausted by the hot steam, he dropped to the floor from the ceiling where he had been hiding, to his great embarrassment.

These two incidents are easily classified as voyeuristic. Yet, in the intersection of the flows of different events—the prohibition on dating, the punishment of Mr. Gu and Ms. Li, and the broadcast of *The Place of Romantic Love*—it is not difficult to discern a relationship between repression and voyeurism, between prohibition and resistance, between the sublimation of desire into fervor for the revolutionary cause and the intensification of unauthorized feelings, and, in the final analysis, between the body made invisible by repression and the body made visible by voyeuristic means. If the body, in public discourse and in the realm of behavior, is made invisible, the search for the visible body takes a route outside the realm of control and also outside normality. In this sense, voyeurism is more than "a return of the repressed," because the confrontation is more than a psychic drama, and voyeurism is more than the manifestation of the repressed libido, or sexual drive. The Chinese case adds a whole new dimension to the Freudian insight into voyeuristic behavior.

Jacques Lacan's notion of desire as "lack" opens up the possibility of understanding the story of repression as a constant process of reproducing desire in desiring.[11] Pushing this reading one step further, I evoke the Deleuzian notion of desire. "Desire" has libido as its subjective essence (see Deleuze and Guattari 1983: 333), but in its relationship with an assemblage,[12] it enables the unconscious to be part of the production and reproduction of social relations.[13]

Seen in this light, instead of indicating a permanent lack, what happened in the school reflected a series of social events featuring the tension between the coding (restricting) and decoding (loosening) of flows as seen in a sequence of actions: prohibition heightened curiosity about the body, the erotic gaze, and open resistance. Voyeurism became the assemblage of life details that included specific postures (e.g., peeping), attitudes (e.g., disobedience), perceptions (e.g., normal biological need), and expectations (e.g., sensual pleasure of viewing) in search of the visible body. This series of events constructed desire in defiance of an ethos that "despised the body" and that "left it out of the account . . . treated it as an enemy" (Nietzsche 1968:131).

The structured tension between coding and decoding did not produce only one type of subject. Instead, a range of subject positions was produced with varying effects: to obey (the complier), to believe in revolutionary asceticism (the devotee), to be voyeuristic (the voyeur), to fight back (the resister), and to be punished (the punished). In her study of the Red Guards during the Cultural Revolution, Anita Chan (1985) found four modes of young activists: the purist, the pragmatist, the rebel, and the conformist. They parallel, in part, subject positions seen in the technical school some ten years later.

But the type of subject represented by the pair of lovers—the resister—stood out. If the voyeurs were a disgusting surprise to the system, the resisters were a shock. In contrast to all the "voyeurs" in the dark, Mr. Gu and Ms. Li became, among sympathetic students and even teachers, heroic figures of faithful lovers defying power. The decision to put the two dating students on probation was announced in a meeting of all students, teachers, and staff members at the school. Mr. Gu defiantly stood up as soon as his name was read aloud by an administrator. A classmate later praised him as *yi tiao haohan* (一條好漢, a real man). Sympathetic to a smart student like Mr. Gu, a middle-aged female teacher wept openly. In the context of the technical school, the prohibition against dating made the invisible, nude female body a key signifier of repressed experience, whereas the unyielding attitude of the two students, particularly Mr. Gu, made them forerunners of a profound transformation in sexuality. The punished in the Maoist era became the prophets of the new era.

Just as in the technical school, a search for the body visible was undertaken in artistic representations. During the Cultural Revolution (particularly in the early 1970s), when virtually no foreign movies were shown to the public, two early Soviet films were shown again and again—one was *Lenin in October*, and the other was *Lenin in 1918*. I remember that many of my male peers liked to watch *Lenin in October* repeatedly, for one reason, in particular: one scene showed a performance of the ballet *Swan Lake*. In this scene, probably less than one minute long, the tight, white costumes of the female dancers clearly revealed their bodies. This movie provided, for many, their first sight of the female body unencumbered by layers of clothing. A miraculous niche of eroticism, in what was considered a movie full of revolutionary heroism, was carved out and preserved by viewers' gaze. This unofficial gaze and unofficial reading of a fixed transcript was not anticipated by state censorship. Although nothing in the Soviet film compared to the graphic images of female bodies saturating today's consumer culture, its ballet scene was as enormous a symbol of the search for the body visible as one could imagine at that time.

Using the term "the body invisible" in reference to ancient Chinese art representations, John Hay (1994) drew a distinction between the Western and Chinese art traditions on the basis of the "nudity" appearing in the former and the "nakedness" found in the latter. Western art presents the nude (the anatomical, individual body), whereas in the Chinese tradition, even when nakedness is represented, there is no nude, because what is presented is a generalized, somewhat androgynous body. To Hay, the absence of the visible naked body reflects a distinctive aesthetic revealing the superiority of the cultured and civilized body. In light of this aesthetic, the naked body could be considered less cultural and, even, not yet "Chinese."

The phenomenon of "the body invisible" in the Maoist period, however, was less an aesthetic matter than an effect of sexual repression in the specific contexts I discuss. Chinese scholar Dai Jinhua mentioned how impressed she was, during her visit to an American university campus in the mid-1990s, by her American academic friends' appreciative reading of the ballet *The Red Detachment of Women* (*Hongse niangzijun*, 紅色娘子軍), one of eight revolutionary model operas, or shows, from the Cultural Revolution. The revolutionary and somehow masculinized female bodies in this Chinese ballet were excitingly fresh to the eyes of Dai's American friends, who were used to the bourgeois genre of ballet with its clearly dichotomized gendered bodies (Dai 1999). This reading, in the context of advanced feminism in the United States in the 1990s, particularly within debates concerning gender and sex (e.g., their performativity as opposed to their essentialization), was stimulating to me. The appreciation of normally unappreciated bodies in two different ballets by two different audiences—by Chinese students in the case of *Swan Lake* and by American academics in the case of *The Red Detachment of Women*—constituted an intersection of historical dislocations. The Chinese audience's covert appreciation of the Soviet ballerinas in the asexual climate of the Cultural Revolution was a despatialized transgression, whereas the American audience's free appreciation of the Chinese performers in the aftermath of the sexual revolution constituted an ahistorical elevation.

In the context of the Cultural Revolution, art representations (visual and performative) not only inherited the tradition of the naked body from ancient arts but also intentionally bracketed out the sexual lives of the characters portrayed, transforming the aesthetics of the body invisible into a moral code of hostility toward individual desire. This moral code became an integral part of Maoist collectivism that the whole system had to defend.

In closing this chapter, I offer a reflection on the following question: if sexual repression was a result of structural limitations and the ethos of sacrifice, was Mao ultimately responsible for this outcome? Mao's personal taste, interestingly, ran to eroticism. In 1965, he decreed that the practice of sketching nude human models in art colleges could continue, even amidst the rising tide of class struggle (Cai 1998). Mao even said, "To prohibit it is a feudalist thought and not appropriate" (qtd. in Cai 1998). However, art colleges hired no nude models until the 1980s. Also, Mao recommended *Jinpingmei* (The golden lotus), the well-known erotic novel of the Ming period, as appropriate reading. But only 2,000 copies were reprinted, and they were made available only to cadres at the ministerial or provincial level or above. Even college courses on Chinese classical literature made no reference to the novel until the reform period (Pan 2006). It was not Mao's per-

sonal taste and directives on sexually related matters but the Maoist structure of collectivism and the Maoist ethos of class struggle that reduced the
body to invisibility.

In the 1980s, the danwei and hukou systems started to loosen up, and
the ethos of sacrifice and class struggle started to fade. The phenomenon of
the body invisible became history. The era of the body visible had arrived.

CHAPTER 3

One Thousand Bodies

of Impotence

It is true, as Marx says, that history does not walk on its head, but it is also true that it does not think with its feet. Or one should say rather that it is neither its "head" nor its "feet" that we have to worry about, but its body.

—Maurice Merleau-Ponty, *Phenomenology of Perception*

Mr. Liang, a sixty-five-year-old retired engineer, came to the clinic seeking help for his impotence. He consulted with the doctor and answered the five questions posed by the International Index of Erectile Failure (IIEF-5). The questions ask about a man's confidence in penetrating a partner, his ability to penetrate, his ability to maintain an erection after penetration, his ability to maintain an erection until ejaculation, and his satisfaction with attempts at intercourse over the previous four weeks. On the basis of the consultation and his responses to the questionnaire, Mr. Liang was diagnosed with moderate erectile dysfunction. Further physical examination would be needed to identify the cause.

IIEF was developed along with Viagra and was part of the high tide of the "biological turn" in impotence treatment in the 1990s, having been adopted as the "gold standard" outcome measure in clinical trials (Rosen et al. 2002). Its limitations were obvious. For example, the IIEF focused only on a man's recent sexual history and provided superficial assessment of domains of sexual functioning other than erection. It did not provide any specific information about the partner relationship or sexual functioning of the partner (Rosen et al. 2002).

Not surprisingly, Mr. Liang's score on the questionnaire and his physical examination revealed little about the circumstances under which his impotence occurred. He graduated from college in the early 1960s, a rare opportunity in China at that time. Despite this success, he had a difficult time getting to know women. He met the woman who would later become his wife in 1965. They were married two years later, during the Cultural Revolution. His difficulty in finding a spouse right after graduation lay in two factors. The first was his political status. In the Maoist period, one's social standing was very much decided by one's family origin and political status. The majority of the population was made up of members or descendants of members of revolutionary classes, which primarily included cadres, workers, peasants, and army members. A small percentage, however, was made up of members or descendants of members of "five black categories," which primarily included landlords, rich peasants, counterrevolutionaries, "bad elements," and rightists. One's classification according to this scheme became the basis for one's identity in a context of constant class struggle, and it affected one's social and private life. This was particularly true for those associated with the five black categories.

A *zhishi fenzi* (an educated person or an intellectual) like Mr. Liang fell into an ambiguous category in Maoist China. Such a person was not a member of a revolutionary class and had to be "attached" to the revolutionary classes to gain the trust of the socialist state and the people. In general, a zhishi fenzi was treated as someone who needed to be reeducated, reformed, and integrated into the revolutionary classes. Successfully integrated, Mr. Liang, nevertheless, continued to rank lower on the social scale than full members of those classes, which compromised his educational credentials and made him less attractive as a potential mate.

The second factor complicating his search for a mate was that, having been born in the south, he preferred to marry a southerner, but it was not easy to find one in Beijing. Mr. Liang was assigned to work with the team responsible for *siqing* (the "four clean-ups," a political campaign in the early and mid-1960s against rural cadres considered to be "moving on a capitalist road"). He worked for the campaign for two years in the countryside and then moved to Beijing. Eventually, the head of the "four clean-ups" work team, his supervisor during the campaign, introduced him to a woman from the south. They dated for two years and then married. Mr. Liang recalled,

> She was a worker. But, as a worker, she enjoyed a higher political status than me. She was also into family life, and honest. So I married her in 1967 and had two children. I was satisfied with my sexual life in the late 1960s and early 1970s. But, since the reform period began, things have

gradually changed. I worked for the Ministry of Electronic Industry under the State Council, whereas she continued to be a worker. I had a college education, whereas she only graduated from junior high school. We don't have anything to talk about, except just living a life together. She likes to watch television, but she only watches low-quality shows, whereas I like to watch programs of good taste and high quality. We can't watch television together. My salary is 1,500 yuan every month, whereas she makes less than 400 yuan. I am always the one who initiates sex whereas she has never asked for sex. She has never touched me "down there" and has never allowed me to touch her vagina.

After I retired, we moved out of our old apartment because a new one was going to be built. We lived temporarily in a makeshift house in the suburbs. My potency started to decline when we lived there. I could get an erection when I was preparing for sex, but once I got on top of her body, it became soft and could not get in. Now we have moved into the new apartment. But for the past three months, I haven't touched her body even once, even though I have had desire and have had morning erections in bed. I decided to see a doctor, whereas she is too old-fashioned and asked me to just give up.

I now really agree with the idea of *mendang hudui* (門當戶對, the doors of the bride's and the groom's natal family households should be compatible with each other, i.e., a good marriage requires a perfect match between husband and wife in terms of their status). The landlord's daughter just cannot marry a peasant, otherwise the two will never get along.

In the late 1970s, most members of the five black categories were vindicated, and the official classification based on family origin and political status lost its power when it was largely replaced by economic stratification (or restratification, if we consider that pre-1949 society was largely structured by economic class). Under Deng Xiaoping's leadership, from 1978 on, the social status of educated persons improved greatly in China's pursuit of modernization as did their economic situation, and a widening income gap separated intellectuals like Mr. Liang from workers like his wife in the reform. Mr. Liang became aware of this fundamental change in Chinese society through his impotence. His body became the sensitive site where the change unfolded.

Ethnographic research has shown the different ways that new social distinctions were produced. My research focused on showing how social distinctions were experienced and made corporeal through male impotence. Together, the cases I collected formed a terrain of corporeality, which I call "one thousand bodies of impotence."

"One thousand bodies of impotence" resonates with the nuances of Gilles Deleuze and Félix Guattari's *A Thousand Plateaus* (1987). Borrowing the term *plateau* from anthropologist Gregory Bateson, Deleuze and Guattari (1987:22) avoided any orientation toward a culminating point or an external end in the development of intensities. Analogous to their "thousand plateaus," my "one thousand bodies of impotence" is intended to create a sense of continuity and consistency between bodies and between body and society.

A Biopolitical View of Classes under Maoist Socialism

The most prominent personal change Mr. Liang experienced probably had to do with his perception of his marriage. In the 1960s, he and his wife were considered a good match, because his high education was offset by his low political status, whereas her high political status as a member of the working class was offset by her lack of education.

Some thirty years later, this equal relation was tipped off balance. What Mr. Liang had been able to tolerate in the past as minor differences with his wife in taste, habits, and lifestyle had now become sources of complaint. Mr. Liang felt victimized by the marriage as a bad match. As he told me this, his face flushed and his voice faltered, signs of his resentment and regret. His feelings ended up being manifested in the loss of potency.

By using the metaphor of *mendang hudui* and referring to the marriage of a landlord's daughter and a peasant as a mismatch, Mr. Liang retrieved a presocialist class system from his memory, expressing a welcome return to that system in the reform era. This was a profound negation of the preceding decades of socialism. For many people, the negation became a way to avenge their lives as outcasts during the Maoist period. Mr. Qiu was such an outcast. I tell his story next.

OUTCAST AND IMPOTENCE

I got to know Mr. Qiu, a fifty-year-old college professor, not in the clinic but at a social gathering. He was a member of the *laosanjie* (老三届, old three classes). Laosanjie was the cohort that graduated either from high school or junior high school in the first three years of the Cultural Revolution (1966–

1968). Swept into the heat of that movement, they participated in it first as Red Guards. Then, in response to Chairman Mao's call, they went down to the countryside in the late 1960s in great numbers as *zhiqing* (educated youth) to "receive reeducation" from the peasants.[1] Most of them stayed in the countryside until the mid- or late 1970s, after the Cultural Revolution officially ended.

Since most members of the laosanjie were born around the time the People's Republic of China was founded in 1949, they often called themselves "people of the same age as the New China." As Red Guards during the Cultural Revolution and as the first large group of sent-down youths, they experienced dramatic political changes within a period of about twenty years. On their return to the cities, they had to readjust to the urban environment and to confront new struggles for survival or renewal of their lives. Since the economic reform began in the 1980s, and especially since its dramatic leap forward after 1992, laosanjie has been radically stratified, and most of its members have not been able to compete with younger generations, who have college educations and professional training. Their identity changed dramatically as they went from loyal revolutionary fighters at the beginning of the Cultural Revolution to sacrificial youths in the countryside and then to sufferers in the new era of reform, left out of its opportunities. A sense of being used and abandoned prevails among them.

Mr. Qiu repeated a popular ditty for me that describes the experience of the laosanjie:

Chairman Mao wanted us to *xiaxiang*	(下鄉, go down to the countryside),
Deng Xiaoping wanted us to *xiahai*	(下海, plunge into the sea to work for private business and make money),
Jiang Zemin wants us to *xiagang*	(下崗, step down from a job, be laid off).

After answering the call to go down to the countryside, then, many of the loyal Red Guards of the Cultural Revolution faced layoffs in the reform era. Mr. Qiu was better off than most of his cohort after he returned to the city from the countryside in the late 1970s. He was able to pass the national college entrance exams and study at a university; after graduation, he was assigned to a teaching position at a university in Beijing. But, when talking about his marriage, he spoke of being unhappy and called himself a "tragic figure."

Mr. Qiu was born in 1948. He had tremendous difficulty finding a girl-friend in the 1970s, when he was in his twenties, because of his bad family background—his father had worked for the Guomindang government (the government of the Nationalist Party, which fled to Taiwan in 1949) and had been classified as a "historical counterrevolutionary," and his mother was twice damned, as the spouse of a historical counterrevolutionary and as a landlord before the Liberation. Mr. Qiu went down to a farm in Heilongjiang Province, which borders the Soviet Union, in the late 1960s and returned to Beijing in 1977. "I was introduced to thirty-four women in a period of three years and was rejected by all of them," he recalled.

At that time, children were encouraged to draw a clear line (*huaqing jie-xian*, 劃清界限) between themselves and bad parents by taking concrete actions against such parents. After Mr. Qiu's father was sent down to a rehabilitation farm in a remote province in the northeast during the Cultural Revolution, his mother continued to live with Mr. Qiu and his siblings. She faced criticism on a daily basis in denunciation meetings organized by the neighborhood committee. At home, Mr. Qiu was determined to keep up the heat on her. He ceased calling her "mother" in a show of disrespect, referring to her by her given name for seven years (he did not have a chance to call his father by name because his father was imprisoned on the rehabilitation farm at the time). Calling one's parents by name was unusual throughout Chinese history but not during the Cultural Revolution.

Mr. Qiu said, "*Chushen* (family origin) in the Cultural Revolution was much more important than money today. When I was allowed to participate in the *dachuanlian* (a Red Guard campaign to mobilize youths around the country through free travel, primarily by railway) and went to several cities, as soon as I was asked about my family origin I was more likely to be assigned to bad and humid lodgings than people with good family origins. There were many forms one had to fill out documenting one's identity. The item 'family origin' was on every form." Despite his determination to set himself apart from his parents, even after the end of the Cultural Revolution he continued to have major difficulties finding a woman who wanted to date him.

I asked, "Did you say that you pursued thirty-four women and did not succeed even once, because of your 'historical counterrevolutionary' family background?"

"Yes," he said and then elaborated,

I even pursued two peasant women. Their *hukou* (household registrations) were purely agricultural ones. But the peasant women ended up rejecting me too. Nowadays people say that I look more handsome than those pop stars in Hong Kong and Taiwan. I was even more handsome when I was young. I am 1.80 meters (5 feet 10 inches) tall. But, my looks did not mean anything in my dating; the only thing that mattered was one's family origin. In fact, there were two things that mattered in dating: one was family origin and the other was what *danwei* (work unit) you were in. But, what danwei you were in was determined by your family origin. If you were from a revolutionary family origin, you would be assigned to a state-owned unit; if your origin was a little weaker than first-rate, you might be assigned to a unit of collective ownership; people like me were assigned to the worst type of unit—a *jiedao* factory (one owned by the grassroots-level administrative unit of a city government). The factory I was assigned to was actually a small workshop. This factory did not provide any *laobao* (labor safety, referring to benefits, broadly defined). Nowadays, when people are out on a date, they first look at each other to see what the other person is like physically; but back then, so many women did not even take a close look at me. I often saw a woman in the evening after hours. It was already dark. If she didn't raise her head and take a close look at me, how could she get to know me?

A bit puzzled, I asked, "How could it be that the woman you were meeting didn't take a close look at you? Were they all introduced to you by a matchmaker?"

"Yes," he answered, "all thirty-four women were introduced to me by go-betweens."

"Why couldn't you look for a girl by yourself?" I asked.

"It was impossible," he responded,

If I looked for a girl by myself . . . , it was impossible to hide my bad family origin, because she would already know it . . . Only by matchmaking could I hope to meet women, because sometimes the go-between would hide my family origin from them. But I was not able to hide it when the woman asked me about it. Even if I did not tell the truth, she was able to find out by herself. Besides, if I hid the truth, she could tell because of the shabby factory I worked in. She could infer that I must have some political problem; otherwise I wouldn't be working in this kind of factory. At that time, my coworkers either had a bad family origin or had a good family origin but were disabled. I had an education from a major high school in Beijing—the highest education in the whole factory.

I asked, "Why did peasant women reject you, if they did not have any benefits either?"

"Indeed, they did not have any benefits and were among the lowest in terms of economic status," he answered, "but precisely because they didn't have benefits, they would ask me: 'What if we have a child and the child gets sick? What if we retire and you don't have benefits?' I had nothing to say. Most of the thirty-four women I saw did not come back after the first meeting with me." According to Mr. Qiu, he did not touch a woman's hand until he was thirty years old.[2]

He recalled that his difficulty in finding a woman led him to imagine surgically becoming a woman, because it was less difficult for a woman with a bad family origin than for a man in that situation to find a spouse. This disparity probably reflects the persistence of patriarchal rule in certain ways, even under the socialist system of gender equality. Children with a bad father suffered more than children with a bad mother, because one's social status was more related to a father's family background than to a mother's. Therefore, if Mr. Qiu were a woman with a bad family origin, rather than a man, his children would not be as adversely affected by his history. Many women to whom he was introduced feared that, if they married him, their children would suffer because of his bad family.[3]

Things changed for Mr. Qiu after his father's conviction was reversed. He went to college in the late 1970s. A considerable number of the women who had rejected him in the past resurfaced, wanting to date him. He rejected them all. He commented, "Nowadays, most divorces happen because men fall in love with other women and decide to abandon their wives. Women in China are now miserable, but I think this is compensation for men for their bad experience with women in the past. As a scholar, I dislike revenge, but as a man who has emotions and feelings, I sometimes cannot avoid the psyche of revenge and like to be in charge of the game."

When the conversation turned to his ex-wife, Mr. Qiu said,

I dated my ex-wife three months before getting married. I did not know that she was not a virgin until we first had sex. She had had sex before and tried to have sex with me during her period. I noticed that she just bled a little bit. I didn't know anything but felt it was not quite right. Afterward, I read medical books and became suspicious of her virginity. One month later, when I questioned her, she admitted that she had had sex before meeting me. She had gone to the countryside during the Cultural Revolution. Because she was from a bad family origin, like me—her father had been a capitalist before the Liberation—she wanted to find a man from a good family background to enhance her own political status. It was the rule of the game at that time. She had lived with the son of a worker's family for several years.[4] She had even had an abortion. Since then, I had been brooding on this. Marriage is supposed to be a very pure thing; a man should get a virgin. If the hymen is broken, what is the point of marriage?

The same year Mr. Qiu and his wife divorced, he became impotent. By the time he described these events, they came as no surprise to me. Mr. Qiu quickly said, "If you look for 100 men with this type of problem, I am the first one [I understood this to mean that his impotence was, to some degree, an inability to satisfy his wife instead of difficulty getting an erection]. My problem came up several years ago, when I was seriously ill. I could not get an erection at all at that time, even though now I would be able to get a 100-percent erection."

Mr. Qiu was obviously grappling with the etiology of his impotence. He went on,

In fact, so-called impotence is not *ju er bu jian* (舉而不堅, one can get an erection but cannot maintain complete rigidity) . . . I can get an erection and it is hard, but the problem is that my desire and my erection are not synchronous . . . when you want it to be hard, it does not respond, but when you do not want it, it becomes hard—it becomes hard before or after you want it. Sometimes an erection happens only a few minutes earlier or later than you want it . . . It means that it happens when the female partner is not ready, because the female body is slower. But, when she is ready, your penis becomes soft; as soon as the female partner gets upset at your failure, it becomes hard again . . . However, I never permanently lost my potency . . . Judging from my experience, many men's problem is that the penis is just not subject to control, despite the obvious existence of erectile function . . . It illustrates clearly that impotence in many people is due to a lack of the ability for self-adjustment, and that the room for such adjustment is obviously there.

Without telling me the reason, he said that he was divorced one year after his hospitalization for several illnesses. It seemed to me that his history had loaded his body with multiple frustrations that prevented him from building intercorporeal intimacy. First, the stratification of bodies according to family origin in the Cultural Revolution built in his body a memory of being an outcast in terms of sexual relationships. Second, the reversal of this status in the reform period generated great frustration when his demand that his wife be a virgin was thwarted by the woman he eventually married. What was absurd in his desire to "control the game" was his inability to control the history his wife's body had absorbed according to the same discriminatory logic he himself had experienced in his thirty-four failed attempts to find a girlfriend. His wife had played the game according to the rules of the body politic in the Cultural Revolution, but she could not successfully play it according to the reversal of class status in the reform period. She encountered an old rule of the game, resurrected from prerevolutionary Chinese history: the concern with virginity, an asset she had lost under the Maoist rules of play. Violation of the rule of virginity turned her supposedly good match with Mr. Qiu into a mismatch and eroded the possibility for intercorporeal intimacy.

I asked Mr. Qiu, "Did you ever lose interest in having sex with your wife because of the memory of her loss of virginity?"

He answered, "Well, sometimes I was just like an animal and wanted to satisfy a biological urge." He implied that, even though his desire was affected by his wife's nonvirgin status, he was able to have occasional sex with her: "Even right after the wedding, I had sex with her only once a month." He left me with the impression that his was a wounded, resentful, narcissistic, and vengeful body.

On Mr. Qiu's living room wall hung three pictures: two black-and-white charcoal drawings, one of his father and one of his mother, and a color poster of Zhao Wei, a popular young female movie star. His past, embedded in the black-and-white images, hung side by side with the current fantasy projected by the colorful pop star's shiny smile.

THE POLITICAL CLASS SYSTEM: A BIOPOLITICAL INVENTION

When compared to Mr. Liang's story, Mr. Qiu's story reveals a more extreme reversal of social status in the post-Mao period, one that Mr. Qiu keenly experienced. One cannot help but ask why the socialist state made *jiating chushen* (family origin or background) so central to one's identity, to the degree that one's body, as Mr. Qiu recalled, did not count. Why did such an arbitrary system of political class, in which one's status was determined by the combination of one's family origin and one's political stances and attitudes, remain in effect for so long?

The need to understand the socialist past is not self-evident today. One author recalled how shocked he was when, after he had delivered a lecture on novels about the Cultural Revolution in the public library in a city of Guangdong Province in 2009, a young reader stood up and commented, in all seriousness, "In the final analysis, ONLY one tenth of the population suffered in the Cultural Revolution. It is true, isn't it?! The majority of the people were not in the middle of the disaster" (Xu 2012, my emphasis). Social amnesia reflects not only ignorance but also willful judgment that reinforces ignorance. But, surprisingly, aside from many emotionally assertive descriptions of the cruelty of class struggle, a thorough and systematic theoretical understanding remains to be sorted out. Here I reflect on Mr. Qiu's history as an outcast in the Maoist politics of class in a way that goes beyond his own emotional recollection.

Judged by the Marxist view that one's class status derives from one's economic status, the political class system in Maoist China was arbitrary (Li 2009; Billeter 1985) because neither one's family origin before socialism nor one's political attitude was necessarily a reflection of one's economic status. In tackling this arbitrariness, Ann Anagnost argued that the class system in the Maoist period operated not as a representation of reality but as an evocation of "the human face of the impersonal forces of imperialism and capitalism . . . binding the nation together to face off external threats as they were projected inward" (1997:41). Among external enemies, in fact, "Soviet revisionism" was perceived as especially threatening.

Li Ruojian argued that "producing a small group of 'enemies,' and placing the majority in a state of war with those 'enemies,' [the state] made the members of the majority feel safe so long as they obeyed order and avoided falling into the camp of the enemy. By doing this, social control was effectively exercised" (2009:265–66). In addition, permanent enemy classes served as scapegoats in constant political campaigns that had shock effects on the general population.

But the following question remains to be answered: Why did one's biological ties play such an important role in determining one's social status, particularly for descendants of the five black categories? The huge influence of such biological ties can be seen in the state's close monitoring of the boundary between "revolutionary classes" and "counterrevolutionary classes" and its erection of barriers to dating and marriage, as Mr. Qiu experienced. These barriers prevented a portion of the population from reproducing and, thus, polluting the larger society and were, perhaps, specifically aimed at the extinction of that segment of society.

Mr. Qiu suffered from class struggle (class discrimination) in much the same way that a member of "an inferior race" suffers from racism (racial discrimination). Therefore, class struggle was not a resurfacing of a feudalist-status polity in contemporary times but a biopolitical invention of Chinese modernity. The concepts of "biopower" and "biopolitics," as discussed by Michel Foucault and Giorgio Agamben, help shed new light on the political practices of class in the Maoist period.

Foucault introduced the term *biopower* in the 1970s in explaining the effect of power on the biological existence of human beings under modernity. *Biopower* refers to the situation in which power (manifested in measures taken by the state and in the form of institutionalized knowledge) is exercised on the biological existence of human beings at the population level as a means of bringing life into the realm of explicit calculation (Foucault 1990a:143). Such explicit calculation can produce completely divergent effects on a population. In one direction, it maximizes the productive potentials of the population and protects it from being harmed by disasters; in the other direction, it spawns racism, the extreme case being the Holocaust under the Nazis, when the biological existence of a portion of the population was declared harmful to the entire population.[5] Foucault describes how racism functions by compartmentalizing the population: "The appearance within the biological continuum of the human race of races, the distinction among races, the hierarchy of races, the fact that certain races are described as good and that others, in contrast, are described as inferior: all this is a way of fragmenting the field of the biological that power controls. It is a way of separating out the groups that exist within a population. It is, in short, a way of establishing a biological type of caesura within a population that appears to be a biological domain" (2003:254–55).

Modern biopolitics can, by inserting caesuras in the domain of the biological, separate groups within a population and subject them to variable discrimination. Race is one of the most prominent markers of separation. Elaborating on Foucault's point, Agamben (2002:84–85) argues that, in Germany, biopolitical caesuras continued to be inserted to make ever finer distinctions—between citizens of "Aryan descent" and "non-Aryan descent," between "full-blooded" Jews and Jews with only one Jewish grand-parent, and so on—until they reached their final limit in the concentration camp.

The political class system under Maoism operated through such biological caesuras—Mr. Qiu's biological ties with his "counterrevolutionary" parents separated him from members of the revolutionary class and almost doomed his sexual, reproductive life. In the early 1960s, a group of middle-school graduates from the city of Chongqing in Sichuan Province (about fourteen thousand in all) were blocked from entering high school partly because of their family backgrounds and eventually were sent to the Daba Mountains as the first wave of rustication of urban youths (Deng 2006). Early in the Cultural Revolution, the "blood line theory" (*xuetonglun*, 血統論), a radical advocacy of purification of the revolutionary camp through exclusion of those whose biological ties and family background were not revolutionary enough, brought the practice of political class to an extreme. Yu Luoke, a youth in Beijing at the time, was arrested for publishing an article criticizing the "blood line theory." Although this theory had been repealed by the leadership to mobilize members of less revolutionary classes into the Cultural Revolution, Yu Luoke misread the repeal as overturning class lines and was later executed for this error (Walder 2009; Wu 2014).

The practice of classifying people according to their biological ties continued, and many campaigns, such as *qingli jieji duiwu* (清理階級隊伍, sort out the classes and set the people apart from the enemy), aimed to *baochi gemingduiwu de chunjiexing* (保持革命隊伍的純潔性, maintain the purity of the revolutionary army), clouding the lives of many people like Mr. Qiu. Rejected by all thirty-four women he approached, Mr. Qiu was prevented from crossing the caesura between the "counterrevolutionary" and the "revolutionary" and thus "polluting" the revolutionary camp through reproduction. Despite the absence of an official policy against marriage between persons of different class backgrounds, certain biopolitical techniques, such as discriminatory policies in job assignment and medical insurance, consolidated the caesura (Li 2009). These techniques revealed the impulse of the Maoist state, particularly during the Cultural Revolution, to maintain the purity of the political body (the people) by maintaining the purity of the biological body (the population). In this sense, the practice of political class under Maoist socialism can be seen as a process of "racialization" in the absence of racial difference.

THE URBAN–RURAL DIVIDE:

ANOTHER INVENTION OF BIOPOLITICS

Xiaomie san da chabie (the elimination of three gaps—between the urban and the rural, between the rich class and the poor class, and between laboring with mind and laboring with body) was a Marxist ideal trumpeted by the Maoist socialist state. Maoist socialism, in fact, created and maintained a divide between the urban and the rural rarely seen even in other socialist countries, resembling the racial discrimination under the South African system of apartheid. The divide, then, was an extreme invention of Maoist biopolitics.[6] Despite being labeled a revolutionary class and allies of the workers' class, peasants as a whole, regardless of internal class distinctions (poor, lower-middle-, and middle-income peasants vs. rich peasants and landlords), became second-class citizens. Any relocation from urban areas to rural areas, particularly as part of the massive movement of educated youths "going up to the mountains and going down to the countryside" during the Cultural Revolution, marked a decline in one's status and had an impact on one's life.

Ms. Ye, a forty-nine-year-old office manager, told how this stratification affected her body as well as her marriage. I got to know Ms. Ye through friends. Like Mr. Qiu, Ms. Ye belonged to the cohort of laosanjie. She was born and grew up in Beijing. After graduating from junior high school during the Cultural Revolution, she went down to a farm in Heilongjiang in 1969, as Mr. Qiu had. She lived a militarized life there for ten years. During her years on the farm, she was a tractor driver, an elementary schoolteacher, and a worker whose duties included looking after pigs, logging, and overseeing the irrigation system. Her narrative of her time in that remote province was full of stories of life and death—deaths from natural causes (fire, bears, etc.), ferocious struggles against class enemies, horrendous murders resulting from marital conflict between sent-down urbanites and peasants and local farmers, and revolutionary heroic sacrifices made by her cohort to save properties owned by the state.

She knew very little about her own body then. In junior high school in Beijing, she had had a girls-only class in physiology and hygiene—boys were given the class separately. She could not remember what was taught. One day, during a checkup in the farm's hospital, the doctor asked her if she had begun *lijia* (menstruation). She did not understand the question and thought *lijia* was a foreign word. Half a year later, she had her first menstrual period. She was nineteen.

Because she desperately wanted to return to Beijing at the end of the Cultural Revolution, she arranged an introduction to a man who had a Beijing hukou (a residence permit qualifying him to legally reside in Beijing). She married him four months after their first meeting. One year later, she had a child. A year after that, in 1980, her husband could no longer get an erection. She was thirty years old when her husband became impotent. She had not had sex since then.

She recalled,

> My husband suffered from hypertension and diabetes. The doctor said that his hypertension was genetic. But my husband complained that I did not want to have sex with him shortly after our marriage. I did reject him sometimes. He said that this hurt him badly. But I just did not have *ganqing* (emotional attachment or good feelings) toward him. I married him not because I was choosing him as a man, but because I was choosing him as a way out of the life on the farm in Heilongjiang and a way to return to Beijing . . . later I thought that it must be very traumatic for him to become impotent, so I never asked for sex anymore . . . [she pulled out a handkerchief to wipe out tears in her eyes] . . . I thought that, earlier, when I was in a difficult situation, he had helped me, so I should not leave him, even though he was having difficulty now. He is sick now. Recently, he even had difficulty walking and using the wall for support. Because of his bad health, he retired early. He is only four years older than me, but people say that he looks 20 years older than me. In my forties, I sometimes still thought about sex, but I could only suppress it; sometimes when I saw good men in my life, I felt that life was not fair to me. Sometimes, in my neighborhood, people would tease my husband for letting me live like a widow. I was angry with those neighbors and said to them that it was none of their business.

Ms. Ye's husband obviously had physiological problems contributing to his impotence (hypertension and diabetes are two of the major medical conditions directly associated with impotence). It is not clear whether his initial erectile difficulty had to do with his participation in a marriage of convenience and how much his medical situation had worsened in recent decades. He was nonapologetic and never expressed guilt about his inability to satisfy his wife. She continued to live with him to fulfill a moral obligation. She said that ever since the birth of their son, she and her husband had slept separately. She had slept with their son until he was 13 years old. I asked myself, would her life have been different if she had fallen in love with her husband, even though theirs was a marriage of convenience, or if she had discovered her sexual desire at an earlier age?

Ms. Ye said that she did not know anything about Viagra or sexual devices, even though information about them was easy to come by in Beijing at the time I conducted my fieldwork. Ms. Ye was an ardent soccer fan. Her extreme enthusiasm for soccer, in fact, struck me as unusual. The last time she had gone to a movie theater was thirty years before I met her. She rarely went shopping in department stores or shopping centers, and she did not go to parks at all. But she was crazy about soccer. She watched as many games on TV as she could, including the major European league tournaments. Attending games between the Chinese national team and visiting foreign teams was the most exciting activity she could imagine. She described why she liked soccer: "I liked to watch soccer when I was a child. I even watched the soccer games of the Chinese national team in which Zhang Junxiu was the goalie in the 1950s . . . Watching soccer games in the stadium is different from watching live broadcasts of them on TV, because there is a lively atmosphere in the stadium . . . Although fans are rude when they are talking, I feel that everyone is equal and free . . . There is no difference among people in the stadium. This feeling of equality is gone as soon as people leave the stadium. My son liked to watch soccer games with me; female fans like to sit together with me and talk to me about soccer . . . We belong to the same fan club so our tickets are sequential and our seats are always close."

When talking about soccer, Ms. Ye's excitement made her a completely different person than she was when talking about her bleak life—her asexual youth, the bloody and horrible death scenes on the remote farm in Heilongjiang, her unhappy marriage and her husband's maladies, and her suppressed sexual desire. She said that she did not like to watch women's soccer games, because they were not as confrontational as men's.

In her short story "The Fucking Soccer," Xu Kun describes the masculine aura surrounding soccer culture. The short story's heroine attempts to enjoy the sport but is eventually repulsed by the rude language of the fans (Xu 2000). That Ms. Ye was attracted to such a virile sport was revealing. For her, attending a soccer game was an occasion to experience equality and freedom, when one could be rude without worrying about etiquette or critical without worrying about appropriateness or correctness. Fans sometimes goaded Chinese players on with shouts that had phallic connotations—such as "Xiongqi!" (雄起, Get it up like a real man!). The Chinese national team had been trying since the 1970s to qualify for the World Cup competition and had failed in all seven preliminary tournaments it had entered. Like every fan, Ms. Ye had been longing for the day when the Chinese team would qualify as real men by making it to the play-offs and, ultimately, the World Cup championship game. For whatever reason, she could forget the shadow of impotence at home and the burden of her moral obligation when she joined others in the soccer stadium in shouting and yelling for the success of the men on the Chinese team.

Deep in Ms. Ye's heart was a desire for real social equality. She had had a rather complex relationship with what was supposed to have been an egalitarian revolutionary life in the Maoist period. Even though she was not born into a bad family and enjoyed a political status as good as that of most people, her forced relocation from the city to the countryside during the Cultural Revolution created a gap between her and other Beijingers. That gap and the subsequent marriage of convenience aimed at overcoming it were responsible for her lack of good feelings toward her husband, which contributed to her loss of intercorporeal intimacy with him. Impotence was one of the consequences. Watching a soccer game and enjoying the company of other fans on an equal footing probably provided her with a moment of escape. She needed to forget her man at home and the disastrous hierarchy of the supposedly egalitarian past.

Xiagang (Laid Off): The Failed System That Failed the Body

Many case studies of sexual psychotherapies have pointed to an association between male sexual dysfunction and traumatic life events (see Rosen and Leiblum 1992; Stekel 1959). But seldom has such an association been examined in a historically specific context, particularly like the one discussed in the preceding two sections, in which physical and emotional dysfunction seems clearly linked to identifiable social transformations. In one case, a pronounced change in a man's feelings toward his sexual partner coincides with dramatic socioeconomic changes. In the second, sexual difficulties follow a marriage of convenience undertaken to escape a socially mandated rural exile. It is from these bodily experiences of impotence that we begin to feel where the post-Mao social transformation was felt: in the depth of society's flesh. Yet another social factor associated with impotence was the experience of xiagang, job loss, and the attendant change in social status when the socialist economy was restructured during the post-Mao reform.

The restratification in the reform period picked up speed in the 1990s. The change in social status was most dramatic for those social groups who had enjoyed high status in the Maoist period, among them, workers in state-run enterprises. One after another, when such enterprises proved unable to compete successfully in the emerging market economy, particularly with private enterprises, the state ceased subsidizing them and maintaining the system of guaranteed employment; their workers had to xiagang (step down from the work unit; i.e., were laid off). The private sector in China's economy accounted for almost no industrial production in 1978; by 1986, it was responsible for 3 percent of industrial production and, by 2005, accounted for 65 percent of GDP.[7] As a result, some forty million workers lost their jobs over a period of several years in the late 1990s and the early 2000s.[8]

In my daily commute in Chengdu, I often passed the intersection of the first ring road that bordered the east part of the city, where large state enterprises were located. In the intersection stood a fifteen-meter-high statue featuring two workers—a woman and a man atop a large stainless steel pipe. The female worker sat upright, her chest elegantly thrust forward, her left leg folding inward and crossing under the right, which was gracefully stretched backward. The male worker stood with face upraised, lifting a welding helmet in two open palms. Both figures were optimistically looking forward and up, as if the two bodies were set in a concerted forward motion. This statue, created by the artist Ren Yibo, was proudly named *The Builders* and had been erected in 1988 to mark the completion of the construction of the first ring road. It not only symbolized the city's future but also the status of the workers of state-owned enterprises who represented that future. At that time, private enterprises and the waves of migrant workers they were to attract had yet to appear.

The statue's public symbolism had changed by the late 1990s. Driving me past it one day, a friend pointed to the statue and asked, "Do you know what the statue stands for?" Before I could respond, he added, "The workers' class is equal to zero!" I subsequently heard the same jest repeated many times in reference to this statue. Its original name—*The Builders*—had become an anachronism, signaling the previous era of socialism and the transitional period, before the rise of consumer society in the 1990s. In the midst of the layoffs from state-owned enterprises, the statue became a popular icon of the decline of workers' status, "reauthored" by the changing social context to tell a story of new social distinctions.

Impotence also became a manifestation of the decline of status for male

Figure 3.1: The statue "The Builders."

workers. "Xiagang" was a phrase I heard frequently during my fieldwork, both in Beijing and in Chengdu. When a man was laid off from a state-owned enterprise, his whole world was turned upside down. Some impotence patients were laid-off workers. I constantly heard stories and jokes about how xiagang was accompanied by impotence. The psychotherapy and psycho-counseling literature recorded cases of anxiety and depression resulting from job loss and impotence. However, my contact with the workers being laid off told me that job loss was a unique experience for Chinese workers, expressed in the distinctive idiom of *xiagang*, instead of *beijiegu* (being laid off) or *shiye* (unemployed). When the layoffs first began in the 1980s, the phenomenon was officially called "daiye" (awaiting employment).

The euphemism the state and the media used to refer to unemployment and layoffs was intended to downplay the moral implication of job loss. Despite that intention, Chinese workers faced a more harrowing reality than the one faced by unemployed workers in a capitalist country. First, when large numbers of workers were laid off in the 1990s and 2000s, a social safety net—including unemployment benefits, social welfare for low-income families, and retirement insurance—had yet to be developed. In many cases I recorded, stepping-down workers in Beijing received a *shenghuo* payment (survival payment, pension) of only 300 yuan (less than $40) or so per month.[9]

Second, most stepping-down workers had not anticipated unemployment when they first entered the workforce in the prereform or early reform period.[10] Ms. Gong was a forty-two-year-old worker in Chengdu. She grew up in a cadre's family. When she was recruited back to the city from her sent-down life in a rural village in Wenjiang County of Sichuan Province, she refused to accept a job as a flight attendant, a nurse, or a department store clerk, instead becoming a lathe operator in the machine shop of a state-owned factory. "Being a worker was so glorious at that time." Less than two decades later, she was let go when her factory could not continue operation. She commented, "Socialism never prepared us for such a threat in life. My parents always taught us how to behave properly but never taught us how to survive." Indeed, her elder sister recalled that their father, an old cadre, had often organized *jiatinghui* (family meetings) for the six siblings in the family to engage in criticism and self-criticism for immoral behavior.

Psychoanalysis makes a distinction among three terms—fear, dread, and fright. Differing from both fear (of an anticipated danger) and dread (fear of a specific object), fright "emphasizes the element of surprise," a state "when we find ourselves plunged into danger without being prepared for it" (Freud 2006:138). In an extended sense, fright resulting from unanticipated disastrous events induces the effect of trauma. This psychological insight is helpful here, because xiagang in the transitional period did come as a surprise to many people. Even though individual workers experienced layoff differently and many had gradually become used to the threat, xiagang in the 1990s constituted a collective, traumatic experience.

For many who were forced to "step down," the body responded, and impotence became an embodiment of xiagang. One day, I decided to visit a clinic patient's home in a suburban area of Beijing where a gigantic state-run steel enterprise was located. Many workers from this enterprise had been laid off, and some were now running illegal businesses like *kai heiche* (driving a "black" car, i.e., driving a taxi without a business license). I was taken to my destination by an illegal taxi driver, who realized that the man I was going to see was one of his former coworkers. On the way to the patient's apartment, the driver revealed that he knew the man, and he made a deal with me: He would drive me wherever I wanted to go so long as I was willing to pay him ten yuan ($1.25). I could neither ask him to charge me according to the odometer nor request a receipt from him. He told me that this type of business was an open secret.

My conversation with this laid-off worker reminded me of a friend's experience in the same district of Beijing. My friend had been chatting with an illegal taxi driver during a ride about two months earlier, when the conversation turned to the topic of advertisements for *zhuangyangyao*, the patent herbal tonics that supposedly strengthen virility. The taxi driver said, "I xiagang (got laid off) and lost my way of life. My stuff couldn't get up. I haven't done it with my wife for two months!" That he admitted his impotence so freely and publicly seemed to me revelatory of the widespread effect of xiagang on the body. Voicing the word *impotence*, an otherwise unspeakable symptom, in public became a more powerful way than any conscious critique he could offer to expose the incompetence of the old system and the injustice experienced in its transformation.

As the clouds of unemployment gradually loomed larger throughout the country in the late 1990s and as unemployment became a regular experience of social life, the effects of xiagang could be felt in *nanke* clinics almost every day. I made a trip to Dr. Cao Kaiyong's clinic in Tianjin and talked to a number of patients about their experience of xiagang. One head nurse told me xiagang was so common that, in a place like Tianjin, which had been one of the major bases of industry, "few families did not have someone *xia le gang* (already stepped down)." The following case generates some insight into how the experience of xiagang was embodied.

Mr. Wu, a thirty-five-year-old worker in Chengdu who had never had problems getting an erection after he got married in 1990, started to have erectile difficulty one month after being laid off from his job. After being unable to get an erection for a month, he consulted a doctor. He had worked in the same state-owned factory since 1981 and had never thought that he would have to step down. Workers in his factory had begun to be laid off two years before he was let go. While he was working, he made 800 yuan per month; after stepping down, he received a basic stipend of 300 yuan per month. He described his experience: "I don't feel too bad about xiagang . . . newspapers and television talked a lot about xiagang . . . but I just couldn't fall asleep in the evening. Whenever I see my wife or run into acquaintances, I *xintiao* (心跳, my heart races), I *xinji* (心悸, my heart throbs, palpitates with terror), I feel *xinlei* (心累, my heart is exhausted). I am nervous and afraid to talk to people. Now, I do nothing the whole day except watch television in the evening. I go to bed late and get up late. I clean the apartment in the morning, then go out to play mahjong for a while, and come back to cook meals. That's all I do at home all day. It is just too embarrassing for a thirty-five-year-old man like me to be idle at home."

Mr. Wu implied an association between xiagang and the symptoms he experienced. In describing his symptoms, he emphasized *xin* (the heart). In the bodily cosmology of Chinese medicine, xin is distinct from the anatomical heart. It is a locus where *shen* (神, spirit) is stored.[11] The heart is the king of the body, representing the ultimate *yang* among all bodily yangs. What is most relevant here to the understanding of xiagang is Mr. Wu's description of his xin overreacting, throbbing, and being exhausted. All three feelings disturb the shen that xin stores. The very indigenous reaction of the body here to the unique social experience of being laid off in the transformation of the socialist system was expressed in local idioms about xin, a semantic network (B. Good 1977; B. Good and M. Good 1980). In parallel with the change from guaranteed to nonguaranteed employment, Mr. Wu's potency underwent a change from guaranteed bodily trait to precarious contingency, a traumatic symptom of his new socioeconomic situation.

In contrast to Mr. Liang and Mr. Qiu, who found that the post-Mao transformation increased their status, the workers in state-owned enterprises experienced a decline in their status, signaling the reversal of the old class system. The restructuring of the economy also restructured the body, potency, and sexuality. One patient of premature ejaculation explicitly revealed a direct relationship between the ups and downs in his potency and in his business: "When business is slow, my sexual life is bad. I can only sustain one or two minutes before ejaculation; but if business is smooth, I can sustain an erection for three to five minutes. But still, it won't be as long as before, when I could sustain more than ten minutes." This man's perception of an intimate relationship between the body of impotence and the body of incompetence (enterprise) vividly reflects the extent to which the social body can impinge on individual physical well-being.

A social safety net for the unemployed was finally built up nationwide, and the phenomenon of xiagang gave way to a more sustainable form of unemployment by 2005 (P. Li 2008). When I revisited Chengdu in the late 2000s, I did not see *The Builders* in its old spot. I was told that its meaning had continued to change along with the space in which it was situated, to the point that the statue had to be removed. When it was erected in 1988, it was placed at the center of a garden at a major traffic roundabout. In 2000, the garden was removed to accommodate increasing traffic, leaving only the statue and its pedestal intact. In 2004, the statue was removed, giving way to six-lane traffic aboveground and four-lane traffic belowground through the area. *The Builders* did not have a final resting place until 2006, when it was placed in the Chengdu Museum of Industrial Civilization, which was housed in a remodeled abandoned workshop building of a state-owned enterprise. The statue has finally found a place in history. But has male impotence accompanying the xiagang experience also become history?

Intergenerational Memories

For those impotence patients who were peasants or had lived in rural areas, life since the reform had changed for the better in terms of material gain, but many retained memories of a past that they understood as affecting their potency and sexual performance. These memories often went beyond the immediate intercorporeal contact of marriage. The stories of Mr. Jiang and Mr. Wan, recounted below, demonstrate the unsettled nature of their memories of their relationships with women, memories that were embodied in their impotence.

POTENCY AND A SOLICITOUS AUNT: THE MEMORY OF HUNGER

Mr. Jiang was thirty-eight years old and had been married for ten years. He was a civil servant in a government agency. Both his desire and his ability to get an erection had decreased after he had fulfilled a mandatory three-year work assignment in Tibet. He had spent only one or two months during each of those three years with his wife in Beijing. Mr. Jiang believed that frequent masturbation in childhood was the cause of his decline in potency. What was distinctive about his story was his attachment to the color white and to the woman who raised him—his aunt. He said:

> I am interested in things that are white. I feel good about dressing myself in white. But I don't have the same good feeling when my wife dresses in white . . . I was born in a county in a central province. I lived with my aunt for a long time when I was a child. My aunt was six years older than my mother and did not have a child. Her home was in a village of the same county. My mother sent me to her home and asked her to take care of me when I was three or four years old. She was separated from her peasant husband when I was an elementary school student.
>
> Life was hard at that time [the late 1960s and early 1970s, during the Cultural Revolution]. Major staples like flour were often in short supply. My aunt took good care of me. She made flour pancakes for me. She only ate *culiang* (粗糧, crude crops, such as corn, beans, and sorghum). She

saved all *xiliang* (細糧, refined crops such as flour and rice) for me until I was about twelve or thirteen years old. She also wove baskets of willow and sold them, so she could buy me new clothes and good cigarettes.

In 1979, I left her to attend high school in the county seat, which was also close to my mother's home. My aunt died suddenly after she took the wrong medicine. But I didn't know about her death until two weeks later. My parents hid this from me on purpose. I was dealt a big blow and was extremely sad. I insisted that I should wear a white costume to mourn her. I recall that I saw her in a dream when I first had nocturnal emission. I would have a better erection whenever I thought about her and dressed myself in white. Now, I miss her and pay homage to her at her grave every year.

Mr. Jiang's sexual fantasy and desire were directed toward his aunt, a female body of another generation. In reconstructing the dream he had at the time of his first nocturnal emission, he reduced the age gap between himself and his dead aunt: he was no longer a boy but an adult, whereas his aunt's age and his image of her were fixed at the time he left her for high school. Certainly his memories of her, of her saving refined food for him, weaving willow baskets to sell so she could buy him cigarettes, and so on, might have had subtle, erotic associations for him. His feeling of arousal when dressed in white was dramatized in his ritualistic action of wearing a white costume and paying homage to his aunt in graveside rituals, constituting an interface within his incestuous nostalgia between an unconscious desire and its cover-up.

He had received a B.A. in humanities and was pursuing an M.A. while working as a civil servant. It is possible that his narrative was the result of self-analysis based on a version of Freudian psychoanalysis, which had been popular in Chinese publications since the 1980s and with which he may have been familiar. Even if he recognized that he was harboring a latent incestuous desire, he may have been so motivated to seek a psychoanalytical explanation for his impotence that he ceased trying to hide that desire.

Mr. Jiang's narrative suggests an interesting relationship between food and sexual imagery. He grew up at a time when food was a top priority for ordinary people. For a long time under socialism, urban Chinese lived with a system of rationing because of limited supplies and even shortages of food. The state determined the amounts and proportions of culiang (crude crops) and xiliang (refined crops) people could have in their diets. Saving refined crops for some members of a family meant that other family members had to eat more crude crops. The difference between crude crops and refined crops was closely tied to sensory perceptions: chewing the *jingsi* (筋絲, e.g., the resilient, tasty gluten of flour) was considered more enjoyable than swallowing cornbread. Behind this contrast, the specter of hunger continually haunted people.

Many people I encountered in my fieldwork talked about hunger under Maoist socialism. A thirty-nine-year-old worker recalled that he often got into fights with his three brothers over food in the mid-1970s, when he was in high school, because his ration (26 *jin*, or 28 pounds, each month)[12] could not assuage the hunger of his tall (188 centimeter; 6-foot 2-inch) body. A fifty-two-year-old man recalled that, in the 1960s, he often picked and consumed wild herbs and other plants to satisfy his hunger. An intellectual recalled that, when he was sent down to the countryside in the early 1960s, he was much better off than the peasants he lived with because he had a secure food ration and they did not; he saw people die of starvation.[13] But still he often felt hungry and ate anything he could get—wild plants, grasshoppers, and even tree bark. Edema was common during the Great Famine, from 1959 to 1961, because people tended to eat anything they could find. Instead of getting enough nourishment, they often ended up poisoned.

In the city of Chongqing, I heard people recall incidents of "food snatching," which were common in the early 1960s. One middle-aged man recalled how desperate he was, as a child, after an older man came up behind him one morning and grabbed the steamed bun he was eating on his way to his elementary school. As the robber ran away, the little boy sobbed. The sense of starvation was widespread in his school. When consumed by hunger while the class was going on, a teacher often took out a small glass bottle containing salt from his pocket. He would stick a finger into the bottle to coat it with a bit of salt and then would suck the salt from his finger to reinvigorate himself. Even when food shortages began to ease in 1962, food thefts still took place. One incident occurred in a restaurant known for its steamed buns stuffed with pork. A man jumped to the front of the long line of waiting customers, quickly grabbed two buns just out of the steamer, and ran out of the restaurant. Afraid of being caught by the shouting crowd behind him, he wolfed down the hot, greasy buns while running. He fell to the ground and died.

The question "what does it mean then to speak of the primary, the existential, experience of hunger" (Scheper-Hughes 1992:136) has its place in understanding the changes that have occurred in everyday life since those days. Once so common, widespread, and mundane, hunger has faded into oblivion in the wake of great improvements in living conditions over the past several decades. Only when other topics touched on the collective memory of starvation in the Great Leap Famine would one be reminded that a sense of hunger had once been deeply ingrained within the nation, particularly in peasants. Compared to what peasants were put through, the experience of hunger among city residents means almost nothing.[14] That his aunt fed him refined crops for twelve years meant a lot to Mr. Jiang and underlay his sentiment toward her. His experience exemplifies how "the mundane concerns of ordinary people," as James Watson (2006:viii) notes, make ethnographic sense of what matters to a person in life.

From a psychoanalytical perspective, Jiang's preoccupation with his aunt can be interpreted as his wish to be the object of mother's desire, his aunt here replacing his real mother. Also, his impotence seems to conform to Wilhelm Stekel's (1927) idea of the "will to impotence." According to Stekel, a certain number of his impotence patients suppressed incestuous desire toward the mother: the "uncut umbilical cord" that tied a boy to his mother prevented him from fully embracing other women. From this very Freudian perspective, the unconscious reluctance to fully love other women was manifested in Mr. Jiang as a driving force toward impotence.

A close look at the social threads woven through Mr. Jiang's narrative shows his "desire" to go beyond the sexual nuances conveyed by the language of psychoanalysis. Mr. Jiang's recollections of his aunt were not consistent with the components of the Oedipus complex, for his father was not present and did not seem relevant. What his story clearly conveys is the conjunction of the cultural sentiment of gratitude, encouraged and justified in rituals of reciprocity and repayment, and sexual desire, which he reconstructed as an educated adult via his memories.

We see here an intergenerational body of concerns and emotions beyond the fixed space of the individual body and the Oedipal triangle. This intergenerational body marked what was most at stake in a specific lifeworld inhabited by many like Mr. Jiang at a certain historical moment: surviving scarcity, poverty, and hunger. On the one hand, his social intercourse with his aunt, which was embodied in touch and through the media of grain, willow baskets, cigarettes, taste, and relief from hunger, led to the formation of the intergenerational body. This body carried memories of social and cultural currents that cut into Mr. Jiang's sexual contact with his wife. On the other hand, his self-knowledge, potentially gleaned from psychoanalysis, might have played a role in making the bodily experience transparent in terms of sexual desire, in guiding the memories into sexual imagery, and in implying his impotence as the consequence of a directed "will" fully embedded in the fabrics of social relationships, interpersonal senses, and the larger political-economic structure.

POTENCY AND A VIRTUOUS DAUGHTER-IN-LAW:
LOST FILIAL PIETY

Mr. Wan, a sixty-three-year-old peasant, complained of erectile difficulty and described the decline of his sexual potency. He was married in the early 1950s and had three children—one son and two daughters. About ten months before I met him, he suddenly had difficulty getting an erection but could eventually achieve one and finish intercourse. About a month before we met, it had become more difficult for him to get an erection and he could maintain it to the point of ejaculation only one in nine times. He had recently had nocturnal erections, which, according to the doctor, showed that his problem was not as serious as Mr. Wan thought. He neither drank nor smoked. He did not have high blood pressure, and his cholesterol level and blood sugar were normal. Nothing seemed to have gone wrong with him physically.

I asked, "Has there been anything unpleasant in your life over the past two years?"

He nodded and sighed, and then he said, "My daughter-in-law died ten months ago. She died of cancer of the esophagus. She lived with us in the same *siheyuan* (four-cornered courtyard). She had one child. She was very *xianhui* (virtuous) . . . I miss her so much . . . When she died, I felt so sad that I could not sleep. My wife misses her too."

I asked, "How virtuous was your daughter-in-law?"

He answered, "She respected the elderly and loved children. She had been married to my son for seventeen years. They fought, but she treated us very well. She treated us better than our daughters did . . . She was so nice and knew the right things to do. She bought gifts for us elderly on the occasions of holidays. Even though we [Mr. Wan and his wife] ate separately from them [their son, daughter-in-law, and grandchild], she often brought to us whatever she thought were good dishes she had made. Now, you can hardly find even one daughter-in-law like her in a hundred daughters-in-law."

Very sad, he continued, "She passed away too early. I cried a lot. I didn't attend her funeral."

"Why didn't you attend it?" I asked.

He kept silent for a while and then said, "Someone had to stay home that day." I could see the glint of tears in his eyes. "Later on, my son was dating another woman—his current wife. She wanted to replace all the old furniture my daughter-in-law had used. I did not let her. But when they got married a month ago, my new daughter-in-law took out all the old furniture and put it in my granddaughter's room."

Two chronologies synchronize in Mr. Wan's narrative. He experienced difficulty getting an erection for the first time in his life when his daughter-in-law died; then, he almost completely lost his ability to maintain an erection after penetration when his son remarried. What could I make of these two related chronologies?

I resisted any attempt at speculation and decided to visit Mr. Wan in his home, which was located in the north suburbs of Beijing. According to the address he gave me, his home was in a village. However, when I got to the area, I encountered not agricultural fields but construction vehicles and new apartment buildings.

Scraps of paper were swirling in the air that windy spring day; concrete, broken bricks, and other garbage were strewn over the lanes between two rows of shabby houses, the only vestiges of the onetime village. The brown ground and gray houses contrasted sharply with the new bright white apartment buildings rising around them and appearing to look down disdainfully on the mess at their feet. When I asked construction workers for directions, the answers often came in the dialects of other provinces. This place—its peasant residents, its agricultural fields, and its rural landscape—was being uprooted. The remaining village houses seemed to be waiting to be washed away by the new wave of construction radiating in all directions from the center of Beijing.

I eventually found Mr. Wan's siheyuan. Sets of rooms stood on three of the yard's four sides. Mr. Wan pointed to the left of the yard's main entrance, saying, "Those were my son and daughter-in-law's rooms." He said that the family had not farmed in the five years since the area had been sold to the city for residential development. "We don't grow vegetables anymore; we buy them in the market." The remaining villagers were no longer agricultural but urban. Their houses would be torn down, and new apartment buildings would be built on the site. They would be assigned apartments in the new buildings. "I don't know whether we can afford to buy a one-bedroom apartment or a two-bedroom apartment; it depends on how much value the company gives to our current house in their evaluation," he said, showing disinterest in his future residence.

Mr. Wan's history was a simple one. He was born in the village in the 1930s. In the 1950s, after the People's Republic was founded, he took a job at a pharmaceutical company in a city in another province and married his wife, who was two years older than he. In the early 1960s, he was laid off from the pharmaceutical company and sent back to his village as part of the state's policy of downsizing the urban workforce in response to the failure of the Great Leap Forward and the subsequent bad economy of the so-called Three Years of Natural Disaster (Great Leap Famine, 1959–1961). He had lived in the village ever since.

Mr. Wan had been pushed back and forth between village and city in the industrial wave of socialist China's early days. He had lost his status as a city resident in the 1960s. Now, when he was being forced to become a city resident again, he was ambivalent about the relocation. This time, not only would his identity change permanently from villager to city dweller but the place where his home was rooted would also be completely erased. This time there would be no way for him to be sent back to his place of origin. When people were sent back from the cities to the rural areas in the early 1960s, they were unhappy victims of a failed project of urbanization. Now, at the end of the twentieth century, Mr. Wan was facing the high tide of the state project of modernization. Unlike most people in the 1960s, who took what they got, Mr. Wan complained vocally about the grief brought about by the new state project.

Pointing to the TV set, I asked him whether or not he watched it. This question triggered an outburst of anger:

What's good on television! There are so many corrupt cadres, but the television won't cover them. Hu Changqing [a cadre in Jiangxi Province who was executed for corruption] was singled out, just because he could no longer cover up his wrongdoings. But he didn't grab as much as one hundred million yuan, like those cadres in Xiamen City. Zhu Rongji [the premier of China] said that he will be satisfied when he steps down so long as the people think of him as a *qingguan* [an official not guilty of corruption]. Not being corrupt is a basic requirement of an official, but now it becomes a great merit. Nowadays even a small group leader in the village is corrupt. Speaking of the state's requisition of the land here, I am angry with the relocation company. This company made every effort to underestimate the value of our houses. We remodeled the house on the south side of our yard, but the company did not count in the cost of remodeling. On the other hand, someone in the brigade in charge of the issue of relocation benefited from having a deal with the company. Someone in my village is able to spend several million yuan to buy new apartments. If he is not corrupt, where did he get the money?

Mr. Wan looked quite different than he had when I first talked to him in the hospital. In the hospital, he was sad and looked very dispirited. Now, at home, he was assertive and very angry. He expressed his anger with such force that I wondered whether anything could appease it and make up for his loss. At the end of his outburst, he asked me, "Will my anger affect my body?"

Everything in Mr. Wan's life was in transition. Perhaps the transition that affected him most was his virtuous daughter-in-law's replacement by a less amiable woman. The death of the first daughter-in-law represented to him the permanent loss of filial piety, a highly regarded virtue in rural villages (Yan 2003). The loss was deeply absorbed into his body, contributing to his impotence.

The death of a woman had had a deep impact on the lives of both Mr. Wan and Mr. Jiang. For Mr. Jiang, improvement in the standard of living only heightened his cherished memory of the care his aunt gave him, whereas for Mr. Wan, the feeling of being uprooted by urbanization intensified his memory of the respect and care he received from his daughter-in-law. In both cases, the memories became associated with impotence.

In this chapter, I have related the stories of four men and one woman. In each story, impotence and changes in social status were interwoven themes. The social status of some of my protagonists went up whereas that of others went down during the era of postsocialist reform. But all five registered the transformation through the body, whether in memory or through immediate bodily response, with an intensity that rendered the flow of sexual desire stagnant. Impotence for these individuals was far from a simple "neurovascular event." Neither was it a malaise of civilization. Instead, it was a social event that was constituted by the transformations of the post-Mao era.

Mr. Lin, twenty-one years old, came to the clinic in Beijing all the way from Henan Province to seek medical help for his "illness." Looking sad, he frowned and sighed constantly while answering the doctor's questions.

Doctor: What is wrong?
Mr. Lin: *Ying bu qilai* (My penis could not get hard).
Doctor: Are you married?
Mr. Lin: Not yet.
Doctor: Have you had sex?
Mr. Lin: No.

In the two clinics where I did my primary fieldwork and in other clinics I visited, doctors did their best to persuade patients like Mr. Lin to give up the idea that they were impotent. These patients either had never had sexual intercourse or had tried to have sex once or twice but failed. Twenty-six of the patients I talked to fell into this category. To use the current categories of the DSM-IV, some of them seemed to be suffering from somatization disorder. Others might simply have been suffering from hypochondria. Yet a close look at their cases might reveal something unique to post-Mao China.

These men demonstrated extreme vulnerability to the idea of impotence at a time when talk about impotence and ads for its treatment were widespread. Among the twenty-six men I interviewed, thirteen were migrants from rural areas who were working in Beijing or Chengdu as construction workers, security guards, or chefs. Eight of the thirteen had girlfriends in their hometowns and communicated with them by telephone or mail. They often shared dormitory rooms with other workers and only returned to their hometowns two to three times a year to see their girlfriends. They were troubled that their penises did not get hard when they embraced or kissed their girlfriends while clothed. They did not take off their clothes because they feared they would be unable to get an erection if they tried to have one.

Some of the men were engaged to their girlfriends and worried about having an embarrassing "first night failure" once they married. Some had attempted sex only to experience premature ejaculation before penetration. Some were discouraged from having sex with their girlfriends for reasons unrelated to erectile dysfunction, including the injunction against sex before marriage, the idea that having sex at a young age was harmful, or the fear of pregnancy.

Disparate as they were in this regard, the men shared the ironic experience of not knowing whether they were really suffering from impotence. They were tantalized by desire but inhibited by fear. They hungered for the visible body, but they retreated from it as soon as they faced its reality. These men were caught in a vicious circle. Their conviction that they were impotent was based on very limited physical contact with women or was merely a product of their imaginations. This "self-diagnosis" then became a preoccupation that discouraged further physical contact. I call this syndrome "imagined impotence." In what social and historical context did it occur?

The phenomenon of "imagined impotence" led me to examine the men's important social relationships: with their families (primarily parents) and with women with whom they were trying to have or had had sexual intercourse (I am unable to verify whether any cases I encountered involved homosexual relationships). If the former accounted for the bulk of the men's social interactions, the latter revolved around what I have been calling "sexual intercorporeality." I first examine how the social body (the family) influenced men's sexual life and impotence after the sexual repression of the Maoist era had largely faded. Second, I explore how the kind of "sexual intercorporeal relationship" men developed with women contributed to their impotence.

Much has been written on changes in family and marriage in post-Mao China (e.g., Davis and Harrell 1993; Yan 1996; Kipnis 1997; Gillette 2000; Kohrman 2005; Friedman 2006; Brandtstädter and Santos 2008; Davis and Friedman 2014). But sexual life does not play a big part in most such studies, with a few exceptions. Yunxiang Yan's (2003) pioneering work remains one of the most detailed explorations of sexual trends in relation to changes in rural family life (e.g., the increasing priority of conjugal intimacy over filial piety). The following two cases show that parental influence on children's sexual life was still strong in the early days of the reform period and that it could bear on male potency.

The Adverse Effect of Parental Dominance

The impact of parental power on the son could be felt in various ways. But how did the son's potency have to do with this impact?

"LIVING IN A GLASS HOUSE"

Mr. Lin was the only son of peasant parents. He had one sister. He had never dated. He remembered that, at the age of fourteen, he had spotted a nineteen-year-old soldier from his village masturbating while bathing in the river near his home. The soldier told him that his (own) uncircumcised penis was a problem for him when it came to sexual relations. Mr. Lin discovered that he too was not circumcised, and he started to masturbate. His grandparents were very old and wanted him to get married soon. When he was sixteen, a matchmaker introduced him to a girl, also sixteen, from a village eight kilometers away. He went to her village to see her twice over a period of four years. The year before I met him, his parents had agreed to the couple's engagement. Yet Mr. Lin was worried that he was impotent because, sometimes, he could not get an erection when he masturbated.

The year before I spoke with him, his fiancée visited his house for two days. Although they were left alone in the house during that time, they did not try to have sex. Mr. Lin had become alarmed when he did not get an erection while embracing the girl with his clothes on. In fact, he was in such a state of shock that he wanted to call off the engagement. He thought that he was seriously ill. But his parents and grandparents insisted that the engagement continue because they were satisfied with the girl. He eventually revealed his worry to his parents, and thus began an endless journey to recover his "lost potency."

Mr. Lin went from hospital to hospital, first in the county seat, then in the prefecture seat, the provincial capital city, and, finally, Beijing. He sought treatment from both biomedicine and Chinese medicine. He spent tens of thousands of yuan on medication, affordable because his father was among the first in his region to get rich in nonagricultural business in the 1980s. After Mr. Lin had taken all the medication he was given, he was sometimes able to get an erection (e.g., after taking a nap). He was somewhat relieved by these occasional erections but was thrown into despair again whenever he was unable to get an erection under the same circumstances. He searched for medication in Beijing while his fiancée worked as a migrant laborer in a province in the south. He felt pressured and embarrassed because he thought he might have to terminate the engagement.

He explained, "Unlike me, nowadays men get to know their girlfriends by themselves, and they won't ask for help from a go-between to arrange an engagement until they get to know each other well. In most cases, the boy and the girl have already slept together at the time of engagement." He was referring to changes that had occurred in his own village in the 1990s, changes that Yunxiang Yan (2003) describes in detail in Xiajia village in Helongjiang Province.

Mr. Lin sighed, "I feel like I'm living in a glass house. The glass walls separate me from other people outside."

I asked whether he had ever loved a girl. He said, "I liked a girl when I was in junior high school. But I did not talk to her. Since graduating from high school, I have never seen her again."

He was particularly unhappy about his engagement. According to one doctor who examined Mr. Lin, color Doppler ultrasound showed a problem with his blood flow. It is possible, however, that his psychological issues were affecting him physiologically, that his blood flow or hormone levels were affected by his depressive mood. Depressed men who believe they are impotent tend to confirm their impotence during physical examinations (Bancroft 1992).

Instead of responding to any erotic cues, Mr. Lin was trying to achieve erection simply by taking medicine for impotence. This decontextualized motivation failed him. What had led to his effort to reliably achieve erection in the first place was his obligation to defer to his parents' preference.

French philosopher Maurice Merleau-Ponty (1962:160–61) cites the case of a girl who lost her speech after she was prohibited by her parents from seeing her lover and who recovered her speech after she was allowed to see him again. The girl's symptom (reflecting the oral phase of sexual development) can be explained "in relation to past and future, to the self and others, that is to say, to the fundamental dimensions of existence" (Merleau-Ponty 1962:161). A case reported in a medical journal dominated by biotechnological views illustrates the futility of prescribing medication for impotence in the absence of an intercorporeal bond: A Swiss man suffering from impotence in the 1990s could not regain an erection with the help of medication without developing a strange skin problem. His condition did not improve until he acknowledged the moral conflict between his extramarital affair and his declining relationship with his wife and faced his true feelings (Bianchi-Demicheli 2005).

In seeking medication, Mr. Lin was denying his dissatisfaction with the girl his parents had chosen for him. When he got engaged, he felt encaged ("living in a glass house"). Why were the walls of the house made of glass—both confining and transparent? On the one hand, no difference was discernible between him and persons on the other side of the glass. On the other hand, a barrier, though invisible, separated him from the rest of the world. When he complained about the arranged engagement, his potency was revealed as an issue affecting relations between two families, his patrilineage, and his natal family. His potency was not only a capacity of his individual body but also of his social, familial body, and these two bodies were at war.

A similar conflict is apparent in the following case, which unfolded in an urban setting in a cadre's family and involved a man much more educated than Mr. Lin.

INCAPABLE OF DESIRING

Mr. Song's life trajectory had been unusual. Forty-four years old and a program manager in Beijing, he had never had sex and had not married. He was under pressure from his parents to get married, because he was their only son. Like Mr. Lin, Mr. Song was worried that he was impotent.

Mr. Song had come of age around the end of the Cultural Revolution in the 1970s. He told me that he had been attracted to women.[1] The woman he talked about the most was one he had dated for half a year in the 1980s. He had liked her very much. He remembered that he had hugged her only once "or, in fact, twice, but I hugged her very intimately only once, when I was sending her home." Unfortunately, his parents did not want him to date her, because her brother had psychiatric problems. As a result, Mr. Song's relationship with his own parents became strained. Eventually, after becoming aware of his difficult family situation, the woman ended the relationship. Since then, he had been looking for a girlfriend through matchmaking services but had not yet succeeded in finding one.

Mr. Song had visited erotic bars during a business trip to Europe and had been attracted to the naked female bodies on display there. He had lived with his parents, who were high-ranking officials in the government, until half a year before I met him. His life was very much entangled with his parents' lives. His father's cadre background enabled Mr. Song to attend college in the early 1970s as a "student of worker, peasant, or soldier background," a politically privileged member of society during the latter half of the Cultural Revolution. But he had also been very much under the control of his father.

After graduating from college in the late 1970s, Mr. Song was assigned to a job in a factory in Beijing. He clearly remembered being aware of an affair between a twenty-year-old factory worker and her married supervisor. The woman was stigmatized as a bad woman after the affair ended and was dismissed from her position. The affair and the stigma had left a deep impression on Mr. Song. But, strangely, he could not remember his own experiences of being aroused or having an erection when hugging the woman he had liked. He recalled, "I did not pay attention to the reaction of my penis at that time. I did not understand sex at all. If my relationship with the girl happened now, I would have sex with her." It seemed that the only woman with whom he would have felt sexually comfortable was the one his parents had stopped him from marrying twenty years before.

Mr. Song appeared to have experienced a two-decade-long vacuum of sexual desire and affection, from the early 1980s to the late 1990s. Even though he had seen doctors about his low sexual desire and seemed to look forward to romantic opportunities, he also seemed to be looking for ways to avoid sex.

I asked him, "If you would not face any consequences, would you want to have sex with a woman you liked?"

He hesitated, not wanting to answer this question, then murmured, "It is impossible to be in such a situation. It won't happen." Yet such a situation did occur. In my follow-up interview with him about a year and a half later, Mr. Song spoke of a recent three-month dating relationship. One day, the woman had to take an exam in a school near Mr. Song's apartment. He suggested that she stay in his apartment overnight, and she agreed. Mr. Song recalled, "I let her sleep in my bed in the bedroom. I set up a foldable bed in the living room for myself. I closed the bedroom door. Later, she opened the door. In retrospect, the opening of the bedroom door was an obvious suggestion to me, but I did not recognize it." In the end, the woman broke up with him.

I asked, "Did your father's intervention in your early love affect you?"

He answered, "Perhaps. After I broke up with that girl [the one he liked so much], I was very upset. That was a big blow. It hit me hard. Even now I cannot talk about my dating to my parents. Whenever I talk to them about dating, they speak to me with irritation. I did not feel desire after my experience with the girl." He recalled that he sometimes watched pornographic videos and had occasionally ejaculated. But he was not satisfied with the experience and felt "empty because the body in pornography was not real."

Mr. Yuan, a fifty-two-year-old editor, recalled how his romances ended because of parental objection. In 1975, he was a member of *zhiqing* (educated youth) on a farm in Helongjiang Province, where he became involved with a girl who was also a zhiqing. He later moved back to Beijing, where his father learned of the romance by reading a letter the girl wrote to Mr. Yuan (at the time, and even in the 1980s, it was common for parents to read letters addressed to their children).

His father had graduated from Tsinghua University in the 1930s and then gone to Yan'an to join the revolution. Knowing that the girl's father had worked for the Guomindang and been sent down to Inner Mongolia, he firmly asked his son to terminate the relationship. Mr. Yuan obeyed.

A second romantic relationship did not work out for reasons other than parental interference. The third girl he dated again met with paternal disapproval. His father said, "You cannot take this girl. If she comes to live with us, we all have to listen to her." His father was referring to the girl's assertiveness, which might have posed a challenge to his authority.

Like Mr. Yuan, his younger brother had also been a zhiqing, having gone down to the countryside in Shaanxi Province. There, he started to date a girl in a neighboring county. The girl's work was to look after date trees in the mountains everyday. The father ordered the brother to terminate the relationship. Unlike Mr. Yuan, the brother resisted his father's order and eventually married his girlfriend. The father was so upset that he refused to have anything to do with his younger son's parents-in-law.

Despite many differences between Mr. Lin, in his twenties, and Mr. Song, in his forties, the two men shared one commonality—a life overshadowed by parental power. Mr. Lin's imagined impotence was probably an unconscious protest against an arranged engagement, whereas Mr. Song's had to do with constant resentment toward his parents for his unfulfilled love. Mr. Song was stuck in a stalemate created by his own imagination. He did not seem to want to be celibate but was held back by his own inhibition. He was not satisfied with the sexual imagery he encountered in films but he was plagued by self-doubt about his ability to satisfy women. Mr. Lin's and Mr. Song's hesitation said less about their inability to get an erection than it did about their inability to articulate their own desires.

In post-Maoist China, particularly from the 1990s on, the loosening of state regulation on sexual desire did not necessarily guarantee its free flow. Mr. Lin and Mr. Song were still coping with age-old problems: a dominant father and imposed inhibitions. Their imagined impotence may have been a form of rebellion against inhibition, but it was a rebellion that was both unconscious and self-destructive.

Impotence and Women: Making the Female Body Available

Many men who suffered from imagined impotence tried to reverse their situation in a variety of ways. Some turned to intercourse with sex workers, some masturbated while watching pornography, and some tried to develop "dating" relationships. Some patients tried all three approaches. Instead of seeking sexual pleasure, however, they were engaging in these activities to test their potency.

TESTING POTENCY THROUGH *XIAOJIE* (SEX WORKERS)

Not surprisingly, many failed the test miserably. A thirty-year-old employee of an electronic appliance company in Beijing believed that he was impotent, even though he had never had sex. He shared a dormitory room with three other men, who, on several occasions, egged him on to have sex. He recalled, "All three times were in nightclubs. I ordered the service of a *xiaojie* (小姐, sex worker),[2] and I got an erection. But, it was not hard enough. As soon as I was in contact with her body, I ejaculated. I had very strong desire, but I failed all three times." A twenty-eight-year-old employee of a company in Chengdu recalled his experience of ejaculating before penetration after his business partner arranged for a xiaojie to offer him her services. The woman told him, "You are better [than some men]. One man even ejaculated while he was still dancing with me."

A forty-year-old civil servant tried to start dating relationships with women. His aim was to quickly go to bed with these women, not for fun but to prove that he was potent. He attempted intercourse four times with three different women—two he was dating and one he got to know by accident. On two occasions, he was able to get an erection but ejaculated before penetration; on the other two occasions, he could hardly get an erection and ejaculated long before attempting penetration.

In these cases, sexual desire became completely focused on passing a "test." But precisely because the men were under pressure to prove their potency, they failed dismally. The notion of "performance anxiety," the focus of William H. Masters and Virginia E. Johnson's desensitizing therapy, is helpful in understanding the syndrome of imagined impotence. A man who suffers from performance anxiety focuses only on having and maintaining an erection and is anxious about doing so, anticipating failure, which completely decontextualizes sexual functioning. Anxiety prevents him from being aroused and leads to erectile failure (Masters and Johnson 1970:11).

The difference between fear of performance and imagined impotence lies precisely in the highly imaginative nature of the latter, as men's sexual inexperience in such cases provides no basis for confirming the diagnosis. Doctors told some men that their problem was more likely to be premature ejaculation (PE) than impotence or erectile dysfunction (ED), that they were confusing the two.

Similar cases have been reported in studies of impotence in Western countries (Stekel 1959; Masters and Johnson 1970; Kaplan 1974; Rosen and Leiblum 1992). For example, Wilhelm Stekel wrote of some of his patients, "They have never attempted coitus, and consider themselves impotent, although at home they have strong erections and have no basis for this assumption" (1959:88). In the only example he gave of this type of impotence, the patient not only had had sex with a maid for three months at the age of sixteen but also saw prostitutes (even though he did not attempt penetration). In nineteenth-century Vienna, according to Stekel, prostitution was frequently part of a patient's sexual experience. Many of Stekel's patients used the body of the prostitute to test their potency. In one case, Stekel (1959) reports, a physician even advised a patient's parents to hire a mistress for their son.

As I point out in chapter 1, Sigmund Freud saw impotence occurring when a man's love (affectionate current) and sexual desire (sensual current) did not match because incestuous fixation preempted the sensual currents needed to consummate the sexual act. So, sexual pleasure could be obtained only through "a debased sexual object," that is, "a woman who is ethically inferior, to whom [a man] need attribute no esthetic scruples, who does not know him in his other social relations and cannot judge him in them" (Freud 1989b:399). Masters and Johnson reported similar cases.[3] The syndrome of imagined impotence is not new, nor is the use of sex workers to try out one's potency.

But the syndrome's social context in China was unique. The return of prostitution in postsocialist China, several decades after its eradication under socialism, provided a site for imagined impotence to surface. Since the culture of the sex industry was still relatively new in the consumer culture of the 1990s,[4] the prowess required of a *piaoke* (a xiaojie's customer or client) was also something new. Although it did not take long for some men to become old hands in the brothel, for sexually inexperienced, anxious men, the mismatch between their bodies and the body of the xiaojie contributed to the production of imagined impotence.

These men felt nervous, guilty, and insecure yet simultaneously tantalized and excited. A thirty-seven-year-old salesman recalled his mixed feelings when he first approached a xiaojie. He was excited but nervous, curious about his potency but feeling guilty about violating his moral code, eager for the experience but fearful of being caught in a police raid. He complained that the xiaojie did not even want to flirt with him to get him aroused and relaxed but just wanted to finish the business as quickly as possible. Obviously, this male body did not fit into the culture of the sex industry and consumption, because he expected the xiaojie to do what she was not supposed to do. He failed disastrously, ejaculating before even attempting to penetrate.

The conflict between the exciting female body and the shadow of morality, the mismatch between the search for intimate feelings and for a context-free erection, rendered the body of the xiaojie infertile ground for rebuilding masculinity and a gravesite for confidence. Contrary to their hopes, some men's experiences with xiaojie produced "evidence" the men did not want to see: they were, indeed, impotent. At this point, the distinction between imagined impotence and real impotence became blurred.

THE IRONY OF VIRTUAL SEXUAL CORPOREALITY

Many patients watched pornography. In the 1980s, pornographic videos produced in Hong Kong, Taiwan, Japan, and other places began to find their way into mainland China. Thereafter, they had become accessible to ordinary Chinese, although their production, circulation, and consumption were illegal and the state often launched campaigns against them. The development of VCD and DVD technology went hand in hand with the flourishing of pornography. *Maopier* (raw, uncut VCDs) were fashionable in the 1990s before they were replaced entirely by DVDs, which in turn were largely superseded by online sites in the 2000s and 2010s. Pornographic viewing has also shifted from public space (VCD showrooms and even rural tea houses) to semipublic and private spaces. Just like the illegal but flourishing red-light districts, the thriving of pornography has normalized the otherwise voyeuristic gaze. The gaze on the visible body has become national (Zhang 2011c; Jacobs 2012).

Among my interviewees, at least thirty-five patients had watched pornographic videos. The average age of patients in this group was thirty-one. Among them, only nine men had ever experienced sexual intercourse. They watched porn in various locations—in their own homes, in friends' homes, or in a video or VCD showroom. One of them had watched adult movies in Paris when he was there on a business trip.

Pornographic imagery created a space for these men to deal with desire in a new way, as such imagery had been completely unavailable during the Maoist period. Within this group, those who were older than about forty often had never seen a naked female body before they got married. A thirty-nine-year-old professional recalled, "The first time I saw a naked female body was in 1977 when I saw a Western oil painting of a female body. The first real naked female body I saw was my wife's body after we registered for marriage in the late 1980s . . . This year [1999] I watched porn twice and felt aroused." A forty-year-old businessman recalled that, in the late 1980s, when he was attending graduate school, he was uncomfortable reading a book on sexology translated from English into Chinese, so he had disguised the book with the cover of a collection of Chairman Mao's works.

Some men watched porn with their wives or girlfriends. A forty-five-year-old peasant in one of Beijing's agricultural counties said that he had watched pornography with his wife. He said, "At the beginning, she was not willing to watch it, saying that it was dirty and obscene. But she eventually watched with me." A thirty-two-year-old taxi driver said that he had watched porn with his wife several times and that she had gotten aroused and was willing to engage in foreplay afterward. A thirty-nine-year-old professional said that he had watched porn with his wife and that she had changed as a result:

My wife and I are kind of *baoshou* (conservative) persons. My parents were cadres and were sent down to the countryside during the Cultural Revolution. When I was in high school, I dared not stand too close to female students when I was talking to them. I was afraid of gossip. I had never seen the female body until I got married. Extremely nervous in my first intercourse with my wife, I was trembling. My wife was born to a working-class family. We live near my parents' apartment, and we have dinner together with my parents every day. She goes back to her parents' home every weekend. She looks down on those women who dress too *yaoyan* (coquettishly). In the 1980s, when she had just started to work, she was even afraid of running into acquaintances when she was buying sanitary napkins in the store. This year we watched porn twice. Now she has started to touch my penis before we have sex. In order to get me aroused, she did oral on me once.

From being afraid of running into acquaintances while buying sanitary napkins to being willing to watch porn and engage in behaviors she once could not have imagined, this man's wife had dramatically changed her view of the body and of sex.

For those who imagined they were impotent, however, the effect of watching pornography was not encouraging. Exposed to an exaggerated, supermale potency on the screen, many of them felt too inadequate and intimidated to initiate sexual contact with women. In addition, the seemingly easy sexual encounters portrayed in most videos intensified their tendency to fantasize about uncontextualized, straightforward coitus, without paying attention to developing proper etiquette in approaching the female. As Michael Kimmel points out, "pornography — is more likely to impoverish" their sexual lives, "reducing emotionally complex erotic encounters to a few-minutes' formula of acrobatics" (Kimmel 2009:188). As a result, the help they needed from a real, sympathetic female body to build intercorporeal intimacy became even more distant, obscured behind the fantasized, virtual body of the female. The accessibility to the virtual body, ironically, signified the unavailability of the real body.

The phenomenon of imagined impotence only highlights the plain truth that female cooperation was key to building sexual intimacy. At the time of my fieldwork, a serious professional effort was underway to make this help available to impotent men. I did not become aware of this effort until I made a trip to Mountain of the Female Immortal.

"PARTNER SURROGATES" IN MOUNTAIN OF THE FEMALE IMMORTAL

On a spring day in the early 2000s, I visited Mountain of the Female Immortal (仙女山, *Xiannü Shan*) in Pengshan County, Sichuan Province. About sixteen miles south of Chengdu, it is the location of the grave of Pengzu, the legendary Shang dynasty (17th–11th century B.C.E.) figure of longevity. The grave was built in the Qing period. According to legend, Pengzu lived

Figure 4.1: The chamber for the grave of Pengzu on the Mountain of the Female Immortal.

for eight hundred years (about one hundred thirty years in today's calendar). Pengzu's reputation as a master of *fangshi yangsheng* (bedchamber arts, or sexual cultivation) was linked to his legendary longevity and was incorporated into the contemporary revival of interest in *yangsheng* (the cultivation of life).[5] This was why several doctors of *nanke* (men's medicine) took me to his supposed gravesite and showed me what they were planning to do there: build a center of yangsheng named after Pengzu at the foot of Mountain of the Female Immortal.

This small mountain is surrounded by hills on three sides and faces a flat, open plain to the south. The tomb of Pengzu is located midway up the path to the top of the mountain, where the tomb of Cai E (Color Beauty), Pengzu's daughter, is located. The mountain is named for Cai E, the female immortal, rather than Pengzu, making it a feminized locale, suggestive of how much sexual cultivation depends on the female.

Walking up the mountain with our group, a local entrepreneur who was also a potential investor in the center, was very eager to tell us what the landscape symbolized. As it turns out, the ridges of Mountain of the Female Immortal and the nearby Shouquan Mountain (Mountain of the Water Spring of Longevity) were interpreted as forming the shape of Taiji—the circular intertwining of yin and yang. Mountain of the Female Immortal is a "yang" fish moving upward, and Mountain of the Water Spring of Longevity is a "yin" fish moving downward. The S-shaped valley separates the two mountain ridges and highlights the twisting of the two into the form symbolic of Taiji. This interpretation places Pengzu at the center of the spatial configuration, because his tomb is located at the "eye of the yang fish"; Cai E's tomb is located at the edge of the fish's head, which is considered a marginal space.

Our tour included a stop at the small Pengzu Museum of Yangsheng, where displays presented two of Pengzu's basic techniques for yangsheng—dietary regimens and bedchamber arts. A series of reliefs depicted a variety of sexual positions with their metaphorical names. While walking past these rather crude images, the doctors commented on how to integrate bedchamber arts with Masters and Johnson's sexual therapy. Hearing this, I was a little puzzled, as sexual cultivation and sexological therapy had different goals, the former aimed at prolonging life and the latter aimed at facilitating sexual pleasure. Sexual cultivation has some "therapeutic properties" that "modern medical science will agree with," as Robert van Gulik (2003:156) rightly perceived, despite his great reservation about bedchamber arts in this regard. The limited similarities (e.g., the adoption of a variety of sexual positions and techniques of foreplay) were not enough, however, to identify the former with the latter.

Even so, as I walked through the museum, I started to see the doctors' point. Pengzu, as we were told by the exhibits, was able to live a long life by having sex with a number of young girls, that is, by "plucking yin to nourish yang."[6] If the benefits of this technique were to be substantiated, however, we would have to look for the evidence outside the clinic, in men frequenting brothels, arranging assignations with sexual workers in hotels, or having a *xiaomi* (little sweetie, i.e., a female subordinate as mistress) or *ernai* (a second pair of breasts, i.e., a regularly paid mistress). But those practices seemed to be oriented more toward sexual pleasure than toward any therapeutic function.

I do not doubt that the doctors were seriously looking for effective ways to cure impotence by attempting to expand their practices beyond the clinic and by drawing inspiration from both ancient and modern traditions. By juggling the ideas of the two traditions, the doctors eventually identified an essential similarity between them—using "female assistants."

"Female assistants?" I asked.

Figure 4.2: Reliefs showing sexual cultivation and bedchamber arts in the Museum.

"Yes, like the ones recruited by Masters and Johnson," one doctor confirmed.

It turned out that the doctors were exploring ways to recruit "partner surrogates" to help treat male sexual dysfunction at their proposed mountainside clinic. Recruiting partner surrogates was one of the key techniques adopted by Masters and Johnson to treat impotence, particularly in men who were not married and did not have regular intimate partners. This practice was very controversial when first adopted in the United States in the 1960s, despite the clear definition of partner surrogates as serious participants in a scientific therapeutic program and the very strict standards for their selection. I immediately wondered, how would this practice differ from prostitution? That is, how was one to find "a partner surrogate," an independent female who would devote herself to serious, sexually focused medical work, someone unlike the young girls who served Pengzu's goal of sexual cultivation and unlike today's sex workers?[7] The doctors had no answer.

The doctors also discussed financial aspects of their proposed center. To survive, it would have to make a profit by providing effective therapies. By having men travel all the way to Mountain of the Female Immortal to *jie lingqi* (receive spiritual vapor, or revelation) from Pengzu, the doctors were attempting to introduce a practice invented in the United States. Inspired by a wide range of sexual practices—sexual cultivation, the sex industry, and scientific experiments, they were going out of their way to explore how to institutionalize women's help in curing impotence. Regardless of whether their ideas were feasible, their effort confirmed that impotence, as an intercorporeal problem, has to be dealt with intercorporeally. In the final analysis, curing impotence means building intercorporeal intimacy. This confirmation led me to a close examination of women's relation to impotence.

Impotence and Women: Sexual Intercorporeality

Framing impotence as a relational problem is nothing new. Psychotherapists are among the most vocal in articulating this view and adhere to the position that the efficacy of any therapy for impotence depends on successfully initiating or restoring a good relationship between a man and a woman. For example, psychotherapist Joseph LoPiccolo lists commonly occurring "relational problems" under what he calls "systemic issues" affecting potency. They include lack of attraction to the partner, poor sexual skills of the partners, general marital unhappiness, fear of closeness, differences between the couple in the degree of "personal space" desired in the relationship, passive-aggressive solutions to a power imbalance, poor conflict-resolution skills, inability to blend feelings of love and sexual desire, and lack of knowledge about normal age-related changes in male erectile functioning (LoPiccolo 1992:179).

However, the psychotherapeutic perspective on impotence tends not to carefully inquire about bodily details that reveal forces affecting sexual intimacy. I attend to such bodily details through the idea of "sexual intercorporeality."

SEXUAL INTERCORPOREALITY

The idea of "sexual intercorporeality" builds on Maurice Merleau-Ponty's notion of "intercorporeality." Intercorporeality is a common experience in everyday life. Examples are abundant. Hubert Dreyfus offered the example of the contagion of yawning. He said, "Merleau-Ponty says that it's our body with its skills which enables us to relate to things by going around them, and relate to people by this interesting capacity called intercorporeality . . . yawning would be the clearest case of this. Yawning is intercorporeality. If things are boring and I yawn, you don't have to figure out what it meant, you can't help but yawn" (Dreyfus 2005).

Intercorporeality (intertwining) is achieved through the capacity of two bodies to relate to each other, as it were, through suggestion. Erving Goff-man's example of two persons walking together and, with little or no effort at all, mutually adjusting their pace, in Nick Crossley's (1995) view, illumi-nates intercorporeality. Any touch between two persons walking together (e.g., a father holding a child's hand) intensifies their intercorporeal relation-ship and helps them adjust to one another.

As Merleau-Ponty (1962) notes in discussing double sensation (when the left hand touches the right, the one touching is simultaneously being touched), touching is the most powerful way to intensify intercorporeality. Jacques Derrida notes the nuance and richness of touching—no matter what part of the surface of the body is touched—and he quotes Jean-Luc Nancy in enumerating the wealth of forms of touching: "skimming, grazing, press-ing, pushing in, squeezing, smoothing, scratching, rubbing, *stroking*, pal-pating, groping, kneading, massaging, embracing, hugging, *striking*, pinch-ing, biting, sucking, wetting, holding, letting go, licking, jerking, looking, listening, smelling, tasting, avoiding, kissing, cradling, swinging, carrying, weighing" (2005:70).

This view of touching opens up a new perspective on sexual inter-course, which can now be seen—even in its most common form (vaginal penetration)—as an intensified, thorough, pervasive, and multifaceted way of touching. The state of touching in sex most closely approximates what I mean by the term *sexual intercorporeality.*

Sexual life is obviously fertile ground for exploring intercorporeality. Zhang Jingsheng, a professor of philosophy at Peking University in the 1920s, vividly described such intertwining in his account of learning to kiss in Paris in the 1910s.[8] He wrote, "Kissing, not only between lips, between mouths, but in the intertwining of tongues . . . I needed to use my tongue to intertwine hers constantly for a long time until our intercourse came to an end" (J. Zhang 1998, vol. 2:98, my translation).

To my great surprise, with few exceptions, major steps toward schol-arly understanding of the sexual relationship in terms of intercorporeality have yet to be taken. Despite a wealth of popular publications about gain-ing sexual pleasure through different positions, French sociologist Marcel Mauss remains one of the very few academics to have explored sexual posi-tions as bodily techniques. He wrote, "Nothing is more technical than sexual positions. Very few writers have had the courage to discuss this ques-tion" (Mauss 1979:118). Mauss's observation reminds me of an embarrass-ing moment in my fieldwork.

In Beijing, I was invited by a female friend, an NGO activist in women's studies circles, to take part in *Half the Sky*, a television program focusing on gender issues. I was to be interviewed about the study of masculinities. During the ten-minute recorded session, the anchorwoman asked me to "explain what masculinities study covers." I gave an example from my fieldwork in nanke—the need to understand men's (and, by extension, women's) increasing complaints about premature ejaculation. However, as soon as I uttered the phrase *zaoxie* (premature ejaculation), the anchorwoman and the three camera operators started to chuckle, disrupting the interview. Rushing over to me, the female editor of the program asked me to come up with another example. I ended up speaking about the psychological barriers to men's open expression of emotions. I realized that perhaps I had been too immersed in my fieldwork to pay attention to the propriety for the program of my initial example. But Mauss's call for courage in conducting detailed studies of sexuality has made me rethink my embarrassment. Perhaps it takes time for the experience of the sexual body to be taken seriously as a topic of discussion, even though it directly concerns the well-being of women and men and, in this instance, perfectly suited the program's focus on gender (Zhang 2013).

Commenting on sexual positions as bodily techniques, Mauss writes,

> Consider for example the technique of the sexual position consisting of this: the woman's legs hang by the knees from the man's elbows. It is a technique specific to the whole Pacific, from Australia to lower Peru, via the Behring Straits—very rare, so to speak, elsewhere.
>
> There are all the techniques of normal and abnormal sexual acts. Contact of the sexual organs, mingling of breath, kisses, etc. Here sexual techniques and sexual morals are closely related. [1979:118–19]

Like the discussion of touching, Mauss's discussion of sexual positions serves as a point of departure for specifying "sexual intercorporeality," which is closely related to moral attitudes toward sexual pleasure (sexual pleasure is good or bad), the gendered nature of such pleasure (one-sided or equally enjoyed), and perhaps the value of life (life affirming or not).

I define "sexual intercorporeality" as the mutual gearing and intertwining of the bodies in sex. This bodily intertwining has three aspects.[9] The first is contact through touching, kissing, licking, rubbing, and so on. The second is the use of carnal space so two bodies are geared toward one other and pace each other in positioning and concomitant rhythms.[10]

The third aspect is the intensification of sensory input, which may include stimulation of all five senses. Verbal teasing can be part of the bodily intertwining, as the use of speech is a carnal, intercorporeal act (Csordas 2008). A sensate surge felt by the male, which synchronizes with erection, is triggered and intensified by sensory input (seeing, touching, and smelling the naked female body, tasting the tongue of the female, or hearing her scream).[11]

The three dimensions of intertwining produce a state in which two bodies accommodate each other—much as two persons do who pace each other in walking and as occurs during the contagion of yawning—and intensify sensory input that produces copresent carnal beings. Other things aside, the idea of "sexual intercorporeality" clearly encourages intimacy and gendered equality in sexual enjoyment.

A GLIMPSE OF INTERCORPOREAL FAILURES

Impotence can be examined from the perspective of sexual intercorporeality, whether two bodies can come to intertwine and gear themselves to one another.[12] In situations of impotence, bodily contact is forged with reluctance or hesitation, and the carnal space is passively filled.

The most common sign of fragile sexual intercorporeality is the lack of touching. Other things being equal, men in this situation—in a "thin" state of sexual intercorporeality—tend to be more vulnerable to erectile failure and experience more difficulty in recovering potency than those in a "thicker" state. The following cases illustrate this pattern.

Mr. Wu, a thirty-year-old technician in Chengdu, had been married to his wife, a twenty-seven-year-old worker, for a year. He had not succeeded in penetrating her after they were married. As soon as his penis touched her vagina, it became soft. Before marriage, he had had no sexual experience or knowledge. He had never seen a naked female body, except in pornographic images. Not until he went to college did he become aware of sex and pregnancy, from the chatter of his dormitory roommates. He did not have any contact with female classmates and only limited communication with the female branch secretary of the Youth League. After getting married, he felt uncomfortable undressing in front of his wife, and his wife was too timid to undress in front of him. Whenever they attempted sexual intercourse, they turned off the light, so they did not really see each other's bodies. They indulged in only limited touching.

Kissing is an important means of building sexual intercorporeality. However, according to a study by Pan Suiming and colleagues, 22 percent of married Chinese couples never kissed each other during sex (Pan 2005). Mr. Wu recalled that, once, his wife jokingly commented that she was very sober when kissing, never becoming as excited as people kissing in the movies. Each time they wanted to have sex, Mr. Wu tried to obtain an erection by himself. He did not allow his wife to touch his penis, because he felt "it was strange" to be touched "down there." His wife lay quietly next to him, waiting. Finally, with limited touching, he mounted her. Their sexual intercorporeality was seriously underdeveloped.

Recall that Mr. Liang (see chapter 3) complained that his wife never touched him "down there" and that she never allowed him to touch her vagina. This situation was not unusual. For instance, a forty-two-year-old man told me that he liked to stroke his wife when having sex, whereas his wife would only occasionally touch him. When he was trying to touch and stimulate her genital area, she would ask, "What are you doing down there? It feels like you are touching my heel."

The lack of touching was most extreme when husband and wife slept in separate beds or in separate rooms. In these cases, the husband went to his wife's bed only after he had already achieved an erection. His erection was completely decontextualized, a register of the couple's thin intercorporeality.

Some couples found that intercorporeal adjustments could make a difference, enabling a successful sexual experience. One man said that he was always turned on when his wife made erotic jokes. A number of men revealed that after achieving a partial erection, they found it helpful for the woman to "lend a hand," to *fu yixia* (hold up the penis) and guide it into the vagina. Many such men described a partial erection as one in which the penis is less than completely rigid and has an angle of less than ninety degrees. Under these circumstances, they could still penetrate the vagina and finish sex, however, if the woman lent a helping hand.

What accounted for the common lack of touching? One might see this phenomenon as simply confirming a longtime prudish Chinese attitude toward the naked body and sex. However, evidence suggests that sexual life in early periods of Chinese history (e.g., the Tang and Ming periods) was less constrained than in the late imperial period (van Gulik 2003; Pan 2006; Li 2005). The text concerning "He yinyang" (Conjoining yin and yang) in the Mawangdui scripture contains detailed descriptions of *xidao* (戲道, the way to enjoy and play, including the fondling of sexual organs, kissing, and stroking; see Fan et al. 1997).

The contrast between the present day and the Maoist period could not be more stark in this regard, as I discuss in chapter 3. The lack of touching, rather than an essential Chinese trait, may be a response to the discouragement of sex for pleasure in specific historical contexts: the public culture of late imperial times but also the sexual repression in the Maoist period, which affected even the sexual life of married couples and the education of the young.

Other factors, such as increasing prostitution and childhood experiences might also contribute to the breakdown of intercorporeal relationship or to the difficulty of building such a relationship in the first place. It was not unusual to hear nanke doctors refer to such issues. Dr. Qin told me about the following case.

A salesman in Henan Province started to suffer from impotence after he had gone on a business trip to Guangdong Province. A checkup found nothing wrong in him. Then, I asked him whether there was anything else involved. He said, "Nothing." I said, "Well, by your profession, you frequently go on business trips. You may have seen a xiaojie." He admitted it. What happened was that during his stay in Guangdong, he stayed in a small inn and had sex with a service woman in the inn. Yet, just as they were having sex, they heard someone knocking on the door. He hid himself immediately under the bed before the policemen walked in. But, the policemen did not really come after prostitution. They only took a quick look at the room and left. It was part of a manhunt launched by the provincial public security bureau. Afterwards, [the salesman] began to have difficulty getting an erection.

He told this to his wife, but his wife could not forgive him. She did not cooperate with him for sex, so his impotence was getting worse. I wrote a letter to his wife. In this letter, I imparted her husband's secret feelings to her, and advised her to change her attitude. I emphasized that her cooperation was key to him regaining potency. Instead of mailing this letter, I asked him to carry it over to her. I told him not to open the letter, or I would not be responsible for his treatment. I did prescribe decoctions for him. Not long after the letter, his impotence was cured.

Dr. Qin was thirty-nine years old. He had practiced in Yunnan Province for ten years after obtaining his BA in TCM, and he then went on to obtain his Ph.D. in Beijing University of TCM and to postdoctoral studies in Nanjing University of TCM. He had also been exposed to psychotherapy and epidemiology. He knew well that in treating impotence he was dealing with the intercorporeal relationship and was willing to make an effort to help patients improve their intimate interactions with partners. He went on to tell me about another case in which the man helped the woman overcome her aversion to sex resulting from her past experience.

A married couple was on good terms with each other. But the wife was just reluctant to have sex, because she felt great pain each time they had sex. She was so in love with him that she proposed ending the marriage. But, he was so in love with her as well that he was firmly opposed to her proposal and believed that her problem could be cured. Her problem is *yinleng* (cold yin). I asked her about the history of her yinleng. I asked, "Did you have any unpleasant experience related to sex in the past?" She said that she could not remember. I said, "You must try hard to recall, otherwise your illness could not be cured."

Finally, she recalled one thing. She slept with her parents until seven years old. At the age of eight, a curtain was hung between her and her parents. One day, she saw her parents having sex. She started to wonder how her parents could be doing things like that and developed negative feelings toward sex. Then, every night she could hear water drops [which perhaps related to her parents' washing or urinating]. As soon as she heard the drops, she felt queasy, tantalized and weird.

After knowing this detail, I prescribed medication. Then, I told her husband to conduct "behavior therapy." I asked him to gently pour water into the spittoon after she goes to bed. The first night she was reportedly tickled and tantalized. The second night, she felt it hard to contain her desire. In the third night, they had sex successfully. When they came together to the hospital later, they were glowing with health. But she did not know about the secret of success until much later.

Qin appeared to have helped the woman redirect her feelings away from her parents (perhaps her father) to her immediate relationship with her husband and change her negative feelings toward sex by fusing her love with sexual desire. Women were more likely than men to react negatively to the idea of touching sexual organs, considering them dirty. A twenty-five-year-old woman said that she developed an aversion to touching genitalia because her mother had scolded her when she unconsciously touched herself as a little girl: "Take your hand off. It is dirty!" As this vigilance was not uncommon in the past, many women extended this negative idea of the sexual organ to a general perception of sexual life as shameful, except for the sake of reproduction. This "body untouchable," so to speak, resonated well with the "body invisible" discussed in chapter 2.

My fieldwork showed that women's desire was rising. Notwithstanding the rhetoric of "the new impotence," for which women's increased sexual appetite was held accountable (see introduction), women's responses to male impotence were diverse. The following section samples this diversity.[13]

Women's Desire

A number of impotence patients spoke of their wives' or sexual partners' complaints about them. Among the worst insults I heard leveled at men were "You eat men's meals, but you don't do men's work," "You are a useless thing (废物, feiwu)," and "You are like a living corpse." One man complained that everything his wife "says to me is nasty." Another man complained that his wife taunted him by saying, "You'd better not eat beef anymore because it would not help you!" She was referring to a folk belief that eating beef could strengthen male potency. These insults present a picture of women's desire that contrasts with the picture of the passive female body, one that never initiated sex, did not demand satisfaction, and was "invisible" as well as "untouchable" during sex.

Research by Pan Suiming and colleagues shows that women's sexual desire has, indeed, been on the rise. Between 2000 and 2006, women's awareness of sexual pleasure, as measured by specific physiological knowledge, has increased. Almost 17 percent more women knew about female orgasm in 2006 than did in 2000, 12 percent more knew the general location of the clitoris (9 percent could clearly locate it), and 12 percent more knew about male orgasm.[14] This research shows that, even though more men than women knew about sexual pleasure, knowledge among women was increasing faster than among men. More people were "very satisfied with sex life" in 2010 (33.3 percent) than in 2000 (26.8 percent), but the increase was greater in women (up 8.7 percent) than in men (up only 4.4 percent; see Pan and Huang 2011c).

One of the indicators of women's increase in desire was said to be a rise in the incidence of divorce due to male impotence. However, no research supports this argument. One study based on interviews with sixty-two divorced persons suggested the increasing importance of sexual life in marriage (Zhong et al. 1988). Twenty-six of those interviewed (40 percent) attributed their divorce to "inharmonious sexual life." However, more men (fourteen) than women (twelve) complained about inharmonious sexual life. This study did not confirm whether women's chief complaint in this regard was male impotence.

My fieldwork did not focus on the link between divorce and impotence, as it would have been extremely difficult to make a comparison between the Maoist and post-Mao periods and the 1990s and 2000s. My discussion here is primarily based on my contact with the men and women I interviewed. In my sample, I found five cases of divorce due to impotence. In one case, an impotent husband remained married while letting his wife regularly have sex with another man. In another case, it was not the wife, a forty-four-year-old laid-off worker, but her forty-five-year-old husband, also a laid-off worker, who proposed divorce. He did so because impotence made him very irritable, and he often started fights with his wife. She said, "Even though I still want it [sex]—particularly before each period, I feel *fanzao* (烦躁, agitated) and feel aching in my breasts—I don't pay much attention to it. I always think that his impotence is curable." In her view, her husband had overreacted to his impotence. Because of his overreaction, his temper as well as his impotence had gotten worse.

A woman's most common reaction to impotence was to suggest that a man see a doctor, but women did not seem to put a lot of pressure on men to do so. Women were less likely than men to panic in the face of initial erectile failures, had more faith that potency could be recovered, and more often tended to seek compensation through emotional comfort. A thirty-five-year-old street vendor from Zhejiang Province was more vocal about her frustration with her impotent husband. She complained, "When we had just gotten married, every time after sex he just fell asleep. He does not like to stroke me, but wants me to stroke him. I really don't think he understands me. Sometimes I *qisile* (am angry to death, i.e., infuriated), but seeing him also very tired after work, I just simply give up." Her point was that if a man has problems getting an erection and satisfying his wife through intercourse, he should try to satisfy her in other ways. What angered her was that, instead of being sympathetic toward her dissatisfaction and becoming more communicative, her husband became even more reticent after his first erectile failure and refused to communicate with her at all. His attitude upset her more than his impotence.

My impressions, based on interviews with women, could only partially support the rhetoric that women were putting increasing pressure on men.

In the cases I recorded, women's responses to impotence varied greatly. This unevenness was consistent with survey results. Fewer women in 2010 (41.5 percent) than in 2000 (55.5 percent) reported having little interest in sex. However, the percentage of women very interested in sex did not increase much: from 14.1 percent in 2000 to 18.5 percent in 2010 (Pan and Huang 2011b). Also, more women than men continued to feel ashamed about having sex (Parish et al. 2007).

Why did women want to stay in a marriage when their husbands were impotent? One might argue that these women were trapped in relationships dominated by men and had no recourse other than to hope for the best. But, in many cases, women's lack of consciousness of their own desire and of their right to pursue sexual pleasure is insufficient to explain their willingness to remain with men who suffered varying degrees of impotence.

One might also argue that many women did not give high priority to their own sexual pleasure and considered many other qualities in their marriage partners as compensating for the loss of pleasure from vaginal intercourse. A third argument is that some women preferred to satisfy sexual desire in nonphallocentric ways. My fieldwork found cases supporting all three arguments, as I demonstrate below.

IMPOTENCE AS A WEAPON

Mr. Gan, a thirty-four-year-old manager working for an enterprise in a suburban district of Beijing, had to *goudui* (勾兑, thicken the relationship with) cadres of different bureaus of the district government by having dinner, taking saunas, or going to karaoke bars with them. He often arranged for xiaojie to have sex with the cadres, and he had sex with xiaojie himself as part of goudui activities. He said, "Now I am bored with women—my wife as well as xiaojie. If I am not happy, I beat her [his wife] in the mouth. She gets beaten black and blue. Afterwards, I apologize, and things are over. She won't report me. So I still often stay away from home in the evening." Mr. Gan came to the hospital for medication for impotence. That a dominant man like Mr. Gan got his way at home, whether impotent or not, was not surprising. By the same token, it was not difficult for me to imagine that he would sleep around after he recovered his potency, leaving his wife at home alone.

I did not get to talk to Mr. Gan's wife, but the story of Ms. Zheng revealed how impotence can be used by some men as a weapon against women. Ms. Zheng, a thirty-seven-year-old worker, complained that her husband came home late or sometimes did not come home at all. She once found out he had stayed in a hotel overnight, leaving at noon the next day. He had sex with her only when he could no longer refuse. About a month before we spoke, instead of simply refusing to have sex with her, he had started to say he was impotent. "Sometimes I just angrily sat on the floor all night until the next day," she recalled. "Four months ago he started to avoid me, not allowing me to touch him. He did not directly turn me down. But when I was undressing myself, he closed his eyes. As soon as I touched his body, he pushed me away. He even ran to another room, huffing angrily. I noticed that almost once a week there was carefully folded toilet paper in the trash can. I suspect that he masturbates once a week."

I asked, "What does he think about the marriage?"

She answered, "He has been trying to get a divorce. But I feel an attachment to him." She revealed that he had beaten her three times. She described her situation this way: "I am holding on to the marriage as though I am holding a porcupine—it is hurting my hand badly, but I cannot throw it away."

In the two cases described above, the husband made significantly more money than the wife. In both cases, the women's economic dependence was largely responsible for their helplessness, and they could do nothing when their husbands turned impotence into a weapon to suffocate their desire. In the flourishing business culture in the 1990s and 2000s, many wives were victimized by their husbands' nightlife.

Once I was invited to two gatherings of professionals in the same evening. The first was a gathering for dinner around 6 P.M., and the second a gathering for tea around 8:30 P.M. The contrast between the two events was sharply drawn. All attending the dinner were men, whereas all who came for the tea were women. At the dinner, I heard talk about drinking, goudui, and looking for xiaojie; at the tea, I heard complaints about how husbands stayed out all night and were unfaithful but tried to cover up their escapades with xiaojie and affairs with other women. One middle-aged woman said that she was most fed up with her husband, a cadre in his late fifties, when he held her around the waist in public, pretending to be close with her. Meanwhile, he was covering up his sexual relationships with two mistresses in their early twenties. It was clear that women's desire was rising and that male dominance could not have been sustained without the complicity of the business culture.

Mr. Meng, a forty-one-year-old laid-off worker, had been panicked about the prospect of being out of work. He recalled that he was particularly sensitive to any news report or TV show that touched on the topic of *xiagang* (stepping down, being laid off) and worried all the time about losing his job. At one point, he was hospitalized in a psychiatric ward because of his panic disorder, and he eventually was asked to retire. He then became impotent.

According to Ms. Peng, his wife, a thirty-seven-year-old worker, Mr. Meng sometimes still had the desire for sex but gave up trying because of worry about erectile failure. I asked Ms. Peng, "Since he is not able to have sex, have you ever thought about [finding another man]?" It was a difficult question for me to ask. I purposely spoke slowly so that she could guess my question before I voiced it. She was quick to answer, "He is extremely nice toward us [her and their ten-year-old daughter]."

"How nice is he toward you?" I asked.

She answered, "We do fight. But unlike other people, after each fight he always *yizhe women niangrliangr* (依着我們娘兒倆, listens to me and my daughter, lets us do what we want to do). He never *bai laoyemenr jiazi* (擺老爺們兒架子, puts on the face of a big father). He is a good person. He is worried all the time, but he never *laixiede* (來邪的, does 'evil things'). Otherwise, how could I stick with him for so many years?"

A year and a half later, I called the couple about a follow-up interview. Mr. Meng's voice over the phone had changed. He sounded confident, unlike the deflated man I had last seen in the hospital. What had happened? Ms. Peng very excitedly told me that "he could do it now!" She wanted me to *baogexi* (報個喜, report the blessing) to the doctor Mr. Meng had seen. Ms. Peng sounded thrilled and genuinely happy. Now they were having sex once a week. Even though each instance of intercourse did not last as long as she might have wanted, they both had good feelings about this development. Asked how this improvement had come about, Ms. Peng could not give a particular reason, but she said that about nine months earlier Mr. Meng had gotten a part-time job. Although he did not make much money at the job (only 400 yuan each month), he felt good about working again.

I asked Ms. Peng, "What if he cannot do it again?"

Ms. Peng said, "I have been with him for so many years. If he could not do it again, I would not complain."

I was unsure whether the part-time job had changed her husband's feelings about sex. But Ms. Peng had every reason to be happy about her decision to stick with him, a man she considered a good person and caring toward her and their daughter. She seemed to be telling me that one could gain pleasure from many things in life. I suspect that Mr. Meng was able to recover his potency because of her attitude toward him. Ms. Peng seemed to me to take pleasure in her relationship with him and in life. I would be reluctant to describe her either as having little consciousness of her own rights or as calculating and tactical in coping with the situation while anticipating his recovery. She simply lived a life based on her judgment of her husband as a whole person, rather than on the ups and downs of his potency. The story of Ms. Peng and Mr. Meng was one of the few happy stories I encountered in my fieldwork, and one I kept retelling myself to keep from being depressed by all the sad stories I heard every day.

ALTERNATIVE SEXUAL INTERCORPOREALITY

Did women give up on satisfying their sexual desire if they stayed in a relationship with an impotent partner? Again, there were two types of reactions. One was for a husband and wife to make no attempt to explore sexual pleasure, even when they remained otherwise close. Asked if her husband did anything to satisfy her sexually before he recovered his potency, Ms. Peng said, "He is a *lao fengjian* (old feudalist, i.e., very conservative) and did not do anything."

Mr. Zhao, Ms. Cui's husband, likewise, appeared to make no effort to satisfy his wife. Mr. Zhao, a thirty-two-year-old law enforcement officer, and Ms. Cui, a thirty-year-old teacher, had been married for four years after dating for four years, but they had never succeeded in having sex because Mr. Zhao could not have an erection rigid enough to penetrate her. When they went to bed, they now slept under separate quilts. Ms. Cui had a pretty face and earned as much as her husband. In the clinic, neither of them showed any sign of dismay or distress, emotions one could easily imagine they might have felt. Neither wife nor husband mentioned that Mr. Zhao did anything to satisfy Ms. Cui physically. Instead, it was she who was more active; she even helped wash his penis. Again, I asked the same difficult question I had posed to Ms. Peng. Ms. Cui explained to me what held them together.

I feel we get along well. We cook together when it's just the two of us or when we have guests. He is nice toward me. For example, when I want to buy a dress worth 100 yuan, he insists that I get the one worth 200 yuan. I don't mean our relationship is all about spending money. In fact we combine our salaries every month. Whoever wants to spend money just goes ahead and does it. We save whatever is left each month. He cares about me. The other day when I was taking a daylong exam for a certificate in my field, he rode a bike in the burning sun to the examination place and kept me company during the lunch break. We often talk a lot to each other, and we enjoy good jokes together. I think his problem is lack of interest in sex. We have a lot of friends. He has more friends than I do. When friends asked us why we still don't have a child, I tried to change the subject. If we can't avoid this question anymore, I just say that we gave up our reproductive quota for the country. I didn't tell the truth to my parents. My father has a heart problem.

After Viagra became available, I contacted them about how things were going. But disappointingly, according to Ms. Cui, Mr. Zhao felt nauseous after taking the drug only once. It did not help him get an erection. Where were they to find a solution to their problem? They did not offer me a clear answer, and I kept on wondering how their emotional bond could be sustained, without significant improvement in building sexual intercorporeality. I confess that this is one case I still puzzle over today.

The second type of response was for men to satisfy their partners' desire using other parts of the body—using fingers to thrust, letting women rub against their bodies, giving massages, and so on. This kind of alternative intercorporeality is practiced in many parts of the world, and it is not unusual for women to report that they enjoy and want more of it during sexual encounters (Potts et al. 2003). Annie Potts and colleagues (2004), for instance, found that married couples in New Zealand adopted ways of having sexual pleasure other than through vaginal intercourse, even when Viagra enabled it.

Can this type of sexual intercorporeality sustain a pleasurable sexual relationship? The answer depends on the specifics of a couple's situation. I found two types of outcome. One, illustrated by the following example, is positive. A forty-year-old technician had not had intercourse for half a year owing to impotence. He had been married for seventeen years, and he and his wife had a daughter who was about fifteen years old. His wife did not like oral sex, but she liked to manually help him to ejaculate. As for her desire, he said, "I always take her out shopping and try to entertain her. In the evening I use my fingers to help her reach orgasm and satisfy her." His doctor gave no clear diagnosis of what might be responsible for his impotence. But he was one of the few men I had seen who did not exhibit much worry or seem pained by his situation. His "alternative sexual intercorporeality" was probably one of the reasons his wife stayed in the relationship. He was not the only man I met who helped his wife reach orgasm by manually stimulating the clitoris. Some women liked it; others did not. In one case, a woman achieved orgasm by rubbing her genital against her husband's leg.

When women practiced alternative sexual intercorporeality, the immediate effect was to alleviate the male's phallocentric fear of performance. Not surprisingly, that helped in the recovery of potency. Alternative sexual intercorporealities (e.g., lesbian homoeroticism) de-essentialize female desire for vaginal intercourse and downplay the centrality of penile penetration to female sexual pleasure. In other words, an alternative sexual intercorporeality, the opposite of phallocentrism, may be integrated into women's as well as men's pursuit of sexual pleasure, whether men are impotent or not.

In the following case, however, this kind of alternative intercorporeality had a mixed effect. Mr. Liu was one of the most desperate patients I observed. He was thirty-three years old and was living with his wife in Beijing. They had been married for four years, and he had never succeeded in penetrating her. He told me that he had wanted to have sex with her back in the 1980s when they were dating. They were both attending college in a southern province at that time. "We were sleeping together naked a dozen times a year," he recalled, "I wanted to penetrate every time, but her family's injunction that she should not have sex before marriage was strict, so I ended up ejaculating outside of her body many times." After graduation, they went to Shenzhen together and worked in business. It was then that he noticed he was sometimes unable to get an erection when embracing her, but because the pressure from work was intense, he did not pay much attention to these episodes. He and his wife-to-be still often slept together without having sexual intercourse. Later, Mr. Liu started to test his potency with xiaojie when he went with friends to a hair salon that also served as a brothel. He passed the test. Unfortunately, after he got married, his erection was still not good enough to penetrate his wife.

He said, "I could not sleep well. This year on my business trip to Shenzhen, I went to see xiaojie in a hair salon again and could get an erection. But I just could not get an erection with my wife. This is very painful. Once I walked up to the roof of the building and wanted to jump off and kill myself, *yiliao bailiao* (all trouble ends when the main trouble ends, or woes end by quitting this world)." As he said this, he was almost in tears. He looked very depressed and obviously felt very bad about his inability to satisfy his wife. He said he often stimulated her clitoris, whereas she did nothing to stimulate him. She could get pleasure from his stimulation and fall asleep afterward, but he felt guilty and could not sleep well. It seems that the less his wife complained, the guiltier he felt. How they remained together was a mystery to me.

In the survey I conducted among female college students, one question I asked was, "What should you do if your male sexual partner becomes impotent?" The survey listed four choices: (1) give up sex, (2) break up with the man, (3) continue the relationship but have sex with other men, and (4) cooperate with the man to cure impotence while seeking alternative ways to make love. Eighty-nine percent of respondents chose the fourth option.[15] It seems that not all women who stayed in relationships with impotent men were oblivious to their own desire.

The key issue reflected in my survey question was not just how men and women could best gain sexual pleasure and what it was that enhanced sexual intercorporeality. Rather, fundamental ethical concerns were also at stake: whether one should identify desire with happiness and how desire could translate into happiness.

As the examples in this chapter illustrate, women's involvement in managing impotence is not any less important than men's, and, in fact, at times may be more important. Impotence, after all, is not only a neurovascular event affecting the individual male body. It is also a social, familial event and an intercorporeal, gendered event.

PART II

Potency and Life

CHAPTER 5

The Loss of *Jing* (Seminal Essence)

and the Revival of *Yangsheng*

(the Cultivation of Life)

───────────────

In *nanke*, the word *jing* (精) often came up in conversations between patients and doctors. The Chinese term for "nocturnal emission" is *yi jing* (遺精, loss of semen), ejaculation is *she jing* (射精, the shooting of semen), coitus interruptus is *tiwai pai jing* (体外排精, ejaculation outside the body), and premature ejaculation is *zaoxie* (早泄)[1] or *she jing taikuai* (射精太快, ejaculating too fast).

Jing means "semen," a bodily fluid central to the narrative of male sexual problems. But in the long tradition of Chinese medicine, *jing* primarily has meant "seminal essence," an intangible essence according to this tradition's bodily cosmology. Qibo, the medical counselor of the legendary Yellow Emperor of the pre-Qin period, explained that "jing is the foundation of *shenti* (the body)."[2] Likewise, Zhuangzi, an ancient Daoist philosopher, valued jing highly, saying, "The masses value material gains, an honest and upright man cherishes reputation, a virtuous man esteems a noble ideal, and a sage treasures jing."[3] Here, he was referring to jing as the value of purity (in the sense of simple and pure essence which either *jingqi*, refined vital energy, or *jingshen*, essence-spirit, embodies). Historically, then, treasuring jing has been of the utmost importance and the highest virtue.

However, in modern times, particularly since Chinese medicine's encounters with Western medicine in the nineteenth and twentieth centuries, *jingye* (semen) and *jingzi* (sperm) have become central to the medical meaning of *jing*. Over time, the materiality of semen has gradually monopolized the ancient category of "seminal essence." I describe this trend as the "loss of jing (seminal essence)." In a broad sense, this linguistic and conceptual trend downplays the importance of "preserving jing" (e.g., by having sexual intercourse less frequently) and reflects public encouragement of sexual pleasure, and it sets the tone for this chapter's discussion of "the history of jing," echoing Lawrence Cohen's (1999) "history of semen."

"The loss of jing" is one aspect of the story of the transformation of the Chinese body. If the loss of jing affirms the rise of individual desire, are people now focused on satisfying desire to the exclusion of treasuring seminal essence? Are there limits to the satisfaction of desire? It is revealing that, at the same time I identified the loss of jing, I noticed another development, the revival of *yangsheng* (養生, the cultivation or nurturing of life), which advocates preserving seminal essence.

The two trends—the loss of jing and the revival of yangsheng—constitute an important problematic in the "anthropology of the contemporary" (Rabinow 2007), speaking to the issue of how to live an ethical life when traditional values are both being lost and being revived as a result of dramatically changed social conditions in post-Mao China. Judith Farquhar and Qicheng Zhang (2012) explored the flourishing of yangsheng among contemporary Beijingers, particularly retirees, who gathered in parks to participate in a wide range of activities deemed good for their health and *shen*-spirit or *shen*-vitality. They viewed yangsheng as a manifestation of Beijingers' reinvention of tradition in the post-Maoist utopia, to cope with both social and personal changes, to experience bodily joy, and to live a good life. Congruent with their exploration of "life's" meaning through methodical ways of living, I examine the historical conditions that underlay the revival of yangsheng, particularly in relation to managing sexual desire. Yangsheng was discouraged by the Maoist ethos promoting the sacrifice of individual interest, whereas its resurgence was made possible by the post-Mao reform, when the familial self and the individualized self gained free space for cultivation. A historical analysis makes it clear that *xingyangsheng* (sexual cultivation) in contemporary China, like "care of the self" in ancient Greece, is an ethical approach to coping with desire.

Jing Is More Than Semen

Nanke is perhaps one of the few sites in China today where jing is still often referred to as "seminal essence" instead of semen. In a clinic of Chinese medicine in Beijing, a patient complained about a five-year decline in his potency. His other symptoms included decreased salivation. Dr. Wang prescribed a decoction containing ten herbs. He explained to the patient that this decoction would help to "*shengjing* (produce jing), *shugan* (purge liver fire), and *shengyin* (replenish yin)." He emphasized, "Producing jing here does not mean producing jingye (semen) but strengthening the whole body."

The notion of jing as seminal essence figured prominently in Chinese medicine during ancient times. There were two types of jing: *xiantian zhijing* (先天之精, jing one is born with, or prenatal jing) and *houtian zhijing* (後天之精, jing one acquires after birth, or postnatal jing). The first type comes from the bodies of one's parents;[4] the second type is acquired through the absorption of nutrients such as water and grain and their processing in the body. So, the former is reproductive essence, whereas the latter is the essence drawn from alimentary nourishment, forming the material basis of physical growth and development (Sivin 1987:242).[5]

Here I propose envisioning jing as operating along a functional continuum, its form varying in terms of tangibility depending on its functional positioning. Jing's function in governing reproduction can be materialized as jingye (semen) and belongs at the most tangible end of the continuum. The function of governing the growth of the body and harmonizing the viscera as well as the meridians through which qi flows cannot be materialized in a specific element such as semen and, therefore, belongs at the least tangible end of the continuum. Jing's transformative function falls between the two ends, because this function may give rise to tangible blood as well as less tangible qi.

In this view, semen and seminal essence are interrelated and transformative, rather than clearly distinguished. Etymological evidence shows that the Chinese character for jing (精) includes the radical 米 (rice), indicating a conceptual relationship between rice and seminal essence. In fact, one of the earliest appearances of the jing character was in a reference to rice.[6] The link between the two was embedded in certain Chinese cultural practices. For instance, I vividly remember that, when I was little, my grandmother liked to scoop a small bowl of *mitang* (米湯, soup made of the liquid drained from half-cooked rice) for me to eat. She said that eating this soup was good for men. The rice soup and semen shared a similar tangible form, gray and viscous, and the purpose of eating the soup was to nourish the whole body: once absorbed into the body, it nourished intangible seminal essence, which, in turn, could be transformed into semen.

According to the *Inner Canon*, jing is closely related to *shen* (腎, the kidney):[7] shen houses jing; hence, shen is of the utmost importance to life and male potency.[8] The kidney stores both types of jing—prenatal and postnatal.

Prenatal jing is always stored in shen, whereas postnatal jing may be stored in all five viscera.

In sum, even though it plays a decisive role in producing new life in the form of semen, jing is more than semen. Semen is only one form of jing, one moment in the existence of jing, one phase of a transformative circle, and one manifestation of vitality.

My impression, gained from reading the ancient literature, is that concern about yijing (loss of jing in nocturnal emission or other forms) was pronounced throughout premodern history. The loss of tangible semen was understood as symptomatic of the weakness of shen (the kidney). Excessive loss of semen causes damage to the yin–yang balance by, for example, causing a deficiency of yin (jing is called "yin-jing"; that is, jing is inherently associated with yin),[9] which leads to the exhaustion of qi.[10] The disturbance in the yin–yang balance resulting from a deficiency of yin causes a disturbance of shen (spirit).[11] Therefore, the loss of semen could disturb the fundamental balance between yin and yang, between the kidney and the heart, and threaten to deplete seminal essence and block its smooth transformation into qi and blood.

The consequence of the loss of semen has been downplayed in modern times because the intangible dimension of jing (seminal essence) has been downplayed. It is hard to tell when this trend first began. By the twentieth century, it had become obvious.

Jing Reduced to Semen

THE DILUTION OF *JING* DURING THE REPUBLICAN PERIOD
The notion of "jing" underwent gradual transformation as Western medicine became more popular in China. *A Collection of New Perspectives of Chinese Medicine* (1932), edited by Wang Shenxuan, is a window onto these changes. This rather long book included chapters on *shengli* (physiology), *zheli* (philosophical rationale), *bingli* (pathology), diagnosis, medicine, *fangji* (medicinal formulas), and diseases of various *ke* (divisions such as internal medicine, external medicine, gynecology, and pediatrics), but jing was mentioned in only two short chapters. That jing was given so little attention in this comprehensive collection showed its decline in importance in the intensifying dialogue between Chinese medicine and Western medicine. One chapter discussed spermatorrhea—the loss of jing—from the standpoint of jing as reproductive fluid, that is, semen (Wang 1932, vol. 9:80–81). Only lip ser-

vice was paid in this discussion to the importance of jing as seminal essence that nourished the whole body.

The nuanced, gradual reduction of jing to semen reflected in the *New Perspectives* volume was cast in terms of harmonizing Western medicine with Chinese medicine. But the "harmonization" ended up stripping Chinese medical notions of their operating principles. The reduction of jing to semen was already under way in the Republican period, despite continuing strong concern and worry about spermatorrhea, as seen in advertisements in newspapers for medicines targeting the condition, sensationalist warnings about the harm resulting from the loss of seminal essence, and frequent letters to doctors and journal editors seeking medical advice and help for spermatorrhea.[12]

THE CONTINUATION OF THE TREND

The reduction of jing to semen continued in contemporary China, owing, among other factors, to the increasing influence of biomedicine from the Maoist period on. Many men were still concerned about the "loss of jing," but the focus of their concern had shifted away from seminal essence to semen, as the following two stories illustrate.

In the late 1980s, Mr. Gong, in his early thirties, told me that he worried whenever the semen he ejaculated looked thin and watery (*xibo*). He explained that occasional thin semen meant a temporary lack of nutrition in the body. However, if semen remained thin for a long time, it meant a serious decline in health. Mr. Gong had a high school education. He grew up in a working-class family. Because he had four siblings and a blind and unemployed mother, he had known economic hardship, and as an adult, he continued to worry about meeting his subsistence needs.

He became a blue-collar worker and got married in the mid-1980s. After divorcing, he had not remarried, but he did not abstain from sex. He often bragged about how he ejaculated three times in one night and about how virile he was when he could ejaculate "real jing" (thick semen) rather than *xitangtang* (semen that looked like diluted soup). Using the language of mahjong, he boasted about his virile power: "Xiabian bu kaijiao, shangbian bu gepai" (the one above does not cut the deal until the one under opens the turf, i.e., in sex the man above does not ejaculate until the woman under him starts to scream in pleasure [reaches orgasm]). He recalled that, in the late 1980s, one of his best friends, then thirty years old, had not yet had sex. Mr. Gong goaded his friend into action, saying to him, "It is shameful that you haven't tasted the pleasure of having sex at this age. Go find [a woman] and try it." One day, his friend finally reported to him in a thrilled tone of voice, "I tasted it! I tasted it!" The diminished concern about the loss of seminal essence went hand in hand with increased justification of sexual pleasure.

At first glance, Mr. Gong's concern about watery semen resembled the concern expressed in the folk saying "Yi di jing, shi di xue" (一滴精, 十滴血, a drop of jing, i.e., semen, is worth ten drops of blood), reflecting a shared epistemology with orthodox Chinese medical thought about the need to be vigilant in preserving seminal essence. Yet a closer look shows that Mr. Gong's alertness to thin semen had nothing to do with this essence. Instead, ejaculating "real jing" was evidence of his virility and a sign of success in attaining sexual pleasure. His working-class background and his history of poverty had not spawned in him a sense of limited good in terms of bodily resources, as George Foster might have predicted.[13] He embraced pleasure instead of worrying about the loss of jing. In his lifeworld, jing had less to do with health than with enjoyment.

My second story also illustrates the decline in concern about preserving seminal essence but in a highly idiosyncratic way. A woman told one of the doctors I worked with, with some concern, that her husband always sucked jingye (semen) from her vagina or from her mouth after ejaculation. Moreover, at dinnertime, with both of them naked, he liked to remove a dozen dates he had inserted into her vagina the day before and eat them while drinking alcohol. He would then insert another dozen dates into her vagina for the next day. This habit appeared to combine diverse interests: seeking pleasure, nurturing life by "plucking yin" from the female body, and taking in nutrients. In ingesting semen to nourish his body, however, this man was not acting in accordance with the bedchamber arts. His behavior did not differ from taking nutrients through eating and satisfied other purposes than preserving jing to nurture life.

CONTRADICTORY TRENDS IN POST-MAO CHINA:
PROMOTING DESIRE VERSUS CULTIVATING LIFE

As I discuss in chapter 1, the birth of nanke reflected the legitimation of sexual desire, a tendency that further diluted concern about the loss of seminal essence. Yet, at the same time, nanke drew strongly on the bodily cosmology of Chinese medicine to deal with male problems, cautioning against the harmfulness of sexual desire.

Two influential works on nanke—*Zhongyi nanke xue* (A study of men's medicine of Chinese medicine), by Wang Qi and Cao Kaiyong (1988), and *Wang Qi nanke xue* (Wang Qi's study of men's medicine of Chinese medicine), by Wang Qi and his students (1997), exemplify this contradiction. In the first book, jing (seminal essence) was given a very important place in structuring the system of nanke. At one point, the book even mentioned the Daoist technique of *huanjing bunao* (returning jing to nourish the brain), which took concern about preserving seminal essence in ancient China to an extreme.[14]

The second book represented Wang Qi's effort to break away from the orthodox perspective the earlier book had espoused. In it, the chapter devoted to preserving jing was short and insignificant: it accounted for less than 2 percent of the overall content, compared with 7 percent of the book published ten years earlier. It differed in emphasis from the earlier discussion in at least two ways. First, it dodged the distinction between prenatal jing and postnatal jing, indicating a more biomedically oriented perspective and emphasizing the reproducibility of jing. Second, it focused only on *shengzhi zhi jing* (生殖之精, reproductive jing)—jingye (semen) as a fluid necessary for reproduction. The transformativeness and transformability of jing were barely mentioned except in the context of the reproduction of semen through the intake of *shuigu* (水榖, water and grain).

Even though Wang Qi did not go as far as he had in the earlier book in emphasizing the importance of jing, he still expressed concern about spermatorrhea. A forty-five-year-old patient complained about the loss of sleep and fatigue because of nocturnal emissions, and Wang Qi treated his problem seriously. This patient had been experiencing nocturnal emissions for three years. Sometimes it would happen once a night for three nights in a row. After two visits to Wang Qi, his emissions became less frequent—about once every other week. But Wang Qi still prescribed herbal medicine for him on his third visit, explaining that frequent emission at the age of forty-five was physically harmful. Wang Qi also took a serious approach in treating spermatorrhea among young men (specifically, high school graduates who had nocturnal emissions while preparing for college entrance examinations). He called their problem "binglixing yijing" (the pathological emission of jing) and considered it indicative of the psychological impact of stress on the body. In this regard, his perspective had gone beyond the early distinction between emission during erotic dreams and emission during dreamless sleep. Nevertheless, he did not go so far as to identify with biomedical urologists, who dismissed jingye as consisting only of protein, chemicals, and water. He devoted one chapter in *Wang Qi nanke xu* to a discussion of the principle of the cultivation of life. As he had in the earlier book coauthored with Cao, he cautioned against excessive sex.

That two important books on nanke saw the potential for harm in sexual desire and advocated the cultivation of life illustrates a contradiction within nanke itself, given that it promotes sexual desire by curing impotence. How do we understand such a contradiction? In the pages that follow, I examine how the "loss of jing" became a moral concern in the midst of rising sexual desire in post-Mao China. Then I demonstrate how this concern differed from the moral concern under Maoist collectivism, calling for the cultivation of life as a counterweight to the rise of sexual desire rather than for the eradication of both individual desire and the cultivation of life.

The Loss of *Jing*

Do ordinary people in urban China today treat jing only as semen? Many do, particularly younger people who are passionate about pursuing sexual pleasure and do not worry about the loss of essence. Yet, at the same time, it is quite common to hear people talk about *baoyang shenti* (保養身體, nurturing and nourishing the body) by taking care of jingqi (精氣, the vital force of seminal essence). For some people, managing seminal essence is an integral part of a healthy lifestyle as well as of a moral economy. The following two stories demonstrate the threat to the moral economy of seminal essence.

THE MORAL ECONOMY OF *JING*

Mr. Xiao was fifty-one years old. He married in the early 1970s and had two children. He worked for a county government subsidiary to the Beijing Municipal Government. Ms. Liao, his wife, was five years younger than he and worked for the same county government as a driver. Mr. Xiao had been having sexual difficulty for a year, being either unable to penetrate or unable to sustain an erection until ejaculation. He thought his problem was *shenxu* (weakness of the kidney; see chapter 6). He went to see doctors in small clinics in his county, getting both biomedical injections and prescriptions for herbal medicine, but his symptoms did not improve. Occasionally, after taking the herbal medicines, he could get an erection when he engaged in erotic joking with his wife, but he could not sustain the erection until ejaculation. Yet what he thought was a biological problem of undetermined origin his wife regarded as a potential social and moral problem.

Mr. Xiao recalled how Ms. Liao responded to his erectile problems: "Since I have had problems getting an erection, she has avoided talking about her desire. But I can tell that she is not happy. Recently, I observed that her breasts have shrunken a lot. One night last year, when I had difficulty getting an erection, she burst out crying. She complained that maybe I had erectile problems because I had had affairs with other women, that my jing had all flowed out and I had been depleted of jing."

Ms. Liao did not perceive jing as a bodily fluid, a material that a man could reproduce continuously. Nor did she think of it as infinite in supply. In Ms. Liao's view, in addition to biological limits on the production and reproduction of jing in a man's body, there were moral and ethical limits. If a man did not live a moral life (e.g., was not a faithful husband), he would soon run out of jing. Ms. Liao attributed her husband's impotence to possible affairs with other women, which had caused his loss of jing. In her understanding, jing was seminal essence as well as semen and also a moral essence that was opposed to what she considered the moral chaos of consumer society. Seminal essence gave her a language for talking not only about the body but also about morality.

Ms. Liao's tears put Mr. Xiao in a difficult position. He defended himself to me just as he had to his wife:

It is hard to explain to her why I had a problem getting an erection. I have never sought to have sex with *xiaojie* (prostitutes). I am a very compassionate man—if I see a *maomaocong* (a kind of insect) on the road, I pick it up carefully and put it back in the field, not doing any harm to it. I care about my family and am always thinking about doing things for my family. On weekends I always stay home, doing household chores, and do not even bother to leave my apartment. The reason I am caring about my family is that I ate bitterness [suffered hardship] in the 1960s. In the 1960s, when I was a teenager, I suffered from starvation. I remember that once I was so hungry that I could not help but grab a turnip from the stand of a vegetable vendor and run away. The vendor, an old man, chased me for the turnip. I was so scared that I peed involuntarily as I ran and threw the turnip away. At that time, I was attending junior high. I had a ration of 28 *jin* (about 31 pounds) of food each month and could not get enough food to eat. Once I went with my brother to pick *yecai* (wild vegetables, i.e., edible plants) and cooked them with corn. But I had stomachache after I ate them. They did not taste good.

As he spoke about how bitter life had been when he was young, I began to wonder why he was defending himself so forcefully, especially if, as he claimed, he had not had sex with other women. I wondered why his wife suspected otherwise. He continued,

My *laoniangr* (老娘兒, literally, old mother; here referring to his wife in a half-teasing and half-blaming tone) is just too inflexible. She never initiates sex with me; sometimes when she wants it, she sticks her foot into my quilt in bed. She does not like to socialize with men and does not even shake hands with men. I remember that once at dinner, I introduced her to the head of my bureau, my boss. She did not want to shake hands with him, even though my boss was already stretching out his hand to her. I had to carefully explain to him that she did not mean to offend him, that that was just the way she was. She looks very innocent, as though she *meixin meifei de* (has no heart and lung, i.e., is simple and does not brood on things or have bad intentions) and is easy to handle. But this is not the case. Once, as the driver for the branch secretary of the party in her unit, she was waiting to give the secretary a ride home after the meeting. When the meeting was over, the secretary was eager to go home. Finding her buying a snack at a food stand nearby, the secretary patted her on the hand. She shook off the secretary's hand, saying: "What are you doing?" In our twenty-some years of marriage, she did not know about orgasm until recently.

What Mr. Xiao wanted to convey through this portrait of his wife was that her complaint about his loss of jing reflected her own personality, particularly her "inflexible and conservative" comportment toward men. She was idiosyncratic. But her crying revealed a sense of moral urgency that he could not help but quickly dismiss. What led her to lose confidence in her husband's faithfulness at the moment when he had difficulty getting an erection? Why did it not occur to him to explain to his wife that his erectile problem was a biological rather than a moral issue? What made his defense so complicated? The source of the complication seems to have been the seductive temptation he faced in consumer culture. He said,

At home, normally it was easy to have an erection. Each time after I made a business trip and got back home, I could get an erection without much foreplay. I call this *jiao gongliang* (turning in grain taxes, i.e., finishing a mandatory task with a spouse). Sometimes I do feel like trying with other women. There is a woman in my unit who likes to give men hugs. When she hugged me, I could feel an erection. Yet, suspecting that she might have slept with countless men, I am afraid that I may get a sexually transmitted disease from her if I have sex with her. Once I was attending a conference in a hotel I was familiar with; the organizer sent six prostitutes and asked me to pick one. I ran away from them to the restroom. I fear being caught having sex with prostitutes and videotaped. If I was caught doing that, I would be embarrassed, at my age. I know someone who was impotent. He told me that his impotence was caused by his *zai waibian luangao* (sleeping around with women).

It became clear to me that, in the end, the sense of moral urgency reflected in Ms. Liao's tears was not groundless. Increasingly rampant prostitution and the decline in her husband's enthusiasm to have sex with her served as the backdrop for her dramatic emotional outburst when he developed erectile problems. She sensed in his problems a threat to the integrity of the moral body, not in the form of a breakdown of the biological mechanism for erection but in the form of the dissolution of the body's moral coherence. This moral coherence was predicated on the fullness of jing as the support for a man's readiness for erection. Anything that compromised the fullness of jing and therefore damaged that readiness damaged the moral economy of seminal essence. In Ms. Liao's view, sex outside of marriage was a vampiristic act that sucked jing out of the body and depleted the body of the capacity for erection. Potency was a moral capacity precisely because jing was a moral agent in the body.

Ms. Liao's emotional outburst reflected a reality in which men and women had unequal access to sexual pleasure, particularly in the flourishing post-Mao business culture. The call for preserving seminal essence, articulated by Ms. Liao, had the clear political implication of protesting not only the loss of seminal essence but also the privileging of male desire and pleasure.

THE THREAT OF EXCESS TO SEMINAL ESSENCE

Seminal essence can be damaged in ways other than by having too much sex. Excessive alcohol intake is one of the ways damage is done, according to many doctors of Chinese medicine. In my fieldwork, excessive alcohol consumption was an integral part of the lifestyles many men developed in the consumer culture of the 1990s and 2000s. I asked Mr. Guo, an impotence patient, why he insisted that he had to drink, when his doctor had advised him to quit.

Mr. Guo was twenty-five years old. He had first had sex when he was in high school in the early 1990s. He had had a girlfriend for three years and had experienced no problems for the first year of their relationship. Several times after the first year, however, he had been unable to maintain an erection. He was a self-employed truck driver and delivered goods (primarily coal) in a suburban district of Beijing. He often had sex late at night, after finishing the day's delivery and returning home to his girlfriend. But he was always drunk when having sex. He had drunk heavily at dinner, often consuming more than half a *jin* (260 milliliters, about 8.5 fluid ounces) of Chinese liquor, which normally has an alcohol level of over 50 percent (by comparison, beer has an alcohol level of only 12 percent). He explained why he had to drink:

> I have to drink when I go to a coal mine to load coal; I have to drink after I deliver the coal to the buyer and ask for payment. I have to treat the buyers with dinner and drink with them in order to get the payment. The problem is that the work unit that had ordered the delivery of coal often did not want to pay, because they said that their business partners owed them money, so they were short of money. One company, which makes honeycomb (briquette), had owed me 70,000 yuan in total. This company gave me a *baitiao* (白條, an IOU, a written statement acknowledging the receipt of the delivery and the debt to the seller) each time. Some of these debts can be traced back to the predecessor of the predecessor of the current leader of the unit. The current leader of the unit disclaimed the debt his predecessor owed to me because his predecessor had died in a car accident. I took him to court. The court ordered that they compensate me by transferring their property to me. They ended up offering me their old shabby trucks. Who wants their shabby trucks? Therefore, almost every time I deliver coal, I have to invite the buyer of coal to dinner and drink a lot with him or his colleagues, in order to get them to pay me. That's why I have to drink.

Baitiao was common in some regions in the 1990s during the transformation to the market economy. It was largely associated with triangular debt, in which one was simultaneously a debtor to one party and a creditor to another party. The phenomenon of triangular debt was considered to be the result of a lack of a mature market economy ruled by law. It was the product of many complex forces, among them corruption, the partially marketized socialist work unit system, and the unregulated nature of business transactions. Far from being an entirely personal activity, Mr. Guo's heavy drinking habit was the means by which he survived the transformation from the centralized economy to a market economy with "Chinese characteristics."

Alcohol and impotence took a toll not only on small business owners such as Mr. Guo but also on far more powerful CEOs. Mr. Jin was the forty-four-year-old CEO of a company that made electronic products. He got married in the early 1980s and had a child. In the early 1990s, he left his work unit, a state-owned company, under the condition of *tingxin liuzhi* (stop salary but keep the position, i.e., unpaid leave of absence with the right to resume the position at a later time). He went to Shenzhen, a city in the south, to start his own company. Having worked there for ten years and made a fair amount of money, he had recently come back to Beijing, leaving his business behind. After his return, he started to experience an inability to maintain an erection until ejaculation. He perceived the change in his body to be associated with his experience of working and living in the south for ten years. "Can you tell me what it was like to work in Shenzhen?" I asked.

"I was very busy in Shenzhen every day, and I was pursuing high efficiency at work. My hours were very much in chaos. Every day after work I had many social activities. Social events normally started at nine o'clock in the evening and went into early morning, like two to three o'clock in the morning. Either I invited people or people invited me to get together. If I was invited, it was hard to decline. Getting together was very frequent. It's like routine."

He said that when he and other people got together on these occasions, they would have dinner and drink. "Drinking is important, because drinking can reduce the distance between two persons. The market in China is still not standard enough, so *guanxi* (connecting) is the foundation for business. Particularly when I was working with a new business partner, drinking was inevitable." Then he described to me how he *haoyin* (participated in unrestrained drinking, similar to binge drinking).

According to Mr. Jin, in a single evening, he would often drink one bottle of *erguotou* (two pot heads, a type of liquor with an alcohol content of more that 50 percent) and five bottles of beer (the Chinese bottle is one-third larger than the average U.S. bottle). He recalled, "One evening I drank up to 20 bottles of beer, because that was when the negotiation with the business partner was at the most crucial moment."

Whether Mr. Jin's routine haoyin and his irregular work hours damaged his potency is unclear. He was diagnosed with diabetes in 1998, and, according to his doctor, his declining potency was related to the disease. Yet he had not reduced his business schedule, even though it was imperiling his health. As he spoke with me, he constantly reminded me that he could not talk too long because he was very busy with his business. Wearing an expensive silver-gray shirt and commenting on how he had taken a detour to the hospital that morning to avoid the traffic jam typical of Beijing's rush hour, he demonstrated both his status as a successful businessman and his determination to continue to achieve success despite suffering from ED.

Doctors told both Mr. Jin, the CEO, and Mr. Guo, the self-employed driver, to drink less and even, to stop drinking for a while. Chinese medical literature, starting with the *Inner Canon*, is full of admonitions against excessive drinking and, particularly, against having sex after drinking. It was believed that heavy drinking followed by sex would damage one's seminal essence. In the *Inner Canon*'s opening chapter, titled "Shanggu tianzhen lun" (On the heavenly essence of the remotest ancient time), the Yellow Emperor asks why people in ancient times could live to the age of 100 and remain nimble, whereas people of his era became weak by the age of 50. After describing how ancient people had a good life style, Qibo, the Yellow Emperor's counselor, points out that "people of our times are not like that. Wine is their drink, caprice is their norm. Drunken, they enter the chamber of love, through lust using up their germinal essence, through desire dispersing their inborn vitality. They do not know how to maintain fullness, they entertain untimely thoughts, they covet short term gratifications, they resist life's joys. And their daily habits are not regular, so by the age of fifty, they are all worn out."[15]

I often heard doctors of TCM say to patients that excessive drinking harms the liver and can affect male potency (see chapter 6). Yet Mr. Jin and Mr. Guo simply smiled bitterly in response to their doctors' advice, implying that it was incompatible with business practices. Their reactions were virtually identical: "Wo buneng buhe ya!" (I could not do business without drinking!). Now, they faced a choice: continue to drink to remain in business or quit drinking and risk either being forced out of business or, at least, gaining a reputation for violating the rules of the male-dominated business world. The need to drink was perhaps exaggerated, but the practice of *gou-dui* ("thickening" the relationship) through dinners and drinking with business partners was consistent with the emerging business culture in China, pervaded as it was by baitiao and triangular debts, and by the imperative to consolidate the relationship with government officials or business partners. The special convergence of social conditions made the body, the agent of such performance, the site of business competition at the cost of seminal essence.

Standing in stark contrast to the above two cases of the "loss of jing" was the concurrent revival of interest in the literature of yangsheng (the cultivation of life). In the post-Mao reform period, particularly in the 1990s, many ancient Chinese medical texts dealing with the topic were published as were a number of popular interpretations. In general terms, yangsheng is the tradition of taking care of the body by properly attending to the details of everyday life (Farquhar and Zhang 2012), to everything from sleep to dietary regimens, bathing, one's temperament in response to changes in climate, and sex. Yangsheng is integral to Chinese medicine and reflects its fundamentals, including its bodily cosmology, its philosophy of life, and its ultimate goal of harmony, balance, and longevity. To characterize Chinese medicine as fundamentally a yangsheng-centered medicine is no exaggeration. It emphasizes the importance of the patient's conduct in recovering from illness and maintaining health. The perception of jing as seminal essence (not just semen) and as a foundation for life is one of the cornerstones of the yangsheng practice. Nourishing and preserving jing is central not just to sex but also to managing life activities such as drinking, eating, sleeping, and walking—in short, everyday *qiju* (rising and resting)—as pointed out by Farquhar and Zhang (2012) and recorded extensively in Daoist literature.[16]

When doctors in clinics gave advice on yangsheng, medication became more of an ethical issue. To many patients, some of the restrictions that were proposed appeared outlandish, archaic, or inflexible. For example, limiting the frequency of sex may seem overcautious to today's young lovers, or maintaining bodily warmth by changing clothing in response to changes in the weather may seem unnecessary when heating and air conditioning are available. Doctors of nanke were often fighting an uphill battle against patients' desire, and much advice just fell on deaf ears. The contradictory trends—the post-Mao revival of the practice of yangsheng and the loss of jing amidst the rise of desire—raise the question of how those trends were related to the waning and ultimate demise of Maoism and how those issues were regarded under the Maoist ethos. We cannot understand the revival of the cultivation of life and the rise of individual desire without, once again, going back to the historical context of the Maoist period.

The Impossible Goal of *Yangsheng* in the Maoist Period

SACRIFICING THE BODY FOR THE REVOLUTION

At first glance, yangsheng seems to share with the "revolutionary asceticism" of the Maoist period the same emphasis on restricting sexual desire. Does it produce the same effect of sexual repression?

Yangsheng could not be justified in the Maoist era, because it was considered the basis of a self-centered lifestyle incompatible with the heroic spirit of revolutionary collectivism. A cadre recalled that in the 1960s, Chairman Mao once pointed out that "tilong jianiao yangyu zaihua" (carrying a bird cage and playing with birds, feeding goldfish, and watering flowers) were decadent activities of feudalists and the bourgeoisie and should be replaced by a *jianku pusu* (hardship-enduring and simple) revolutionary lifestyle. The cadre had himself once worked for the bureau of gardening and park administration in the city government. That he would have taken a stand against people tending flowers, birds, and fish shows just how unthinkable it was in the milieu of the 1960s to promote activities meant to cultivate one's life and how much attention was focused on the collective cause.

The discourse of *xisheng* (sacrifice) best described and defined the relationship between the individual, as well as the familial, body and the collective body. It was based on the principle that the interests of the individual and family should yield unconditionally to the interests of the people. This moral discourse drew its inspiration partly from Marx's motto that only after the proletariat liberates the whole of humankind can it liberate itself. In addition to structural limitations, the moral imperative of placing collective interests above individual interests stemmed from the judgment that most people in the world were suffering from exploitation under capitalism, imperialism, and Soviet "revisionism." A sense of mission as well as urgency did not allow for self-indulgence and hedonism. The story of one impotence patient very much reflected the impact of the ideology of "sacrifice" on his body.

Mr. Hou, a forty-four-year-old half-blind worker, came to the clinic for medication for impotence. With his poor eyesight, he could not read, though he was still able to walk in the street without a cane. Since his marriage in the early 1990s, he had not succeeded even once in penetrating his wife, although he had experienced erection through masturbation. He had seen many doctors before he came to see Dr. Ma, but the medication he had received from them had not improved his potency.

He attributed his poor eyesight to a childhood illness. He was born in Beijing in the late 1950s. His parents, both professional journalists at a large newspaper in Beijing, were too busy to take care of him and had to send him back to his *laojia* (the birthplace of his parents), a village in a northern province, where his grandparents took care of him. At the age of two or three, he had a fever that lasted for several days before his grandparents became aware of it and tried to get him medical help. He subsequently lost his eyesight. Even though it was not entirely clear how he lost his potency, he believed his physical condition had to do with the "sacrifice" his parents had made for the revolutionary cause.

"What did they do then in Beijing such that they did not have time to look after you?" I asked.

He said, "You should know . . . since you are old enough to know what people then were busy with. According to my parents, they did not have time to do anything except work and study. You know the late 1950s, the years of Great Leap Forward. People in every unit wished they could work around the clock."

I asked, "Do you know what made them so busy all day long then?"

He sighed and said, "Who knows what they were crazy about then! They said that they often *jiaban* (worked after hours) and had small group meetings for political studies."

Such memories were common. Mr. Shen, about the same age as Mr. Hou, was luckier than Mr. Hou because, rather than being sent to a rural area for child care, he was sent to a kindergarten in the city in the early 1960s. But the kindergarten was *quantuo* (whole care, a facility where kids stayed for the whole week, except Saturday night and Sunday). He had vivid memories of his parents picking him up from the kindergarten on Saturday evenings and dropping him off again on Sunday afternoons. Mr. Shen said that his parents told him they had to participate in small-group study in the evenings during the week, sessions in which they engaged in criticism and self-criticism. In the 1950s and 1960s, people rarely had any free time, as the one-day weekends were often filled with public or collective activities or political studies (the two-day weekend was not instituted until the mid-1990s).

During small-group sessions of criticism and self-criticism, a common form of political control in work units, people's behaviors and thoughts were constantly censored, self-censored, reflected on, and judged against the revolutionary consciousness. To physically engage in such constant and tense group sessions meant disciplining the individual body to conform to the collective, sacrificial body. The political dedication of Mr. Hou's parents' ended up taking a toll on their son's body—through negligence of his care and his health. It is easy to understand how, under such circumstances, the cultivation of life came to be viewed with suspicion.

A close look at the relationship between sex and health sheds more light on the impossibility of pursuing yangsheng in the Maoist period. Concern about health and the body was actually prominent under socialism and was translated into practice in a series of public-health campaigns and routine physical activities.[17] The socialist state actively promoted both competitive and mass sports, the former to serve nationalism (Brownell 1995) and the latter to enhance the collective ethos. Schools and many work units held sporting events on a regular basis. For example, almost every member of a *danwei* had participated in *bahe* (pull the river, i.e., tug of war), a sporting contest that consisted of two teams tugging on opposite ends of a rope. Bahe required not only muscular power but also, more importantly, the coordination of all members. It fit perfectly into the collectivist structure and ethos.

CASUAL CONVERSATIONS ABOUT HEALTH:
NURTURING THE COLLECTIVE BODY

In 1959, Fu Lianzhang (1894–1968), deputy minister of health at the time, published a book entitled *Yangshen zhi dao* (養身之道, The way of nurturing the body). This book gave advice on how to maintain health. It was a collection of short pieces Fu had either published previously in print media or had broadcast on special radio programs. He wrote them in response to letters he received from all over the country.

At first glance, Fu's title suggested his book was concerned with something akin to the prerevolutionary tradition of yangsheng. Yet a close reading of it reveals that any suggestion of yangsheng was either overshadowed by, or reframed within, the intense ethos of class struggle.

Had this book been written by someone other than Fu Lianzhang, the title would immediately have gotten the author into trouble for promoting an individualistic, selfish lifestyle. But Fu Lianzhang had sufficient credentials to be politically safe. He was a unique combination of professional medical practitioner and veteran revolutionary. Fu joined the Red Army in the 1930s, becoming the director of Central Red Hospital and head of the army's medical school. After the founding of the People's Republic, Fu was appointed deputy minister of health. He was a model of *youhong youzhuan* (又紅又專, both "red" and equipped with expertise, i.e., both politically trustworthy and professionally competent). His loyalty to Mao was unswerving. He had treated Mao's illness in the 1920s and received Mao's special attention in the 1930s. He eventually published a book titled *Zai Maozhuxi de jiaodao xia* (Under Chairman Mao's guidance), detailing the establishment of the Red Army's medical system during the Chinese revolution and expressing his personal indebtedness to Chairman Mao (Fu 1959b). Fu's political identity secured his position within the party.

When the book was about to go into its fourth printing in 1966, on the eve of the Cultural Revolution, Fu Lianzhang decide to change the title from *The Way of Nurturing the Body* to *Casual Conversations about Health*. Fu's caution, however, did not protect him from later being charged with having grown "a poisonous plant" (毒草, *ducao*), that is, publishing a counterrevolutionary book.

Yet, reading through Fu's book, I had the impression that it could not have been more compliant with the party's collectivist guidelines. First of all, it avoided discussion of sexual matters, to the extent that it did not even mention reproduction. Of its twenty-six chapters, the one that ventured closest to "the erogenous zone," so to speak, was the one about hemorrhoids. The whole book gave the impression that sex was not only thematically inappropriate but also completely irrelevant to a consideration of the human body and physical health. The absence of sex in the book echoed the more general invisibility of the body and sex in the Maoist period, as I discuss in chapter 2. The omission of any discussion related to sex reflected Fu Lianzhang's political judgment about the inadvisability of raising the issue of sexual desire in public discourse.

Moreover, Fu Lianzhang argued that one's belief in the collective, revolutionary cause and one's optimism about its bright future were central to one's health, both in recovering from illness and in maintaining health. In the chapter entitled "A Chat on Longevity," Fu attributed his own long life—he was seventy-two when he made his last revision to his book—to "the will for revolutionary struggles and the spirit of revolutionary optimism" (1979:126). He wrote that, if one "always has the interests of the nation in the mind, thinks big about the future of the whole world, dissolves oneself in the revolutionary collectivity, shares the sentiment and feelings of the people, breathes the same breath as the revolutionary cause . . . one can have the broad vision and be in a good mood all the time . . . so that one can be in good health and live longer" (1979:131).

Fu singled out *gerenzhuyi* (個人主義, individualism) as responsible not only for the decline of one's political conscience and competence in work but also for one's health. This was because "gerenzhuyi is always the source of sorrow, worry, and vexation. Individualism features insatiable desire, making one calculate endlessly for his or her gain. [The person's] whole mind is so full of worry, wishful thinking, and frustrations that he or she does not have a single moment of peace and quiet. Such persons swallow their own bitter fruits. As a result, they age early" (1979:131).

Fu repeatedly emphasized identifying with revolutionary collectivism as a necessary condition not only for a long life but also for overcoming problems such as tuberculosis and insomnia. Fu quoted Lenin's claim that "those who don't know how to rest don't know how to work" and implied that the purpose of resting was to work better, making it clear that the purpose of remaining healthy and achieving longevity was to serve the cause of collectivism.

The revolutionary approach to "nurturing the body," then, shared with yangsheng a cautious attitude toward desire. But beyond this point of overlap, the differences between the two were stark. First, the regulation of desire in yangsheng was intended to keep the body in a state of serenity, whereas the revolutionary medical ethos required one to sublimate one's desire into a collective energy to foster the collective body. Second, in yangsheng, desire was regulated through embodied practices such as dietary regimens, *daoyin* (a Daoist way of breathing, part of *qigong* technique), and meditation, whereas the revolutionary way to control desire was to impose a collectivistic mentality on the body. In an article entitled "On Revolutionary Energy," Fu emphasized the fundamental role of mental strength in maintaining one's health: "One cannot build up a strong revolutionary will overnight. Some comrades may share this experience: whenever a heated political campaign comes, in the intensified political atmosphere, progressive factors in one's mind increase, and one is energized and invigorated. Yet as soon as the campaign is over, gerenzhuyi again develops, and the habitual resistance comes back to some degree. This situation illustrates the tenacity of old ideas and the utmost difficulty of fostering a strong revolutionary will. Only if we pursue [it] persistently and tenaciously, only if we never let our guard down, only if we never excuse ourselves, only if we carry out the struggle without any compromise, can we eliminate this 'habitual resistance'" (1979:35).

Such is the advice of a medical doctor for maintaining health!

Given Fu's revolutionary credentials, there was little doubt about his sincerity when he spoke of the importance of transforming individual seminal essence into collective energy, a requirement of the ethos of sacrifice. By the same token, given Fu Lianzhang's status as a venerated revolutionary, I do not doubt his sincerity in speaking about his philosophy of longevity, based as it was on his own experience that revolutionary idealism, heroism, and optimism enabled people to be in a good mood all the time, which was conducive to good health. In contrast, anxiety and worry about one's own gain and loss, which were associated with gerenzhuyi, harmed the body. Even his own selflessness, however, could not insulate Fu Lianzhang from the harm spawned by political campaigns. He was tortured to death in prison during the Cultural Revolution.[18]

In the early 1970s, a number of folk "therapeutic exercises or regimens" were invented and gained some popularity, such as drinking a lot of water in the morning, *shuaishou liaofa* ("throwing hands," referring to swinging both arms forward and then backward), and injections of chicken blood. "Shuaishou therapy" was like a very simple version of collective exercise but felt more personal and individualistic because it could be done alone in a small space. For a while, I saw people (most often middle-aged or older women) swinging their arms for fifteen minutes or so in the morning on the balconies of apartments in the city of Chongqing. However, their idiosyncratic and rudimentary nature aside, the underlying rationale of such practices—trying to carve out a space of care for individual health in a time of scarcity—did not gain currency in public discourse. They soon vanished without a trace.

Overall, under the ethos of collectivism, then, yangsheng could not find a place in socialist medical discourse, and it was very much opposed in practice. The subsiding of the collectivist ethos set the stage for yangsheng to reemerge in the post-Mao reform period.

Yangsheng as Ethics

The revival of the cultivation of life and the rise of sexual desire were contradictory. On the one hand, people started to talk openly about enjoying sexual pleasure, and, on the other hand, they started to pay greater attention to nourishing the body. In the nanke clinic, patients mentioned various activities they engaged in to nourish the body: qigong, walking, and other physical exercises; dietary and behavioral regimens; and even *yangge* (a type of folk dancing), to name just a few.[19] Nanke doctors encouraged the pursuit of sexual pleasure at the same time they recommended nurturing life, including cultivating seminal essence. What sense can we make of these contradictory trends?

As I worked with nanke doctors, I found myself paying attention to their own bodily practices, because they often epitomized the principle of yang-sheng and the preservation of seminal essence.[20]

BODIES OF LONGEVITY: A NOSTALGIA OR A RISING ETHICS?

Dr. Chen Wenbo is a nanke doctor of Chinese medicine and former president of the Committee of Nanke Division of the Association of Chinese Medicine. He received his training not through formal education but primarily through *chao fangzi* (抄方子). A common means of acquiring knowledge of Chinese medicine (particularly in the past), chao fangzi is an apprenticeship that involves copying down prescriptions for decoctions dictated by an older, more experienced doctor. It is still a very important way for college students of TCM to learn embodied skills from venerated doctors. When I observed his consultations with patients, I noticed that Dr. Chen recommended many restrictions on patients' lifestyles. In treating patients of *shaojing zheng* (low sperm count), *wujing zheng* (lack of sperm), or impotence, he often gave advice nonstop throughout the consultation. The following are excerpts from some of those conversations.

> You should not drink any alcohol. Nowadays, drinking two *liang baigan* (two small cups of white spirits) is normal. But, before 1949, whoever drank two small cups of spirits would be called a *jiugui* (drunkard, alcoholic). Nowadays, even the president of the hospital drinks two liang of spirits everyday, even though he is an expert of Chinese medicine!
>
> You should not smoke, should not drink, and should not eat spicy food. Don't eat pork fat; instead, eat peanut oil. You must sleep at least seven hours and a half every day. Go to bed at 10:30 in the evening every day.
>
> Don't eat too much meat, fish, and eggs. Nowadays, even peasants cook dishes [i.e., dishes containing meat, eggs, and other high-protein food] for their meals very often. In the past [before the 1950s], even landlords did not have dishes cooked every day. For peasants in the past only

Figure 5.1: Dr. Chen offering advice on the nurturing life when seeing a patient.

on three occasions did people cook dishes: on Spring Festival [Chinese New Year's Day], during the harvesting season in the autumn, and on visits of important guests.

Don't engage in strenuous physical exercise, because strenuous exercise causes the body to sweat too much. Too much sweating does no good to the body. We doctors of Chinese medicine encourage mild exercise such as going for a walk after dinner.

As I listened to the conversations between Dr. Chen and his patients, an image surfaced in my mind of his notion of the ideal body. It was a body that stuck fast to the principle of moderation: never committing any extreme action or maintaining any extreme habit, never eating too much or eating anything that would be considered too stimulating, never moving too strenuously, never getting too emotional. This kind of body, though probably the accepted norm in Daoist circles, fit in neither with the revolutionary, collective, sacrificial body of socialism nor with the adventurous, risk-taking body of consumer society. I confess that I could never have followed all of Dr. Chen's proscriptions. But I remain very interested in whether those self-regulations make a difference in realizing the ideal of health and longevity.

Being around doctors of Chinese medicine, I was able to witness the extent to which they actually preserved and practiced the principle of the ideal body. During my field experience, I often shared meals with doctors in restaurants, which led to unexpected revelations. One day, I was having a meal with Dr. Wei, a middle-aged physician with a PhD in TCM. I was impressed by Dr. Wei's choice of dishes: shredded pork with bitter melon, lamb stewed with white turnip, stir-fried shrimp, and stir-fried squid with celery. Bitter melon was a "cool" or "cold" food; it balanced the stir-fried pork, which, in this case, was neutral but slightly on the "warm" side. The lamb was considered capable of *zaohuo* (stirring up the fire of the body, causing yang to rise to excess) but was balanced by turnip, which was considered capable of *tongqi* (smoothing qi) and leaned toward the cool side. The cooler bitter melon also helped to balance the heat of the lamb stew. Dr. Wei's choice of dishes struck me as reflecting the sensitivity of doctors of Chinese medicine to maintaining a balanced body in everyday life.

The coexistence of the loss of jing and the revival of yangsheng was well illustrated by the following encounter I had during my visit to a county in Sichuan in 2009. My host during the visit, a friend of mine, presented me with a pair of gifts: a bottle of the county's famous brand of *baijiu* (white spirit) and a box of herbal patent pills produced by a local pharmaceutical company. He explained to me, "This box of pills helps *shugan* (smooth out the liver)." Heavy drinking may lead to stasis in the liver that needs to be smoothed out. With their opposite effects—one could harm the liver and the other coped with the harm—my friend's gifts conveyed mixed signals. Post-Mao reform has given people more choices in terms of consumption than ever before; how to make choices has become a growing challenge in everyday life. More openness, more choices, and more free time (for some) means that people must do what they did not have to do in the past: make decisions about a series of everyday details to live a long and good life. Doctors of TCM became a ready resource to tap into for inspiration.

In an attempt to understand how doctors of Chinese medicine treated their own bodies, I consulted a book entitled *Renowned and Old Doctors of Chinese Medicine Speak of the Way of Yangsheng* (Li Junde 1996). One hundred seventy-one doctors of Chinese medicine contributed to this collection. Among them, ninety-seven were between 70 and 100-plus years of age. They shared the same moderation in lifestyle that Dr. Chen urged on his patients. Their attitude toward sex was cautious. They emphasized the importance of conserving jing and advocated refraining from sex. Although they adopted different strategies for dealing with sex, they displayed a tendency to have sex in accordance with a rhythm and to limit the frequency of sex, particularly when they reached certain ages. For example, Dr. Tang, an eighty-five-year-old doctor, had refrained from sex for thirty-five years. Dr. Guo, a seventy-six-year-old doctor, had had sex three times a month from age thirty to age sixty and thereafter three times a year. Dr. Shi, an eighty-year-old doctor, had worked out the following schedule: During one's twenties, one should have sex every four days; during one's thirties, every nine days; and during one's forties, every sixteen days.

Dr. Guo said that he never indulged in the desire to ejaculate profusely during intercourse. Instead, he "always concentrated on the inner upward flow of spirit and did not excessively ejaculate, so that the yin and yang were in harmony, the spirit and qi were flowing and smooth" (Guo 1996:259). Many doctors seemed to be practicing, to the letter, principles of yangsheng laid out in the *Inner Canon*. For example, some ceased to have sex at the age of fifty because, according to the *Inner Canon*, renal qi started to run out around that age. We can trace Dr. Guo's caution with regard to ejaculation and his concentration on inner upward flow to the influence of the bedchamber arts. Such flow brings jing to the brain and turns it into qi, then turns qi into shen (spirit) and sends shen back to a seemingly pervasive "nothingness" (煉精化氣,煉氣化神,煉神還虛, *lianjing huaqi, lianqi huashen, lianshen huanxu*).

Dr. Gao, a one-hundred-year-old doctor, spoke more directly about *fangshi yangsheng* (房事養生, sexual cultivation or the cultivation of life through sex). He wrote,

Forty years ago [in the early 1950s, shortly after the founding of the People's Republic], I discreetly asked a very robust and healthy elderly person about cultivating life through sex. He said that this was a sage's way of life, commonly known as *zhangong* (the art of battle), and one has to practice very hard to obtain it. His words were hard to understand, such as *ziqian wuhou, shuisheng huojiang* (right before the time of *zi* and after the time *wu*, water is on the rise and fire is on the wane, referring to the importance of adjusting the body to the cosmos in deciding when to have sex). I can still remember the secret rules concerning how to do it. First, one's body needs to be built up strong, just as only a rich country can have the edge in a battle; second, one has to *jieyu* (restrain desire) . . . third, husband and wife must share the same desire. (Gao 1996:247)

It is noteworthy that these doctors based their precautions on the importance of conserving jing. Dr. Yan, a seventy-five-year-old doctor, said, "*Fanglao* (房勞, laboring in the bedchamber, i.e., having sex) consumes seminal essence, so I started to be moderate in sex when I was young. Being moderate in sex is a must for the way of yangsheng, in order not to damage seminal essence." Dr. Yan's explanation was typical of doctors of Chinese medicine. Again, this moderation in sex may resemble the asceticism of the Maoist period, but, in fact, it differed in rationale and purpose. The doctors were concerned about damage to the vitality of the body and to longevity, whereas revolutionary asceticism, by preaching hostility toward sexual desire, led people to be more dedicated to the collective cause. For the doctors, the body was an ethical body that regulated itself, whereas the revolutionary ascetic body was a moral body that followed an order or opened to inducement. I elaborate on this difference in the last section of this chapter.

Leaving aside the question of how many ordinary people were really practicing these restrictions, the idea of nurturing and protecting seminal essence was common cultural knowledge. Many of the old doctors featured in the yangsheng volume had practiced self-regulation in the Maoist period and even in the pre-1949 Republican period. The publication of their experiences, turning them into public knowledge, was partly a repudiation of the collective body of the Maoist period and partly an exhortation against the new individualistic body of desire in the post-Mao consumer society. Yet the teachings of yangsheng were often seriously undermined by the impulse to immediately satisfy the desire for sexual pleasure, as the following experience shows.

Among the flyers pasted to lampposts and buildings along city streets, those advertising "clinics" specializing in curing impotence, premature ejaculation, and sexually transmitted diseases were especially common. One day, pretending to be an impotence patient, I visited one such "clinic" in Beijing. Following the address given on a flyer, I found the clinic, which was actually a single residential room, in a small *siheyuan* (four-cornered courtyard). A thin, thirty-something man introduced himself as the "doctor." I told him what my problem was. It took me a little while to realize that he assumed I had come for treatment to enable an erection right away, perhaps so I could see a prostitute. He said he could inject me with *jisu*.[21] When I demurred, he was disappointed. Seeing that he was not going to talk me into his deal, he charged me a "diagnostic fee." Detecting my southern accent, he said that he was from the south too. As I was about to leave, he said, a sincere expression on his face, "You should nourish your body. Don't eat spices [southerners like spicy food]. Don't drink alcohol."

All of a sudden, he had switched faces: from suggesting an aphrodisiac, which most doctors of TCM thought harmful to the body, to advising the cultivation of life. To me, his first face simply showed his greed for money by helping to satisfy a client's urge for sexual pleasure, whatever the cost to his body. In contrast, his second face turned humane, as if he knew that he had suggested doing harm only moments earlier and was making amends. The doctor's desire to make money and the patient's desire for a night of pleasure at all costs transformed the principle of the cultivation of life into something the doctor could throw away despite his belief in its value.

It is nothing new to say that curing an illness, in fact, means curing the person, by introducing good habits into his or her life. Nor is the use of aphrodisiacs to get an erection new to Chinese history. Both the experience of the venerated doctors of TCM and the quack's way of making money demonstrate what is at stake when yangsheng is practiced. It is an ethic reemerging in the transformation from socialism to postsocialism and from Maoist asceticism to consumerism. The cultivation of life, including the fostering of seminal essence, works in opposition both to the collective, sacrificial ethos of Maoism and to the desire-centered subjectivity of consumerism. Does the reappearance of yangsheng reflect the emergence of a new form of sexual repression in the wake of Maoist asceticism? Is the ethic of yangsheng completely indigenous to Chinese medicine? To understand the nature of this ethic and its political implications, I compare the Chinese cultivation of life with the ancient Greeks' "care of the self," drawing on Foucault's discussion of the history of sexuality.

YANGSHENG AND "CARE OF THE SELF"

In Shigehisa Kuriyama's view, ancient Chinese medicine and the medicine of the ancient Greeks once had similar understandings of the body, but they diverged through time. He wrote, "Once upon a time, all reflection on what we call the body was inseparable from inquiry into places and directions, seasons and winds. Once upon a time, human being was being embedded in a world" (1999:262).

Similarly, I have the impression that the cultivation of life, in terms of nourishing, preserving, and managing seminal essence, shares a central concern with "the care of the self," an ethical practice promoted among the ancient Greeks: how to deal with eroticism as well as what we now call "desire." This impression is obtained from reading Foucault's discussion of "the care of the self" as well as "the use of pleasure" in ancient Greece in his project of writing the history of sexuality (Foucault 1988, 1990). The contexts between ancient Greece and post-Mao China were vastly different. However, Foucault's concern about the "arts of existence" in ancient Greece raised the question that applies to the discussion of yangsheng in post-Mao China. The question is: How is it possible for one to become ethical while experiencing sexual desire and pleasure? Being ethical differs from conforming to a certain moral code against sexual desire (e.g., interdictions on illicit sex under Christianity after the Greco-Roman periods), because the subject of desire *acts on one's own desire* by cautioning against the threat and danger sexual pleasure poses to one's life, to become an ethical subject. An ethical subject is the master of one's own desire. Caution against the excess of sexual desire in contemporary China shares the ethical implication of self-mastery after sexual repression under Maoism had faded. This is why some similarities between the two types of ethical practices can shed light on the other part of the story of desiring production—the ethical limits of desiring production—for this book.

I see two similarities. First, both practices share a concern about the excretion of semen. Among the Greeks, through improper excretion ("venereal excess"), "the body is not simply deprived of its seminal fluid: 'all the parts of the animal find themselves robbed of their vital breath'" (Foucault 1988:109). Aristotle shared with Plato and Hippocrates the "same principle of precious loss" regarding the expelling of semen (Foucault 1990b:131–32), in that

. . . the discharge of this semen constitutes an important event for the body: it withdraws a substance that is precious, being the end result of a lengthy distillation by the organism and concentrating elements which, in accordance with nature, might have gone "to all parts of the body," and hence might have made it grow if they have not been removed from the body. (Foucault 1990:132)

In the Greeks' view, the formation of semen and the swelling of the penis were attributable to "pneuma," breath. Like the Chinese, ancient Greek doctors expressed concern about the danger of indulging in sexual pleasure when the timing was not right. Whereas the Chinese "economy of jing" placed the danger of sexual activity in the loss of the seminal essence crucial to the transformation of vital elements such as blood, qi, and shen (spirit), the "economy of pneuma" placed the danger of sexual life in "an involuntary violence of tension and an indefinite, exhausting expenditure" (Foucault 1988:113).

Second, the two ethics share a profound ambivalence toward, and even mistrust of, sexual pleasure itself and strongly advocate self-regulation. Concern about the weakening of the soul because of an excess of sexual pleasure figured prominently in Greek discussions of the cultivation of the self. Likewise, the ancient Greeks and Romans, according to Foucault, emphasized the shaping of the soul through the conscious control of or vigilance toward sexual pleasure. This concern about the soul entails a comparison between animals and humans. Animals have innate biological mechanisms that prevent sexual excess, whereas humans must rely on the soul to regulate sexual pleasure: indulgence in such pleasure results from the weakening of the soul. The mistrust of pleasure and the cultivation of the self did not just emphasize self-mastery but entailed an orientation toward the formation of an ethical subjectivity in the use of pleasure. Passivity, one of the connotations of *pathos* in Greek rhetorical as well as medical analytics, was the most harmful and intolerable illness one could have because it prevented one from forming an ethical and controlling subjectivity.

The ambivalence toward sexual practices—"Are they good? Are they bad?" (Foucault 1988:112)—was sometimes related to concerns about serious bodily problems and illnesses associated with sex. Galen (second century C.E.) said, "It is not difficult to recognize that sexual relations are fatiguing for the chest, the lungs, and the head and the nerves" (qtd. in Foucault 1988:117). Rufus, a physician who lived about the same time as Galen, listed the following problems as effects of an abuse of sexual relations: digestive disorders, a weakening of sight and hearing, a general weakness of the sense organs, memory loss, convulsive trembling, pains of the joints, a stabbing pain in the side, aphtha in the mouth, toothaches, inflammation of the throat, spitting of blood, and kidney and bladder diseases (Foucault 1988:117). The ancients' profound ambivalence toward sex, which would be hard for a twenty-first-century Westerner to believe, gave rise to measures to counter the negative effects or abuse of sexual relations. Abstinence from sex was very much a positive action to take, because, according to Aretaeus (another physician of Galen's time), those who retained the "vivifying humor" (semen) "become bold, daring and strong as wild beasts" (qtd. in Foucault

1988:121). Those who "are naturally superior in strength, by incontinence [*akrasia*] become inferior to their inferiors; while those by nature much their inferiors by continence [*enkrateia*] become superior to their superiors" (qtd. in Foucault 1988:121).

Unlike the ascetic moral order under medieval Christianity, for physicians like Galen, "the sexual act is not an evil; it manifests a permanent focus of possible ill" (Foucault 1988:142). Sexual pleasure was never given unconditional approval and endorsement. Instead, sexual pleasure was handled with great care and caution because of concerns about maintaining balance. The focus on excess revealed the desire for balance. "As Galen says, to experience the sexual pleasures, one ought to be in an exactly *medial* state, at the zero point . . . avoid 'fatigue, indigestion, and anything, moreover, which might be suspect in consideration of a person's health'" (Foucault 1988:116, my emphasis). Similarly, Rufus stressed that, "around sexual activity, and in order to preserve the balance it risks upsetting, one must keep to *a whole mode of living*" (qtd. in Foucault 1988:132, my emphasis). To achieve moderation and balance and avoid "unlimited expenditure," one of the two pathologies of sexual activity (the other being "an involuntary violence of tension" [Foucault 1988:113]) requires a focus on individual temperament and metabolism. The injunction to seek moderation and balance resembles the advice given by doctors of Chinese medicine to their patients.

Foucault writes of the classical Greeks, "Sexual moderation was an exercise of freedom that took form in self-mastery; and the latter was shown in the manner in which the subject behaved, in the self-restraint he displayed in his virile activity, in the way he related to himself in the relationship he had with others" (1990b:93). Foucault drew from the ancient Greeks to answer the question of "how reason is exercised" today, as opposed to the Weberian question, "how have certain kinds of interdictions become the price required for attaining certain kinds of knowledge about oneself?" (qtd. in Rabinow 1998:xxiv). Transforming the Weberian question into the Foucauldian question, one sees that self-mastery is no longer a necessary price one pays for attaining knowledge about oneself. Instead, it becomes a way to practice freedom.[22]

In the Chinese context, the revival of sexual cultivation in particular and yangsheng in general was not possible until individual and familial life gained the legitimacy to be cultivated in private as well as in public in the post-Mao decollectivization. Also, it is not inconceivable that the "loss of jing" became the impetus for the revival of yangsheng. If decollectivization provided more space to care for the individual and familial life, the "loss of jing" prompted the emergence of a clearer sense of self-mastery and self-enhancement of life. Through yangsheng, a movement was taking place away from constraint and toward exercising self-mastery, a transformation in the ethics of being.

CHAPTER 6

Bushen (Nourishing the Kidney),

Shugan (Smoothing out the Liver), or

Taking the Great Brother (Viagra)

Impotence patients commonly complained about lower back pain at the *nanke* clinics I visited. They described two types of pain, one of which they related to sex. Mr. Zhou, a forty-year-old worker, complained that, for three years, he had had frequent lower back pain after sex. At the same time that the pain began, he also started to have difficulty having an erection. He described his problem: "My waist feels sore. In the past I didn't feel lower back pain after I had sex. Now I feel pain for ten days after each intercourse. I have to tighten my belt to make me feel better. Even if I lean back, I feel pain in my lower back. After having sex each time, I feel pain even if I lie on my back."

The second type of lower back pain did not necessarily correlate with sexual activity. Mr. Jiang, a twenty-five-year-old professional, for example, complained that, each morning when he got up, his waist felt swollen and painful. These two types of lower back pain were often attributed by patients themselves and by most doctors of nanke to weakness of *shen* (肾, the kidney, in Chinese bodily cosmology). Common sense has it that impotence is also associated with weakness of shen. My survey asked respondents to rate twenty-two possible factors as causally associated with impotence. "Weakness of shen" ranked first among male patients in Chengdu and second among male patients in Beijing; it ranked first among students (male and female) in Chengdu and tied with "psychological pressure" as the first choice for students (male and female) in Beijing.

From the perspective of biomedicine, lower back pain can arise in two ways. In some cases, the origin is physiological (e.g., arthritis or a pinched nerve). In other cases, the pain is a manifestation of a psychological disorder (in Chinese, *xinli zuoyong*), the result of somatization.[1] In their anthropological studies of neurasthenia and depression in early 1980s China, however, Arthur and Joan Kleinman discovered that a portion of patients who complained of physically unexplained headache did not suffer from mental illnesses such as depression, and they concluded that "somatization is not always mediated by psychiatric disorder" (1985:452). In the absence of mental illness, they proposed, chronic pain could be understood as "a coping style, a form of social communication, a cultural symbol and its interpretation" (472).[2]

Taking this argument further, I locate the phenomenon of lower back pain among impotence patients in the convergence of two forces in the context of Chinese medical practice. On the one hand, the relation of lower back pain to impotence is a cultural construction based on Chinese bodily cosmology. On the other hand, the sensory perception of lower back pain developed out of the accumulation of habitual bodily complaints along with the decline of potency, through "lived experience" (in Merleau-Ponty's words), and so could not be dismissed easily as a fabrication. The intermingling of the two forces—discursive construction and lived experience—highlights the differences between biomedicine and Chinese medicine as well as their related ethical regimes in dealing with impotence and sexual desire. Of interest under intensified globalization is which medicine impotence patients would turn to for relief. Patients' preferences have a huge bearing on the overall legitimacy of Chinese medicine in today's world and on the value assigned to difference.

This chapter addresses the issue of the legitimacy of Chinese medicine in the era of globalization, focusing specifically on nanke's repositioning vis-à-vis biomedicine. First, I trace the struggle within Chinese medicine since the 1980s between two perspectives concerning the etiology of impotence and show how the "liver-centered" perspective came to prominence at the expense of the "kidney-centered" perspective, thus positioning TCM closer to biomedicine and reflecting a profound change within traditional practice.

This change was intensified by the entry of Viagra into the Chinese market in the 2000s at the high tide of "the biological turn." Surprisingly, Viagra did not sell as well as expected in China, because of the specific understanding among many Chinese men and women that sexual potency was not just an ability to get an erection but a measure of vitality as a whole. An erection induced by Viagra does not fulfill the goal of enhancing overall vitality, a view representing both the etiological and ethical dimensions of the TCM perspective that many Chinese embrace. Out of this understanding of potency emerged a story of switching—patients alternating between herbal medicine and Viagra—and then a pattern of hybridization between the use of Viagra and the use of Chinese medicine. This pattern reflected a cosmopolitan attitude in patients and TCM doctors that valorized both the specificity of the Chinese bodily experience and "a worldwide macro-interdependency encompassing any local particularity" (Rabinow 1996:56).

Part I: Pre-Viagra Era

What Is Wrong with the Chinese Kidney?

LOWER BACK PAIN AND IMPOTENCE

I documented complaints about lower back pain associated with impotence in TCM clinics of nanke far more frequently than in clinics of biomedicine. In the biomedical clinic, a patient's complaint about lower back pain was far more likely to be dismissed out of hand. Dr. Xue, a doctor of biomedicine, would say to the patient: "Lower back pain? It is just in your mind. It is a xinli zuoyong (psychological effect). The more you brood over this, the more you feel it." Similarly, Dr. Zhang, a urologist, said in the early 2000s:

> If [a man] feels lower back pain, it is probably because he already believes that he suffers from weakness of the kidney. Actually, it is quite normal to have lower back pain after intercourse. Intercourse involves movement of muscles in the back. Besides, lower back pain could result from many diseases, such as lumbar muscle strain, condensing osteitis, and overlaboring. It has nothing to do with whether or not his kidney is weak. Everyone comes to complain about weakness of the kidney, and asks if he needs to replenish the kidney. I have to explain to them: look, I have seen patients whose kidneys were in bad condition. They were receiving dialysis, or suffering from uremia, or waiting to receive a kidney transplant. But they still had sexual function. How can you attribute sexual dysfunction to dysfunction of the kidney?

"Unreasonable worry" about weakness of the kidney and lower back pain had been well documented in the psychiatric literature. This phenomenon was named "syndrome of shenkui or shenxu" (腎虧 or 腎虛, weakness of the kidney, or syndrome of kidney deficiency; see Wen and Wang 1981; Jiang and Jiang 1983). It was "a state of marked anxiety or panic that involved complaints about somatic symptoms for which no organic pathology [could] be demonstrated" (Wen and Wang 1981:357). The symptoms included dizziness, backache, fatigue, general weakness, insomnia, frequent dreams, the appearance of white hair, weight loss, premature ejaculation, and impotence. Psychiatric studies of the syndrome of kidney deficiency categorized it as a "culture-specific sexual neurosis," or culture-bound syndrome. How, then, does Chinese medicine establish the link between lower back pain and the weakness of the kidney?

A DIFFERENT KIND OF KIDNEY

Unlike biomedicine, Chinese medicine pays attention to the kidney in the case of lower back pain if the patient also complains of impotence. Almost every book on nanke refers to the *Inner Canon*'s (*Huangdineijing*'s) classic discussion of the importance of the kidney to a man's vitality and capacity for *shengzhi* (reproduction). First and foremost, the kidney is the place where *jing*, seminal essence, is stored. Because jing can be transformed into renal qi (vital energy), and vice versa, jing and qi together embody the vital force responsible for reproduction and sexual cultivation. Fullness of renal qi is therefore crucial to an erection.[3]

In light of this model, inadequacy of the kidney could manifest in symptoms felt in the area of the waist. The *Inner Canon* asserts, "When the waist, the abode of the kidney, cannot turn and shake freely, it indicates the exhaustion of the kidney" (*Huangdineijing, Suwen*: Maiyaojinweilunpian, Anonymous 2000:50). It also states, "When the illness is in the kidney, the acupuncture point is between the waist and the buttocks" (*Huangdineijing, Suwen*: Jinguizhenyanlunpian, Anonymous 2000:14). Wang Qi, in his *Study of Nanke*, elaborated: "Because the waist is the abode of the kidney, illnesses that have to do with the kidney are all reflected in the waist. If the kidney weakens due to sex, the cold and dampness take the opportunity to invade the body through the kidney, and then the waist feels 'weighty,' overused and aching. If one has sex excessively, the kidney jing is overconsumed and damaged . . . the kidney qi is in short supply, and one suffers weakness and waist pain. Then waist pain could worsen whenever one has sex" (1997:761).

It is important to clarify what is meant here by the key term *kidney*. The shen in Chinese medicine is different from the kidney in biomedicine. *The Wang Qi Study of Nanke* notes, "The so-called 'kidney' in Chinese medicine often denotes a functional system and rarely denotes a substantive organ" (Wang Qi 1997:71), reiterating a different "kidney" from the anatomical one. But urologists such as Dr. Zhang considered this a flawed view. He

Figure 6.1:
An advertisement
of Capsule of
Replenishing
the Kidney for
Longevity, a
zhuangyang
capsule.

commented, "I don't think Chinese medicine has figured out the mechanism of erectile dysfunction, because its line of reasoning—yin yang, the five phases (metal, wood, water, fire, and earth), the weakness of the kidney—has impeded its development." In Dr. Zhang's view, Viagra had provided powerful evidence not only that Chinese medicine's primary etiology of impotence (the weakness of the kidney) was erroneous but also that its ontology of the body was no longer viable.

From Nourishing the Kidney to Smoothing out the Liver

Long before Viagra was invented, the primary etiological focus on the weakness of the kidney had been challenged by some doctors of TCM. In 1985, Wang Qi published an article entitled "Lun yangwei cong gan zhi" (On

Treating Impotence through the Liver). He wrote it from the standpoint of a disciple documenting the master's (i.e., Wang's) practice and words. He argued that, instead of the weakness of the kidney, "I often discover that [patients'] impotence results from damage to their emotionality (情志傷, *qingzhi shang*). Sex is a function of *zongjin* (宗筋, primary sinew, i.e., the penis), and the *Inner Canon* points out that the shrinking of the penis (impotence) *results from the interior disorder of the liver*" (Wang Qi 1985:15, my emphasis).

According to the *Inner Canon*, because the liver meridian (足厥陰肝經, *zu jueyin gan jing*) runs anteriorly (through the penis), the liver governs the penis. So, the slackness of anterior yin (i.e., impotence) resulting from emotional problems has to be resolved by smoothing out the liver, because the liver also governs emotionality. Wang Qi notes, "Impotence is mostly associated with one's mood and emotions . . . I discovered in my clinical practice that some impotence patients oftentimes could easily get an erection due to the excitement of arousal when not having sex. Yet, when having sex, they could not get an erection. This problem results from the dysfunction of the liver in regulating emotionality" (1985:16). Wang's argument was based on one of the most important functions of the liver—generating blood. He asserted that, if liver qi is smoothed out, stagnancy is dispersed, one's emotionality is improved, and potency is then recoverable, a view that undermines the orthodox, kidney-centered etiology.

The shift from the kidney-centered perspective to the liver-centered perspective was a significant breakthrough and assumed one of three possibilities. The first is that, in overemphasizing the kidney, Chinese medicine had simply "gotten it wrong" for a long time. The second is that Chinese medicine had been slowly self-correcting, developing a multilocale etiology over the course of several hundred years that culminated in enthusiastic promotion of the liver-centered perspective in the 1980s. The third possibility is that Chinese medicine had not only corrected itself but was also responding to the changing reality of the body in the 1980s. All of these possibilities assume that medicine is a representation of the body. Yet how did those involved in the kidney-versus-liver debate decide which perspective accurately represented reality?

In practice, doctors of TCM had historically approached this epistemological question through clinical reasoning. Constant negotiation between principles based on classics of Chinese medicine and clinical practice was the routine (see, e.g., Scheid 2002; Farquhar 1994; Zhan 2009) and is part of

TCM's practical reasoning based on *jingyan* (experience; see Farquhar 1987; Lei 2002). At the same time, a doctor tried to generalize on the basis of the population of patients he had seen, however small it was. For example, a doctor in a certain locale might claim that in his treatment of impotence over a number of years of practice, only one case in ten resulted from weakness of the kidney, whereas the majority of cases resulted from *shire xiazhu* (damp invasion of the lower energizer), *ganyu qizhi* (stagnation of the liver and qi), *ganshen yinxu* (depletion of liver and kidney yin), or some other cause.

But a new basis for claiming etiological truth began to emerge in the 1990s, when Qin Guozheng, a PhD student and experienced practitioner of TCM, conducted an epidemiological study to address the debate between the kidney-centered perspective and the liver-centered perspective (Qin 2000b). Qin undertook his research in nanke clinics in six cities (including Beijing and Chengdu), and 717 impotence patients took part.

The result of this research supported the liver-centered perspective: Qin found impotence to be very closely associated with *ganshen* (the liver and the kidney), and particularly with the liver. Forty-two percent of all symptoms documented were liver related, compared to 31 percent associated with the kidney. In addition, 57 percent of patients demonstrated symptoms indicative of liver problems, compared to 37 percent who had kidney problems (Qin 1999a). These results disputed the typology of impotence officially acknowledged by the State Administration of TCM under the Ministry of Health.[4]

Accordingly, clinical practices shifted the emphasis from qi to blood by focusing on *shugan jieyu* (舒肝解瘀, smoothing the liver to disperse stagnant liver qi) and *chongrun zongjin* (充潤宗筋, replenishing the primary sinew), which involved facilitating the flow of blood into the penis. In an interview in 1999, I had asked Dr. Wang if Chinese medicine had a way to cure impotence caused by the leaking of a vein in the penis, a common urological diagnosis in the late 1990s that was addressed by ligate surgery (see chapter 7). He responded, "Isn't it true that if there is not enough blood in the penis, impotence occurs? To put it in an oversimplified way, if surgery on the penile vein aims to block the returning flow of blood in order to maintain an erection, why can't Chinese medicine help maintain an erection by supplying more blood and maintaining a stronger blood flow from the artery?" Since, according to Chinese medicine, blood is produced in the liver, working on liver function to cure impotence was consistent with the biomedical focus on blood dynamics in impotence treatment.

Here, TCM and biomedicine converged in emphasizing blood flow in the physiological understanding of impotence. A convergence between TCM and psychiatry occurred when Dr. Wang described the relationship between impotence and *ganyu* (stasis of liver qi) as a reversible cause–effect relationship—"yinyu zhiwei" (因瘀致痿, the stasis of the liver qi causes impotence) and "yinwei zhiyu" (因痿致瘀, impotence causes stasis of the liver qi). He sounded here like a psychotherapist or psychiatrist talking about the mutually causal relationship between erectile dysfunction and depression. The only difference was that, in Chinese medicine, depression had a bodily locale (the liver) and a bodily form (the stasis of qi).

The liver-centered perspective still cannot be equated with the blood dynamics of urology, because the two perspectives rely on different maps of structures and functions. "Smoothing out the liver" means ensuring that qi circulates smoothly along the liver meridian so as to smooth the flow of blood. In contrast, blood dynamics in urology focus on how to produce muscle relaxation in the corpus cavernosum of the penis and thus increase inflow of blood. However, the two approaches converge in working toward the improvement of blood flow.

YINWEI (SHRINKING OF *YIN*) OR *YANGWEI* (SHRINKING OF *YANG*)?

Because of the dominance of the kidney-centered perspective, one common medicine for impotence available in TCM pharmacies was *zhuangyangyao* (medicine for mildly strengthening kidney yang). According to Mr. Wang, general manager of Tongrentang, the largest TCM pharmacy in Chengdu, the number of different brands for sale in the category of zhuangyangyao increased by 85 percent from 1995 to 1999—from eight to fifteen. Huiren Shenbao (Kidney Treasure of Converging Benevolence), a patent herbal medicine in this category, once ranked sixth among sales of all medicines in the pharmacy, a rather high rank for a single brand. One evening in the early 2000s, I walked into a pharmacy in Chengdu and found that, of the twenty-one patent medicines available for warming and replenishing yang, most specifically targeted kidney yang. The names of at least one-third of them explicitly referred to the kidney.

The kidney-centered perspective attained orthodox status only after the

Ming period (Qin 2000a). It was during the Ming period that the term *yangwei* (陽痿, shrinking of yang) came to dominate the medical literature, replacing *yinwei* (陰痿, shrinking of yin). A brief review of this change is instructive.

Just as the penis was called "yinqi" (陰器, yin utensil) in the *Inner Canon*, impotence was called "yinwei" (the shrinking of yin).[5] This terminology emphasized yin over yang in determining sexual potency and reflected the complex relationship between the two in the androgynous body of the *Inner Canon* (Furth 1999).[6] The penis was considered yin for three reasons. First, it is located in the lower (yin) part of the body, as opposed to the upper (yang) part. Second, it is located on the front (yin) side of the body, as opposed to the back (yang) side. Third, it is located near the body's inside (yin) meridians, as opposed to the outside (yang) meridians. That the penis is still called "yinjing" (陰莖, yin stem) today reflects the early emphasis of Chinese medical practice on the yin aspect of impotence, just as the vagina was also called "yindao" (yin path).

In the Ming period (1368–1644 C.E.), *yangwei* started to be used in addition to *yinwei* to label impotence. Zhang Jiebin (张介宾, also known as Zhang Jingyue, 張景岳), an influential doctor of that time, emphasized the kidney-centered perspective, asserting that impotence was due in most cases to the deficiency of kidney yang.[7] This perspective subsequently dominated the TCM approach to impotence.

In the early 2000s, Wang Qi argued against the kidney-centered perspective. During an interview, he told me,

What I hate most with regard to traditional Chinese medicine's medication for impotence is the typology that our textbooks and our guidance for new drugs use. Western medicine for impotence has developed around erection, whereas in Chinese medicine our doctors do not ask the patient about erection during diagnosis. Instead, they ask whether or not his scrotum is moist, whether or not he has severe palpitations, whether or not he is afraid of coldness . . . Take, for example, the patient I just saw. He was having difficulty getting an erection. But, unlike what our textbooks taught us, he was not suffering from coldness of the lower back and the knees, he was not suffering from coldness in the penis, he did not look like his teeth were all falling out—in a word, he was not suffering from deficiency of kidney yang. All of our textbooks are seriously out of touch with reality. All those medicines for replenishing kidney yang are seriously influenced by Zhang Jingyue's statement that "eight out of ten patients of impotence suffer from the deficiency of kidney yang." They are seriously out of touch with reality too.

Wang Qi's view was reinforced by Qin Guozheng's (1999) epidemiological studies on impotence. For example, Qin noted that more patients suffered from excess syndrome (repletion) than deficiency syndrome (depletion). He elaborated on this point to me, saying, "Now the standard of living has improved for most people. Unlike in the past, very few people suffer from malnutrition or starvation. In the clinic we rarely see an impotence patient who looks infirm, pale, and weak, and fits into the classical description of *mingmen huoshuai* (命門火衰, the fire at the life gate is burning out, i.e., deficiency of kidney yang). Instead, most patients suffer from having too much fatty, deep-fried, and spicy food and drinking too much alcohol. Excess of rich food and alcohol causes the interior accumulation of turbid phlegm, which may lead to poisonous stasis with damp heat. These factors are the pathological basis of impotence in the change from deficiency syndrome to excess syndrome." Qin's research reinforced the argument for calling impotence "yinwei." But the debate was not over.

Chen Wenbo, a renowned doctor of nanke, still thought the kidney-centered etiological perspective worked well. He thought that the majority of impotence patients suffered from a deficiency of *jingqi* (seminal essence and qi), a result of weakness of the kidney, despite the improved standard of living in the post-Mao era. He argued that stasis can occur in the kidney too and needs to be smoothed out. He said, "The kidney is *ben* (the foundation) of the body and medicine."

Dr. Cao Kaiyong was more accommodating toward the liver-centered perspective but fell short of completely endorsing it. In his view, the kidney was still the central location of the etiology of impotence. In a one-hour question-and-answer call-in talk show on a Beijing radio station in the early 2000s, Cao mentioned the kidney eighteen times, whereas he did not mention the liver once. Accompanying him in his car on the way to the radio station, I asked him what he thought about Wang Qi's liver-centered perspective. He said, "There are some elements of truth in Wang Qi's argument, because *ganshen tongyuan* (肝腎同源, the liver and the kidney share an origin).[8] But it would be problematic if we only focused on the liver. The problem is that the liver cannot be supplemented; it can only be smoothed out.[9] In the long run, you have to nourish the kidney."

The difference between the two perspectives could be understood as the difference between two "styles of reasoning," to use Ian Hacking's term. But the liver-centered perspective became attractive because it positions TCM closer to biomedicine as a source that inspires positive actions instead of reaction. The entry of Viagra into the Chinese market intensified the kidney–liver debate and led to a more extensive repositioning of Chinese medicine.

Part II: The Era of Viagra

Switching between Chinese Medicine and Viagra

Viagra was officially introduced to the Chinese market in July 2000. Before then, some doctors and sex education specialists in Beijing had predicted that Chinese men would enthusiastically embrace this "magic pill." Certain events, such as controversy over the drug's name, heightened this expectation.

Pfizer, the manufacturer of Viagra, had planned to market it under the name Weige (偉哥, Great Brother) but failed to register that name before a Chinese pharmaceutical company did so for its own patent pill. Pfizer settled for calling its product Wanaike (万艾可), a name with no specific meaning. Nevertheless, in China, Viagra continues to be popularly known as Weige.

The term *weige* has an erotic connotation. "Great brother" recalls the word *laoer* (老二), which means "no. 2 brother" and, in some dialects, is a euphemism for the penis. It also recalls the common phrase *gemenr, xiongqi* (哥们儿, 雄起, my brother, get up), connoting the upward movement associated with becoming a real man. Therefore, the name Weige became a powerful signifier of the anxiety around impotence and of the excitement associated with regaining potency.

The competition over an erotic name foretold a major battle between Viagra and zhuangyang tonics. When I was doing fieldwork in Taiwan on the eve of Viagra's release in China, I heard a news story on a Taipei radio station reporting that, across the straits, Chinese pharmaceutical companies were planning a "summit meeting" whose main agenda item was devising strategies to counter the expected large-scale switch from herbal medicine to the "great brother."

Some doctors were concerned that the Chinese government might not approve the drug's entry into the country because conservative officials

Figure 6.2: Advertisements of "Authentic Viagra," touting caring for men's health and letting the ideal of harmony take off.

would regard it as a *yinyao* (霪药, lustful drug, or a *chunyao* 春药, spring drug, "spring" being a metaphor for sexual desire, referring to an aphrodisiac) that promoted sex. However, this concern soon vanished. A doctor cited an authority in the National Academy of Military Sciences as saying, "China cannot say 'no' to Viagra!" This phrase reversed the title of a mid-1990s bestseller, *China Can Say No*, indicating the speaker's confidence that the Chinese government would eventually approve Viagra's distribution.

It is not surprising that Viagra was expected to sell well in China, partly because of its widely publicized effects and partly because it was set to debut in a new sexual landscape of openness and attention to men's health issues. Globally, in the effort to invent less intrusive ways to treat impotence, a transnational medical regime had emerged that was devoted to male sexual dysfunction (see chapter 7). It included urological research on the etiology of impotence, epidemiological studies of male aging (including impotence), breakthroughs in biomedicine such as self-injection therapy and clinical trials for oral therapies, forums on impotence, consumer activist groups speaking on behalf of impotence patients, consensus statements from international conferences on impotence and from research institutions such as the U.S. National Institutes of Health (NIH), impotence patient self-awareness groups, and so on. Using the results of the Massachusetts Male Aging Study, Pfizer had projected the prevalence, by country, of mild, moderate, and complete erectile dysfunction (ED). Not surprisingly, China topped its list, with 102.1 million men between forty and seventy estimated to suffer from some degree of impotence. These numbers fueled the company's optimism that Viagra would sell well in China.[10]

"Viagra fever" spread, primarily in the media, during the first month of the drug's availability. In Beijing and Chengdu, journalists went to departments of both urology and nanke to find out just how much Viagra was being sold and, more important, to get a sense of what kind of men came to ask for it. With its splashy introduction in the media, Viagra made impotence patients as well as the condition itself highly visible. It also focused a spotlight on sexual desire, the driving force behind the demand for Viagra. As one doctor said, "Viagra makes it easier to talk about sex." One controversial story out of Chengdu described how a daughter had bought Viagra as a birthday present for her father and extended her good wishes to her parents.

However, Pfizer's hope that impotent men would all switch from herbal medicine to Viagra was not borne out. To the contrary, the sales of Viagra in China were disappointing not only to Pfizer representatives but also to some doctors of biomedicine and of TCM. According to some reports, between 1998, when Viagra appeared on the market in the United States, and 2004, about 170 million prescriptions for it were written worldwide. Only 1.5 million (less than 1 percent) were written in China. And sales in China were even lower than this number indicates as, on average, each prescription was for fewer pills than was the norm in the United States (Zhang 2004). In most cases I observed, impotence patients asked only for a few pills, to try them out. Indeed, it was unusual to see someone asking for more than ten pills. The first year after Viagra was introduced, a major hospital in Chengdu prescribed only about two hundred pills a month. Given that Dr. Zhuang, a urologist and an expert on impotence at that hospital, saw eighty to a hundred impotence patients every month (as an older, venerated doctor, he only saw patients two and a half days a week), we get a sense of the rather small number of Viagra pills dispensed in each prescription.[11] A doctor from a medium-size city in Hebei Province said that he wrote about ten prescriptions a month for Viagra, each prescription for only one pill. In the Department of Sexual Medicine at Yuquan Hospital in Beijing, doctors prescribed fewer than a hundred pills a month. A patient rarely wanted more than three or four pills. The low sales of Viagra in China stood in sharp contrast to Pfizer's high expectations.

What accounted for this discrepancy between high expectations and low sales?

Expenditure of Life: A Different Understanding of Potency

On an ordinary day in July 2001—one year after Viagra had been officially introduced into the Chinese market—I was observing activities in the Department of Urology in a biomedical hospital in Chengdu. Mr. Bao, a thirty-three-year-old impotence patient, was consulting with Dr. Zhuang. He was complaining that herbal medicine had not improved his condition, and Dr. Zhuang suggested that he take Weige. Mr. Bao asked, "Does this 'great brother' have any side effects?" Dr. Zhuang answered, jokingly, "The biggest side effect of this 'great brother' is that it is too expensive. It costs 99 yuan [about US$12] per pill." Mr. Bao became curious: "How many pills does one need to take before it cures impotence?" Dr. Zhuang looked at him seriously and said, "One pill works one time." Mr. Bao responded with disbelief: "What? If I take so many pills at such a young age, what will happen to me in the future?" He refused to take Viagra.

Mr. Jiao, another impotence patient in his thirties, was also worried about Viagra's side effects. His concern was that he might become dependent on it. He said, "I am just over 30 years old. Is it good for young people?" He ended up asking for a prescription for a single pill. Similar conversations also occurred in the clinic in Beijing. A couple who had just been married came to Dr. Ma for medication for impotence but refused to accept Viagra. Husband and wife were both worried that, as they were very young, Viagra might have a negative impact on the husband's body.

The price of Viagra was also off-putting for many patients. The drug was simply too expensive for people like Mr. Bao. Ninety-nine yuan was a lot of money for an ordinary wage earner in Chengdu, where the average monthly income in 2005 was less than 1,000 yuan (about US$125). If a young workingman like Mr. Bao came to depend on Viagra to achieve sexual potency, he would end up spending more money than he was making. Many doctors in China told Pfizer sales representatives that the price of Viagra was too high. Given the standard of living for ordinary people, one could even argue that the introduction of Viagra into postsocialist China reinforced the

newly developing class hierarchy by ensuring unequal access to sexual pleasure. A deputy head of a state-owned enterprise that was going into bankruptcy commented to me, "Viagra is not for the *xiagang* workers" (下崗,
stepping-down or laid-off workers). As I discuss in chapter 3, many laid-off
workers suffered from a loss of potency, which is not surprising, given that
losing one's job is often experienced as a loss of power.

Yet a Pfizer sales representative disagreed that the drug was too expensive. She said, "In fact, many people who complain about the high price of
Viagra are willing to spend several hundred yuan on a banquet . . . They just
don't place a high priority on paying for medicine for sex." In her view, the
complaint about price had more to do with a person's priorities than with
the price charged. She was disappointed that, when it came to choosing between banquets and sex, many people chose the former. Pfizer did slightly
lower the price, primarily through a marketing strategy that advertised "the
more you buy, the cheaper it gets." However, the price was still not low
enough to quiet people's complaints.

Many Chinese pharmaceutical companies were confident that, if they
won the right to produce a generic form of Viagra, they could cut the price
by two-thirds and thus greatly increase the consumption of the drug. They
were encouraged by the decisions of the State Intellectual Property Office
to lift the patent for Viagra in July 2004, a decision that Pfizer quickly appealed. In June 2006, a midlevel court in Beijing overturned the decision and
handed a victory to Pfizer. In October 2007, the Supreme Court of Beijing
validated the decision of the lower court (Fang 2007). The intention of the
court decision was unclear, but as the battle over Pfizer's patent rights raged,
the optimism of Chinese pharmaceutical companies, which were promising
to take over the anti-impotence drug market, waxed and waned.

It soon became clear that, even if Viagra were to become as affordable as
aspirin, some Chinese men would still be reluctant to take it because they
feared becoming dependent on it (a fear based on how the drug works: one
pill equals one night of sexual potency). They believed that dependency on
Viagra would be harmful to their bodies. And this is where the rational view
of economics falters and is unable to account for another "economy"—the
economy of sexual potency as it plays out in the lives of many Chinese men.

A DIFFERENT ECONOMY OF SEXUAL POTENCY

Patients' worries about becoming dependent on Viagra were based on two
ideas. One was that Viagra works like an aphrodisiac. Many Chinese have a

strong aversion to aphrodisiacs—yinyao (lustful drugs) or chunyao (spring drugs)—which are thought to stimulate excessive sexual desire. According to folk histories, over the course of two millennia a good number of Chinese emperors had died at relatively young ages supposedly because they took chunyao and overindulged in sex. These folk histories often blame eunuchs for recommending chunyao to emperors and thus corrupting the imperial court.[12] Even though no one knows exactly what went into chunyao, its reputed negative consequences live in the collective memory and continue to influence people today. On one occasion, I heard a urologist try to explain to a reluctant patient that Viagra was not chunyao: "Chunyao resembles drugs that increase the level of sexual hormones, which is what is largely responsible for sexual desire. Viagra does not induce desire and does not change the level of sexual hormones. These [two drugs] are different." That doctors had to battle the perception that Viagra was a form of chunyao indicates that many Chinese were wary of excessive sexual desire, even though desire was much more acceptable than it had been some twenty years earlier.

The second idea was that inducing erection would harm vitality. A urological etiology of impotence shows that one's potency is nothing but the ability to get an erection. In many Chinese people's understanding, however, potency involves much more than erection: it relates to one's overall vitality (see chapter 7). Robust and long-lasting vitality requires, among other things, a fullness of jing (精, seminal essence), qi (气, vital energy), and shen (神, spirit). Impotence involves not only the impairment of one's ability to get an erection but also the decline of one's overall vitality. Thus, regaining one's potency requires more than regaining one's ability to get an erection: it requires strengthening one's vitality by nourishing the body. Looked at within this context, one does not gain potency even if one can achieve an erection by taking Viagra because, after each instance of sexual intercourse, impotence returns. Viagra does not cure the ben (本, root cause); it only treats the biao (標, surface cause). Many Chinese men and women do not consider potency to be something that can be constructed by Viagra at the moment it is "needed"; rather, they consider it to be an attribute inherent to, and permanently possessed by, the body. Nourishing and strengthening one's overall potency is seen as more important than regaining the ability to get an erection; it generates a different pleasure from that associated with having sexual intercourse.

In sum, many Chinese men were reluctant to embrace Viagra because the drug would not enable them to fully recover their potency, their overall vitality. Worse still, getting an erection and having sex after taking a pill, without making an effort to fully recover one's potency, could unduly consume seminal essence and, therefore, further compromise one's vitality. In this view, impotence is far more about one's vitality and life than it is about one's sexual pleasure.

Mr. Wei's story illustrates this view of sexual potency. Mr. Wei, a sixty-year-old retired worker, was having difficulty getting an erection. He had not had sex for a year. In the clinic, looking gloomy, he told me that neither he nor his wife had much interest in sex. "Then why did you come to see the doctor?" I asked. He answered, "My wife wanted me to come to see the doctor." I was puzzled, but my visit to his home uncovered the missing pieces in this puzzle. Mr. Wei had worked for a huge state-owned enterprise in Beijing for almost thirty years and had just retired. His wife had Parkinson's disease and was not in good health. She could not even go to the bathroom by herself. Mr. Wei had to take care of her every need. To add to his worries, all four of his children had been laid off from the same state-owned enterprise at which he had worked. This company, like many state-owned enterprises in China, had lost out to competition in the restructured market economy and had had to downsize its workforce. Mr. Wei's 1,000-yuan retirement pension (about US$125 at the time) was the only stable income for the whole family. His wife told me that she did not have any interest in sex; her concern was that her husband's difficulty in getting an erection was a sign that his health was in decline, which would be disastrous for the whole family. She said, "I am only worried that it is a disease." In this case, sexual pleasure, for both the man and the woman, was secondary to the importance of overall potency. Mr. Wei's sexual potency was felt to be central to the survival not only of his individual body but also of the familial body. The centrality of sexual potency to his life had nothing to do with the discourse of sexual desire; rather, it had to do with his need to ensure a long, healthy life. Viagra could not provide him with what he wanted: guaranteed physical health and longevity. Mr. Wei was pursuing sex to live a longer, healthier life—a perspective that the desire-centered ethics of the "Viagra regime" can neither replace nor comprehend.

Needless to say, this understanding of potency clashed with the biomedical view. Dr. Zhuang, the urologist, often found it difficult to persuade patients to accept a different notion of potency, as his interaction with Mr. Geng shows. Dr. Zhuang impatiently questioned Mr. Geng's notion of potency: "What does it mean to be potent? So long as you can do it each time with the help of Viagra, you are not impotent. You are potent." The patient looked totally unconvinced. Dr. Chang told me that one of his reluctant patients said, to the doctor's amusement, that he would take Viagra if he could have a 20-milligram pill every day for five days rather than a single 100-milligram pill. This patient wanted to treat Viagra according to the logic of herbal medicine, pursuing an accumulative recovery of potency rather than a suddenly induced erection.[13]

The reluctance of Chinese men to use Viagra reinforces a critique of the simple-minded celebration of the drug's power. Even as Viagra further sexualizes everyday life in the United States and a number of other societies by helping men obtain erections and alleviating their fears of impotence, it may also be desexualizing the act of copulation (see Loe 2004). Slavoj Žižek, a Lacanian psychoanalytical theorist, sees in Viagra's positive effect on the penis a negative effect on the phallus. He refers to Viagra as "the ultimate agent of castration" (Žižek 1999: 383–84). As he explains, "If a man swallows the pill, his penis functions, but he is deprived of the phallic dimension of symbolic potency—the man who is able to copulate thanks to Viagra is a man with a penis but without a phallus" (383). Žižek questions the effect of Viagra by looking at how it turns an erection into a mechanically achievable state while robbing men of the ability to sexually express themselves (even if only through impotence).[14] Cases like those related by Dr. Zhuang and Dr. Chang point to a reason for the reluctance of many Chinese men to embrace the drug: quite simply, they have an ethic of sexuality that is incompatible with the "Viagra regime," an ethic concerned with the cultivation of life, or overall potency, and, as such, in conflict with a globalized sexual ethic that focuses solely on reproduction and sexual pleasure.[15] To a large degree, it is this ethical difference that explains why many Chinese are not as interested in Viagra as predicted. Not surprisingly, a doctor quoted a Pfizer representative as saying that, in countries such as Singapore and Malaysia, where there is a strong tradition of TCM, Viagra did not sell well either.

Switching between Viagra and Herbal Therapies

Did those Chinese men who were reluctant to take Viagra take herbal therapies instead? The answer, of course, is that some did and some did not and that others switched back and forth.

From what I observed, contrary to what the modern–traditional dichotomy might imply, it was not necessarily the young who chose Viagra and the old who chose herbs. Some older patients were willing to take Viagra. Mr. Fang, a seventy-year-old retired worker, suffered from a decline in potency after prostate surgery. When I interviewed him, he had taken three Viagra pills (50 milligrams each). At first, to save money, he only took half a pill each time, but the results were disappointing. Even though he could ejaculate, "It was too fast. She was not satisfied. I was not satisfied." Later, he took a full pill and was satisfied. So he returned to the hospital to ask for four more pills, but he did so without telling his wife, as she would not have approved. She did not know that his renewed ability to achieve erection was due to Viagra. Mr. Fang and his wife slept in different rooms, and whenever he felt sexually inclined, he went to her room. He said, "She does not want it that much, but I want it. Viagra is expensive, but I can afford it if I do it once every other month." He was very satisfied with his retired life. Unlike Mr. Wei, Mr. Fang's three daughters had good jobs. He was able to buy a seventy-square-meter apartment. He gave the impression that, as he had had a good life, he was quite willing to enjoy the time he had left rather than worry about extending it as long as possible. It seems that, precisely because he had retired and was reasonably secure financially, and also because he planned to take the medication infrequently, he was not concerned about developing a dependency on Viagra. It was younger patients who tended to be most fearful of this.

Some men wanted to get an erection as well as nourish their bodies to recover overall potency. In other words, aside from those who took only Viagra and those who took only herbal medicine, a third group of patients took both. The existence of this group, which was large, was backed by a survey I did in Beijing and in Chengdu in 2000. I asked impotence patients what kind of doctor an impotent man should see (a doctor of biomedicine only, a doctor of TCM only, a folk doctor, doctors of both TCM and biomedicine, or some other kind of doctor); 76.7 percent of men in Beijing and 78.7 of men in Chengdu answered that one should consult doctors of both TCM and biomedicine. This is consistent with the responses from college students: 71.7 percent of male students and 80.8 percent of female students in Beijing and 77 percent of male students and 77.3 percent of female students in Chengdu supported seeing doctors of both TCM and biomedicine.[16] I conducted the survey shortly before Viagra was officially introduced to the Chinese market, but the majority of respondents had heard of the drug. Responses from the male patients in my survey point to a space of ambiguity and indeterminacy in the encounter between Viagra and TCM. These men showed a certain cosmopolitan curiosity, a willingness, if not yet a desire, to try things that originated "outside" their own habitual lifeworld, without entirely giving up their traditional beliefs.[17] Below, I take a closer look at this phenomenon.

Mr. Wang, a sixty-six-year-old retired professor, had come to the nanke clinic in the Hospital of Chengdu University of TCM (CUHTCM) in March 2001, saying that he had been unable to have sex since 1993. His wife thought this inability could indicate an inadequacy in his body and was afraid that it could be a sign of other problems. TCM doctors found that Mr. Wang had a white coating on his tongue and a weak pulse. Guided by the bodily cosmology of TCM, they pointed to a weakness of his yang qi, in general, and of his kidney yang, in particular. A TCM doctor prescribed a patent herbal pill, Yikanwan, to strengthen his yang (*yikanwan* translates as "*kan*-benefiting pill"; kan is one of the eight divinatory symbols; it refers to water and corresponds to shen, the kidney, in Chinese bodily cosmology; the remedy thus can be described as "kidney benefiting"). Another TCM doctor also gave Mr. Wang a prescription for Viagra. When he came back to the clinic in July, he reported that, after having taken one Viagra pill, he had been able to obtain an erection. Even though his penis was not fully rigid, he could penetrate and ejaculate. He thought his condition was improving and, therefore, asked for more pills—both Yikanwan and Viagra. I asked him why he still wanted to take herbal medicine, and he told me that he believed in traditional Chinese medicine. He asked the doctor of TCM whether he could obtain erections without taking Viagra, as he was worried about becoming dependent on it. Interestingly, the TCM doctor who prescribed the herbal medicine advised Mr. Wang to continue to take Viagra because it could help increase his confidence in gaining an erection, which in his case seemed very important.

So Mr. Wang continued to switch between Viagra and herbal pills. He took Yikanwan twice a day, as advised. Over four months, he went through more than a dozen bottles of it, which means that he took ten tiny herbal pills every day. During the same period, he took only two Viagra pills, the implication being that he had sex with the help of Viagra only occasionally.

In many cases, what prompted men to seek treatment for impotence was their being in a state of *juer bujian* (舉而不堅, erect but not rigid enough): they could get an erection but their penis was not fully rigid (see chapter 4). In this state, they either lacked the confidence to penetrate or their penis became soft shortly after penetration and they could not achieve ejaculation.

I often heard patients describe how they used Viagra to *zengjia yingdu* (increase the rigidity of the penis). Mr. Zhou, a twenty-six-year-old worker, could not satisfy his girlfriend because his penis was not rigid enough when erect. He had taken eight bottles of Huiren Shenbao (the popular patent herbal liquid that nourishes kidney yang and is thought to cure impotence) before he saw a doctor of nanke at CUHTCM. The doctor asked him to try Yikanwan and Viagra. During the following ten months, Mr. Zhou took ten Yikanwan pills every day for an extended period of time. He also took eight Viagra pills during the ten months. When he returned to the hospital, Mr. Zhou reported that he was able to have sex once a week. The eight Viagra pills he had taken seemed to have boosted his confidence (and, therefore, possibly, the rigidity of his penis) when having sexual intercourse with his girlfriend. But he also said that the ejaculations he had after taking Viagra were not satisfying: "She le jiu she le, meiyou ganjue" (射了就射了, 没有感觉, I ejaculated for the sake of ejaculation but did not feel anything). A TCM doctor first prescribed a decoction containing ten herbs (to get rid of dampness and excessive heat and to smooth out the liver) and then prescribed Viagra.

It would be an oversimplification to attribute the improvement in Mr. Zhou's ability to get an erection solely to his taking Viagra. A TCM doctor commented on the difficulty of evaluating the efficacy of either herbal medicine or Viagra when patients were taking both. She said that, in the clinic, doctors often asked their patients to temporarily stop taking pharmaceuticals to let the herbal pills take full effect. This made it easier to evaluate their efficacy and to adjust the dosage, or *peiwu* (配伍, a deliberate adjustment to the combination of herbs), accordingly. When patients insist on taking both medicines or, for some reason, cannot stop taking biomedical drugs, doctors often ask them to take each type of medication at precisely spaced intervals. For example, the patient may be asked to take the herbal drugs several hours after taking the biomedical drugs so that the researcher can assess the effect each has on the body. Taking different types of medicines results in a hybridized form of healing.

Even some biomedical doctors felt that herbal medicines should be given in conjunction with Viagra. According to Dr. Jia, a biomedical doctor in Beijing, "Chinese medicine produces better effects in terms of improving sexual desire and controlling ejaculation. It also improves the general status of the body, whereas Viagra can improve the rigidity and the frequency of erections. The relationship between Viagra and Chinese herbal medicine is the relationship of coffee and Coffee-Mate" (CCTV International 2004). That a urologist would characterize Chinese medicine as "Coffee-Mate" to biomedicine's "coffee" shows a subtle reconceptualization of the value of herbal medicine. Gone is the black-and-white prediction that Viagra would wipe out all other forms of treatment for impotence; instead, we have a far more complex situation—one that involves a "both/and" rather than an "either/or" form of thinking.

GENDERED POLITICS AND SWITCHING
BETWEEN TWO MEDICINES

Whether a medication is effective is often context dependent, particularly in the case of medicine prescribed for sexual problems. We cannot discuss the effectiveness of a treatment without discussing the context in which it is given. Most relevant to my study, the effectiveness of Viagra has to be judged according to its impact on "felt flows of interpersonal communication and engagements" (Kleinman 1999:358). The results of a man's taking Viagra may well vary, depending on whether he takes it to improve sexual relations with his wife, a girlfriend, a lover, or a sex worker—an action embedded in dramatic changes in gender relations and sexuality in post-Mao China.

Viagra, a medical agent, carries with it the promise of satisfying sexual desire and contributes to desiring production (see Deleuze and Guattari 1983). In many cases, Viagra's official story—that it enhances one's ability to get an erection—continued to depend on an unofficial story: that it induces sexual desire. I heard doctors tell patients that Viagra would not work if they did not have sexual desire to begin with. Doctors also advised their Viagra patients to stroke their sexual partners or otherwise become intimate before trying to have sexual intercourse with them. But many patients made no effort at all. One patient said that, after taking Viagra, he simply lay in bed motionless while looking at his watch and waiting to get an erection. Nothing happened. The doctor explained that the patient should not have expected the drug to fill him with sexual desire; that is not the drug's purpose.

The "misuse" of Viagra for sexual arousal said important things about men's interpersonal relationships and highlighted the contrast in the same men between instances of "having" and "not having" sexual desire, because sexual desire itself was situationalized, and sexual pleasure was made contingent on those with whom one developed intimate relationships.

In this new sexual landscape, desire may ebb and flow and potency may fluctuate. In the context of increasing numbers of extramarital affairs, a common saying alluded to this ebb and flow: "Kewai zuoye kao ganjue; jiating zuoye kao chiyao" (課外作業靠感覺,家庭作業靠吃葯, when working extracurricularly, one relies on the senses, but, when doing homework, one relies on drugs). In other words, men act on urges when conducting "work outside the home" (i.e., having sexual encounters outside marriage), whereas they depend on medicine when conducting "homework" (i.e., engaging in sexual relations within marriage). For whom, then, did men use Viagra? The cases discussed thus far have involved strictly monogamous men who took Viagra so that they could have sex with their wives, who, for their part, did not seem that interested in intercourse. The man's switching between herbs and Viagra centered on concerns about the male body. Female desire was far less an issue than male desire was. However, when men take Viagra to enhance extramarital relationships, does the switching between herbs and Viagra reflect the same tension between the cultivation of overall potency and the promotion of individual sexual desire—the two ethical regimes represented by TCM and biomedicine, respectively—that one finds in monogamous relationships?

Two cases shed light on this issue. In the first, Mr. Cao, a twenty-nine-year-old migrant worker, had a bad relationship with his wife, who fought with him when she found out that he was seeing a prostitute. He had erectile problems both with his wife and with prostitutes, and he took Viagra to satisfy his own desire when seeing the latter. A TCM doctor prescribed a decoction that contained twelve herbs, the point of which was to nourish the kidney and to remove heat and dampness and thereby improve the flow of qi and *xue* (blood). Mr. Cao took Viagra to pursue his own bodily pleasure and gave no thought to leaving his wife unsatisfied. His desire was purely self-centered: he neglected his wife's sexual satisfaction and used sex workers as tools, whether he was taking herbs to enhance the cultivation of overall potency or Viagra to enhance his individual pleasure.[18]

The second case is much more complicated. Mr. Gao was a thirty-two-year-old migrant worker in Chengdu. Unlike most migrant workers, he had been economically successful, having built a fruit-farming business and his own house in a rural area of Sichuan Province. After he migrated to Chengdu, he operated a shoe shop, which did well enough to allow him to buy a car. He met his wife in his hometown in 1987 through a matchmaker. They dated for three years. During their second year of dating, feeling confident that they would get married, they had sex for the first time in their lives. Although Mr. Gao had dated other women before, he had not even held hands with them. His wife thought his family was better off than hers, and he thought she was pretty and he knew that her home was close to the highway, which would make it easy for him to transport supplies for his business by motor tricycle (a rare convenience in the mountainous area where they lived). They got married when she was four months pregnant.

However, even while they were dating, they often fought. Mr. Gao's girlfriend complained about his gambling and about always having to drag him away from the poker table. He responded by beating her. They also had arguments about how to spend their money, whether he should give money to his parents, and so on. She once attempted suicide.

They eventually had two children and paid a fine for violating the one-child policy. The whole family then migrated to Chengdu. Since Mr. Gao could make enough money to support them, his wife stayed home and learned how to use a computer. When they were dating in the late 1980s, there were only two television sets in the school in their rural town, so they obviously did not watch much TV. In the 1990s, by contrast, they not only watched a lot of TV but they also watched pornographic videos together.

About half a year before coming to the clinic, Mr. Gao started to lose interest in having sex with his wife. In the past, they had had sex every other day, but the frequency had decreased to about once a week. Even though Mr. Gao was having sex less frequently, he was having problems maintaining an erection. As he put it, "It is not rigid enough. It becomes soft as soon as I am a little distracted." He had visited both biomedical doctors and TCM doctors several times, the former telling him that he did not have any serious problems. He tried herbal pills as well as Viagra: "I took one Viagra pill. It indeed made my erection last longer."

Mr. Gao revealed that his erectile problems seemed to be related to a new wrinkle in his sexual life: he was seeing a twenty-two-year-old lover. He saw her during the day and then went back to his wife in the evening. He said that having sex with his lover was more intense and stimulating than anything he was used to. Unlike his wife, his lover screamed during lovemaking, and she also tried different sexual positions. When he was with his wife, he was often distracted by thoughts of his lover and had difficulty maintaining an erection. Since his wife kept asking for sex, and since he did not have much interest in providing it, he thought he had better get medical help. He had already taken several types of patent herbal pills on his own initiative.

Doctors prescribed both herbal medicine and Viagra. His plan was to take Viagra when having sex with his wife so that he would be able to perform for her as well as for his lover.

Taking Viagra gave Mr. Gao the power to manipulate the two women, particularly his unsuspecting wife. By helping to stabilize his marriage, Viagra helped him to carry on his extramarital affair. As he also took herbal medicine, however, he was clearly trying to nourish his body while satisfying multiple desires—his desire to enjoy his own sexual pleasure with his lover, his lover's desire to be with him, and his wife's continued desire for sexual pleasure.

Yet Mr. Gao's switching back and forth between the two medicines destabilized the contrast between the promotion of individual desire, represented by the Viagra regime, and the cultivation of overall potency, represented by the TCM regime, because, first, Mr. Gao took Viagra to fulfill his family duty rather than to satisfy his own sexual desire and, second, because he did care about his partners. How women experienced the combination of a man's cultivation of overall potency and his pursuit of sexual desire within the context of multiple gendered bodies remains to be explored.

DOCTORS AND SWITCHING BETWEEN TWO MEDICINES
From what I observed, doctors, particularly TCM doctors, often persuaded patients to combine herbs and Viagra, reflecting the tendency in the doctors' training to integrate TCM and biomedicine. Having studied the two forms of medicine, many doctors have drawn on both traditions since early in their careers, reflecting the history of *zhongxi huitong pai* (a school of thought that advocated convergence and assimilation between Chinese medicine and Western medicine) in the late Qing and Republican periods (Scheid 2007; Andrews 2014) and the project of the integration of TCM and Western medicine under Maoist socialism (Scheid 2002, 2013). By the time Viagra officially entered China, familiarity with biomedicine had been a norm for TCM doctors, particularly those in younger generations.

In Dr. Zhang's department of nanke, the professional history of three doctors exemplifies China's state project. Two of them—Dr. Wang and Dr. Chang—were graduates of a TCM college, but their curricula had included a considerable number of courses in biomedicine. Dr. Wang started his career in a health clinic in a county in which he had to be prepared to prescribe antibiotics as well as herbal medicine. Before he went to Chengdu to get his master's degree in TCM, he had learned a great deal from a biomedical doctor who worked at his clinic. Dr. Chang's studies focused on acupuncture-induced anesthesia; however, this type of anesthesia was discontinued before he graduated from a TCM college in the 1980s, and he switched to biomedical anesthesia.

Dr. Zhang was originally a biomedical doctor; however, in the 1970s, he entered the state's mandatory program to learn TCM. After he finished his two years of study, he was assigned to a position in the department of urology in a TCM hospital. It was not unusual at that time to find a division of biomedicine in a TCM hospital, so it was not difficult for Dr. Zhang to adapt to working in such a hospital. In the early 1990s, when the department of nanke was established, it joined the department of urology in a combined division of *miniao nanke* (泌尿男科, urological and men's medicine). Later, Dr. Zhang became head of this division. In an average week, he divided his time between two consultation rooms, one in urology and one in nanke. The practice of all three doctors—Wang, Chang, and Zhang—reflected their experiences of having worked within a state project that integrated two forms of medicine. They had no ideological problem switching between Viagra and herbs, and they encouraged their patients to do so.

The Imbalance of Power

THE INCREASING POWER OF BIOMEDICINE

Doctors recalled that, in the 1950s and 1960s, urologists could not offer impotence patients much help, whereas TCM doctors, having inherited many *fangji* (方剂, formulas) as well as acupuncture from historical medical practices and literature, could offer some relief. Dr. Yang remembered a urologist prescribing powdered baked *ciwei* (hedgehog) skin. According to Dr. Guo, the most common prescription given by urologists at that time was for a medicinal wine made of *yinyanghuo* (霪羊藿, longspur epimedium), an herb for strengthening kidney yang. As I have noted, men suffering from impotence made far fewer visits to hospitals in the 1950s and 1960s than they do today. And most outpatient visits for impotence-related problems were to TCM hospitals rather than to biomedical hospitals. Because of the power imbalance between TCM and biomedicine, before the era of Viagra and the decline of Maoism, there was no point in switching between biomedicine and herbs.

Once Viagra entered the impotence field, the power balance began to shift to some extent in favor of biomedicine. The hospitals that had existed within the socialist non-enterprise work unit (事業單位) system were transformed into profit-making enterprises. What drugs doctors prescribed depended on many factors, including how much extra income they could earn. In Dr. Zhang's TCM hospital, his division could keep 17 percent of what it made on the sale of biomedical drugs but only 2 percent of what it made on the sale of herbs. In other words, doctors made more money by prescribing biomedical drugs than they did by prescribing herbal medicine. This, not surprisingly, resulted in their being more willing to prescribe Viagra than herbs. It also partly explains why TCM doctors were more likely to switch to prescribing Viagra than biomedical doctors were to prescribing herbs. Nonetheless, urologists sometimes did prescribe patent herbal pills. Dr. Zhuang in the biomedical hospital explained: "Well, it has to do with some kind of placebo effect of herbal medicine. I give patients some comfort by prescribing herbs. Particularly for those patients with whom you try so hard in order to talk them into taking Viagra but in the end cannot change them, I have to prescribe herbs. Sometimes patients request herbs and want to nourish the kidney. The other factor is that now, because we are in a market economy, our hospital wants to increase profits. Representatives of TCM pharmacies come to bombard you with their patent herb pills all the time."

Dr. Zhuang had no faith in herbal medicine, but the rising market economy, including the marketing strategies of the TCM pharmaceutical industry, played a role in how he prescribed medicine. Thus, he switched between biomedicine and TCM.

FROM *YANGWEI* TO *ERECTILE DYSFUNCTION* (*ED*)

Recall that *yangwei* (陽痿, the shrinking of yang) had, since the Ming period, been the dominant term used to name impotence. A consensus statement on impotence published by the U.S. NIH in 1992 advocated a terminological change from *impotence* to *erectile dysfunction*. As one urologist pointed out, the term *erectile dysfunction* (*ED*) makes impotence sound less frightening and less morally devastating than the term *impotence* does. *Impotence* sounds to the man suffering from the condition like a death sentence for his masculinity. *ED*, in contrast, connotes an obstacle to erection—and an obstacle can be removed.

Viagra's introduction to the Chinese market went hand in hand with the promotion of the term *ED*.[19] In the department of nanke at CUHTCM, I often heard doctors switch between using the English shorthand *ED* and the Chinese term *yangwei* when referring to impotence. Early (mid-1990s) records of patient visits to the department of nanke show that these two terms were used interchangeably. Beginning in the late 1990s, and continuing through the Viagra era, ED replaced both *yangwei* and *impotence* as the only designation used in written records. However, this was not the case in verbal communications, in which the term *yangwei* was still used. Dr. Zhang, the head of the department of nanke, often switched between ED and *yangwei*. When Dr. Zhang was talking to patients or chatting with me casually about his patients, he tended to use the term *yangwei*; however, when Viagra was introduced into the conversation, he often switched to ED. In general, Dr. Zhang tended to use ED more often, reflecting the ascendance of biomedical science and technology.

The Pfizer Company's marketing campaign for Viagra, of course, contributed to the spread of the term ED in China. However, it is one thing to replace the term *impotence* and quite another to replace the term *yangwei*. This is because, as I have discussed, *yangwei* represents a whole set of etiological ideas about how impotence functions in the Chinese body. The terminological tension between *yangwei* and ED is emblematic of a struggle between two bodily perspectives not only on a specific point of medicine but also on sexuality, the physical body, and life itself.[20] But instead of this tension being resolved in favor of one perspective or the other, it is quite likely that a mixed perspective will emerge, reflecting the approach of the doctors who work to cure impotence, who act as agents of hybridization or switching between the two medicines.

Dr. Wang Qi did not have any problem switching from using the term *yangwei* to using the term ED, but he habitually switched back, even within the same conversation or the same article. Since I first met with him in 1999, Dr. Wang has made a conscious effort to stick to using the term ED. I tried to make sense of this change by comparing what was happening in China with what was happening in the United States in terms of impotence treatment. In the 1980s, Dr. Wang first proposed the liver-centered perspective and identified *qingzhi* (情志, emotionality) as the "pathogen" associated with impotence, whereas in the United States at that time the focus had just begun to shift from a psychology-centered perspective to a physiology-centered perspective. Having emerged from Maoist socialism, though, Chinese urologists and doctors of TCM were just beginning to find themselves attracted to psychological explanations of and therapies for impotence (e.g., Masters and Johnson's sensitization therapy).

In the 1990s, increasing globalization had made the working mechanism

Figure 6.3: A representative of Pfizer Company's Beijing Office sharing the knowledge about Viagra in a symposium on sexual dysfunction (ED).

of Viagra—blood dynamics—known to medical professionals in the field of impotence. Dr. Wang commented, "Whenever doctors of TCM use the name *yangwei*, we think of deficiency of the kidney yang. This is not right. Now, when I use the name ED, I center my discussion around *boqi zhangai* (勃起障礙, obstacles to erection, the Chinese translation of ED). We need to think about how to have a full supply of blood." His shift from using *yang-wei* to using ED shows that Dr. Wang's reasoning was moving ever closer to favoring the blood dynamics of biomedicine, which he mapped onto the matrix of TCM. "The globalization of Viagra" has created conditions within which adopting the reasoning of biomedicine is not only a fashionable component of TCM but also a necessary strategy—one that enables TCM to maintain its legitimate status as offering viable treatment for impotence.

THE EMERGING PATTERN OF SWITCHING
BETWEEN TWO MEDICINES

Given that patients alternated between herbal remedies and Viagra, doctors of nanke at CUHTCM designed a research project to study this phenomenon. Their research proposal, in which they sought funding from Pfizer, states, "There has been no lack of clinical cases in which patients, in their search for better results, turn to Viagra when TCM does not work, or vice versa. More often seen are the cases in which taking Viagra and Chinese medicine at the same time produced optimal results. What is encouraging is that the majority of patients express their willingness to accept a medication that combines Viagra and TCM . . . Prescribing herbal medicine for patients of ED while also prescribing Viagra can increase patients' compliance with the prescription of Viagra."

The researchers proposed classifying subjects according to the six types of impotence outlined in *Guidelines for Clinical Studies of New Drugs of TCM for Impotence* (中醫新藥治療陽痿的臨床研究指導原則), published by the Ministry of Health in 1993. These classes were then to be subdivided into three groups—a TCM group, a Viagra group, and a TCM/Viagra group. Each group would receive therapy for four weeks and then be studied for eight weeks to determine the effectiveness of the treatment.

The research, from its rationale to its methodology and terminology, was biased toward "hegemonic scientism" (Farquhar 1987). The four-week time frame was based on how quickly the effects of Viagra can be seen. However, four weeks may not be long enough to see the effects of many herbal therapies.[21] That TCM doctors, in this research proposal, suggested promoting social acceptance of Viagra demonstrates not only their belief in its efficacy but also a change in sexual ethics. There is no doubt that one goal of this research was to help increase the sales of Viagra in China.

However, these doctors were by no means suggesting making a complete switch from herbal therapies to Viagra. For one thing, the proposal clearly states that Viagra cannot provide an optimal result unless it is combined with TCM. And, here, we see that the doctors had their own agenda— demonstrating that TCM is a viable system. Moreover, the design of this research project indicates a willingness to accommodate two types of sexual ethics: one that encourages sexual desire and sees it as posing no harm to one's potency, and one that advocates a cautious attitude toward excessive sexual desire because it results in an expenditure of overall potency. The latter implies that TCM is essential to striking a balance in treatment by encouraging the cultivation of potency (which, of course, is quite likely why Pfizer did not fund the research).

COSMOPOLITANISM

On the surface, a patient switching between Viagra and herbal remedies is no different from a diner switching between two types of restaurants, a bilingual speaker switching between two languages, and so on. But what is happening on a deeper level?

I make a crucial distinction between switching *from* one thing to another and switching *between* one thing and another. When one switches *from*, one changes track once and for all, whereas when one switches *between*, one constantly moves back and forth between two entities, with the result that an "either/or" situation becomes a "both/and" situation. Switching between two potentially antagonistic (or even complementary) choices, be they conceptual, linguistic, material, or whatever, intensifies the mingling of different elements, regimes, practices, and so on. And this results in hybridization.[22] The process of switching back and forth illustrates precisely how hybridization—a common form of biological life, things, thoughts, feelings (e.g., ambivalence), identities, and social life—operates at the microlevel. For example, in his discussion of postcolonial development in India, Akhil Gupta writes, "Thus, we have the example of Suresh, who explained the properties of the fertilizer DAP by drawing an analogy with the hen incubating its eggs, *switching back and forth* between the recommendations of development officials and theories based on a humoral agronomy" (1998:232, my emphasis). The idea of switching back and forth helps us to visualize hybridization and provides us with a way of seeing it as emergent rather than static. As one switches back and forth—taking Viagra before having sex and taking herbs to nourish the body at other times—one negotiates between medical regimes as well as ethical regimes.[23]

Where does this negotiation lead? On the level of individual bodies, it leads to the ethos of cosmopolitanism. Paul Rabinow argues that cosmopolitanism is "the acceptance of [a] twin valorization" (1996:56). On the one hand is the valorization of "a specificity of historical experience and place, however complex and contestable they might be." On the other hand is the valorization of "a worldwide macro-interdependency encompassing any local particularity." Rabinow argues, further, that "*Homo sapiens* has done rather poorly in interpreting this condition. We seem to have trouble with the balancing act, preferring to reify local identities or construct universal ones" (56). The willingness to try new ways of life while still remaining in touch with one's habitual way of life is a move toward cosmopolitanism.

This cosmopolitanism has ethical implications for TCM. On the one hand, the pattern of switching among the patients modified, if not completely altered, the expectation from the globalized regime of Viagra. With such a modification, the world of anti-impotence technology did not look as flat as that only represented by Viagra or similar drugs, because the terrain of differences—a different use of potency and a different ethics related to the use of potency and jing—have enriched both life and medicine. This terrain of difference provides new evidence for the legitimacy of TCM as both a lively tradition and a representative of the value of differences in the twenty-first century—multiplicity, plurality, and vitality.[24] On the other hand, the pattern of switching also pushed for changes in TCM in the direction of cosmopolitanism. That is, the practice of "switching" also tells the story of TCM's potentiality for change in itself by mingling with biomedicine to serve the society.

CHAPTER 7

Potency Is Fullness of Life

含德之厚, 比于赤子. 毒蟲不螫,猛獸不據, 攫鳥不搏. 骨弱筋柔而握固. 未知牝牡之合而全作, 精之至也 (老子道德經. 第五十五章).

Those who are thoroughly virtuous are like newborn babies. Poisonous insects would not sting, fierce beasts would not grab, and ferocious vultures would not attack. A newborn baby, though weak in bones and soft in tendons, can clench his fists tight. Without any knowledge of sexual intercourse, a baby boy can have a full erection. This is because his body is full of jing (seminal essence).

—Laozi

Two thousand five hundred years ago, Laozi, the earliest Daoist philosopher and one of the most important thinkers in Chinese history, observed one of the wonders of life—a baby boy's erection. He attributed this wonder to the infant's fullness of *jing* (seminal essence). Fullness of jing, then, does not indicate a state of *yu* (慾, desire) but, rather, a state of *wuyu* (無慾, freedom from desire). Those who are *han de zhi hou* (含德之厚, thoroughly virtuous, here referring to being thoroughly immersed in the power of Dao—道, the Way) are comparable to newborn babies in their purity of *sheng* (life).

Laozi's view diverges sharply from the Freudian view of infant sexuality. Freud considered an infant's erection to be a manifestation of libido, revealing his physical reactions to sensory stimulation of other body parts in different phases of infantile development (from mouth to anus to penis). Laozi saw, instead, the "asexual" and "alibidinal" nature of infant erection, leading him to argue that, precisely because of the "purity" of this erection, male potency is, in essence, the fullness of life.

Today, we hear people say "jingqizu" (jing and *qi* are abundant) to praise a vigorous and spirited man and to indicate strong potency.[1] Potency manifests itself in many ways, for example, in a glittering gaze, a robust stride, a booming, resounding tone of voice, and a calm but firm demeanor. Charlotte Furth offers one example, taken from a seventeenth-century text, of a mature masculine figure: "A man's deeper generativity may be hinted at by an appearance that hides his years—the strong teeth, abundant black hair, and fresh complexion associated with ample Kidney function" (1999:206).[2]

This understanding of sexual potency has etymological roots in Chinese language. In ancient China, there was no equivalent for the English term *sexual potency*. In contemporary Chinese, that term is translated as *xing-nengli*, which literally means the ability to have sex. How, then, did people refer to male potency in Laozi's time?

We can get a clue by looking at the antonym for *potency*, that is, the term for male impotence in ancient Chinese. The *Inner Canon* (*Huangdineijing*, *Suwen*: Wuchangzhengdalunpian) states, "When tai yin rules the sky, damp qi descends, the kidney qi rises up accordingly, water darkens, dust rises to receive cloud and rain, the chest is clogged, *yin shrinks*, qi drastically declines and weakens, so the yin organ does not rise and is unable to be put to use" (Anonymous 2000:217, my emphasis).

As *yin* refers to the male sexual organ, *yinwei* (yin shrinks) refers to impotence.[3] However, no single word describes potency, the opposite of *yinwei*. In other words, we cannot easily find an ancient Chinese word or phrase that denotes the opposite of *yinwei*. Phrases such as Laozi's "the fullness of jing" (*jing zhi zhi*) come close.

In the Mawangdui scriptures, which are believed to have been produced in the pre-Qin period (prior to 221 B.C.E.), impotence is referred to as "si" (of the penis). *Si* means "death." "If the penis does not show the propensity of rising up, he can be treated with special food consisting of crow eggs and wheat congee. If he takes it, it would turn death back to life" (Fan et al. 1997:4–5). The "death" of yin was seen as resulting from severe loss of jing and could lead to the death of the man in whom it occurred.[4] Yu Zhen, a medical scholar and a doctor of TCM in the Qing period, stated, "There are men who become impotent at the age of 60. They would not be able to live a long life. They should just follow the natural way and give up on any intention to have sex and satisfy desire. Then, they might be able to extend their lives. If they seek medication for strengthening yang by washing their penises or taking a decoction in order to conquer women, they would die in a few years. Those middle-aged men who suffer from no other illnesses than impotence are likely to die early. Those young men who are weak, frail and impotent would die soon, because the moving qi in the kidney has declined prematurely" (1998:377).[5]

This idea was promoted by contemporary scholars as well. In 2004, a scholar of Daoism in the Chinese Academy of Social Sciences commented, "If a man cannot get an erection, he will die in five years!" His comment resonated with TCM's view of impotence: it is a matter of life and death.

Discussions of impotence as death reminded me of a conversation I had had one spring day with an eighty-eight-year-old white American man in a small town near Boston. We were chatting at a coffee shop, looking out the window at the sunny, quiet street scene. I noticed the old man was paying attention to the young girls walking by, and, from time to time, he commented with great interest on their looks and their way of dressing. Our conversation eventually turned to his sexual life. He answered rather straightforwardly and frankly when I asked how he had done. He said proudly that he had had a "wonderful" sexual life, "because I had a wonderful wife and we never had any problem." The couple had had sexual intercourse until about two years earlier—when the man was eighty-six. Then, "one day, all of a sudden," he said, "I discovered that I could not do it anymore. My penis simply became a piece of meat. That's it." As he spoke, an expression of self-pity settled on his face, and he looked as a much younger man might when describing sudden erectile failure. Rather than simply accepting impotence as a result of aging, this older man seemed to consider his loss of potency fortuitous and unnatural.

Even though it is difficult to establish empirically the link between potency and life, the idea that the ability to get an erection is rooted in the overall strength of life (sheng) is integral to ancient Chinese thought. In contrast, "the biological turn" has reinforced the belief that impotence is only "a neurovascular event" and has little to do with the overall potentiality of life. Challenging this view, in previous chapters I have presented impotence, first, as a social, gendered, and intercorporeal event and, second, as a cultural event, as the practice of *yangsheng* and alternation between Chinese medicine and Viagra testify.

In this chapter, I argue that impotence is a life event. *Life* here carries the double senses of *shengming* (being alive) and *shenghuo* (living a life).[6] The Daoist emphasis on the undifferentiation of the human and the universe situates one's life (potency is part of it) in beings of myriad things (e.g., the yin yang balance within shenti, the Chinese term for the body, is continuous from one's potency to myriad things in the world). To push this Daoist insight further, I feel it helpful to extend Laozi's view by introducing Martin Heidegger's (1962) notion of "being-in-the world," because it can demonstrate the inadequacy of the biological turn from within the Western philosophical self-reflection on the whole intellectual tradition particularly since Descartes. The Heideggerian notion of "being in the world" unravels the ontological divide between human and the world by addressing how being-already-in-the-world including "being with the other" is the fundamental mode of human existence. His idea was greatly illuminated and specified by Merleau-Ponty's discussion that it is the body that illuminates being in the world. Heidegger was known for his interest in Laozi's philosophy (Parkes 1990), and Merleau-Ponty was indebted to Heideggerian ideas. A dialogue between potency as life's fullness in ancient Chinese thought and being in the world in Western phenomenology reveals clearly the inadequacy of the understanding of potency in terms of the biological turn. Furthermore, potency not only refers to life (sheng) but also to opening life up to the world.[7] Conversely, impotence is not only the decline of life but also the inability to open one's life up to the world.

Opening Life Up

BODYING FORTH

Getting an erection is neither solely conscious nor solely unconscious behavior, and the bodily movement of the sexual organ differs from controllable movement of many parts of the body. One day in a philosophy class I attended at Berkeley, the professor, John Searle, demonstrated how some bodily moves are conscious ones. He said, "Now I want to raise my right arm. Look, my right arm is up."

It would be difficult to replicate this intentional movement with the penis. Indeed, many impotent men cannot force an erection however hard they try. In a clinical encounter, speaking to his anxious patient, one doctor highlighted this irony: "Having an erection is like sneezing. Are you able to do it simply because you want it? You are not!" I often heard doctors point out to their impotence patients, "The more desperately you want an erection, the less likely you will get one." In William H. Masters and Virginia E. Johnson's words, "No man can will an erection" (1970:196).

Think about curing impotence: a patient needs treatment because he cannot order himself to get an erection. His consciousness, or his intentionality (his conscious representation of the objectified bodily move), just does not produce the effect of having an erection. This is why many psychotherapists focus treatment on relaxing the anxious patient to minimize the influence of his consciousness.

However, it is difficult to separate erection from consciousness, particularly when a patient is consciously learning techniques to cure impotence. For example, unlike nocturnal erection—an unconscious behavior—when one gets an erection in response to an erotic stimulus, however spontaneous, it is not completely free from conscious reinforcement.

A view that sharply distinguishes between the conscious and the unconscious is inadequate for understanding how erection occurs. A more productive approach is to view erection in terms of "somatic awareness" (Shusterman 2005:168) or as involving "somatic modes of attention" (Csordas 1993).[8] The two phrases capitalize on somatic capacity, which Merleau-Ponty describes well: "If I am ordered to touch my ear or my knee, I move my hand to my ear or my knee by the shortest route, without having to think of the initial position of my hand, or that of my ear, or the path between them. We said earlier that it is the body which 'understands' in the acquisition of habit" (1962:144).[9]

When one gets an erection at the "right" time on the "right" occasion, one's body is poised to experience erotic inspirations and release its capacity to be evoked. As consciousness is involved when one is learning how "to use the body correctly" to cure impotence, consciousness "in the first place is not a matter of 'I think that' but of 'I can'" (Merleau-Ponty 1962:137). Seen in this light, impotence occurs when this "I can," a capacity, is lost.

This capacity can be expressed in terms of "bodying forth," a phrase Heidegger used in his discussion of being-in-the-world (Boss 2001). The verb *bodying* indicates the poise and comportment of one's existence in bodily form. "Bodying forth" refers to movement that puts an idea into shape or tangible form and exhibits it in an observable way—in the context of this discussion, in the form of the swelling up of the sexual organ. To take a phenomenological turn, "bodying forth" refers to the tendency to open up life through the body. The question raised by Heidegger—"How is the human being in space insofar as he is bodying forth?" (2001:88)—is about how life is expressed through the body. Based on his intellectual conversations with Heidegger, Swiss psychiatrist Medard Boss interpreted "bodying forth" as the unfolding of the inherent potentiality of human existence.[10] Thus, getting an erection entails unfolding one's potentiality, that is, "bodying forth."

"Bodying forth" turns Laozi's view of potency into a concrete bodily movement toward the world.

LEARNING TO BODY FORTH

Dr. Yang Wenzhi, a urologist at Beijing Medical University, was one of the few doctors in the 1970s and early 1980s to treat infertility among patients who could not have sex successfully. It is hard to imagine today that this kind of treatment was once necessary. Consultation on how to have sex was risky at that time. Dr. Yang could have been accused of encouraging premarital sex or sex outside marriage, a serious political crime, if a couple seeking his advice only pretended to be married. At that time, a couple had to prove that they were married just to stay in the same hotel room. But because he had seen so many ironies in his lifetime and was aware of the pain caused by infertility and sexual dysfunction, Dr. Yang was determined to help. He had worked in one of the teaching hospitals of Beijing Medical College since the 1950s and once worked with the well-known urologist Wu Jieping. He retired from the hospital in the 1990s, when in his seventies, but still saw patients. I interviewed him both in his consulting room and in his home and found him to be both kind and eloquent.

To Dr. Yang, it was not at all odd that one has to learn to have sex. It was stunning to him that knowledge of such a basic human activity and embodied capacity had been suppressed for so many people. Whereas some people simply did not know how to have sex, many more did not know how to have good sex. For many males, a gap lay between having an erection and having sex. Impotence occurred when this distance became a *tianqian* (天塹, a huge chasm).

The difficulty in having sex successfully was partly attributed to social constraints on imparting sexual knowledge. Dr. Yang took from his bookcase an original copy of the second edition of *Knowledge about Sex*, by Wang Wenbin, Zhao Zhiyi, and Tan Mingxun, three doctors at Union Medical College in Beijing in 1956. He received this book as a gift from the lead author. Merely seventy-eight pages long, it was perhaps the most influential book on sex education during the Maoist period. Its first printing sold 800,000 copies, and its second printing in 1957 sold 1.4 million copies at the price of 18 cents a copy.

Several characteristics of this book reveal its pro-sex attitude. First, it includes ten sketches detailing male and female sexual and reproductive organs. The sketches of the vagina and penis provided a rare chance for millions of men and women to see what these structures look like and where they are located in the body.

The second feature is its positive attitude toward satisfaction of sexual desire and sex for pleasure. It uses the terms *xing chongdong* (sexual impulse), *xingyu* (sexual desire), and *xingyu gaochao* (orgasm) frequently. It even details *dongqing qu* (the zone of sensations, erogenous zone), or *xingyu qu* (the zone of sexual gratification). The following sentence is representative of its straightforward exposition, "Properly stimulating the three parts (labia majora, breasts, and mouth) all can cause sexual excitement; among them, stimulating lips, the tip of the tongue, nipples, the clitoris, the edge of the vaginal opening and the inner wall of vagina particularly easily triggers extreme sexual excitation, the clitoris being the most sensitive" (Wang et al. 1956:35).

Third, even though this book makes it clear that enjoyment should not take priority in sexual matters, that having "correct" thoughts is the most important part of life, it introduces a myriad of details related to satisfying sexual desire (stimulating the clitoris, continuing to stroke the female after ejaculation, thrusting the penis from shallow to deep, etc.). It also discusses women's misperceptions about themselves, for example, that "sexual desire is only an issue of the male"; "some women consider sexual desire base and ugly, so become ashamed and unwilling to reveal their desire"; and "some women treat sexual relationship as an obligation, so they are passive and even have aversion to it" (42).

This book's open-minded attitude toward sexual desire reflects the relatively open atmosphere of the mid-1950s. Discussion of sexual matters became much more restricted after a series of political campaigns in the late 1950s and early 1960s. In 1963, however, Premier Zhou Enlai met with ten doctors and asked them to promote sex education for youths and adolescents. In response, one of the participants in the meeting, along with several other doctors, published articles on such topics as the physiology of menstruation and nocturnal emission, receiving more than 1,000 letters from readers within a year of publication (Ye 1983; Evans 1997). But unlike *Knowledge about Sex*, the scope of sex education in the aftermath of Zhou's meeting was limited to human biology and had nothing to say about sexual life in marriage. Even this limited sex education completely disappeared after the Cultural Revolution began, resonating with the disappearance of the phrase *aiqing* (romantic love; see chapter 2).

Figure 7.1:
Dr. Yang Wenzhi
holding a copy of
*Knowledge about
Sex* in his home.

A man recalled how he had read *Knowledge about Sex* as a high school student in 1973, after secretly obtaining a copy: "I acted like a thief, hatching the already very old and worn-out book under my armpit and went to the restroom (Note that he had to go to the restroom to read it). Squatting over the toilet and pretending to be 'fangbian' (to get convenience, referring to moving the bowel), I read this book in a rush. Under the dim light, I nonetheless saw the lines very clearly. When reading the illustrations, my eyes almost popped out of the sockets" (qtd. in Deng 2008).

Showing me his copy, Dr. Yang gently touched Wang Wenbin's signature on the cover of the book, the inscription "For Respected Dr. Yang Wenzhi," and the imprint of Wang's personal stamp. He said, "Wang Wenbin was tortured to death in the Cultural Revolution because of the book." The miserable fate of the lead author was partly the reason why, when the book was re-published after the Cultural Revolution, the section on the "Three Phases of Sexual Life" in the chapter "Sexual Life after Marriage" was deleted. Nonetheless, the 1980 edition sold 5.6 million copies (Lin et al. 2011).

The ups and downs of *Knowledge about Sex* and Dr. Yang's experience raise the issue of how men and women learn to have sex. I asked a group of men whether one has to learn to have sex, a question I had supposed everyone would readily answer with little disagreement. To my surprise, responses varied.

One man said, "No, one can do it by instinct." But others immediately disputed this. In fact, "Tianxia zhidao tan" (On the Ultimate Way All under Heaven), a section of the Mawangdui scriptures, has this to say: "When a person is born there are two things that do not need to be learned: the first is to breathe and the second is to eat. Except for these two, there is nothing that is not the result of learning and habituation. Thus, what assists life is eating; what injures life is lust. Therefore, the sage when conjoining male and female invariably possesses a model" (Harper trans. 1998:432).

Mr. Hua, a forty-year-old professional, recalled how clumsy he had been in his twenties when he was naked for the first time with his girlfriend in bed. The two had not planned to have sex. One day, his girlfriend came to his home while his parents were away. She and Mr. Hua kissed each other and then found themselves undressing each other and getting into bed. Mr. Hua felt himself getting an erection, and his girlfriend lay down on her back and pulled him on top of her, a thrilling encouragement of his sexual advance. What was funny, he said, was that he was on top of her with his legs spread, but she did not open her legs, not because of any resistance on her part but because she did not know (and neither did he) that by opening her legs he would be in a comfortable position to penetrate. Very excited, he clumsily ejaculated outside her vagina. It took a while for them to become "skillful" in their intercorporeality.

As our discussion went on, most men in this group leaned to the view that one had to learn and that there were different ways of doing so. For many, coming of age in an era when there was no sex education, learning to have sex was not as easy as one might imagine. Recall that, in school, girls and boys received their only instruction in "physiological hygiene" separately or that only girls received the class and boys were simply asked to go home. The articles about nocturnal emission and menstruation that followed Premier Zhou's 1963 meeting gave rise to a lot of questions from readers. One of the authors, Dr. Ye, recalled, "What surprised us is that more questions came from boys than from girls. Perhaps, when girls have their first menstruation and feel at a loss as to what to do, they may turn to their mothers for explanation. But for boys who have their first nocturnal emission, they feel it hard to ask their parents about it . . . There was one case in which a young man killed himself by lying on the train rail after he had nocturnal emission. In his letter left before his death, he said that he had an incurable illness and it was better to kill himself" (Ye 1983:3).

How, then, did people learn to have sex? A thirty-year-old professional said, "One learns it by imitating animals. I saw a male dog having intercourse with a female dog and got to know how the male body is supposed to move."[11]

Not surprisingly, couples who sought consultation in Dr. Yang's clinic were mostly urban residents. Dr. Yang commented, "Peasants who look after horses and donkeys know how to do it." He was initially puzzled by one case, that of a man working for a college of agriculture who had not succeeded in having sex. Dr. Yang recalled asking him, "Have you never seen cows, pigs, and rabbits *jiaopei* (copulating)?" "No," the man replied. Dr. Yang asked, "Didn't you say that you graduated from the agricultural college?" The man answered, "No, I graduated from an industrial college and am working for the agricultural college."

According to Dr. Yang, men often did not know what to do after the penis entered the vagina. As a result, many men had difficulty ejaculating. In Beijing in 1999, a woman of *laosanjie* (the old three classes) recalled to me that, when she was sent down to the farm in Heilongjiang, she knew nothing about sex. She thought that if a man and a woman sat facing each other, they would be able to produce a child. Unlike the situation today, "infertility" in Dr. Yang's clinic had more to do with ignorance about sex than with the quality of a man's semen or other problems. Dr. Yang reported he literally had to tell a man how to open his wife's legs, lower into position, slowly put the penis in, withdraw a little and then push in again, alternating between deep and shallow moves, asking his wife what she liked, and doing what she liked. Of 160 couples he treated, 80 percent were able to have sex successfully after the consultation. The men had learned to "body forth."

Some men learned the rudiments of sex as children playing games with peers. Mr. Liang, a manager in his late thirties, learned by playing the popular fighting game of *douji* (鬥雞, cockfight). In this game, boys stand on one leg and try to knock one another down using only the knee of the upraised leg. During one game, Mr. Liang said, a player moved his body and his hands suggestively, imitating the thrusting of the penis. When other boys burst out laughing at these movements, Mr. Liang became aware of the sexual nuances.

Mr. Liu, a man in his early forties, recalled how he had learned to have sex during an encounter with a woman in the late 1970s. He had been single, a blue-collar worker in his twenties. One day he found himself in bed with a divorced female coworker, both of them clothed. They fell asleep, and, later, he awoke to feel the woman embracing him. He was aroused and had an erection. He undressed her and then lowered himself on top of her and entered her body. Embracing her tightly, he had the very uncomfortable feeling that he was stuck in her body. He felt pain instead of pleasure. A question flashed through his mind: "Is this the enjoyment of sex people talked about? It is so uncomfortable!" This feeling changed as soon as the woman started to teach him what to do, by pushing against his chest and forcing him to lean back. He did so and then forced his body forward again. Again, she pushed him back. Gradually, he started to feel pleasure, thrusting back and forth rhythmically until he ejaculated. "I got it," he recalled. That was the beginning of his sexual enjoyment. For other people I talked to, the learning process was full of frustration. Consider the following example.

Mr. Tang, a twenty-five-year-old peasant in Hebei Province, had not suc-ceeded in having sex with his wife after a year of marriage. He had gotten an erection by masturbating when he was sixteen or seventeen years old and thereafter had masturbated once a week. But he stopped after he got married. On two occasions, he had gotten an erection while watching pornographic videos. Ms. Hou, his twenty-four-year-old wife, had watched with him once and afterward wanted to have sex. But, on that occasion, he could not get an erection. He sometimes had erections in the morning, but Mr. Tang said, morning was not a good time for sex, because he was busy getting ready for work in the fields. Strangely, he reported, he could get an erection while he was working. He described his erectile failure to a doctor. He recalled that on his wedding night, his penis *taiping le* (抬平了, raised horizontally, i.e., got rigid). But, as soon as his *guitou* (龜頭, turtle head, glans penis) entered his wife's body and he felt she "was not tight," he lost the erection.

His erectile failure had become a family concern, because his parents were eager to have a grandchild. Mr. Zhuang, Mr. Tang's cousin, accompanied Mr. Tang and Ms. Hou to the clinic and told the doctor that the couple did not speak to each other when watching TV together and that they did not sleep together when they stayed at his apartment in Beijing. Ms. Hou revealed that she had never seen her husband naked. To help the couple become more intimately involved with each other, Mr. Zhuang's wife had instructed Ms. Hou to stroke her husband. With this help, Mr. Tang could get an erection, but as soon as he got on top of his wife, he lost it.

The need to cure impotence made many patients reflect on the cultural process of learning to have sex. In terms of simple mechanics, it is not too different from learning other bodily skills, for example, using a hammer. Successfully using a hammer, though, does not require intercorporeal intimacy (see chapter 4). The intercorporeal requirement makes the translation of one's potency into good sex contingent on factors far more complex than those involved in learning carpentry skills. In Heideggerian language, the complexity lies in the fact that "you exist and I exist. We are here in the world with one another" (Heidegger 2001:123). Neither "you" nor "I" should be only an object; neither "you" nor "I" should be only a subject. "You" and "I" are intercorporeal beings.

By the 1990s, the kind of consultation Dr. Yang had provided was no longer needed. Since the 2000s, the more open sexual culture, including the viewing of erotic or pornographic videos, has greatly improved sexual socialization. Nevertheless, Dr. Yang's work helps underscore the point I make in this chapter, that is, that potency (life) is not just fullness of jing but also the capacity of "bodying forth," to give the fullness of jing a bodily form in relation to the "world." In other words, potency is the propensity for opening life up to the world. However, this understanding of potency found itself increasingly at odds with the "biological turn." A brief history of the breakthroughs in the biological field of impotence shows why.

A HISTORY OF INDUCING ERECTION

Doctors had sought to induce erections using drugs for a long time, to replace other therapies that were either ineffective or too intrusive (McNamara and Donatucci 2010). Even during the heyday of psychogenic-centered diagnosis and treatment of impotence based on the rationale "it's all in your head," efforts were being made to understand the physiology of impotence. Significant steps were taken when implantation of an inflatable penile prosthesis—the Scott–Bradley–Timm inflatable prosthesis—was introduced in 1973 in the United States. This surgical procedure was the first treatment for ED to become reasonably widespread among urologists. The device was the first to allow a man to have a prosthetic erection only when needed and to provide "nearly" natural flaccid and erect states. This implant would now be designated a three-piece inflatable prosthesis, consisting of a pair of inflatable intracorporeal cylinders, a small scrotal pump, and a large-volume abdominal fluid reservoir that was surgically placed in the body (Simmons and Montague 2008). It works in the following way: "The two cylinders are inserted in the penis and connected by tubing to a separate reservoir of fluid. The reservoir is implanted under the groin muscles. A pump is also connected to the system and sits under the loose skin of the scrotal sac, between the testicles. To inflate the prosthesis, the man presses on the pump. This does not involve putting pressure on the testicles. The pump transfers fluid from the reservoir to the cylinders in the penis, inflating them. Pressing on a deflation valve at the base of the pump returns the fluid to the reservoir, deflating the penis" (Cleveland Clinic 2010).

Implanting this typical cyborg penile device radically alters the body. The surgery itself is highly intrusive, and mechanical failure of the device can occur. Other drawbacks are possible infection and high cost (Jhaveri et al. 1998). In my fieldwork in the 1990s, Chinese urologists told me that Chinese men were more reluctant to accept such intrusive surgery than U.S. men were, so the demand was low.[12]

Venous ligation was yet another intrusive surgery to help maintain erections. I once observed the procedure in the early 2000s. The patient lay on the operating table, looking calm after receiving local anesthesia. A curtain hung above his waist to block his view of his lower body. Walking to the other side of this curtain, I saw his penis becoming a piece of bloody flesh. The foreskin had been open from the top and pushed down to the bottom of the shaft. The doctor carefully poked a scalpel into the membrane to reach a tiny vein amid the flow of blood. He separated the vein from the surrounding flesh and tied it off with a suture. I was later told that the purpose was to enable the man to maintain increased blood flow in the penis for a longer time when having an erection. This process corrects "venous leakage"—rapid decrease or leaking of blood—an abnormality responsible for the loss of erection. I saw the doctor ligate several veins to alter the inner circuit of blood. After a nurse administered fluid injections to test whether the leakage was fixed, the doctor tested for rigidity. He then put the foreskin back in place and sutured all the incisions. Finally, the penis was bandaged. According to the doctor, three weeks later, the man would be fully recovered.

He wished the patient well, much as one might tell a diner to enjoy eating a sausage without having to see the mess that went into making it.

A far less intrusive aid in achieving erection was intracorporeal self-injection (with intracavernous alprostadil or a drug mixture) into the penis. The following story describes the excitement that greeted this breakthrough.

In 1983 North American urologists at a convention in Las Vegas received a startling demonstration of the efficacy of drug-induced erection. During an evening seminar, a British researcher rose to present a lecture on the physiology of erection. His audience was composed of several hundred urologists jammed into a large conference room. Unlike previous speakers at the meeting, the guest lecturer was dressed in a pair of loose-fitting sweatpants.

Approximately thirty minutes into his presentation, he remarked that, in fact, at that very moment, his own penis was getting hard. Most of the urologists chuckled, thinking he was joking. A few more minutes passed. Suddenly he stopped, then said, "I must demonstrate this." He stepped out from behind the lectern and lowered his sweatpants, revealing his own penis in a state of blazing rigidity. He then wandered among the first few rows of the audience, inviting the astonished urologists to palpate his erection. He wanted them to confirm for themselves that his penis was indeed quite rigid—without the use of an implant.

Despite the unorthodox presentation, the era of penile injections was ushered into being. His erection was induced by a drug injected into his penis, a drug similar to the one used by impotent men today. Since then, drugs that induced erections have revolutionized impotence diagnosis. (Payton 1995:116–18)

This sensational display of a drug-induced erection was the prelude to the development of self-injection therapy in the 1980s. In displaying his drug-induced erection, this physician demonstrated what John Searle had demonstrated in the classroom when he raised his right arm. This physician "raised" his penis through conscious management. That is, consciously reordering the body based on an understanding of the biological and neural structures (the arteries, veins, muscles, blood flows, nerves, neural transmitters, etc.) achieved the bodily response necessary for vaginal intercourse.[13]

The least intrusive anti-impotence technology came in the 1990s with the invention of Viagra, which drew from the discovery in the early 1990s that the release of nitric oxide, a nerve transmitter, in the penis plays a role in smoothing the cavernous muscle and thus aids erection (Rajfer 2008). One of the scientists involved in this discovery won the Nobel Prize in 1998. Rendering invasive anti-impotence technologies moot, Viagra and subsequent oral drugs (Cialis, Levitra, etc.) essentially ensured the triumph of the bio-technological turn, demonstrating that it is indeed possible to consciously "raise the penis." With this turn, the human becomes an agent of science consciously working to effect a change in an object, here a biological bodily function.

Drug-induced erections are a modern marvel, reminiscent of certain new forms of "life" (e.g., the cyborg, a mechanical–biological body; see Haraway 1991). They simplify the existential relationship between life and potency by equating potency with erections. However, Viagra has not brought to an end other understandings of potency, as the previous chapter on switching drugs shows. In the rest of this chapter, I show further how potency is understood beyond the biological notion of erection.

OPENING LIFE UP

The following two cases—one ending on a negative note and the other on a positive one—examine "imagined impotence" from the perspective of potency as "opening life up to the world."

Mr. Geng, thirty-one years old, unemployed, and unmarried, talked to me about his life and told me he was impotent. He had never had sex. He tried to masturbate when he first felt that he might be impotent, at the age of sixteen. He described the result as "an erection between 60 and 90 degrees," but it was not hard enough. This experience had had a lasting impact on him and discouraged him from pursuing relationships with women.

He worked in a factory for four years after graduating from high school, where he met a girl his own age whom he liked. They once got intimate and became physical with each other. Because he did not feel an erection while he was kissing her (still clothed), he lacked the confidence to continue the relationship, so he withdrew from it. He even quit his job to avoid the girl. But Mr. Geng remained interested in women. He went to see *maopianr* (pornographic movies) in the video/VCD screening room in the small town where his factory was located. He had another girlfriend for a brief period, but because of his conviction that he was impotent, he did not dare initiate bodily contact with her. He did not allow her to touch him and ended up breaking up with her. He was fixed on the idea that he would not look for a girlfriend until he could get an erection.

Mr. Geng grew up in northwestern China. He recalled that he was physically fragile as a child and often got sick. Very few kids his age liked to play with him. In school, he was passive, particularly in relationships with girls. He liked to be left alone. He was not close to his parents, and *bu xiaoxin* (不交心, they did not open up their hearts to each other, did not communicate thoughts and feelings). He remembered once having nocturnal emission and being beaten for it by his parents. He said that he became "aware of himself as a man" at age fifteen but did not know much about sex. His school offered a class on personal hygiene, but the teacher, a woman, kept only the girls in the class and asked all the boys to leave. This incident conveyed a strong signal to him that sexual desire should be avoided.

In the dormitory during junior high and high school, he often heard teenagers talking about girls, and he learned about the female body from those conversations. When he worked in the factory, he lived in the factory dormitory. He was introduced to sexual intercourse by his roommates, who sometimes had sex with girls in beds separated from his only by a plastic screen.

Mr. Geng suffered from imagined impotence, but his trouble ran deeper. His upbringing might have been partially responsible for the fact that he simply shut himself off from the world. Merleau-Ponty wrote, "In so far as a man's sexual history provides a key to his life, it is because in his sexuality is projected his manner of being towards the world" (1962:158). He also argued, "There is no explanation of sexuality which reduces it to anything other than itself, for it is already something other than itself, and indeed, if we like, our whole being" (171).[14] Mr. Geng's withdrawal from social relationships was symptomatic of a more serious loss of "potency" in life.

In contrast, Mr. Wan experienced a renewal of his potency. Mr. Wan looked very depressed when he first talked to me in the clinic. He was thirty years old and had been married for two years. After the first year of marriage, he became less interested in having sex with his wife and began experiencing erectile difficulties. The couple had had sex twice a week before his problem began.

Without telling his wife, he took *zhuangyang* herbal tonic pills. He then masturbated and could get an erection. He went to a karaoke nightclub to try his luck with a *xiaojie* (sex worker) and found that he could get an erection simply by embracing her, but he did not have sex with her. This discovery made him even gloomier.

He was most worried about pressure from his wife to have a baby. He wanted to have a child too. One of the reasons he was so worried was that his sister-in-law was actively trying to get pregnant. Being "left behind" by his brother-in-law in a "masculine competition" to produce a child was what worried him the most.

The doctor said to him, "The sky won't fall if you cannot get an erection this time; you can simply give it another try next time. You need to get her aroused so that you will be attracted to her again." As the doctor spoke, Mr. Wan's facial expression showed dawning comprehension.

A couple of months later, Mr. Wan returned to the clinic in a totally different mood. He was high-spirited, saying that he had succeeded in penetrating his wife. He also said that he had tried Viagra. But what most excited him was that, even before taking Viagra, he had succeeded in getting an erection and penetrating his wife.

"How did you succeed even before you took Viagra?" I asked.

He said that he did what the doctor had told him to do on his earlier clinic visit. He said, "It became soft and slipped out after the first penetration, but we worked on it and I put it back in again. I ejaculated, even though it did not feel very deep. So, recently, in order to impregnate her, we did it every day."

"What did your wife say when you became soft?" I asked.

He said, "She understands me very well and did not complain."

Viagra might have boosted Mr. Wan's confidence and relaxed his body. He simply learned that he could try again after a failure, and he seemed to have relished this idea, which sounded so commonsensical and perhaps had worked many times for him in other areas of his life. In saying that he simply "tried to get it hard again and reinsert it," he demonstrated an enormous change in his attitude toward life. Instead of shutting himself off from engagement with the world, he learned to keep his sexual being open. Potency, indeed, is life and life's opening up of itself to the world.

Staying Potent When Impotent

A PRECARIOUS LIFEWORLD

Opening life up to the world was not always a liberating experience, as the lifeworld could be experienced as so precarious that one feels out of place in it.[15] One older man, Mr. Wei, tells a dramatically different story from those recounted by Mr. Geng and Mr. Wan, the two much younger men in the previous section.

Mr. Wei was sixty-six years old and a retired cadre. His whole life centered on two issues—the search for a satisfying marriage and the striving for a happy sexual life. He was born in a rural area in a province near Beijing in the 1930s. He had had three unsatisfying marriages.

His first marriage was an arranged one that took place when he was thirteen years old, before the founding of the People's Republic in 1949. He was married by his parents to a woman who was eight years older than he. According to the custom at the time, the bride did not live in her parents-in-law's home but came to stay with the groom on three occasions—during autumn, after the harvesting of the wheat, and on New Year's Day. Mr. Wei said that he did not have sex with his first wife until several months after her initial stay in his parents' home. He remembered that he could not ejaculate because he was too young and he was too scared to feel any pleasure. He had vivid memories of the wedding-night ritual of *nao dongfang* (闹洞房, the teasing of a newlywed couple). Instead of happy memories, he recalled being scared by all the noise. Years after the wedding, he continued to be scared of the noise of paper blown by wind because it sounded like the noise of nao dongfang. He said that he had not been on good terms with his wife and that they often fought. Nonetheless, they had had two children.

Mr. Wei subsequently left his village for Beijing. Not long after the founding of the PRC in 1949, the new Marriage Law was implemented and arranged marriage was abolished. He went back to his village and ended his first marriage in 1951. He became a cadre under socialism. One of his hobbies was *jiaoyi wu* (friendship dance, social dancing, i.e., ballroom dancing). Having ended his arranged marriage, he began to engage in *ziyou lianai* (自由戀愛, free love, i.e., affection-based dating), seeing a female teacher he got to know at a dance party. They managed to sleep together several times in a small room he rented. Asked how it was possible for them to do so, he said that people in the small courtyard where he rented the room knew about his unpleasant marriage and were sympathetic toward him. In addition, class struggles under Maoist socialism, one aspect of which was hostility toward sexual desire, had not yet peaked.

Mr. Wei said his sex life with the teacher was satisfactory. But both he and his lover were classified as rightists in the antirightist campaign of 1957. He was accused, among other things, of involvement in antirevolutionary hobbies such as dancing and dressing up. Shortly afterward, his lover drowned in a well in suburban Beijing. She had been sentenced to reformation through labor, a political arrangement of reeducation and correction for those deemed enemies of the people. "I suspected that she committed suicide. She was not happy in those days," he recalled.

In 1960, the punishment Mr. Wei received for his rightist activities was reduced and he was able to socialize again. He got to know a woman who was a secretary of the Youth League branch—again, at a dance party. "She was very pretty," he began. Then, overcome by emotion, he fell silent. Finally, he continued, "You can tell that I also was *zhangde hen duanzheng* (长得很端正, good looking)." I could see a glint in his eyes that conveyed deep *yihan* (遗憾, feeling of irreversible loss). "One day after a dance party, we ended up naked in bed together and embraced each other. We kissed each other. I felt an erection, but she did not allow me to get into her body." Later, she rejected him, citing her family's opposition to her marrying a man with political problems. Ironically, the ethos of "free love" to which Mr. Wei was attracted did not apply to him. He had moved away from an arranged marriage only to find himself in a state of "arranged unmarriage."

As the whole country spiraled downward in class struggle in the 1960s, life for Mr. Wei became difficult again. He tried to flee the country early in the Cultural Revolution but was captured. He was sentenced to life imprisonment and jailed in his home province. He said he had felt sexual desire while in jail, but obviously he could do nothing about it except masturbate.

"What did you think about your life all those years in prison?" I asked.

He answered with a sigh, "I did not have much fun in all my life." He continued, "Well, in prison I was very attentive to any news outside and wanted to get out of the jail. I was very concerned about national politics. I listened to the *da guangbo* (loudspeaker) for news very attentively. I was very sure that China would change." As he said this, his eyes flashed again.

As the reform began in 1979, Mr. Wei's political life changed again. He was released after spending more than ten years in prison, his conviction for antirevolutionary and rightist activity was reversed, and he was eligible to go back to Beijing to live. He returned to his work unit, was allocated an apartment, and treated as a cadre with seniority until he retired.

Mr. Wei wanted to get married again, to a woman of his own choosing. He still thought about the secretary of the Youth League he had gotten to know more than a decade and a half earlier. "She had already married," he recalled, "She had two children. I ran into her soon after I came back to Beijing." His voice was full of a sense of loss.

Not long after his return to Beijing, a neighbor acting as a go-between introduced him to a woman he liked, and they married. This marriage, however, did not last long. Mr. Wei said he soon found out that the woman was mentally ill, and they divorced.

Undaunted, Mr. Wei did not give up his search for a good wife. In the 1980s, he tried an approach that was new, both to him and to socialist society in general: he ran an advertisement in a newspaper seeking a spouse. His ad was quickly answered by a woman who came from another city. They had sex immediately after meeting and soon married. She was five or six years younger than he and divorced. She told him that her ex-husband was more virile than he was, but neither she nor Mr. Wei felt it was a big issue. Nonetheless, her comment was a sign that Mr. Wei was starting to experience sexual dysfunction.

Their seemingly durable marriage turned sour because of the shadows cast by their previous marriages. Mr. Wei wanted to bring his granddaughter (his daughter's daughter from the arranged marriage) to Beijing to live with him, and his wife wanted him to do the same for her daughter from her previous marriage. They could not agree on the living arrangements and got divorced.

At the time of his third divorce, Mr. Wei was sixty years old. He decided, at that point, to give up on marriage, but he did not give up on sexual pleasure. He was introduced to a woman in Beijing who was also in her sixties, and good feelings developed between them. They went out to dinner together and had pictures taken together. She stayed with him at his place from time to time. One of the concerns that prevented him from marrying her had to do with his ownership of property—a subsidized apartment he had purchased from his work unit. Recalling his arguments with his third wife over the use of the apartment, he was afraid of disputes over ownership of the unit if yet another marriage did not work out. His sex life with his girlfriend was not as good as he had hoped for either. He said, "We had sex occasionally. I either could get in but ejaculate too fast or I could get an erection but lost it as soon as I got on top of her." This time, the obstacle to the gratification he was seeking was his own body. He tuned in to *Whispering Tonight*, a popular sex-education talk show on Beijing's People Radio (Zhang 2013), and he consulted Dr. Ma, a frequent guest on the show, for medical help.

Mr. Wei's life story unfolded along three parallel trajectories: marriage, desire, and potency. All three were heavily affected by the political and economic history of the nation.

Mr. Wei had experienced all of the major legal types of marriage that contemporary Chinese societies could offer, from an arranged marriage to a one achieved with the help of a go-between and one resulting from a newspaper advertisement. All three marriages ended in divorce. Mr. Wei ended up in a relationship of *tongju* (cohabitation) that was not headed toward marriage—he and his girlfriend had "jiebanr bu jiehun" (结伴儿不结婚, become intimate companions but not married), in his words, an uncommon arrangement among those of his generation. All of the major changes in his marital history were related to changes in Chinese political climate. Like a small boat, he rose and sank with the ferocious currents of a tumultuous political ocean.

Mr. Wei's marital history began in the most traditional way and gradually became more modern. His status had changed repeatedly throughout his adult life: from a peasant in the 1940s to a cadre and city resident in the 1950s, a rightist in the late 1950s and early 1960s, a criminal and then a prisoner serving a life sentence in the late 1960s and most of the 1970s, a vindicated citizen and cadre again in the late 1970s, and, finally, a retiree and property owner (however small) residing in Beijing in the late 1990s.

Being assertive, he was potent in the full sense of the term. He did not have erectile difficulties until his third marriage in the 1980s. He recalled that he had had nocturnal emissions in his twenties and had taken Liuwei Dihuang Wuan (六味地黄丸), a patent herbal pill that aims to reduce such emission by strengthening the kidneys. Many older men recalled taking the same type of pill in the Maoist period, an indication of how common nocturnal emission was at that time. In contrast, impotence has become the symptom of the new era (see chapter 1) and it can be alleviated with Viagra. Viagra, however, did not work well for Mr. Wei. He also did not want to masturbate. After a long pause, he explained to me, "I am satisfied, and she is satisfied with the relationship. I mean not to walk that tract anymore (我现在不走那一经了)."

His desire repeatedly ran up against obstacles in his lifeworld. In my three interviews with him, he referred to his second lover only as "the female secretary of the Youth League." His use of her political title indicated a strong longing to be her equal in political status, to have a proper political identity in the Maoist period. In the commercialized 1990s and 2000s, Mr. Wei's concern focused on the potential for property disputes to arise in the event of another failed marriage. In Deleuzian terms, this change shows that desiring production in consumer society resulted not just in "deterritorialization"—a process of loosening restriction on desire (sex without marriage), but also in "reterritorialization"—a process of restricting desire (his long desire for marital intimacy was constrained by the concern about private property).[16] Facing endless constraints, how would he come to terms with his desire?

A GLIMPSE OF AN EXISTENTIAL LIGHT IN POTENCY

Mr. Wei's pursuit of desire went against ancient Chinese understandings of potency. According to the *Inner Canon*, inborn potency evolves and develops to its fullest as one grows up. To help me visualize the evolution of potency, a doctor of Chinese medicine used a "finger chart." He raised his right hand, the five upstretched fingers representing the rise and fall of potency: the thumb represents a man's potency at the age of ten, the index finger at twenty, the middle finger at thirty, the ring finger at forty, and the little finger at fifty. The middle finger represents the peak of one's potency. After the age of thirty, potency declines.[17]

My fieldwork shows that some men's lives today played out according to this model. But many more did not. A survey I conducted shows that 43 percent of male patients in Beijing considered impotence an illness of old age in general, and 22.6 percent considered it an illness until age seventy. Twenty-five percent of male patients in Chengdu considered it an illness of old age, and 33.9 percent considered it an illness until age seventy.

On the one hand, in accord with Laozi's view that pure potency might not involve desire, Mr. Wei's persistent desiring might seem to confirm the negative impact of desire on potency. On the other hand, the more frustrated Mr. Wei was, the more determined he became to pursue satisfying desire. Desire had become, for him, an integral part of potency. This is where both Laozi's view and the Heideggerian notion of potency might need new input.

Mr. Wei himself did not deny his inability to achieve an erection. However, when he said, "I am satisfied, and she is satisfied with the relationship. I mean not to walk that tract anymore," he looked content. He implied that he was gaining sexual pleasure in an alternative, "deterritorialized" way,[18] as discussed in chapter 4. He continued to open himself up, not despite, but because of, his unsettled desire.

Thus, Mr. Wei's life trajectory redefines potency: *impotence* is a much narrower term than implied in its use as an antonym for *potency*. Suffering from impotence does not take away one's potency, because it does not impede deterritorialized desiring. Potency is life's fullness, the capacity to open oneself to the world.

"If *Shen* (the Kidney)

Is Strong, Life Is Good"

One spring day in the early 2000s, I was riding in a car with two friends in my hometown of Chongqing, which served as a stopover for me as I traveled between Beijing and Chengdu, my two field sites. The three of us had met to catch up. Instead of heading downtown, we were on our way out of town to a big Daoist temple, reached by driving along the zigzag mountain road on the south bank of the Yangzi River. Sitting in the front passenger seat, I spotted an advertisement on the bus ahead of us for Huiren Shenbao (converging benevolence for kidney treasure, an herbal patent pill). It read, "If *shen* (the kidney) is strong, life is good." Popular belief still has it that a strong kidney means strong potency, in the life-enhancing sense I have discussed in this book.

The winding *yang* road ran alongside a *yingou* (*yin* ditch, i.e., drainage ditch), through a landscape of trees budding into green against the curving silhouette of the mountain, life awakening to the rhythm of the misty spring so typical of Chongqing. The message on the bus we were following resonated with the potency of the landscape, the natural intercourse between yin and yang, and the blurred distinction between *shengming* (being alive) and *shenghuo* (living a life). I grabbed my camera and took a photo of this visible manifestation of the cosmological order.

Over the years of the postsocialist reform, life for the Chinese people had changed a great deal. To take but one example: When the reform began in the late 1970s, food shortages had a far-reaching impact on perceptions of a good life. Political scientist Ding Xueliang recalled that when he was growing up in Xuancheng County, Anhui Province, during the Cultural Revolution, two children (brothers) had arrived in his community from Nanjing, their identities concealed until, one day, the younger brother bragged that

Figure C.1: A bus carrying a commercial for a zhuangyang patent fluid in Chongqing. The line on the side reads: "If the kidney is strong, life is good."

all visitors to their family back in Nanjing were *da pangzi* (big fat guys). Hearing this, other children inferred that the boys' father must be a very high ranking official (indeed, he was in command of the People's Liberation Army's Nanjing garrison), because in Xuancheng, with a population of several hundred thousand, only a handful of people, including the party secretary and the county chief, were pangzi (Wang 2011). At that time, being fat meant having better access to food and other resources. Decades later, eating too much fatty food and sugar is blamed for cardiovascular diseases or diabetes, both associated with impotence.

This contrast offers a glimpse into the huge changes that have taken place over the last several decades. However, at the time when I began my field-work in the late 1990s, the enormity of these changes was just beginning to be felt in the public sphere and in people's everyday lives. One way in which they were manifested was in the impotence epidemic.

In the first two chapters of this book, I laid out the case that the impotence epidemic was a positive event that signaled the rise of desire. This discovery came as a surprise to me. The impotence epidemic was intricately related to the reemergence of "love" in public discourse shortly after the Cultural Revolution (chapter 2) and to the rise of carnal desire in China's sexual revolution (Pan 2006; Zhang 2013). Through this epidemic, we can trace the change in public perceptions of sexual desire, from negative to positive, as impotence ceased to be a moral failing, reflecting the selfishness of indulging sexual desire, and became, instead, an ethical inadequacy, emblematic of the inability to enjoy sexual pleasure. The epidemic produced an increase in impotence patient visits to hospitals and contributed to the production of the subject of desire.

When I tackled the issue of why impotence was so invisible before the epidemic, I was surprised to find that many historical aspects of Maoism, including its reputed sexual repressiveness, were not fully understood. That the *danwei* (work unit) and *hukou* (household registration) systems were found to have contributed to sexual repression points to the need to better understand the implications of Maoist sociopolitical structures for people's intimate lives. The discovery that the Maoist political class system was a biopolitical invention also points to the significance of such research. I am convinced that in-depth examination of several decades of Maoist socialism, particularly the Cultural Revolution period, is critical for understanding the major social transformations that have taken place since the reform began.

Another surprise was the discovery that some heterosexual couples were coping with impotence by exploring alternative sexual intercorporeality, satisfying desire in ways other than through penile–vaginal intercourse. They gained sexual satisfaction through what could be called "lesbian eroticism," a genuine reinvention of desiring production.

Those surprises also called attention to complexities and contradictions. One complexity was the coincidence of two trends—the loss of *jing* (seminal essence) and the revival of *yangsheng* (cultivation of life)—competing but intertwined visions of life. Elaborating on Georges Bataille's insight, Andrew Kipnis (2011) points out that overemphasis on one type of desire may result in a hierarchy that dangerously compromises other human virtues. In China, sexual desire has been promoted, but yangsheng represents the ethical limits to the production of desire.

A related complexity involved patients who switched between taking Viagra and taking herbal medicine, pursuing sexual pleasure as well as nurturing life. In these patients, the two competing visions of life entered into negotiation, through the small action of switching, not from one thing to another but between one thing and another. By dispensing with an either/ or mindset and embracing a both/and approach, people were shaped into cosmopolitan subjectivity.

If the first part of this book—the story of the birth of *nanke*, the lifting of sexual repression, changing family relationships, and women's desire—relates how sexuality was shaped by the state, society, and family, then the second part—the story of preserving and losing seminal essence, Viagra, switching between two medicines, and potency as life's fullness—focuses on how concerns about potency revealed a way to live an ethical life.

Instead of being only a neurovascular event, impotence is revealed as a social event, a gendered, intercorporeal event, a cultural event, and, ultimately, "a life event." "Impotence" is not precisely the counterpart of "potency," in that potency encompasses much more than sexual functionality: it is a measure of the fullness of life in its ceaseless rejuvenation. The ad on the bus—"If shen is strong, life is good"—is telling.

What does the seemingly improbable issue of impotence reveal about the larger picture of contemporary Chinese life? When I was staying in Beijing during an extended field trip in 1999, China was about to enter the World Trade Organization. Excited anticipation mixed with anxious uncertainty on the eve of the new millennium. As I revise this book more than a decade later, China has become the second-largest economy in the world. In pondering the extensiveness and rapidity of its transformation, I cannot help but recall getting lost during a visit to Chongqing one morning in June 2004.

I had traveled to Chongqing by express bus from Chengdu, some two hundred miles to the southeast. The same trip had taken ten to twelve hours by a winding railway back in my college days in the 1980s. On that June morning, it took me less than four hours to get to Chongqing. (In 2009, it took about two hours by the new train line. A line currently under construction will reduce the time to one hour.) Upon arrival, I got into a taxi and told the driver to take me to the Chongqing People's Hall, a famous landmark (my destination was next to the hall). Much to my surprise, as the taxi approached the hall, it descended underground into a tunnel. Apparently, something dramatic had happened to the city's landscape since my last visit, only a couple of years earlier. As soon as the taxi emerged from the tunnel and back to street level, I found that we had completely passed by the hall. I asked the driver whether he could find a way to turn back so that I could get off where I wanted to. He looked at me with a mixture of surprise and sympathy and said, "We can no longer turn back here."

Disoriented, I got out of the taxi to find myself in a large public square. The road I recalled from my last visit, flanked by a city government building on one side and the front gate of the People's Hall on the other side, had disappeared. In place of the government building was a gigantic new structure—the Three Gorges Dam Museum of Chongqing. This museum is dedicated to the history of the construction of the dam on the Yangzi River, some three hundred miles east of the city. The road that had gone by the government building had been rerouted into the underground tunnel my taxi had just taken me through. The square on which the museum fronts is a public place of *xiaoxian* (消閒, whiling away the time) and *jianshen* (健身, strengthening the body), where people gather, usually in the evening, to practice *taiji*, jianshen dances, and so on. A sense of vertigo seized me in the midst of the change in my own hometown. I heard it said that Chongqing changed its city map every three months and that such frequent updating was common throughout China.

The sensation of vertigo has become familiar to me in China. Constantly reorienting oneself to a new physical as well as social landscape has become an integral part of doing ethnography there. How is one to claim ethnographic authority on China when faced with repeated "we-can-no-longer-turn-back" shocks?

Perhaps never before have anthropologists been so pressured to seek a durable picture amid such constant change. Durability has become one of the greatest seductions, as well as an increasingly rare quality, of ethnography in today's China. I realized that all an anthropologist can do is seize a moment in the flow of vital forces—in which the past, present, and future are not clearly distinguishable. I seized my moment by engaging with the unfinished issue of modernity for the Chinese.

My understanding of this moment developed through a series of self-examinations about the nature of my ethnographic encounters. My first moment of self-examination grew out of the question, "Why do you study impotence?" a question often put to me. In answering it, I found myself particularly inspired by Michel Foucault's intellectual exploration of modernity. In reference to his work on madness, which seems to have touched on a taboo, Foucault stated, "The book constituted a transformation in the historical, theoretical, and moral or ethical relationship we have with madness, the mentally ill, the psychiatric institution, and the very truth of psychiatric discourse. So it is a book that functions as an experience, for its writer and reader alike, much more than as the establishment of a historical truth" (2000:243).

Foucault's goal, then, was to make certain experiences accessible rather than to establish historical truths. This is not to say that he did not care about truth but that he was more interested in changing his reader's perspective toward true or historically verifiable findings. Through his work, he makes it possible for readers to create new experiences of their own. Many excellent ethnographies share the same capacity for changing our perspectives. That has been my goal with this book. I wish to contribute to a transformation in the historical, theoretical, and moral or ethical relationship we have with impotence and its ramifications. I have shown that impotence as a realm of experience is not just about erectile failures but also about a wide range of experience—social restratification, sexual desire, family obligations, gender relations, one's ethical orientations, and, ultimately, life itself. Only a small portion of the population in any society is directly affected by impotence, but the experiences this book can help create go beyond impotence and can be shared by many.

Foucault claimed, "I haven't written a single book that was not inspired, at least in part, by a direct personal experience. I've had a complex personal relationship with madness and with the psychiatric institution." He also emphasized, "It is not at all a matter of transporting personal experience into knowledge . . . this experience must be capable of being linked in some measure to a collective practice, to a way of thinking" (Foucault 2000:244). I do not know what "complex personal relationship" Foucault had with madness and with the psychiatric institution, but that is immaterial to the transformative opportunity he offered his readers, an experience that is linked both to a collective practice and to a way of thinking.

My second moment of self-examination involved my realization that, in studying the somewhat taboo issue of impotence, one must be extremely careful, sympathetic, and willing to take chances. I sometimes detected mixed feelings among my colleagues when I revealed that I was studying impotence. Some expressed reservations about engaging the topic at all using an ethnographic approach, because it is "too private." In the field, I found that many who suffered from impotence could be very open and articulate about their experiences once they felt that someone was listening to them with sympathy and concern. Their experience of impotence was private in that they seldom revealed it to anyone except their closest friends or relatives. Many had not revealed it to anyone at all. I obtained the most unforgettable stories not in clinics but from contacts I made through friends, evidence that many were longing for understanding after having suppressed their suffering for long periods. Oftentimes, their stories about impotence were so closely tied to everyday transformations going on around them that they seemed to be explicitly teaching me about the relationship between body and society. In revealing their stories to me, they were publicizing their private feelings and desires. Many of the things they talked about (such as the sharp rural–urban divide and the cruelty of class struggle in the Maoist period and the increasing inequality in post-Mao China) had already become public knowledge. People talked to me about these issues, however, from the perspective of their own bodies; their nuanced bodily experiences shed new light on where Chinese society stands today and what really matters to people in the wake of so much change. Often, when I was struggling to decide whether to ask yet one more "personal" question about an individual's private life in bed, I was encouraged by that person's readiness to answer. And, in deciding what to write, I felt obligated, on the one hand, to protect my informants' privacy and, on the other hand, to evoke a collective experience and a way of thinking by presenting their stories.

Studying sexuality is always a challenge. But I was able to overcome the anxiety about invading people's privacy partly because my questions were not really about sex per se. As Foucault pithily but strategically stated, "Sex is boring" (1997:253). What really appealed to me in the stories of the people I studied was not sensational confessions about sex but the feelings they revealed toward various individuals, the difficulties people coped with, and their attitudes toward life. I hope this book can help us to better understand both Maoist socialism and its transformation. For me, understanding this transformation is both an academic and a personal issue.

My third moment of self-examination was occasioned by my dissatisfaction with this book, in that it has not made use of all the insightful stories I collected in the field and is very much incomplete. I imagine that, in reporting on their research, many anthropologists share this feeling of incompleteness. For me, a specific dimension of this sense has to do with my continuing thoughts concerning the fate of each person I talked to, as I wrote about that individual. I have been in touch with some, by phone or e-mail—more with doctors than with patients—since my last follow-up fieldwork. How they are doing now is always in my imagination. I understand that my personal concerns are only part of a larger concern about where China is heading. This concern often arouses strong feelings of ambivalence in me toward the fast pace of developments. Broadly speaking, this ambivalence is probably an essential theme of modernity that refuses any simple solution.

The issue of modernity has been constantly with the Chinese throughout the past century or so, particularly since the founding of the PRC. Entering the twenty-first century, the media have reported one landmark event after another in China's rise as a world power. It is becoming more and more difficult to analyze this transformation, given the huge pain as well as great joy it has engendered, given increasing grievances among the population (caused by corruption, inequality, environmental destruction, etc.), given the country's more and more intricate entanglement with the global economy and politics. Strong potency, and, therefore, a good life, had long been valued by the time of the Yellow Emperor, but never has it been under such pressure for renewal as in the contemporary moment. According to Foucault, modernity is an attitude. While heroically coping with the problems of the present through patient work, it is important to be alert to claims that would promise "escape from the system of contemporary reality so as to produce . . . another vision of the world" but that would lead "only to the return of the most dangerous traditions" (Foucault 1997: 316). Foucault noted, "You have no right to despise the present," a sentiment I endorse. At the same time, I maintain a critical attitude toward the present as it is constantly re-created.

Introduction

1 Bicycle riding can cause vascular constriction in the penis (e.g., because of sudden squeezing or pressing due to an accident), leading to a decline in blood flow, a primary mechanism of erectile dysfunction (Jeong et al. 2002; Blakeslee 2005).

2 See, for example, Adams and Savran 2002, Whitehead and Barrett 2002, Cohen 2000, Gardiner 2002, and Connell 2005.

3 Leonore Tiefer (2006) discusses in detail the multiple forces leading to this biological shift.

4 *Experience* can be translated into Chinese as both *jingyan* (經驗) and *tiyan* (體驗). *Jingyan* has a connotation very similar to one of the definitions of *experience* given by *Webster's Ninth New Collegiate Dictionary*: "practical knowledge, skill, or practice derived from direct observation of or participation in events or in a particular activity." *Tiyan*, by contrast, comes close to matching another definition of the English term *experience*: "something personally encountered, undergone, or lived through."

5 In classical Chinese *shen* (身) and *ti* (體) were more often used separately. The phrase *shenti* was used in the pre-Qin period (before 221 B.C.E.)—for example, in *Xiaojing* (*The Book of Piety*; Wang 2004) and *Huangdi Neijing* (*Inner Canon*; Anonymous 2000)—appearing to denote the limbs and the whole trunk, including the head. It is not clear why *shen* and *ti* were not combined into a single term more frequently until the twentieth century.

6 The responses of some male college students diverged from those of patients. Of students in Beijing, 52.8 percent would choose to live a shorter life without suffering from impotence (consistent with the trend in patients), while 55.8 percent of students in Chengdu would choose to live longer, even suffering from impotence (against the trend in patients). I asked female college students which option they would choose for their *nanfang* (male partner or male spouse). In Beijing, 79.2 percent of female students said they would prefer their men to live

longer, even if impotent, and, in Chengdu, 78.9 percent chose this option. It seems that the actual experience of impotence tilted the response toward giving priority to sexual potency over life span.

7 Studies have produced contradictory results on the relationship between socio-economic status and impotence. For example, some have found that monthly income is negatively associated with impotence (e.g., Cheng et al. 2007; Choi 2003), while others have found no relationship (e.g., Shiri 2004).

8 In developed democracies, there has been a tendency in the media to portray male potency as a component of elderly life, correlated with the power older men manage to gain through their higher rates of political participation compared with other age groups. I thank Martin Collcutt for drawing this point to my attention. In this context, it is no wonder that the most comprehensive and largest population-based epidemiological study of impotence was originally part of a study on aging (Massachusetts Male Aging Study, conducted in the late 1980s and early 1990s). The incidence of impotence goes up as age increases, according to this study. For example, men between the ages of 60 and 69 were reported to be four times more likely to experience moderate or complete ED than 40- to 49-year-olds (McKinlay 2000). This discovery was interpreted as abnormal and "alarming" and boosted studies of impotence and the development of anti-impotence technologies, including drugs like Viagra. Such sexualization of elderly life was criticized by some as one of the detrimental effects of biomedicalization of sexuality (Tiefer 2006; Potts et al. 2003). In post-Mao China, however, the rejuvenation of sexual desire among the elderly as well as transformations in women's attitudes toward sexual life can be seen as having potentially positive implications.

9 Deleuze and Guattari raised the notion of "desiring production" in the early 1970s in the aftermath of the radical social activist years of the 1960s. They re-examined capitalism, including its historically revolutionary momentum and its inevitable limitations (note the subtitles of the two volumes of the work— *Capitalism and Schizophrenia*). They did so through critiquing the popular approaches of Marxism combined with psychoanalysis and through focusing on the social conditions in which the capitalist machine operates. Marxism did little to analyze "desire," whereas psychoanalysis was seriously limited by their negative view confined in the Oedipus complex. See Dosse (2010) for the historical background of Deleuze and Guattari's thoughts. They came up with their schizo-analytics that enriches, not abandons, Marxism. Therefore, the notion of "desiring production" is abundantly relevant to examining the production of desire in the aftermath of Maoist socialist years amid the rise of capitalist elements in post-Mao China.

10 Numerous works have addressed this trend. See Yan 2010, Hansen and Svarverud 2010, and Kleinman et al. 2011.

11 See Yang 1999.

12 A large number of studies document this privileging of men over women (Hers-

hatter 2006; Yang 1999; Zheng 2009; Zhang 2001, 2011c; Xiao 2011; Otis 2011; Osburg 2013, etc.).

13 None of the examples I have cited led to the conclusion that men had significantly declined in power or privilege. For example, the question of why male athletes could not do as well as female athletes led more to self-congratulation of China's achievement in women's development than to criticism of men's incompetence, particularly in the 2000s. The debate about whether Shanghai men were suffering a decline in masculinity was triggered by the misreading of a Taiwanese female writer's praise of the local, "soft" norm of masculinity (e.g., men doing household chores, being "obedient" to wives, etc.). The call for "men's liberation" put more emphasis on the need to change traditional precepts that curtailed men's emotional expression and their "right" to be impotent than on the need to maintain any rigid masculine norms. Ethnographies demonstrate that women's advancement in social status also did not engender masculine crisis (e.g., Yan 2003).

14 At first glance, the masculine figures portrayed by Sylvester Stallone and Ken Takakura did threaten to undermine the primacy or superiority in the long-established literary tradition of a *wen* (cultural attainment) orientation over a *wu* (martial valor) orientation in Chinese masculinity (Louie 2002). However, the primacy and superiority of wen over wu—seen in the tradition of *yi jing zhi dong* (conquer the force in motion with the force in stillness) or in *yin zhong jian yang* (yang embedded in yin)—did not represent any major compromise in men's privileging over women. What is encouraging is that the countercurrents against "entrepreneurial masculinity" were also rising. For example, in addition to defense of "Shanghai men," approval of *zhujia nanren* (the man who stays home to take care of the child while his wife takes over his job as the head of a small company) was trumpeted loudly in public space. "Zhujia nanren" was the title of an episode of a popular CCTV talk show *Shi hua shi shuo* (*Straight Talk*), hosted by Cui Yongyuan in early 2000. The episode was also called "Xin hao nanren" (The New, Good Men). See also Louie 2012 on the emergence of more gendered neutral masculinity. Aside from creating confusion, the talk about masculine crises served political purposes, concealing real issues facing society. If, in the Maoist period, the emphasis on political classes drowned out the voices of gender differences (Riley 1997), in the 1990s and 2000s, the noise about masculine crisis could conceal the issue of class. For example, talk of a masculine crisis targeting *xiagang* workers (stepping-down workers, i.e., laid-off workers) could serve to distract attention from the emergence of an underclass out of the "leaders' class" of the Maoist period (Yang 2010). Discourse privileging men's suffering over women's suffering obscured the fact that female workers were often laid off before male workers.

15 The *Shishang Xiansheng Ban* article mentioned above, which is devoid of empirical data, confuses men's lack of desire for their wives with their inability to get an erection and advocates only a thorough examination of the sexual lives of men

seeking medication for impotence. In one case cited by the article, a woman filed for divorce because of "inharmonious sexual life." The thirty-five-year-old husband said that he was too busy to satisfy his wife. In another case, a thirty-one-year-old manager was afraid to go home because of the burden of *jiao gongliang* (delivering tax grain, i.e., fulfilling the obligation to have sex with his wife). A number of feminist studies of Western contexts several decades after the sexual revolution tended to focus on how the male-centered, phallocentric view of impotence jeopardizes women's enjoyment of a broader range of intimate behaviors than just penile–vaginal intercourse (Tiefer 1986, 1994, 2006; Riley 2002; McCabe et al. 2010; Potts et al. 2003). Those studies did not address, however, whether women's demands for more sex could result in male impotence.

16 A line of flight is a primary move of deterritorialization and is a compromise between two other types of lines—lines of molar or rigid segmentarity and lines of molecular or supple segmentation (Deleuze and Guattari 1987: 202–7). I was also very much influenced in my approach by the idea of the "pervasiveness" of ethnographic moves, as exemplified in Lawrence Cohen's *No Aging in India* (1998).

17 The anthropology of China has produced excellent ethnographies that benefited from studying cohorts. See Rofel 1999 and Jing 1996 for examples.

18 Anthropological studies of the body have generated many discussions of embodiment (Csordas 1990, 1994; Scheper-Hughes and Lock 1987; Desjarlais 1992, 1997; Jackson 1996; Good 1994; Stoller 1995), a concept that continues to be a cornerstone of the discipline's phenomenological approach to the body (Mascia-Lees 2011). Preobjective and prelinguistic perception best exemplifies embodiment. Another important development over the past few decades is the focus on how the body is constructed by forces, whether social, ritualistic, discursive, or material, that can be corporealized (e.g., Fassin 2007; Martin 2001; Lock 1995). I draw on Robert Desjarlais and C. Jason Throop's definition of "embodiment [as] the bodily aspects of human beings and subjectivity" (2011:89). Thomas Csordas (1993) offers a more concrete heuristic way to understand embodiment: the process by which one's perception becomes sensorily engaged with (develops somatic attention to) the world, which largely consists of one's own and others' bodies.

19 I concur with Csordas's (2011) succinct presentation of Pierre Bourdieu's view of the relationship between the body and the world as one of opposing orientation, forming what Bourdieu calls "habitus," as distinct from Maurice Merleau-Ponty's "being toward the world" and Michel Foucault's power inscription on the body. To illuminate the two directions of the body, Matthew Kohrman's (2005) dual foci—"disability" and "disablement"—in his ethnography of disabled persons in China are helpful, the former referring to perception and the latter referring to the forces that affect how disability is defined and governed.

20 In Beijing, 67.7 percent of patients preferred ED to *yangwei* and, in Chengdu, 62.3 percent preferred ED.

Chapter 1: The Birth of *Nanke*

1 I selected hospitals from *A Handbook for Beijingers*, published in 2000. It lists
  five types of hospitals. I called every hospital in the categories "Large Comprehensive Hospitals of Beijing" and "Hospitals of Chinese Medicine" (a total of
  forty-three), and I selected twenty-six hospitals from the categories "Hospitals
  of Districts of Beijing," "Hospitals of the People's Liberation Army," and "Hospitals of Ministries and Large State-Owned Enterprises."

2 For a discussion of the development of fuke in the Song and Ming periods, see
  Furth 1999. Jender Lee 2008 and Yi-Li Wu 2010 also trace the history of fuke.

3 Why the practices associated with treating impotence and other male problems
  had not been institutionalized in a recognized specialty in the long history of
  Chinese medicine is not clear. The term *nanke* first appeared in the seventeenth-
  century Ming period in Yue Fujia's *Nanke zhenzhi quanbian* (*A Complete Compilation of Nanke's Diagnoses and Treatment*) and *Fu Qingzhu nanke* (*Works of Fu Shan
  on Men's Medicine*). While the former was not handed down to latter generations,
  the latter uses the term *nanke* to refer to a group of *neike zazheng* (内科雜症, internal miscellaneous diseases), not necessarily the conditions nanke treats today
  (Fu 1993). Yue Fujia's *Miaoyizhai yixue zheng yin zhongzi bian* also refers to nanke
  in discussing how to produce descendants. Like earlier texts, later medical works
  do not codify treatments for male sexual dysfunction. Reviewing over a thousand volumes, Qin Guozheng (1999b) found 131 books of traditional Chinese
  medicine from ancient, medieval, and late imperial times that discuss causes of
  and treatment for yangwei in a clinical sense. Some of the collections of nanke
  cases that have been published in post-Mao times include examples dating back
  to earlier periods (e.g., Gao 1994; Zhang 1990). Classic works on Chinese sexuality also discuss the long Chinese tradition of enhancing male sexual potency
  (e.g., van Gulik 2003). Many nanke treatments for impotence today are "a modern rearrangement of the historical tradition" (Furth 1999:92), particularly the
  tradition of the cultivation of life. But the institutionalization of treatment for
  men's sexual problems into nanke in post-Mao China was a novel phenomenon.

4 The term *spermatorrhea* was coined by François Lallemand in the early nineteenth century (Shapiro 1998:586). The Chinese term *yijing* (遺精) emerged
  no later than the Song period (C.E. 960–1279; see Wang 1980). Earlier, *shijing*
  (失精) had been the term for this bodily phenomenon, seen, for example, in the
  text *Jingui yaolue* dating to the Han period (206 B.C.E.–220 C.E.; see Zhang
  1997). *Spermatorrhea* is not an accurate English translation of *yijing*, so I retain
  the Chinese term in my discussion.

5 Historically, *fenke* (分科, the division or classification of medicine into subdisci-
  plines) has been a rather complex issue. Analyzing the official divisions of medical practice in the Song period, Chang Che-chia (2000) argues that the emergence of new divisions depended on many factors and that the change in the

structure of institutionalized medicine under the state did not necessarily reflect the needs of society.

6 For an analysis of the complex effects of medicalization, see Lock and Nguyen 2010.

7 Wan Quan, a medical scholar in the Ming period, enumerates a set of "five un-maleness" that includes some different terms (*Guangsi jiyao*, vol. 3).

8 *Mengzi, Lilou A*. See Li 1992:172.

9 This was true in many other places in the world as well. For example, in documenting the infamous "impotence trials" presided over by church authorities in prerevolutionary France, Pierre Darmon wrote, "The Church forbade all sexual activity undertaken in a spirit of pleasure for its own sake. The hope or ulterior motive of conception had always to be present during the conjugal act, according to St. Augustine" (1986:57). For discussion concerning the centrality of reproduction in sexuality in Christianity, see Brown 1988 and McLaren 2007.

10 The Maoist state did make efforts to carry out family planning, but those attempts had nowhere near the forcefulness and intensity of measures associated with post-Mao birth policy (Greenhalgh and Winckler 2005; Greenhalgh 2008).

11 This count does not include those who were not married or who were married but did not express the desire to have a child soon or even at all.

12 One case published in *Jiangxi TCM* described a thirty-year-old patient who had been impotent for ten years. He had gotten a divorce because he was not able to get an erection and impregnate his wife. According to the author of this case study, after being treated by a doctor in Gannan People's Hospital for three months, the man's "qi of yang recovered. He found a woman and got married. The couple was happy. In less than a year they had a son. Their relatives and friends were all full of joy about the birth of the baby. I also visited them to celebrate" (Yang 1963:27).

13 Again, I use *yijing* instead of its English translation partly because "defining yijing as spermotorrhea is an approximation, for yijing is generally understood as semen loss without orgasm" (Shapiro 1998:586).

14 Advertisements for drugs to correct yijing were prominent during that period (Huang 1988; Shapiro 1998). Case studies and medical discussions concerning yijing were also common (Dai 1925; Shen 1926; Ma 1931; Qian 1931; Wang 1931; Zhang 1931; Zhou 1936; Zeng 1937). My reading of medical publications from the 1920s and 1930s confirmed significant attention to the disease. Particularly prominent was the concern about the serious consequences of yijing in the media. One author stated, "Yijing is a common disease among city youth and does great harm to education and careers of the sufferers. In a large sense, it jeopardizes the future of the nation and the country's lifelines" (Zeng 1937: 42). In one issue of a medical magazine, one advertisement for "The kidney defending and jing consolidating pill" lures the readers by stating: "Neurasthenia is evidence of the weak body and the deficient kidney; losing jing in dream and dripping jing are a huge disease that endangers the entire life!"

15 This *chengyu* (成語, idiom) was a variation on the saying "Tanhu sebian" (談虎色變, talk of the tiger causes the color of the face to change and frightens people). The phrase first appears in writings dating to the Song period. See, for example, *ErChengji* (Cheng and Cheng 2004), a collection of the works of philosophers Cheng Yi and Cheng Hao, and *ErCheng yulu*, a collection of quotations of Cheng Yi and Cheng Hao, compiled by Zhu Xi (1995).

16 Journals of TCM in the 1950s and early 1960s did occasionally publish case studies of impotence. Those articles revealed no systematic effort to manage it, as is the case now. Some of the doctors involved in those cases acted like indigenous folk doctors, offering *mifang* (秘方, secret recipes) to patients. See, for example, Li 1955 and Tian 1960.

17 Doctors of Chinese medicine made a distinction between *youmeng yijing* (nocturnal emission in erotic dreams) and *wumeng yijing* (nocturnal emission in the absence of erotic dreams). The former was considered a problem of *xin* (the heart) and the latter a problem of shen (the kidney). One of the earliest discussions of the etiology of spermatorrhea is found in *Mingyi zazhu*, written by Wang Lun in 1502, during the Ming period. It identified three etiological locations of spermatorrhea: shen (kidney), xin (heart), and spleen (*pi*; see Wang 2007).

18 A middle-aged man from Xinjiang told me a similar story of self-castration that occurred in that region in the mid-1970s. One day, a branch of Jianshe Bingtuan (the Construction Corps) was holding a mass rally to repudiate a young man who had been caught in adultery. The young man managed to break the ropes binding his arms and run away from the rally. Several *minbing* (soldiers of a quasi-military organization, or militia) ran after him and tried to catch him. They aimed their guns at him and were about to shoot, when he evaded them by running into an outdoor restroom. When the soldiers followed him into the restroom, they saw the man lying on the ground in a pool of blood. He had cut his penis off. The man who told this story did not witness this scene himself but only repeated what he had heard.

19 For an example of other interpretations of "the real," see Žižek 2010.

20 *De-moralization* is different from *demoralization*. The former refers to downplaying the moral nature of an event or a thing or neutralizing it, whereas the latter refers to corrupting moral principles or destroying the will to bear up against dangers or difficulties.

21 Though an unintended consequence, China's one-child policy has contributed to the rise of sexual desire (Pan 1995; Zhang 2011c).

Chapter 2: Sexual Repression in China

1 The Maoist state did orchestrate major flows of people and labor, such as the migration of rural labor into cities in 1958 for the Great Leap Forward, the relocation of state-owned factories to third-line construction bases in the mid-1960s,

and the rustication movement that sent seventeen million youths to rural areas in the late 1960s and early 1970s to solve the problem of urban unemployment. These relocations were under complete control of the state and allowed the individual little flexibility. The 1958 migration ended up being reversed—laborers were sent back to rural areas after the Great Leap Forward went bust. The *dachuanlian* (the great movement of free travels in the second half of 1966) gave travelers some flexibility. But dachuanlian did not last long—only three to four months out of the ten-year span of the Cultural Revolution.

2 On danwei ren, see Li 2008.

3 *Sexual repression* is translated into Chinese as *xing yayi* (性壓抑). The idea of sexual repression was expressed in the Republican period, through a variety of terms, among them, *xing de jiefang* (sexual liberation; see Zhang 1992). Zhang Jingsheng (1998, vol. 1:204) wrote of *yayi* (壓抑), arguing in 1925 that understanding the sexual impulse was preferable to repressing it. In 1935, Pan Guangdan (1999, vol. 1:107) referred to suppressing the sexual impulse as "yizhi" (抑制). I thank Keith McMahon, Pan Suiming, and Martin Heijdra for discussing this issue with me.

4 The official announcement of their probation emphasized their violation of mandatory attendance at self-study sessions (*wanzixi*) and their rejection of criticism from the leaders of the party branch.

5 Their punishment can be viewed as a "repression of romantic love" or a "repression of 'sex love,'" in Friedrich Engels's (1978:746, 751) terms. Because dating is part of the practice of sexuality, however, I consider the couple's punishment a form of sexual repression.

6 The first view is that repression is a way not only to prevent sexual interest from creating a world outside the control of the state but also to induce a hysteria that can be channeled into war fever and leader worship. The second view is that repression sublimates libido to strengthen group ties while displacing sexual feelings outside the group. The third view simply places sexual repression at the root of authoritarianism and violence. Wilhelm Reich is a proponent of the third view. He argues that "man's authoritarian structure . . . is basically produced by the embedding of sexual inhibitions and fear in the living substance of sexual impulses" (Reich 1970:30). In turn, sexual repression "changes the structure of economically suppressed man in such a way that he acts, feels, and thinks contrary to his own material interests" (Reich 1970:32). In other words, sexual repression creates the man who desires fascism.

7 In criticizing the repressive hypothesis in relation to contradictory sexual phenomena in Victorian-age Europe, Michel Foucault (1990a:49) does not deny the existence of sexual repression. He explains, "It is not a question of denying the existence of repression. It is one of showing that repression is always a part of a much more complex political strategy regarding sexuality. Things are not merely repressed . . . The way in which sexuality in the nineteenth century was both repressed but also put in light, underlined, analyzed through techniques

like psychology and psychiatry shows very well that it was not simply a question of repression" (Foucault 1997:126).

Foucault's critique of the repressive hypothesis emphasizes the role of knowledge and the mode of subjectification, two of the three dimensions of sexuality (regulation is the third) in his overall theory of it (Foucault 1990a, 1990b). In my view, what Foucault does not emphasize in his critique—regulations, or "the systems of power that regulate [sexual] practice" (1990b:4)—must be highlighted in any analysis of Chinese sexuality in the Maoist period. This emphasis does justice to Foucault's study of the history of sexuality and its limits.

8 Yet such ownership is a more complex notion than it appears at first glance. One's control over one's body is often taken for granted, but, in reality, one is not autonomous at all. Sulamith Potter (1987), for instance, reminds us that women may not own their bodies when it comes to the decision to reproduce. Ownership of the body itself embodies the tension between freedom and unfreedom. According to Alan Hyde, such "ownership" invokes the notion of the body as property. The body, as property constructed through law, may either naturalize others' domination of it, as Aristotle asserted, or reinforce one's freedom and autonomy, as John Locke argued (Hyde 1997).

A classical Marxist view tends to be critical of the thesis that ownership of one's body is evidence of freedom and individual autonomy, because capitalist relations of production legalize individual ownership of the body but leave the worker with no choice but to sell his body "freely" as the physical foundation of the process of capitalist production. This view presumes freer use of the body in a communist society, one based on collective ownership of the means of production, as a foundation for fully and comprehensively developed human nature.

Marx did not develop an explicit theory of or notion about the body, in my view, because the body is not as important a unit of analysis in capitalist relations of production as the notion of labor. A laborer is alienated under capitalism, which deprives him of his opportunity to fully develop his human nature (Marx 1844). Therefore, the notion of ownership of the body, to Marx, would be primarily about the ownership of the laborer in the concrete sense and the ownership of labor in the abstract sense (Marx 1867).

In critiquing the Marxist labor-centered analysis, Foucault emphasized bodily techniques that bring about the existence of labor under modernity. Considering the body entails a careful examination of the time and space out of which labor is produced (Foucault 2000:86). Disciplining further problematizes the body as one's own property.

9 Several decades after Lei Feng's death, information was discovered suggesting that he had had rather rich interpersonal relationships with females. Some reports identified a woman named Wang Peiling as his first girlfriend. Such reports were intended to humanize or "decollectivize" Lei Feng, a move consistent with the logic of consumer society in post-Mao China, to portray him as a man with as much mundane need of individual emotion and desire as anyone

else, therefore, making him more believable and lovable than the man in the official portrayal (Shi and Liu 2006). This reconstruction of Lei Feng satisfies both the nostalgia for Maoist socialism and the need to create a new model of manhood in the era of decollectivization and individualism.

10 See Lee (2006) and Larson (1998) for analyses of the change of the vocabulary defining romantic love in literary representation.

11 For Freud, *desire* is never far from a string of other terms such as *instinctual impulse*, *wish*, *drive*, and *instinct*. In the Lacanian notion of desire, sexual libido is already more than an instinctual impulse. It is a consequence of the constant semiotic recuperation of permanent lack—the impossibility of satisfying desire itself. Desire, which is different from either needs or demands, stands out as central to defining the Lacanian subject.

12 Deleuze defines the assemblage in terms of four characteristics—the state of things, kind of style, the creating of territories, and deterritorialization (Deleuze and Parnet 1996).

13 Deleuze and Guattari emphasize that what defines libido is the association of two modes of operation, mechanical and electrical, in a sequence with two poles, molar and molecular. This is, in my view, their way of extending Reich's efforts to overcome the divide between mechanism and vitalism, to avoid the simplistic view of libido as a purely instinctual impulse in the Freudian sense (Deleuze and Guattari 1983:291). Here, libido is neither only a mental event nor only a biological drive but something that "results from a highly developed, engineered setup rich in interaction" (Deleuze and Guattari 1987:215). Desire, therefore, always constructs an assemblage while itself being part of an assemblage. "Desire is established and constructs in an assemblage always putting several factors into play" (Deleuze and Parnet 1996).

Chapter 3: One Thousand Bodies of Impotence

1 City youths started to go down to the countryside in 1962. Large waves of zhiqing did so from 1968 until the late 1970s. Altogether, more than 17 million youths went to the countryside (Liu 2009).

2 I suspect that he had shaken hands with women, as was common among "revolutionary comrades" in the grand mobilization campaign (dachuanlian) in 1966 and 1967. What he alluded to here was probably the lack of any physical contact of a romantic nature.

3 Ironically, in this case, patriarchal dominance under socialism, however hidden, was manifested as having a negative impact on men. However, this should not obscure the privileging of men over women in many respects. For example, Judith Stacey points out how the practice of the *dingti*, an employment policy by which children inherited fathers' instead of mothers' jobs, "help[ed] to sustain a mode of patrilineal legacy in urban China" (1984:239).

4 Mr. Qiu did not tell me whether his ex-wife had married that man. It was un-

usual for a man and a woman to live together without getting married during the Cultural Revolution, but, in some rural areas, it did happen.

5 Racism is not intrinsic to biopower, although biopower functioning through sovereignty may promote racism. Foucault states, "The juxtaposition of—or the way biopower functions through—the old sovereign power of life and death implies the workings . . . of racism. And it is, I think, here that we find the actual roots of racism" (2003:258). Rather than biopower per se, Maoist sovereignty was the decisive root of such discrimination in China (Zhang 2011a, 2011b).

6 On the historical formation of the dual rural and urban systems and their functioning, see Cohen 1993, Solinger 1999, Zhang 2001, Qin 2010, Liang 2011, and Zhang 2011b, to name just a few sources.

7 The three figures I quote here come, respectively, from *Zhongguo tongji nianjian 1999* (China statistics almanac 1999), *Zhongguo tongji zhaiyao 1999* (China statistics digest 1999), and *Zhonghua quanguo gongshangye lianhehui 2006*.

8 This estimate is based on the total number (38.85 million) of xiagang workers from 1998 to 2005, according to an annual statistical report of the Ministry of Labor and Social Security.

9 The survival fee varied from city to city and was as low as 120 yuan a month in some cases. In one of the worst cases I encountered, a state-owned furniture factory ended up only offering 30 yuan to stepping-down workers. Workers who received survival fees were usually given one-time lump-sum compensation. Before a social safety net was finally put in place in the 2000s, the unmaking of the working class and the dispossession of factory workers caused huge pain and discontent (Lee 2007; Yang 2010). The situation varied widely, but it has generally improved over the years. For example, workers can now purchase danwei apartments with subsidies (Lee 2007).

10 Unemployment had not been unheard of since 1949 (Lee 2007; Walder 1988). The campaign of sending seventeen million city youths to the countryside in the name of their "reeducation" during the Cultural Revolution was an alternate way to deal with the problem of urban unemployment. But the scale of stepping down in the 1990s and 2000s was unprecedented and caused insecurity and hardship for massive numbers of workers. The dispossession of factory property and assets nominally owned by the people and their transference into the hands of a few in a nondemocratic fashion exacerbated the grievances of stepping-down workers and provoked public protests (Qin 2003; Lee 2007).

11 However, as overall vitality, shen also has its concrete origin in jing-seminal essence and has its manifestation in all kinds of aspects of shenti (the body).

12 Foods such as meat and sugar were rationed as well as grains.

13 This intellectual had been classified as a "rightist" in the antirightist campaign of 1957. He was, to some degree, however, protected from the worst treatment meted out to such "enemies," probably because he had an uncle who was a famous scientist.

14 That survivors of the Great Leap Famine were peasants who lacked the where-

withal to articulate their grievances explains why experiences of the famine were not published until the twenty-first century (Watson and Caldwell 2005).

Chapter 4: Impotence, Family, and Women

1 I have no evidence that he was lying or being ambiguous about his sexual orientation.

2 See Zhang 2011c on the meaning of *xiaojie*.

3 They describe four men who developed erectile dysfunction after failed coitus with prostitutes. The men had had no previous sexual experiences. One man had been assured that "he would never be able to get the job done for any woman—if he couldn't get it done here and now with a pro" (Masters and Johnson 1970:142).

4 On the Chinese socialist state's eradication of prostitution, see Hershatter 1997. On prostitution's revival in the reform period, see Pan Suiming 1998 and Zheng 2009.

5 There had been a debate as to whether his sexual reputation was warranted. In one view, the relationship between Pengzu and sexual cultivation was a construction of the late Qing scholar Ye Dehui, who mixed different sources together (Li 2006b).

6 Sexual cultivation in the Daoist tradition is often male-centered, because the nourishing of male potency, or vitality, is concerned with ensuring the longevity of the male. The tradition involves the complex practice of "plucking yin to nourish yang," in which the female sexual partner functions to cultivate the potency of the male. Two examples are seen in Tao Hongjing's description in the Southern Dynasties (420–589 CE) (Tao 1997) and Volume No. 21 of Ya-suyori's *Yixin fang* (Yasuyori 1997). For a feminist critique of this practice, see Furth 1994. However, the Mawangdui scripture reveals that some bodily movements were concerned with the satisfaction of the female, as both the effect and the condition for successful sexual cultivation of the male (Li 2006a:302–42; Harper 1998:413–38). It states, "Gou neng chijiu, nü nai da xi, qing zhi xiongdi, ai zhi fumu" (茍能持久,女乃大喜,親之兄弟,愛之父母, If only he can be slow and prolonged, the woman then is greatly pleased. She treats him with the closeness she feels for her brothers, and loves him like her father and mother. Whoever is capable this way is designated "heaven's gentleman" [Harper 1998:438]). Scholars such as Liao Yuqun (1994:51–52) argued that women could benefit from orgasm. Li Jianmin (2000:73–76) shared Liao's view. Some early works of bedchamber arts describe sexual enjoyment as shared by the male and the female, seen in the idea that "nan zhi bushuai, nü chu baibing" (男緻不衰,女除百病, the man will be strong and the woman will be free from illnesses) in *Sunü jing* [The plain girl sutra] and the idea of "yi yang yang yin" (以陽養陰, nourishing yin with yang) through sex in *Yufang mijue* [The secret in the jade chamber] (Fan et al. 1997).

7 The growth of sex tourism in China would make it hard to distinguish such women from sex industry workers at tourist attractions (Hyde 2007; Zhang 2006).

8 Zhang Jingsheng (1888–1970) was controversial for his view and practices, primarily articulated in the 1920s, promoting an ideal society through fully developed, aesthetic enjoyment of the body, sex, and love. His discussion of intercorporeal pleasure was open and detailed. For an English account of Zhang Jingsheng and his work, see Leary 1994.

9 To further define "sexual intercorporeality," I turned to the innovative and sophisticated techniques used by Masters and Johnson (1970) to cure impotence.

10 Sexual intercorporeality requires as its minimum condition a bodily "cooperation"—one opens the legs to allow the other to be on top, one bends the upper body forward and protrudes the buttocks so the other can approach from behind, and so on—the two bodies must be synchronized with one another to consummate sex. In intertwining, the bodies "fill or use the space available . . . in a tight and contractive fashion or in an expansive way" (Johnson 2007:22). The use of space for bodily intertwining (*amplitude*, in Mark Johnson's terminology, or *umwelt*, to use Erving Goffman's term) is evidenced in the mingling of breaths, in the adopting of various sexual positions, and in gearing the two bodies for the match of the genitals.

11 Sexual intercorporeality, in my understanding, draws on both the conscious and the unconscious, on a "somatic awareness" or "somatic mindfulness" (Shusterman 2008:49–76). Examples taken from athletic training illustrate bodily movement that is neither purely conscious nor unconscious. No matter how unreflective an athlete's bodily movement is, it is judged as either good or bad and, more important, can be improved by conscious application of instruction. In this sense, training explores somatic awareness to its optimum and turns it into habitus. Masters and Johnson's techniques are good examples of ways to develop "somatic awareness" of touching to enable bodily intertwining.

12 Bodily contact does not necessarily result in sexual intercorporeality because such contact can be forced. In the extreme case of rape, for example, the contact is forced, the use of carnal space coerced, and the appreciation and enjoyment of sensory input one-sided. Two persons cannot enjoy sex together without building sexual intercorporeality. Developing such intercorporeality, however, may involve play that includes sadism and masochism, wherein "wield[ing] power over the other in a sort of open-ended strategic game where the situation may be reversed is not evil; it's a part of love, of passion and sexual pleasure" (Foucault 1997:298).

13 I did encounter cases in which partners engaged in extensive touching but still experienced erectile failures, a phenomenon the intercorporeality model does not fully account for. The following is a case in point. Ms. Zhou was a twenty-four-year-old middle-school teacher, and her boyfriend was her former college

classmate. They started to date after they graduated from college and got along with each other so well that they felt they were ready to have sex. Unfortunately, her boyfriend could not get an erection in bed. They often embraced with their clothes on and then undressed and held each other. She undressed in front of him to arouse him, but he usually did not look at her naked body and did not like to touch her vagina. In contrast to his reluctance, she made advances, orally stimulating his genital. He closed his eyes and smiled, obviously feeling content. But still, his erection was not good enough to penetrate. Once he almost entered her but withdrew as soon as he felt *du* (clogged) at the entrance. She pushed him to enter further but was frustrated by his passivity and timidity. His own passivity was partially to blame for his not being fully aroused. He apparently fell short of embracing her as fully as she did him. However, less than optimal intercorporeal intimacy only partly accounts for his erectile difficulty. Likewise, a man in his forties recalled, "In the past, when I was taking a shower in the public shower room of our work unit, I saw some of my coworkers washing their penises really hard—they turned the foreskins inside out to let hot water brush the dirt out. I could never do it. Even at a mere touch, my penis stiffens." Unfortunately, he lost his ability to achieve easy erection a couple of years before we spoke.

14 These figures are from a longitudinal, nationwide, random-sample survey conducted by Pan Suiming and colleagues and funded by the Ford Foundation (Pan 2008). Of the 10,203 persons who were selected to participate in the survey, 7,553 responded, returning 6,010 valid questionnaires. The response and valid-return rates, then, were roughly the same, about 79 percent (Pan 2008).

15 Eight percent chose option 1, 2 percent option 2, and 2 percent option 3. A total of 281 female students answered this question.

Chapter 5: The Loss of *Jing* and the Revival of *Yangsheng*

1 I suspect that the term *zaoxie* (premature ejaculation) was borrowed from modern urology or sexology, but the idea of the inability to sustain erection before ejaculation existed in ancient Chinese medical and bedchamber arts literature.

2 The text is "fu jing zhe, shen zhi ben ye (夫精者, 身之本也)" (*Huangdineijing, Suwen*: Jinguizhenyanlunpian, Anonymous 2000:14).

3 The text is "Zhongren zhong li, lianshi zhong ming, xianshi shang zhi, shengren gui jing" (*Zhuangzi: Keyi*). See Cao 2000:227.

4 As reflected in the phrases "gu sheng zhi lai wei zhi jing" (故生之來謂之精, so the original material that constitutes life is jing; *Huangdineijing, Lingshu*: Benshen, Anonymous 2000:323).

5 This view of jing, discussed by Nathan Sivin (1987), was originally presented in *The Revised Outline of Chinese Medicine*, a textbook published in China in 1972, and is representative of contemporary Chinese medicine's understanding of jing. It is also consistent with the definitions of *jing* given in *A Concise Dic-*

tionary of Chinese Medicine (Editorial Committee 1979) and in *A Dictionary of Chinese Medicine* (Li Jingwei et al. 1995). Manfred Porkert views jing much as Sivin does, as basically two-dimensional. He maintains that neither *semen* nor *essence* grasps all the implications of *jing* (Porkert 1974:176–80) and that *jing* also implies "structive potential." This latter idea seems consistent with the idea of jing as the essence gained through bodily sustenance, described in the standard view. I suggest that the two dimensions do not necessarily diverge clearly from each other. Xiantian zhijing (jing one is born with, or reproductive jing) does not necessarily mean only semen. Since jing is important to men's vitality, to classify it only as functioning in reproduction is too simplistic.

6 Zhuangzi refers to "gujia bo jing, keyi shi shiren" (古筴播精,可以食十人, shaking off the chaff by shaking the winnowing basket to obtain rice to feed ten people (*Zhuangzi: Renjianshi*). See Cao 2000:67. Also see Li Shuang 1994:52.

7 As I discuss in chapter 6, *kidney* does not adequately capture the Chinese medical notion of "shen," and it risks replacing this notion with an anatomically based biomedical view.

8 "Shen cang jing" (腎藏精, kidney houses jing; *Huangdineijing, Lingshu*: Benshen, Anonymous 2000:324).

9 "Junhuo zhixia, yinjing cheng zhi" (the sovereign fire goes down, the seminal essence of yin bears it; *Huandineijing, Suwen*: Liuweizhidalunpian, Anonymous 2000:196).

10 Zhang Jiebin (Jingyue) argued in 1636 (Ming period), "The exhaustion of jing leads to the deficiency of yin, and the deficiency of yin leads to a complete loss of qi. As a result, one's body suffers greatly from the losses to the degree that one will soon die. Should we not be afraid of the consequence of the loss of jing?" (J. Zhang 1991, *Jingyue quanshu*, vol. 29:634).

11 Wu Zhiwang, another Ming-period scholar of Chinese medicine, quoted Lin Chengzhong, in 1626, as saying, "Jing is the fundamental root of human beings. The kidney houses jing, but the kidney obeys the heart. If one can regulate desire and keep the heart calm and pure, then jing and qi are kept in place, yin is free from disturbance, and yang is stable. As a result, the *zhenyang* (the kidney yang) will be solid and dense" (Wu 1996:805). The point is that semen, as the tangible dimension of jing, relates to the fundamental balance between yin and yang, a balance that is maintained throughout the viscera (e.g., between the kidney and the heart) because of the spreading of the intangible dimension of jing beyond the kidney.

12 See *Zhongyi zazi* (issue 14, March 1925; issue 21, December 1926), *Guangdong Yiyao Yuebao* (vol. 1, issue 2, 1929), *Guoyi Dizhu Yuekan* (issue 1, January 1937), and *Yijie Chunqiu* (vol. 6, issue 65, November 1931), for examples of these types of materials. See also Huang K'o-wu 1988.

13 Foster's (1967) notion of limited good came from his study of the Mexican lower classes and peasantry.

14 The technique, which involves withholding jing during sex to allow it to move

up through the body and directly nourish the brain, is considered unrealistic today. Although the authors of *Zhongyi nanke xue* discussed the technique in some detail, they seemed ambivalent about its benefits.

15 Translation by Farquhar and Zhang (2012:146).

16 The medical and Daoist literature on yangsheng is extensive. See, for example, Hu 1997, Zhou 1997, Wang 1998, Wu 1996, Zhang and Qu 2005, Fan et al. 1997 and Song 1991. The rise of qigong fever was certainly a part of the revival and reinvention of yangsheng. See Palmer 2007 and Chen 2003.

17 The public health system under Maoist socialism benefited the population, but the harsh political campaigns, the urban–rural divide, and, worst of all, the Great Leap Forward and subsequent Great Leap Famine contributed to tremendous human suffering.

18 It was commonly agreed that Fu's death was the result of political revenge by Lin Biao, the number-two leader during part of the Cultural Revolution. Fu had been the primary medical authority who, in the early 1950s, reported to the Central Committee of the Chinese Communist Party that Lin's complaint of bad health was not borne out by physical examination and should not excuse Lin from serving as commander in chief in the Korean War. Fu also advised Lin to kick his morphine addiction. Mao's approval of Fu's performance in pre–Cultural Revolution times did not outweigh Fu's "mistakes" and left room for criticism of him to escalate into deadly persecution. The above information is partly derived from personal communication with Fu Weikang, Fu Lianzhang's son, in June 2006.

19 For more discussion of yangsheng activities, see Farquhar and Zhang 2012.

20 Doctors do not necessarily engage in the kinds of behavior they promote in their professional capacities. See Kohrman 2008 for an analysis of complex social factors behind this contradiction. According to my observations, venerated doctors of traditional Chinese medicine are more likely than others to "practice what they preach."

21 The direct translation of *jisu* is "hormone." But the "therapy" the "doctor" recommended seemed different from hormonal therapies sometimes prescribed by urologists or doctors of nanke. I read and memorized the label on the little glass bottle that contained the drug he suggested I take and later consulted a urologist about it. The urologist had no clue what the vial contained. It might have been some kind of aphrodisiac. Or it might have been a type of medicine used in self-injection therapy for impotence, which enjoyed greater popularity in places such as the United States in the pre-Viagra era. An estimated thirty thousand U.S. men were using penile injections, on average twice a week, as therapy for impotence in the early 1990s (Rothstein and Goldstein 1995). The "doctor" I saw might have had access to this kind of therapy, since he told me that the medication was imported from abroad. The use of both aphrodisiacs and self-injection therapy ran against the principles of the majority of doctors of TCM I had worked with.

22 The relationship between ethics and freedom is central to Foucault's critiquing of Western epistemology since Descartes (Faubion 2012). According to Martin Heidegger (2005), the Kantian notion encompasses both "negative freedom" and "positive freedom." The former refers to being free from coercion ("being away from") whereas the latter refers to "self-legislation" or "self-activity" ("being toward," "being free for"). In Isaiah Berlin's (2002) elaboration, negative freedom refers to acting unobstructed by others, whereas positive freedom results from having self-mastery or self-direction.

Chapter 6: *Bushen*, *Shugan*, or Taking the Great Brother

1 Arthur Kleinman (1986, 1980; see also Kleinman and Kleinman 1985) examined the prevailing neurasthenia in China as a possible "somatization" of depression in the aftermath of the Cultural Revolution. Even though somatization features a conceptual divide between the somatic and the mental, Kleinman paid special attention to the social conditions that encouraged the somatal articulations of distresses. This discovery situates the prevaling bodily complaints in distinctive social conditions and broadens the meaning of somatization to the terrain of social construction of the somatic, a self-reflectiveness in the development of the notion observed by other commentators from different angles (e.g., Davis 2012). The other lines of inquiry about the somatic complaints of possible psychological or psychiatric disorders include the cultural habitus undifferentiating body from mind in Chinese medical clinics (Ots 1990; Y. Zhang 2007). For example, some patients were able to present their bodily discomforts as caused by emotions such as anger but tended to seek bodily reliefs from Chinese medicine that does not differentiate the physiological from the psychological (Y. Zhang 2007). However, we may be cautious not to underestimate the increasing institutional as well as semantic influence of the body-mind differentiation on clinical encounters since the 1990s.

2 Also see Good et al. 1992 and Good 1994 for discussion of chronic pain and its symbolic and experiential stakes.

3 See "Tianxia zhidao tan" (天下至道談, Discussion of the Culminant Way in All Under Heaven), included in Harper 1998. It states: "When it is angered yet not large, skin has not arrived; when large yet not firm, muscle has not arrived; when firm yet not hot, qi has not arrived." Also see Zhang Jiebin 1991 and Li Zhongzi 1642.

4 The *Guidelines for Clinical Research on New Drugs of Treating Impotence in Chinese Medicine* (State Administration of TCM 1993) recognized six etiological types of impotence: deficiency of kidney yang (*mingmen huoshuai*), weakness of both the heart and the spleen (*xinpi liangxu*), asthenic yin causing excessive pyrexia (*yinxu huowang*), panic causing damage to the kidney (*jingkong shangshen*), stagnation of hepatic qi (*ganqi yujie*), and damp invasion of the lower energizer (*shire xiazhu*). As a result of Qin's study, the number of recognized types of im-

potence was expanded from six to eleven. Seven of the eleven types were associated with the liver, and four were associated with the kidney.

5 It is simply called "yin" and has eight other names as well in the Mawangdui scriptures (Li 2006a).

6 Before the Ming period, impotence was predominantly referred to as "yinwei." *Buqi* (不起, not up) is the earliest known name for the condition (appearing in the Mawangdui scriptures). Other names include *yinqi buyong* (陰器不用, the prolonged inactivity of the penis due to the shrinking yin; see Qin 2000c; Wang and Cao 1988; Wang 1997). In the Yuan period, *yang* started to be incorporated into references to impotence, in such terms as *yangdao weiruo* (weakness of yang's way), *yangshi buju* (yang's inability to rise up), and *yangshi buxing* (lack of prospering of yang matter; see Qin 2000c).

7 In *Jingyue quanshu*, Zhang Jiebin claimed that most cases of yangwei are caused by extreme deficiency of renal yang: "Every seven or eight out of ten [impotence patients] suffer from deficiency of renal yang whereas those [patients] who suffer from excessive yang are practically nonexistent" (1991:713). Zhang Jiebin's emphasis on yang as the basis of vitality of the kidney was partly a critique of Zhu Zhenheng's thesis that "there is often a deficiency of yin and excess of yang" (1982:1).

8 *Ganshen tongyuan* refers to the relationship between the liver and the kidney in terms of mutual nourishment. Specifically, the yin of one benefits from nourishing the yin of the other. Also, the liver houses blood, whereas the kidney houses seminal essence. Blood and seminal essence are mutually transformable.

9 *Gan bu ke bu* (one does not replenish the liver) is an accepted rule in Chinese medicine.

10 This projection was laid out on Pfizer's webpage when I viewed it in 2000. For more on the Massachusetts Male Aging Study, see introduction, n. 7.

11 Dr. Zhuang is a pseudonym.

12 *Shenxuejiao* (a small medicinal ball) was one such chunyao that allegedly helped men gain one night of pleasure (Liu 1998:423).

13 Viagra comes in 50- and 100-milligram dosages.

14 Some professional psychoanalysts express similar concerns with regard to their own experiences of treating impotence (Melchiode 1999). Whether Viagra encourages phallocentrism is subject to debate. Some have argued that the dominant discourse around Viagra reinforces the heterosexual norm (Mamo and Fishman 2001). A group of empirical studies found that Viagra reinforces male-centered sexual pleasure by neglecting women's feelings (Potts et al. 2003). But some researchers have found that Viagra may enhance efforts to seek nonphallocentric ways of making love and satisfying desire, depending on how it is used (Potts 2004).

15 Commentators have pointed out Robert van Gulik's (2003) inadequate appreciation of the importance of the cultivation of overall potency. For example,

Kristofer Schipper refers to van Gulik's failure "to appreciate the macrobiotic and cosmological beliefs that link [people] to cultic visions of longevity or immortality rather than to the goal of sexual pleasure for either women or men" (Furth 2005:72).

16 My survey included 194 impotence patients and 594 college students.

17 There is no consensus about what the term *cosmopolitanism* means. According to one definition, it is "an ethos of macro-interdependencies, with an acute consciousness (often forced upon people) of the inescapabilities and particularities of places, characters, historical trajectories, and fates" (Rabinow 1996:56). According to others, it is an allegiance to "the worldwide community of human beings" (Nussbaum 1996:4) or an open attitude toward strangers (Appiah 2006). James Ferguson's study (1999:82–122) of cosmopolitanism focuses on cultural styles of performance. See also Cheah and Robbins 1998.

18 How women feel about Viagra is an important issue. Most of my interviews were with men. The limited information I obtained from a very small number of women shows that they were split in their attitude toward Viagra, some liking it and some disliking it. For example, a forty-five-year-old woman in Chengdu said that she did not feel aroused even after her husband was able to penetrate her after taking Viagra. She felt that her husband concentrated more on erection per se than on sharing pleasure with her. This feeling bothered her. Another woman in Chengdu, in her thirties, said that Viagra had enhanced her sexual partner's erection and made it last longer, which was good.

19 In the modern history of medicine in China, Western medical terminology has often been translated into Chinese through the adoption of preexisting Chinese terms (often via Japanese), thus creating new meanings for old words. The assimilation of germ theory in China is an example (Andrews 1997), as is the assimilation of nerve theory (Shapiro 2000). By the same token, TCM terms can be translated into English in a variety of ways (Pritzker 2007).

20 Lydia Liu's (1995) discussion of the "condition of translation" as key to understanding not only the transformation of meanings but also their invention is helpful here. In their study of the "integration" of Tibetan medicine and biomedicine, Vincanne Adams and Feifei Li (2008) examine the semantic relationship between the Tibetan term *bu* and the Western terms *bacteria* and *virus*. They document a linguistic slippage in which the terms refer to rather different things but are used interchangeably and thus maintain a state of apparent (albeit forced) "integration." In her study of how Nepalese adapt the English vocabulary around HIV/AIDS, Stacey Leigh Pigg (2000) argues that code switching is not balanced but, rather, reflects the relative power and social privilege displayed between speakers as well as between the languages used to construct scientific knowledge.

21 In commenting on Robert Anderson's (1992) study of the efficacy of ethnomedicines, Mark Nichter discusses the problems that arise when claims of effi-

cacy are "subjective, provisional, [and] based on contingencies" (1992:226). Successful claims of efficacy tend to depend on who gets to decide what counts as efficacious in any given case.

22 There has been much discussion of hybridity, particularly in the areas of post-colonialism, transnationalism, identity politics, and ethnic studies. The term *hybridity* is often used to describe the "in-between" status or "indeterminacy of diasporic identity" (Bhabha 1994), the mixing of culture and nature (Latour 1993), the coexistence of tradition and modernity (Vasavi 1994), and mixed identities within postcolonial situations (Young 1995), to name just a few applications. The debate about the advantages and disadvantages of using this term is quite intense. See Mahmood 1996 and Rosaldo 1995 for criticisms of its use, and see Pieterse 2001 for a defense of it. Efforts have been made to conceptualize the situation as "assemblage" (Ong and Collier 2004), "the mangle of practice" (Pickering 1995), and so on.

23 The understanding of this kind of negotiation has intensified in anthropology (e.g., Ong and Chen 2010) and in the history of medicine (e.g., Furth 2010). Here is where the notion of "cosmopolitanism" is relevant.

24 The idea of medical pluralism—the existence of multiple medicines and practices—had become popular since the 1960s, and has continued to develop (e.g., Leslie and Young 1992; Scheid 2002, 2007; Hsu 1999; Farquhar 1994; Zhan 2009). But the development of biomedicine has posed an increasingly tense challenge for medical pluralism. Apparently, both in the United States and in Europe, acupuncture has done much better than herbal medicine in attracting a following. Mei Zhan's (2009) ethnography confirms this trend, even though it is optimistic about the eventual acceptance of both. See also Barnes 2005 and Kaptchuk 2002. Unlike herbal preparations in China, herbal supplements in the United States are not primarily consumed to cure disease. In China, the validity of Chinese medicine was debated throughout the twentieth century (e.g., Zhao 1989; Lei 2014), and that debate continues today. Biomedicine is the primary weapon in the battles against pandemics such as AIDS, SARS, avian flu, and other infectious diseases; nonbiomedicines pale in comparison or have difficulty being promoted in such contexts (e.g., Hanson 2010).

Chapter 7: Potency Is Fullness of Life

1 Other terms referring to "potency" today include *xiong de qi* (the maleness could stand up strong) and *neng qi xing* (capable of initiating sex). "Xiong" (maleness) is similar to "yang" in the contemporary gendered distinction between male and female, and has two connotations: broadly, it means acting like a real man in standing up to challenges, and, more narrowly, it means "getting one's stuff up to do the job" (have sex). *Neng qi xing* indicates the ability to get an erection. *Bu qi xing* (could not initiate sex) signals impotence.

2 *Shen qi zu* (fullness of renal qi) is another term indexing strong potency. *Shenxu*

(the kidney is weak) refers to both impotence and weakened vitality. The fullness of renal qi is related to the fullness of jing, according to the *Inner Canon*, because of the close relationship between the shen (kidney) and jing. See chapter 5.

3 Other terms referring to impotence included *buqi* (not up) and *yinqi buyong* (inactivity of the yin utensil). See chapter 6, n. 6.

4 Emperor Hanchengdi (Han dynasty) reputedly died of the leaking of *jingye* (semen) resulting from taking an aphrodisiac (Lin X 1966). Although its veracity is in doubt, this story carries with it folk knowledge that is influential today.

5 Feng Zhaozhang, a medical scholar in the Qing period, made a similar point: "Old men who can have sex as usual would live a long life, because their yang is strong and solid. Needless to say, young men who are impotent must die early" (1996:410–14).

6 I define "life" here primarily in terms of the tradition of Daoist philosophy and Chinese medicine. I share with Judith Farquhar and Qicheng Zhang (2012) an emphasis on life's generativity and transformativity, on the one hand, and everyday lively sociality, on the other hand, as well as their effort to collapse the distinction between shengming (being alive) and shenghuo (living a life).

7 Despite numerous discussions of illness experience from an existential perspective (e.g., Gadamer 1996; Boss 2001; Scarry 1985; Murphy 2001; Csordas 1994; Good 1994; Jackson 1996; Kleinman 1999; Das 2006), no ethnographic account of the existential implications of potency or of impotence has appeared.

8 These two phrases highlight different aspects of the same effort. With "somatic awareness," Richard Shusterman tried to cast light on how bodily reflectiveness of some sort is not just possible but necessary, as in the interplay between the reflective, lived body and intentionality ("lived somaesthetic reflection"; see Shusterman 2008:63). "Somatic modes of attention," the body's attention to its "situation in the world . . . in surroundings that include the embodied presence of others" (Csordas 1993:138), goes beyond the divide between the conscious and the unconscious.

9 The notion "habitus" is consistent with Merleau-Ponty's view of the body toward the world (Bourdieu 1977; Wacquant 2004).

10 Boss was a longtime friend of Heidegger. He organized a well-known series of seminars from the late 1940s to the early 1960s in which Heidegger addressed groups of professionals and intellectuals on his ontology and philosophy in relation to practical issues such as illness and psychiatry. According to some sources, Boss also served as Heidegger's psychiatrist (Polt 1999). Boss continued to advocate daseinsanalytic, a school of psychiatry first associated with Ludwig Binswanger, and to emphasize the potential of applying abstract and profound philosophical theories such as Heideggerian phenomenology to psychiatric practices (Heidegger 2001; Boss 1979).

11 Li Yinhe documented the difficulty her female interviewees experienced in acquiring knowledge about the sexual body during the Maoist period. For

those women too, watching animals copulate was a way to learn about sex (Li 1996:36).

12 Personal communication with Dr. He Zihua in Chongqing and Dr. Zhang Si-xiao in Chengdu.

13 Other efforts had also been made. For example, the first vacuum constriction device (VCD) was approved by the U.S. Food and Drug Administration in 1982. The device uses negative pressure to cause the penile corporal sinusoids to swell and to increase blood inflow to the penis, and an external constricting ring is placed at the base of the penis to prevent blood outflow from the corpora cavernosa. This allows maintenance of an erection for sexual intercourse (Yuan et al. 2010).

14 Feminist critics point out that Merleau-Ponty's discussion of sexual being is misogynist (Butler 1989; Sullivan 1997). I try to apply Merleau-Ponty's view of embodiment without losing sight of the gendered nature of potency.

15 Criticism of the phenomenological view of the body becomes relevant here. One critique is that the lifeworld, from the phenomenological perspective, looks too pure, as if the complex social distinctions and the forces inscribed on the body have little influence on being-in-the-world. See Zhang 1998. Foucault's criticism of phenomenology can be seen in his rejection of the "inner" through his emphasis on the influence of power (Foucault 2000). Deleuze pushed this skepticism to new heights by saying that there was only the "outer" (Deleuze 1995). Their criticisms highlight the emphasis in the phenomenological view on an individual's "outward" movement in interacting with the world, which does not take into account the "inward" movement of power, in the Foucauldian sense, in affecting that individual (Csordas 2011).

16 For the increasing divorce disputes over the ownership of apartments, see Davis 2010.

17 The *Inner Canon* (*Huandineijing, Suwen: Shanggutianzhen lunpian*) presents the rise and fall of potency through the rise and fall of *shenqi* (renal, or kidney, qi). Shenqi represents one's vitality, regardless of gender. An erection is the manifestation of shenqi in the male. See Anonymous 2000.

18 *Deterritorialized* here means nonphallocentric, suggesting new forms of pleasure may be found outside the confines of the erotogenic zones in what Deleuze and Guattari (1983) called "the Body without organs" (see also Zhang 2013; Potts 2004).

Adams, Rachel, and David Savran, eds. 2002. *The Masculinity Studies Reader*. Malden, MA: Wiley-Blackwell.

Adams, Vincanne, and Feifei Li. 2008. "Integration or Erasure? Modernizing Medicine at Lhasa's Mentsikhang." In *Tibetan Medicine in the Contemporary World*, edited by L. Pordie, 105–31. London: Routledge.

Agamben, Giorgio. 1998. *Homo Sacer*. Translated by Daniel Heller-Roazen. Palo Alto, CA: Stanford University Press.

Agamben, Giorgio. 2002. *Remnants of Auschwitz: The Witness and the Archive*. Translated by D. Heller-Roazen. New York: Zone Books.

Allison, Anne. 1994. *Night Work: Sexuality, Pleasure, and Corporate Masculinity in a Tokyo Hostess Club*. Chicago: University of Chicago Press.

Altman, Dennis. 2001. *Global Sex*. Chicago: University of Chicago Press.

Ames, Roger T. 1993. "The Meaning of Body in Classical Chinese Philosophy." In *Self as Body in Asian Theory and Practice*, edited by Thomas P. Kasulis, Roger T. Ames, and Wimal Dissanayake, 157–78. Albany: State University of New York Press.

Anagnost, Ann. 1997. "Making History Speak." *National Past-times: Narrative, Representation, and Power in Modern China*, 17–44. Durham, NC: Duke University Press.

Anagnost, Ann. 2008. "From 'Class' to 'Social Strata': Grasping Social Totality in Reform-era China." *Third World Quarterly* 29 (3): 497–519.

Anderson, Robert. 1992. "The Efficacy of Ethnomedicine: Research Methods in Trouble." In *Anthropological Approaches to the Study of Ethnomedicine*, edited by Mark Nichter, 1–18. London: Routledge.

Andrews, Bridie. 1997. "Tuberculosis and the Assimilation of Germ Theory in China, 1895–1937." *Journal of History of Medicine* 52: 114–57.

Andrews, Bridie. 2014. *The Making of Modern Chinese Medicine, 1850–1960*. University of British Columbia Press.

Anonymous. 1999. "Tianxiazhidaotan" [On the highest Dao under heaven]. In *Zhonghua Xingxue Guanzhi* [An ultimate collection of Chinese sexological classics], edited by Fan Youping, Shi Zhichao, Chen Zihua, and Zhao Fengqin, 24–36. Guangzhou: Guangdong renmin chubanshe.

Anonymous. 2000. *Huangdi Neijing* [Yellow Emperor's Inner Canon]. In *Zhongyi sibu jingdian* [Four classics of Chinese medicine], edited by Tianjin kexue jishu chubanshe. Tianjin: Tianjin kexue jishu chubanshe.

Appiah, Kwame Anthony. 2006. *Cosmopolitanism: Ethics in a World of Strangers.* New York: W. W. Norton.

Araujo, Andre, et al. 1998. "The Relationship between Depressive Symptoms and Male Erectile Dysfunction: Cross-sectional Results from the Massachusetts Male Aging Study." *Psychosomatic Medicine* 60: 458–65.

Araujo, Andre. 2000. "Relation between Psychosocial Risk Factors and Incident Erectile Dysfunction: Prospective Results from Massachusetts Male Aging Study." *American Journal of Epidemiology* 152 (6): 533–41.

Bancroft, John. 1992. "Foreword." In *Erectile Disorders: Assessment and Treatment*, edited by Raymond C. Rosen and Sandra R. Leiblum, vii–xviii. New York: Guilford Press.

Barnes, Linda. 2005. "American Acupucture and Efficacy: Meanings and Their Points of Insertion." *Medical Anthropology Quarterly* 19 (3): 239–66.

Berlin, Isaiah. 2002. *Liberty: Incorporating Four Essays on Liberty.* Oxford: Oxford University Press.

Bhabha, Homi K. 1994. *The Location of Culture.* New York: Routledge.

Bianchi-Demicheli, F. 2005. "Erectile Dysfunction: To Prescribe or Not to Prescribe?" *International Journal of Impotence Research* 17: 381–82.

Biehl, João. 2005. *Vita.* Berkeley: University of California Press.

Billeter, Jean-François. 1985. "The System of 'Class-status.'" In *The Scope of State Power in China*, edited by Stuart R. Schram, 127–69. London: School of Oriental and African Studies.

Blakeslee, Sandra. 2005. "Serious Rider, Your Bicycle Seat May Affect Your Love Life." *New York Times*, October 4. Accessed October 26, 2011. http://www.nytimes.com/2005/10/04/health/nutrition/04bike.html?pagewanted=print.

Boss, Medard. 2001. *Existential Foundations of Medicine and Psychology.* Translated by Stephen Conway and Anne Cleaves. New York: Jason Aronson.

Botz-Bornstein, Thorsten. 2011. *The Philosophy of Viagra: Bioethical Responses to the Viagrification of the Modern World.* Amsterdam: Rodopi.

Bourdieu, Pierre. 1977. *Outline of a Theory of Practice.* Translated by R. Nice. New York: Cambridge University Press.

Brandtstädter, Susanne, and Goncalo D. Santos, eds. 2008. *Chinese Kinship: Contemporary Anthropological Perspective.* London: Routledge.

Bray, David. 2005. *Social Space and Governance in Urban China: The Danwei System from Origins to Reform.* Palo Alto, CA: Stanford University Press.

Brown, Peter. 1988. *The Body and Society.* New York: Columbia University Press.

Brownell, Susan. 1995. *Training the Body for China.* Chicago: University of Chicago Press.

Brownell, Susan. 1999. "Strong Women and Impotent Men: Sports, Gender, and Nationalism in Chinese Public Culture." In *Spaces of Their Own*, edited by Mayfair Yang, 207–31. Minneapolis: University of Minnesota Press.

Butler, Judith. 1989. "Sexual Ideology and Phenomenological Description." In *The Thinking Muse: Feminism and Modern French Philosophy*, edited by Jeffner Allen and Iris Marion Young, 85–100. Bloomington: Indiana University Press.

Cai Jieren. 1998. "Mao Zedong guanyu renti xiesheng moter wenti de pishi" [Mao Zedong's directive on the issue of nude models for practicing sketching human bodies]. *Zhongguo wenhua bao (China Cultural News)*, December 18.

Candib, Lucy, and Richard Schmitt. 1996. "About Losing it: The Fear of Impotence." In *Rethinking Masculinity: Philosophical Explorations in Light of Feminism*, edited by Larry May, Robert Strikwerda, and Patrick D. Hopkins, 211–36. Lanham, MD: Rowman and Littlefield.

Cao Chuji. 2000. *Zhuangzi qianzhu* [A preliminary annotation of Zhuangzi]. Beijing: Zhonghua shuju.

Cao Kaiyong. 1997. "Zhongyi nankexue de lishi, xianzhuang yu qianjing" [The past, present, and future of nanke of TCM]. In *Zhongyi nanke yanjiu yu linchuang jinzhan* [The development in research and clinical practice of nanke of TCM], edited by Cao Kaiyong and Qi Guangchong, 1–5. Shanghai: Shanghai kexuejishu chubanshe.

Cao Kaiyong, ed. 1989. *Nanke yian* [Medical cases of nanke]. Beijing: Zhongguo yiyaokeji chubanshe.

Cao, Nanlai. 2010. *Constructing China's Jerusalem: Christians, Power, and Place in Contemporary Wenzhou*. Palo Alto, CA: Stanford University Press.

CCTV (China Central Television Station) International. 2004. Interview with Dr. Jia Jinming. December 23.

Chan, Anita. 1985. *Children of Mao*. Seattle: University of Washington Press.

Chang Che-chia. 2000. "Guangfang yixue fengke yu yixue fazhan: Yi beisong jibing fenlei yu shanghan yanjiu wei xiansuo" [The official classification of medical divisions and the development of medicine: Classification of diseases and studies of the Treaties on Cold Injury in the Northern Song period as clues]. Paper presented in the symposium "A History of Diseases," Academia Sinica, Taipei, June 16–18.

Cheah, Pheng, and Bruce Robbins, eds. 1998. *Cosmopolitics: Thinking and Feeling beyond the Nation*. Minneapolis: University of Minnesota Press.

Chen Bojun. 1990. "Shui jiekai le moping: Dui xinshiqi she xing wenxue de fansi" [Who opens the magic bottle: A reflection on literary representations of sexuality in the reform era]. *Wenxue pinglun* [Literary criticism], no. 3: 27–28.

Chen Linong. 1996. "Zhongguo jingji tiyu 'yinsheng' xianxiang tan yin" [An exploration of the causes of the phenomenon of 'yin waxes' in China's sports]. *Journal of Shanghai Physical Education Institute* 20 (1): 15–21.

Chen, Nancy N. 2003. *Breathing Spaces*. New York: Columbia University Press.

Cheng, J., E. Ng, J. Ko, and R. Chen. 2007. "Monthly Income, Standard of Living and Erectile Function in Late Life." *International Journal of Impotence Research* 19: 464–70.

Cheng, Tiejun, and Mark Selden. 1994. "The Origins and Social Consequences of China's Hukou System." *China Quarterly* 139 (September): 644–68.

Cheng Yi and Cheng Hao. 2004. *ErCheng ji* [A collection of the two Chengs' works]. Beijing: Zhonghua shuju.

Choi, B. L. 2003. "Prevalence and Risk Factors for Erectile Dysfuntion in Primary Care: Results of a Korean Study." *International Journal of Impotence Research* 15: 323–28.

Chu, Julie Y. 2010. *Cosmologies of Credit: Transnational Mobility and the Politics of Destination in China*. Chicago: University of Chicago Press.

Clarke, Adell E., Laura Mamo, Jennifer Ruth Fosket, Jennifer R. Fishman, and Janet K. Shim, eds. 2010. *Biomedicalization: Technoscience, Health, and Illness in the U.S.* Durham, NC: Duke University Press.

Cleveland Clinic. 2010. "Surgical Penile Implants." Accessed October 17, 2011. http://my.clevelandclinic.org/services/surgical_penile_implants/hic_surgical _penile_implants.aspx.

Cohen, Lawrence. 1995. "The Pleasure of Castration: The Postoperative Status of Hijras, Jankhas, and Academics." In *Sexual Nature, Sexual Culture*, edited by Paul R. Abramson and Steven D. Pinkerton, 276–304. Chicago: University of Chicago Press.

Cohen, Lawrence. 1998. *No Aging in India*. Berkeley: University of California Press.

Cohen, Lawrence. 1999. "The History of Semen: Notes on a Cultural-bound Syndrome." In *Medicine and the History of the Body*, edited by Yasuo Otsuka, Shizu Sakai, and Shigehisa Kuriyama, 113–38. Tokyo: Ishiyaku EuroAmerican.

Cohen, Myron. 1993. "Cultural and Political Inventions in Modern China: The Case of the Chinese 'Peasant.'" *Daedalus* 122 (2): 151–70.

Cohen, Theodore F., ed. 2000. *Men and Masculinity: A Text-Reader*. Belmont, CA: Wadsworth.

Connell, R. W. 2005. *Masculinities*. 2nd ed. Berkeley: University of California Press.

Crossley, Nick. 1995. "Body Techniques, Agency and Intercorporeality: On Goffman's *Relations in Public*." *Sociology* 29 (1): 133–49.

Csordas, Thomas J. 1990. "Embodiment as a Paradigm for Anthropology." *Ethos* 18 (1): 4–57.

Csordas, Thomas J. 1993. "Somatic Modes of Attention." *Cultural Anthropology* 8 (2): 135–56.

Csordas, Thomas J., ed. 1994. *Embodiment and Experience: The Existential Ground of Culture and Self*. New York: Cambridge University Press.

Csordas, Thomas J. 2008. "Intersubjectivity and Intercorporeality." *Subjectivity* 22: 110–22.

Csordas, Thomas J. 2011. "Embodiment Agency, Sexual Difference, and Illness." In *A Companion to the Anthropology of the Body and Embodiment*, edited by Frances E. Mascia-Lees, 137–56. Malden, MA: Wiley-Blackwell.

Dai Jinhua. 1999. *Ershi shiji zhongguo nuxing shi fangtan* [An interview for a history of Chinese women in the twentieth century] on the program "Banbiantian" [Half the sky] on China Central Television. Video cassette diskette. Beijing: Zhongguo guoji dianshi zonggongsi.

Dai Jupu. 1925. "Yixielun [On yijing]." *Zhongyi zazhi* 14 (March): 11–12.

Darmon, Pierre. 1986. *Damning the Innocent: A History of the Persecution of the Impotent in Pre-Revolutionary France.* Translated by Paul Keegan. New York: Viking.

Das, Veena. 2006. *Life and Words: Violence and the Descent into the Ordinary.* Berkeley: University of California Press.

Davis, Deborah, ed. 2000. *The Consumer Revolution in Urban China.* Berkeley: University of California Press.

Davis, Deborah. 2010. "Who Gets the House? Renegotiating Property Rights in Post-Socialist Urban China." *Modern China* 36 (5): 463–92.

Davis, Deborah, and Sara Friedman, eds. 2014. *Wives, Husbands and Lovers: Marriage and Sexuality in Hong Kong, Taiwan and Urban China.* Palo Alto, CA: Stanford University Press.

Davis, Deborah, and Steven Harrell, eds. 1993. *Chinese Families in the Post-Mao Era.* Berkeley: University of California Press.

Davis, Elizabeth Anne. 2012. *Bad Souls: Madness and Responsibility in Modern Greece.* Durham, NC: Duke University Press.

Deleuze, Gilles. 1995. *Negotiations.* New York: Columbia University Press.

Deleuze, Gilles. 1997. "Desire and Pleasure." In *Foucault and His Interlocutors*, edited by Arnold Davison, 183–92. Chicago: University of Chicago Press.

Deleuze, Gilles, and Félix Guattari. 1983. *Anti-Oedipus: Capitalism and Schizophrenia.* Minneapolis: University of Minnesota Press.

Deleuze, Gilles, and Félix Guattari. 1987. *A Thousand Plateaus.* Minneapolis: University of Minnesota Press.

Deleuze, Gilles, and Claire Parnet. 1996. *Gilles Deleuze's ABC Primer* (film dir. Pierre-André Bountang). Summarized by Charles A. Stivale on URL (consulted May 2005): www.langlab.wayne.edu/CStivale/D-G/ABC1.html.

Deng Mingyu. 2008. "Zhongguo dangdai xingxue fazhan gailun" [An overview of the development of contemporary sexology in China]. Accessed June 18, 2012. http://www.douban.com/group/topic/17854634/.

Deng Peng, ed. 2006. *Wusheng de qunluo 1964–1965* [The silent group 1964–1965]. Chongqing: Chongqing chubanshe.

Deng Yiwen. 1998. "Cong zhongxin dao bianyuan" [From the center to the margin]. *China Market Economy Times*, March 6.

Derrida, Jacques. 2005. *On Touching: Jean-Luc Nancy.* Palo Alto, CA: Stanford University Press.

Desjarlais, Robert. 1992. *Body and Emotion: The Aesthetics of Healing in the Nepal Himalayas.* Philadelphia: University of Pennsylvania Press.

Desjarlais, Robert. 1997. *Shelter Blues: Sanity and Selfhood among the Homeless.* Philadelphia: University of Pennsylvania Press.

Desjarlais, Robert, and Jason Throop. 2011. "Phenomenological Approach in Anthropology." *Annual Review of Anthropology* 40: 87–102.

Dosse, François. 2010. *Gilles Deleuze and Félix Guattari: Intersecting Lives.* Translated by Deborah Glassman. New York: Columbia University Press.

Dreyfus, Hubert. 2005. "Hubert L. Dreyfus Interview: Conversations with History." Interviewed by Harry Kreisler. Institute of International Studies, University of California, Berkeley. Accessed March 14, 2009. http://globetrotter.berkeley.edu/people5/Dreyfus/dreyfus-cono.html.

Du Ruzu. 1985. "Zhongyi 'shen' de yanjiu ji jidian kanfa" [A view of the studies of the kidney in Chinese medicine]. In *Zhongguo zhongyi yanjiuyuan sanshinian tunwen xuan 1955–1985* [A collection of papers over the past thirty years of the Chinese Academy of TCM 1955–1985], edited by Chinese Academy of TCM, 486–87. Beijing: Zhongyi guji chubanshe.

Elvin, Mark. 1993. "Tales of Shen and Xin: Body-Person and Heart-Mind in China during the Last 150 Years." In *Self as Body in Asian Theory and Practice*, edited by Thomas P. Kasulis, Roger T. Ames, and Wimal Dissanayake, 213–94. Albany: State University of New York Press.

Engels, Friedrich. 1978. "The Origin of the Family, Private Property, and the State." In *The Marx-Engels Reader*, 2nd ed., edited by Robert C. Tucker, 734–59. New York: W. W. Norton.

Escoffier, Jeffrey, ed. 2003. *Sexual Revolution.* New York: Thunder's Mouth Press.

Evans, Harriet. 1997. *Women and Sexuality in China: Dominant Discourses of Female Sexuality and Gender since 1949.* Cambridge, UK: Polity Press.

Fan Youping, Shi Zhichao, Chen Zihua, and Zhao Fengqin, eds. 1997. *Zhonghua xingxue guanzhi* [An ultimate collection of Chinese sexological classics]. Guangzhou: Guangdong renmin chubanshe.

Fang Gang. 1999. *Nanren jiefang* [Men's liberation]. Beijing: Zhonguo huaqiao chubanshe.

Fang, Jianchun. 2007. "Beijing gaoyuan zhongshenpanjue wanaike zhuanli youxiao" [Beijing Supreme Court upholds that the patent of Viagra valid]. *China Medical News*, July 29. Accessed August 23, 2008. http://www.39kf.com/yyjj/Intellectual-property-rights/2007–11–03–425937.shtml.

Farmer, Paul. 2004. *Pathologies of Power.* Berkeley: University of California Press.

Farquhar, Judith. 1987. "Problems of Knowledge in Contemporary Chinese Medical Discourse." *Social Science and Medicine* 24: 1013–21.

Farquhar, Judith. 1994. *Knowing Practice.* Boulder, CO: Westview Press.

Farquhar, Judith. 1999. "Technologies of Everyday Life: The Economy of Impotence in Reform China." *Cultural Anthropology* 14 (2): 155–79.

Farquhar, Judith. 2002. *Appetites: Food and Sex in Post-socialist China.* Durham, NC: Duke University Press.

Farquhar, Judith, and Qicheng Zhang. 2012. *Ten Thousand Things: Nurturing Life in Contemporary Beijing.* New York: Zone Books.

Farrer, James. 2002. *Opening Up: Youth Sex Culture and Market Reform in Shanghai*. Chicago: University of Chicago Press.

Fassin, Didier. 2007. *When Bodies Remember: Experiences and Politics of AIDS in South Africa*. Berkeley: University of California Press.

Faubion, James D. 2012. "Foucault and the Genealogy of Ethics." In *A Companion to Moral Anthropology*, edited by Didier Fassin, 67–84. Malden, MA: Wiley-Blackwell.

Feng Yuming and Cheng Genqun. 1997. *Zhongguo qixiang yu dili bingli xue* [A study of traditional Chinese medicine on meteorological and geographical pathology]. Shanghai: Shanghai kexuepuji chubanshe.

Feng Zhaozhang. 1996. *Feng shi jinnang milu* [Secret records in Scholar Feng's brocade]. Beijing: Zhongguo zhongyiyao chubanshe.

Ferguson, James. 1999. *Expectations of Modernity*. Berkeley: University of California Press.

Fink, Bruce. 1995. *The Lacanian Subject*. Princeton, NJ: Princeton University Press.

Fishman, Jennifer R. 2006. "Making Viagra: From Impotence to Erectile Dysfunction." In *Medicating Modern America*, edited by Andrea Tone and Elizabeth Siegel Watkins, 229–52. New York: New York University Press.

Fong, Vanessa. 2011. *Paradise Redefined: Transnational Chinese Students and the Quest for Flexible Citizenship in the Developed World*. Palo Alto, CA: Stanford University Press.

Foster, George M. 1967. *Tzintzuntzan: Mexican Peasants in a Changing World*. Boston: Little, Brown.

Foucault, Michel. 1988. *The History of Sexuality*. Vol. 3: *The Care of the Self*. New York: Vintage Books.

Foucault, Michel. 1990a. *The History of Sexuality*. Vol. 1. Translated by Robert Hurley. New York: Vintage Books.

Foucault, Michel. 1990b. *The History of Sexuality*. Vol. 2: *The Use of Pleasure*. New York: Vintage Books.

Foucault, Michel. 1994. *The Order of Things*. New York: Vintage Books.

Foucault, Michel. 1997. *Michel Foucault: Ethics—Subjectivity and Truth. Essential Works of Foucault 1954-1984*, vol. I, edited by Paul Rabinow. New York: New Press.

Foucault, Michel. 1998. *Aesthetics, Method, and Epistemology. Essential Works of Foucault 1954-1984*, vol. II, edited by James D. Faubion. New York: New Press.

Foucault, Michel. 2000. *Power. Essential Works of Foucault 1954-1984*, vol. III, edited by James D. Faubion. New York: New Press.

Foucault, Michel. 2003. *Abnormal: Lectures at the Collège de France 1974-1975*. New York: Picador.

Frank, Katherine. 2002. *G-strings and Sympathy*. Durham, NC: Duke University Press.

Freud, Sigmund. 1964. "Fixation to Traumas—The Unconscious." In *The Standard*

Edition of the Complete Psychological Works of Sigmund Freud, Volume XVI, translated by James Strachey. London: Hogarth Press.

Freud, Sigmund. 1989a. "Repression." In *The Freud Reader*, edited by Peter Gay, 568–72. New York: W. W. Norton.

Freud, Sigmund. 1989b [1912]. "On the Universal Tendency to Debasement in the Sphere of Love (Contributions to the Psychology of Love I)." In *The Freud Reader*, edited by Peter Gay, 394–400. New York: W. W. Norton.

Freud, Sigmund. 2006. "Beyond the Pleasure Principle." In *The Penguin Freud Reader*, 132–95. New York: Penguin Books.

Friedman, Sara L. 2006. *Intimate Politics: Marriage, the Market, and State Power in Southeastern China*. Cambridge, MA: Harvard University Asia Center.

Fu Lianzhang. 1959a. *Yangshen zhi dao* [The way of nurturing the body]. Beijing: Renmin weisheng chubanshe.

Fu Lianzhang. 1959b. *Zai Maozhuxi de jiaodaoxia* [Under Chairman Mao's guidance]. Beijing: Zuojia chubanshe.

Fu Lianzhang. 1979. *Jiankang mantan* [Casual Conversation about Health]. Beijing: Kexue puji chubanshe.

Fu Shan. 1993. *Fu Qingzhu nannüke* [Fu Qingzhu on men's and women's medicine]. Beijing: Zhongguo yiyao chubanshe.

Furth, Charlotte. 1994. "Rethinking van Gulik: Sexuality and Reproduction in Traditional Chinese Medicine." In *Engendering China: Women, Culture, and the State*, edited by Christina Gilmartin, Gail Hershatter, Lisa Rofel, and Tyrene White, 125–46. Cambridge, MA: Harvard University Press.

Furth, Charlotte. 1999. *A Flourishing Yin*. Berkeley: University of California Press.

Furth, Charlotte. 2005. "Rethinking van Gulik Again." *Nan Nü* 7 (1): 71–78.

Furth, Charlotte, ed. 2010. *Health and Hygiene in Chinese East Asia*. Durham, NC: Duke University Press.

Gadamer, Hans-Georg. 1996. *The Enigma of Health*. Palo Alto, CA: Stanford University Press.

Gao Jihe, ed. 1994. *Zhongyi nanke zhengzhi leicui* [A collection of cases of diagnosis and treatment of nanke diseases of Chinese medicine]. Tianjin: Tianjin Kexuejishu Chubanshe.

Gao Shiguo. 1996. "Shouzhang cao yu fangshi yangsheng" [The walking cane exercise and sexual cultivation]. In *Minglao zhongyi tan yangsheng zhi dao* [Renowned and old doctors of Chinese medicine speak of the way of yangshen], edited by Li Junde, 246–48. Beijing: Huaxia chubanshe.

Gardiner, Judith Kegan. 2002. *Masculinity Studies and Feminist Theory*. New York: Columbia University Press.

Gillette, Maris Boyd. 2000. *Between Macca and Beijing: Modernization and Consumption among Urban Chinese Muslims*. Palo Alto, CA: Stanford University Press.

Gilmore, David. 1990. *Manhood in the Making: Cultural Concepts of Masculinity*. New Haven, CT: Yale University Press.

Godelier, Maurice. 1986. *The Making of Great Men*. New York: Cambridge University Press.

Goldstein, Irving. 1998. "Impotence: Questions and Answers." *NOVA*. PBS, May 12. Accessed April 14, 2003. http://www.pbs.org/wgbh/nova/body/impotence-goldstein.html.

Good, Byron J. 1977. "The Heart of What's the Matter: The Semantics of Illness in Iran." *Culture, Medicine, and Psychiatry* 1: 25–28.

Good, Byron J. 1994. *Medicine, Rationality, and Experience: An Anthropological Perspective*. New York: Cambridge University Press.

Good, Byron J., and Mary-Jo DelVecchio Good. 1980. "The Meaning of Symptoms: A Cultural Hermeneutic Model for Clinical Practice." In *The Relevance of Social Science for Medicine*, edited by Leon Eisenberg and Arthur Kleinman, 165–96. Dordrecht, Holland: D. Reidel Publishing.

Good, Byron J., Michael M. J. Fischer, Sarah S. Willen, and Mary-Jo Delvecchio Good, eds. 2010. *A Reader in Medical Anthropology*. Malden, MA: Wiley-Blackwell.

Good, Mary-Jo DelVecchio, Paul E. Brodwin, Byron J. Good, and Arthur Kleinman, eds. 1992. *Pain as Human Experience: An Anthropological Perspective*. Berkeley: University of California Press.

Greenhalgh, Susan. 2008. *Just One China: Science and Policy in Deng's China*. Berkeley: University of California Press.

Greenhalgh, Susan, and Edwin Winckler. 2005. *Governing China's Population: From Leninist to Neoliberal Biopolitics*. Palo Alto, CA: Stanford University Press.

Gregor, Thomas. 1977. *Mehinaku: The Drama of Daily Life in a Brazilian Indian Village*. Chicago: University of Chicago Press.

Grosz, Elizabeth. 1994. *Volatile Bodies*. Bloomington: Indiana University Press.

Guang, Lei. 2007. "Rural 'Guerrilla' Workers and Home Renovation in Urban China." In *Working in China: Ethnographies of Labor and Workplace Transformation*, edited by Ching Kwan Lee, 56–76. London: Routledge.

Guo Qianheng. 1996. "Jianshen fangbing ba yao" [Eight crucial points on strengthening the body and preventing illnesses]. In *Minglao zhongyi tan yangsheng zhi dao* [Renowned and old doctors of Chinese medicine speak of the way of yangsheng], edited by Li Junde, 257–60. Beijing: Huaxia chubanshe.

Gupta, Akhil. 1998. *Postcolonial Developments: Agriculture in the Making of Modern India*. Durham, NC: Duke University Press.

Gutmann, Matthew C. 2007. *Fixing Men*. Berkeley: University of California Press.

Hammond, William. 1974 [1887]. *Sexual Impotence in the Male and Female*. New York: Arno Press.

Hansen, Mette Halskov, and Rune Svarverud, eds. 2010. *iChina: The Rise of the Individual in Modern Chinese Society*. Copenhagen: NIAS.

Hanson, Marta. 1998. "Robust Northerners and Delicate Southerners: The Nineteenth-Century Invention of a Southern Medical Tradition." *Positions* 6 (3): 515–550.

Hanson, Marta. 2010. "Conceptual Blind Spots, Media Blindfolds: The Case of SARS and Traditional Chinese Medicine." In *Health and Hygiene in Chinese East Asia*, edited by C. Furth, 228–54. Durham, NC: Duke University Press.

Haraway, Donna. 1991. "A Cyborg Manifesto: Science, Technology, and Socialist-Feminism in the Late Twentieth Century." *Simians, Cyborgs, and Women*, 149–82. New York: Routledge.

Harper, Donald J. 1998. *Early Chinese Medical Literature: The Mawangdui Medical Manuscripts*. Translation and study by Donald Harper. London: Kegan Paul.

Hay, John. 1994. "The Body Invisible in Chinese Art?" In *Body, Subject and Power in China*, edited by A. Zito and T. Barlow. Chicago: University of Chicago Press.

Heidegger, Martin. 1962. *Being and Time*. New York: Harper and Row.

Heidegger, Martin. 2001. *Zollikon Seminars*, edited by Medard Boss, translated by Franz Mayr and Richard Askay. Evanston, IL: Northwestern University Press.

Heidegger, Martin. 2005. *The Essence of Human Freedom: An Introduction to Philosophy*. Translated by Ted Sadler. New York: Continuum.

Herdt, Gilbert. 1994. *Guardians of the Flutes*. Chicago: University of Chicago Press.

Hershatter, Gail. 1996. "Sexing Modern China." In *Remapping China: Fissures in Historical Terrain*, edited by G. Hershatter, E. Honig, J. Lipman, and R. Stross, 77–93. Palo Alto, CA: Stanford University Press.

Hershatter, Gail. 1997. *Dangerous Pleasures*. Berkeley: University of California Press.

Hershatter, Gail. 2006. *Women in China's Long 20th Century*. Berkeley: University of California Press.

Ho, Loretta Wing Wal. 2011. *Gay and Lesbian Subculture in Urban China*. London: Routledge.

Honig, Emily. 2003. "Socialist Sex: The Cultural Revolution Revisited." *Modern China* 29 (2): 143–75.

Honig, Emily, and Gail Hershatter. 1988. *Personal Voices: Chinese Women in the 1980s*. Palo Alto, CA: Stanford University Press.

Hou Hongping. 2003. "Guanyu 'wushu ke du' de sanzhong kanfa" [Three views on 'Nothing is worth reading']. *New Weekly*, November 12.

Hsu, Elisabeth. 1999. *The Transmission of Chinese Medicine*. New York: Cambridge University Press.

Hu Wenhuan, ed. 1997 [1592]. *Shouyang congshu quanji* [A complete collection of books on cultivation of life for longevity], collated by Li Jingwei et al. Beijing: Zhongguo zhongyiyao chubanshe.

Huang K'o-wu. 1988. "Cong Shengbao yiyao guanggao kan minchu Shanghai de yi wenhua yu shehui shenghuo, 1912–1926" [Examining medical culture and social life in early Republican Shanghai through the lens of commercials on Shenbao]. *Journal of Institute of Modern History of Academia Sinica* 17 (2): 141–94.

Huashan Hospital of No. One Medical College. 1977. *Zhongyi* [Chinese medicine]. Shanghai: Diyi yixueyuan.

Hyde, Alan. 1997. *Bodies of Law*. Princeton, NJ: Princeton University Press.

Hyde, Sandra T. 2007. *Eating Spring Rice: The Cultural Politics of* AIDS *in Southwest China*. Berkeley: University of California Press.

Jacka, Tamara. 2005. *Rural Women in Urban China: Gender, Migration and Social Change*. New York: M.E. Sharpe.

Jackson, Michael, ed. 1996. *Things as They Are: New Directions in Phenomenological Anthropology*. Bloomington: Indiana University Press.

Jacobs, Katrien. 2012. *People's Pornography: Sex and Surveillance on the Chinese Internet*. Chicago: Intellect.

Jankowiak, William. 1993. *Sex, Death, and Hierarchy in a Chinese City*. New York: Columbia University Press.

Jeffreys, Elaine, ed. 2006. *Sex and Sexuality in China*. London: Routledge.

Jeong, S-J., K. Park, J-D. Moon, and S. B. Ryu. 2002. "Bicycle Saddle Shape Affects Penile Blood Flow." *International Journal of Impotence Research* 14: 513–17.

Jhaveri, F. M., R. Rutledge, and C. C. Carson. 1998. "Penile Prosthesis Implantation Surgery: A Statewide Population Based Analysis of 2354 Patients." *International Journal of Impotence Research* 10: 251–54.

Jia Pinwa. 1993. *Feidu* [The defunct capital]. Beijing: Beijing Chubanshe.

Jiang Bishan. 1932. "Zhongxiyi lun shen dichu zhi pipan" [A critique of the view on the conflict between Chinese medicine and Western medicine with regard to the kidney]. In *Zhongyi xinlun huibian* [A collection of new perspectives of Chinese medicine], vol. 1, edited by Wang Shenxuan, 30–31. Suzhou: Suzhou guoyi shushe.

Jiang Hansheng and Jiang Wanxuan. 1983. "Zhongguo chuantong shehui wenhua beijing zhong de xing wuneng" [Impotence in the cultural background of traditional Chinese society]. *Dangdai yixue zazhi* [Journal of modern medicine] 10 (5): 388–94.

Jiang Yubo. 1965. "Jiang Yubo yian" [Medical cases treated by Jiang Yubo]. *Guangdong Yixue*, no. 1: 37–38.

Jing, Jun. 1996. *The Temple of Memories*. Palo Alto, CA: Stanford University Press.

Johannes, Catherine B., Andre B. Araujo, Henry A. Feldman, Carol A. Derby, Ken P. Kleinman, and John B. McKinlay. 2000. "Incidence of Erectile Dysfunction in Men 40 to 69 Years Old: Longitudinal Results from the Massachusetts Male Aging Study." *Journal of Urology* 163: 460–63.

Johnson, Mark. 2007. *The Making of the Body: Aesthetics of Human Understanding*. Chicago: University of Chicago Press.

Jullien, François. 2007. *Vital Nourishment*. Translated by Arthur Goldhammer. New York: Zone Books.

Kaplan, Helen S. 1974. *New Sex Therapy: Active Treatment of Sexual Dysfunctions*. New York: Times Books.

Kaptchuk, Ted J. 2002. "Acupuncture: Theory, Efficacy, and Practice." *Annals of Internal Medicine* 136 (5): 374–83.

Kimmel, Michael. 2009. *Guyland: The Perilous World Where Boys Become Men*. New York: Harper Perennial.

Kipnis, Andrew B. 1997. *Producing Guanxi*. Durham, NC: Duke University Press.

Kipnis, Andrew B. 2011. *Governing Educational Desire: Culture, Politics, and Schooling in China*. Chicago: University of Chicago Press.

Kleinman, Arthur. 1980. *Patients and Healers in the Context of Culture: An Exploration of the Borderland between Anthropology, Medicine, and Psychiatry*. Berkeley: University of California Press.

Kleinman, Arthur. 1986. *Social Origins of Distress and Disease: Depression, Neurasthenia, and Pain in Modern China*. New Haven, CT: Yale University Press.

Kleinman, Arthur. 1989. *The Illness Narratives: Suffering, Healing, and the Human Condition*. New York: Basic Books.

Kleinman, Arthur. 1999. "Experience and its Moral Modes: Culture, Human Conditions and Disorder." In *The Tanner Lectures on Human Values*, vol. 20, edited by Grethe Peterson, 357–420. Salt Lake City: University of Utah Press.

Kleinman, Arthur. 2007. *What Really Matters: Living a Moral Life amidst Uncertainty and Danger*. New York: Oxford University Press.

Kleinman, Arthur, Veena Das, and Margaret M. Lock, eds. 1997. *Social Suffering*. Berkeley: University of California Press.

Kleinman, Arthur, and Joan Kleinman. 1985. "Somatization: The Interconnections in Chinese Society among Culture, Depressive Experiences and the Meanings of Pain." In *Culture and Depression*, edited by A. Kleinman and B. Good, 429–90. Berkeley: University of California Press.

Kleinman, Arthur, Yunxiang Yan, Jun Jing, Sing Lee, Everett Zhang, Pan Tianshu, Wu Fei, and Guo Jinhua. 2011. *Deep China: The Moral Life of the Person*. Berkeley: University of California Press.

Kohrman, Matthew. 2005. *Bodies of Difference*. Berkeley: University of California Press.

Kohrman, Matthew. 2008. "Smoking among Doctors: Governmentality, Embodiment, and the Diversion of Blame in Contemporary China." *Medical Anthropology* 27 (1): 9–42.

Kuriyama, Shigehisa. 1999. *The Expressiveness of the Body*. New York: Zone Books.

Lacan, Jacques. 1991. *The Seminar of Jacques Lacan Book I*. New York: W. W. Norton.

Lacan, Jacques. 1992. *The Seminar. Book VII: The Ethics of Psychoanalysis, 1959–60*. Translated by D. Porter. New York: W. W. Norton.

Lacan, Jacques. 2007. *Ecrits*. New York: W. W. Norton.

Laqueur, Thomas W. 2003. *Solitary Sex: A Cultural History of Masturbation*. New York: Zone Books.

Larson, Wendy. 1998. *Women and Writing in Modern China*. Palo Alto, CA: Stanford University Press.

Latour, Bruno. 1993. *We Have Never Been Modern*. Translated by Catherine Porter. Cambridge, MA: Harvard University Press.

Leary, Charles Leland. 1994. "Sexual Modernism in China: Zhang Jingsheng and 1920s Urban Culture." PhD diss., Cornell University.

Lee, Ching Kwan. 2007. *Against the Law: Labor Protest in China's Rustbelt and Sunbelt*. Berkeley: University of California Press.

Lee, Haiyan. 2006. *Revolution of the Heart: A Genealogy of Love in China, 1900–1950.* Palo Alto, CA: Stanford University Press.

Lee Tender. 2008. *Nüren de zhongguo yiliao shi* [Women's Chinese medical history]. Taipei: Sanmin shuju.

Lei, Sean Hsiang-lin. 2002. "How Did Chinese Medicine Become Experiential? The Political Epistemology of *Jingyan*." *Positions* 10 (2): 1–32.

Lei, Sean Hsiang-lin. 2014. *Neither Donkey Nor Horse: Medicine in the Struggle over China's Modernity*. Chicago: University of Chicago Press.

Leslie, Charles, and Allan Young, eds. 1992. *Paths to Asian Medical Knowledge*. Berkeley: University of California Press.

Levine, Stephen B. 1992. "Intrapsychic and Interpersonal Aspects of Impotence: Psychogenic Erectile Dysfunction." In *Erectile Disorders: Assessment and Treatment*, edited by Raymond C. Rosen and Sandra R. Leiblum, 198–225. New York: Guilford Press.

Li Hanlin. 2008. "Gaige yu danwei zhidu de bianqian" [The reform and the change in the system of danwei]. In *Zhongguo shehui bianqian sanshinian 1978–2008* [Social change in China 1978–2008], edited by Li Qiang, 179–216. Beijing: Shehui kexue wenxian chubanshe.

Li Huilin. 2009. "Guoji shiye xia de zhongguo jingji tiyu 'yin sheng yang shuai' xianxiang yanjiu" [A study of the phenomenon of 'yin waxes and yang wanes' of China's sports from the international perspective]. *Wuhan tiyuxueyuan xuebao* [Journal of Wuhan Institute of Physical Education] 43 (3): 19–27.

Li Jianmin. 2000. *Fangshu Yixue Lishi* [Fangshu medicine history]. Taipei: Nantian Shuju.

Li Jianyi. 1928. "Lun jing de yuanyi" [On the fundamentals of jing]. *Yijie chunqiu* 2 (24): 16.

Li Jiazhen and Pang Guorong. 1983. *Zhongyi nanke zhenzhi* [Diagnoses and treatment of men's medicine of Chinese medicine]. Chongqing: Kexuejishu chubanshe Chongqing fenshe.

Li Jingwei et al., eds. 1995. *Zhongyi da cidian* [A comprehensive dictionary of traditional Chinese medicine]. Beijing: Renmin weisheng chubanshe.

Li Junde, ed. 1996. *Minglao zhongyi tan yangsheng zhidao* [Renowned and old doctors of Chinese medicine speak of the way of yangsheng]. Beijing: Huaxia chubanshe.

Li Ling. 2006a. "Mawangdui fangzhongshu yanjiu" [A study of the bed chamber arts of Mawangdui scripture]. In *Zhongguo fangshu zhengkao* [A principal study of ancient Chinese fangshu], 302–42. Beijing: Zhonghua shuju.

Li Ling. 2006b. *Zhongguo fangshu xukao* [A continuous study of ancient Chinese fangshu]. Beijing: Zhonghua shuju.

Li Peilin. 2008. "Gaige kaifang sanshinian yu shehui zhengce de bianhua" [Thirty years of reform and opening up and the change in social policy]. In *Zhongguo shehui bianqian sanshinian* [China's thirty years of social change], edited by Li Qiang, 341–73. Beijing: Shehui kexue wenxian chubanshe.

Li Qiang. 2008. *Zhongguo shehui bianqian sanshinian* [Thirty years of social change in China]. Beijing: Shehui kexue chubanshe.

Li Shizhen. 2005 [1596]. *Bencao Gangmu* [Compendium of material medica]. Beijing: Renminweishen chubanshe.

Li Shuang. 1992. *Mengzi baihua jinyi* [Contemporary vernacular translation of Mengzi]. Beijing: Zhongguo shudian.

Li Shuang. 1994. *Zhuangzi baihua jinyi* [Contemporary vernacular translation of Zhuangzi]. Beijing: Zhongguo shudian.

Li Yangheng. 1955. "Yong zhongyao zhiliao yangwei de chubu zhiyan" [The preliminary exploration of treating impotence with herbal therapy]. *Zhongyi Zazhi*, no. 3: 25.

Li Yinhe. 1996. *Zhongguo nüxing de xing yue ai* [Sex and love of Chinese women]. New York: Oxford University Press.

Li Yinhe. 2005. *Shuo xing* [On sexuality]. Harbin: Beifang wenyi chubanshe.

Li Zhongzi. 1642. *Shanbu yisheng weilun* [Small comments on nurturing life — enhanced version]. Woodblock edition held by the Gest Library, Princeton University.

Liang, Zhiping. 2011. "The Death of a Detainee: The Predicament of Status Politics in Contemporary China and the Way out." In *Governance of Life in Chinese Moral Experience*, edited by Everett Zhang, Arthur Kleinman, and Weiming Tu. 83–102. London: Routledge.

Liao Yuqun. 1994. *Qihuang yidao* [The medical way of Qihuang]. Taipei: Hongye wenhua shiye youxiangongsi.

Lin Shanshan, Liu Lin, Jiang Linlin, and Huang Qianru. 2011. "Xingjiaoyu liushi nian: Zai Mengmei yu ganga zhong mosuo" [Sixty year's of sex education: Groping in ignorance and awkwardness]. *Southern People Weekly*, August 26. Accessed July 7, 2012. http://news.sina.com.cn/c/sd/2011-08-26/152423056748.shtml.

Lin Xuan. 1966. *Zhao Feiyan waizhuan* [An unauthorized biography of Zhao Feiyan]. Taipei: Yiwen yinshuguan.

Liu Dalin. 1998. *Zhongguo lidai fangneikao* [A historical examination of Chinese sexuality]. Beijing: Zhongyi guji chubanshe.

Liu Dalin. 2000. *Ershishiji zhongguo xingwenhua* [Chinese sexual culture in the 20th century]. Shanghai: Sanlian shudian.

Liu Jianjun. 2001. *Danwei Zhongguo* [China under the system of danwei]. Tianjin: Tianjin renmin chubanshe.

Liu, Lydia H. 1995. *Translingual Practice*. Palo Alto, CA: Stanford University Press.

Liu Xiaomeng. 1998. *Zhongguo zhiqing shi* [A history of China's zhiqing]. Beijing: Dangdai zhongguo chubanshe.

Liu, Xin. 2002. *The Otherness of Self*. Ann Arbor: University of Michigan Press.

Liu, Xin. 2009. *The Mirage of China: Anti-humanism, Narcissism, and Corporeality of the Contemporary World*. New York: Berghahn Books.

Liu Xinwu. 1979. "Aiqing de weizhi" [The place of romantic love]. In *Aiqing xiao-shuoji* [A collection of short stories on love], edited by Shanghai wenyi chuban-she, 235–48. Shanghai: Shanghai wenyi chubanshe.

Liu Xinwu. 2008. "Wei aiqing huifu weizhi" [Recovering the place for romantic love]. Accessed April 7, 2011. http://www.gmw.cn/01wzb/2008-12/18/content _870514.htm.

Lock, Margaret. 1995. *Encounters with Aging*. Berkeley: University of California Press.

Lock, Margaret, and Vinh-kim Nguyen. 2010. *An Anthropology of Biomedicine*. Malden, MA: Wiley-Blackwell.

Loe, Meika. 2004. *The Rise of Viagra*. New York: New York University Press.

Long Yintai. 1998. *A, Shanghai nanren* [Ah, Shanghai men]. Shanghai: Xuelin chu-banshe.

LoPiccolo, Joseph. 1992. "Postmodern Sex Therapy for Erectile Failure." In *Erectile Disorders: Assessment and Treatment*, edited by R. C. Rosen and S. R. Leiblum. New York: Guilford Press.

Lou Baiceng and Wang Xiaochun. 1964. "Zhenjiu zhiliao yangwei linchuang liao-xiao guancha" [An examination of the clinical effect of acupuncture treatment of impotence]. *Jiangsu Zhongyi*, no. 6: 9–11.

Louie, Kam. 2002. *Theorizing Chinese Masculinity*. New York: Cambridge Univer-sity Press.

Louie, Kam. 2012. "Popular Culture and Masculinity Ideals in East Asia, with Spe-cial Reference to China." *Journal of Asian Studies* 71 (4): 929–43.

Lu, Xiaobo, and Elizabeth Perry, eds. 1997. *Danwei: The Changing Chinese Workplace in Historical and Comparative Perspectives*. Armonk, NY: M. E. Sharpe.

Lu Zijie and Xue Jianyun. 2000. "Yinwei yangwei bian" [On the difference between yinwei and yangwei]. *Zhongguo yiyao xuebao* 15 (6): 42–43.

Lue, Tom F. 2000. "Erectile Dysfunction." *New England Journal of Medicine* 342 (24): 1802–13.

Ma Shanzhen. 1931. "Zhengqiu zhi yijing he yangwei de liaofa" [Soliciting therapies for spermatorrhea and impotence]. *Yijie chunqiu* 5 (57): 26.

Mahmood, Saba. 1996. "Cultural Studies and Ethnic Absolutism: Comments on Stuart Hall's 'Culture, Community, and Nation.'" *Cultural Studies* 11 (1): 1–11.

Mai Tianshu. 1996. "Xing wangguo de yinmi shijie" [A secret world in the kingdom of sexuality]. In *Nannü shiren tan* [Works of ten men and women writers], edited by Zhongguo dangdai qingai lunli zuoping shu xi bianji weiyuanhui, 1–174. Bei-jing: Jinrizhongguo chubanshe.

Malinowski, Bronislaw. 1927. *Sex and Repression in Savage Society*. New York: Har-court, Brace.

Mamo, Laura, and Jennifer R. Fishman. 2001. "Potency in All the Right Places: Viagra as a Technology of the Gendered Body." *Body and Society* 7: 13–35.

Marcuse, Herbert. 1966. *Eros and Civilization*. Boston: Beacon Press.

Martin, Emily. 2001. *Women in the Body*, rev. ed. Boston: Beacon Press.

Marx, Karl. 1844. *Economic and Philosophical Manuscripts*. Marx-Engels Library (on-

line). http://www.marxists.org/archive/marx/works/1844/manuscripts/preface
.htm.

Marx, Karl. 1867. *Capital Vol. I.* Marx-Engels Library (online). http://www.marxists
.org/archive/marx/works/1867-c1/index.htm.

Mascia-Lees, Frances E., ed. 2011. *A Companion to the Anthropology of the Body and
Embodiment.* Malden, MA: Wiley-Blackwell.

Masters, William, and Virginia Johnson. 1966. *Human Sexual Response.* Boston:
Little, Brown.

Masters, William, and Virginia Johnson. 1970. *Human Sexual Inadequacy.* Boston:
Little, Brown.

Mauss, Marcel. 1979. *Sociology and Psychology.* Translated by Ben Brewster. London:
Routledge and Kegan Paul.

McCabe, M. P., H. Conaglen, J. Conaglen, and E. O'Connor. 2010. "Motivations
for Seeking Treatment for ED: The Woman's Perspective." *International Journal
of Impotence Research* 22: 152–58.

McCullough, Andrew. 1999. "Sildenafil (Viagra™) One Year Later: A Retrospec-
tive." *Sexual Dysfunction in Medicine* 1 (1): 2–7.

McKinlay, J. B. 2000. "The World Wide Prevalence and Epidemiology of Erectile
Dysfunction." *International Journal of Impotence Research Supplement* 4: 6–11.

McLaren, Angus. 2007. *Impotence: A Cultural History.* Chicago: University of Chicago Press.

McNamara, Erin R., and Craig F. Donatucci. 2011. "Oral Therapy for Erectile Dysfunction." In *Contemporary Treatment of Erectile Dysfunction: A Clinical Guide*,
edited by Kevin T. McVary, 93–106. New York: Humana Press.

Melchiode, Gerald. 1999. *Beyond Viagra.* New York: Henry Holt and Company.

Merleau-Ponty, Maurice. 1962. *The Phenomenology of Perception.* Translated by
C. Smith. New York: Routledge.

Merleau-Ponty, Maurice. 1973. *The Visible and the Invisible.* Evanston: Northwestern University Press.

Mol, Annemarie. 2002. *The Body Multiple.* Durham, NC: Duke University Press.

Murphy, Robert F. 2001. *The Body Silent.* New York: W. W. Norton.

Nanda, Serena. 1998. *Neither Man nor Woman: The Hijras of India.* 2nd ed. Belmont,
CA: Wadsworth.

National Institutes of Health. 1992. "Impotence." *NIH Consensus Statement* 10 (4):
1–31.

Nichter, Mark. 1992. "Ethnomedicine: Diverse Trends, Common Linkage." In
Anthropological Approaches to the Study of Ethnomedicine, edited by Mark Nichter,
223–59. Langhorne, PA: Gordon and Breach Science Publishers.

Nietzsche, Frederic. 1968. *The Will to Power.* New York: Random House.

Nobile, Philip. 1972. "What Is the New Impotence? And Who's Got it?" *Esquire*
78 (4): 95–99.

Nussbaum, Martha C. 1996. "Patriotism and Cosmopolitanism." *For Love of Country: Debating the Limits of Patriotism.* Boston: Beacon.

Ong, Aihwa, and Nancy N. Chen, eds. 2010. *Asian Biotech*. Durham, NC: Duke University Press.

Ong, Aihwa, and Stephen Collier, eds. 2004. *Global Assemblages: Technology, Politics, and Ethics as Anthropological Problems*. Malden, MA: Blackwell.

Osburg, John L. 2013. *Anxious Wealth: Money and Morality among China's New Rich*. Palo Alto, CA: Stanford University Press.

Ostrovsky, Nikolai. 1974. *How the Steel Was Tempered*. Moscow: Progress Press.

Otis, Eileen. 2011. *Markets and Bodies: Women, Service Work, and the Making of Inequality in China*. Palo Alto, CA: Stanford University Press.

Ots, Thomas. 1990. "The Angry Liver, the Anxious Heart and the Melancholy Spleen: The Phenomenology of Perceptions in Chinese Culture." *Culture, Medicine, and Psychiatry* 14: 21–58.

Palmer, David A. 2007. *Qigong Fever*. New York: Columbia University Press.

Pan Guangdan. 1999. *Pan Guangdan xuanji* [Selected works of Pan Guangdan], edited by Pan Naigu and Pan Naihe. Beijing: Guangming ribao chubanshe.

Pan Suiming. 1995. *Zhongguo xing xianzhuang* [The reality of sexuality in China]. Beijing: Guangming ribao chubanshe.

Pan Suiming. 1998. *Zhongguo Dixia Hongdengqu* [The underground red light districts in China]. Beijing: Institute of Sexual Sociology of People's University.

Pan Suiming. 2005. "Social Gender and Sex Work." In *The "Social Immunization" AIDS*, edited by Gao Yanning, 262–92. Shanghai: Fudan daxue chubanshe.

Pan Suiming. 2006. "Transformations in the Primary Life Cycle: The Origins and Nature of China's Sexual Revolution." In *Sex and Sexuality in China*, edited by Elaine Jeffreys, 21–42. London: Routledge.

Pan Suiming, Huang Qi, Shi Mei, and Wang Xin. 2008. *Zhongguo xinggeming chenggong de shizheng* [The empirical evidence of the success of the sexual revolution in China]. Gaoxiong, Taiwan: Wangyou chubanshe.

Pan Suiming and Huang Yingying. 2011a. *Sexual Sociology*. Beijing: Zhongguo renmin daxue chubanshe.

Pan Suiming and Huang Yingying. 2011b. "Xingqu heng sheng" [The flourishing of sexual enjoyment]. *Ren zhi chu* (May). http://blog.sina.com.cn/s/blog _4dd47e5a0100t6io.html.

Pan Suiming and Huang Yingying. 2011c. "Xingfu yuan yu hu-ai" [Sexual happiness comes from mutual love]. *Ren zhi chu* (June). http://blog.sina.com.cn/s/blog _4dd47e5a0100t6i6.html.

Parish, William, Ye Luo, Ross Stolzenberg, Edward O. Laumann, Gracia Farrer, and Suiming Pan. 2007. "Sexual Practice and Sexual Satisfaction: A Population Based Study of Chinese Urban Adults." *Archives of Sexual Behavior* 36: 5–20.

Parker, Richard G. 2009. *Bodies, Pleasures, and Passions*. 2nd ed. Nashville, TN: Vanderbilt University Press.

Parkes, Graham, ed. 1990. *Heidegger and Asian Thought*. Honolulu: University of Hawaii Press.

Payton, Terry. 1990. "Self-injection Therapy." In *The Potent Male*, edited by Irwin Goldstein and Larry Rothstein, 116–18. Los Angeles: The Body Press.

Petryna, Adriana. 2002. *Life Exposed*. Princeton, NJ: Princeton University Press.

Pickering, Andrew. 1995. *The Mangle of Practice: Time, Agency, and Science*. Chicago: University of Chicago Press.

Pieterse, Jan N. 2001. "Hybridity, so What? The Anti-hybridity Backlash and the Riddles of Recognition." *Theory, Culture and Society* 18 (2–3): 219–45.

Pigg, Stacey Leigh. 2000. "Languages of Sex and AIDS in Nepal: Notes on the Social Production of Commensurability." *Cultural Anthropology* 16 (4): 481–541.

Polt, Richard. 1999. *Heidegger: An Introduction*. Ithaca, NY: Cornell University Press.

Porkert, Manfred. 1974. *The Theoretical Foundations of Chinese Medicine: Systems of Correspondence*. Cambridge, MA: MIT Press.

Potter, Sulamith. 1987. "Birth Planning in Rural China: A Cultural Account." In *Child Survival*, edited by Nancy Scheper-Hughes, 33–58. Dordrecht, Holland: D. Reidel.

Potts, Annie. 2004. "Deleuze on Viagra (Or, What Can a "Viagra-body" Do?)." *Body and Society* 10: 17–36.

Potts, Annie, Nicola Gavey, Victoria M. Grace, and Tiina Vares. 2003. "The Downside of Viagra: Women's Experiences and Concerns." *Sociology of Health and Illness* 25 (7): 697–719.

Potts, Annie, and Leonore Tiefer, eds. 2006. "Viagra Culture." Special Issue of *Sexualities* 9 (3).

Pritzker, Sonya. 2007. "Thinking Hearts, Feeling Brains: Metaphor, Culture, and the Self in Chinese Narratives of Depression." *Metaphor and Symbol* 22 (3): 251–74.

Qian Shushi. 1931. "Zhengqiu yijing liaofa" [Seeking therapies for spermatorrhea]. *Yijie Chunqiu* 6 (65).

Qian Yanfang. 1990. "Wang Qi zhiliao yangwei suotan" [A discussion of Wang Qi's way to treat impotence]. *Zhongyi zazhi*, no. 2: 21–22.

Qin Guozheng. 1999a. "Yangwei zhongyi fabingxue he zhenghouxue guilü xintan: Fu 717 li liuxingbingxue diaochafenxi" [A new exploration of the etiology and symptomatology of impotence: An analysis of the 717 cases from the epidemiological study of impotence]. *Zhongguo Yiyao Xuebao* 14 (6): 33–37.

Qin Guozheng. 1999b. "Gudai zhongyi bianzhi yangwei de wenxian yanjiu" [A study of the literature of diagnoses and treatment of yangwei in ancient Chinese medicine]. *Journal of Nanjing University of TCM* 15 (5): 311–14.

Qin Guozheng. 2000a. "Jin wushinian zhongyi yanzhi yangwei shuping: Fu 866 pian wenxian fenxi" [On fifty years' research on impotence in TCM: An analysis of 866 articles]. *Zhongyi Wenxian Zazhi*, no. 1: 37–47.

Qin Guozheng. 2000b. "Zhongyi nankexue kaolue kaobian" [Rebuttal of an examination of nanke of TCM). *Zhongguo Yiyao Xuebao*, no. 2: 71–73.

Qin Guozheng. 2000c. "Yangwei bingming yu guishu ji bianbing yanbian kao" [On the naming of impotence and the evolution of its classification and clinical differentiation]. *Zhongguo yixueshi zazhi* [Chinese journal of medical history] 30 (1): 28–31.

Qin Hui. 2003. "Zhongguo dangqian de jingji zhuanggui (On current China's change of economic ownership)." Zhongguowang. January 13. Accessed June 7, 2010. http://www.china.com.cn/chinese/OP-c/260765.htm.

Qin Hui. 2010. "Cong nanfei kan zhongguo hequhecong de qianjing bijiao (A comparison between South Africa and China in the future development)." Caijingwang, April 15. Accessed May 5, 2010. http://blog.caijing.com.cn/expert_article -151381-5023.shtml.

Rabinow, Paul. 1996. "Representations Are Social Facts: Modernity and Post-Modernity in Anthropology." *Essays on the Anthropology of Reason*, 28–58. Princeton, NJ: Princeton University Press.

Rabinow, Paul. 1998. "Introduction: The History of Systems of Thought." In *Michel Foucault: Ethics: Subjectivity and Truth*, by Michel Foucault, edited by Paul Rabinow, x–xlii. New York: New Press.

Rabinow, Paul. 2007. *Marking Time: On the Anthropology of the Contemporary*. Princeton, NJ: Princeton University Press.

Rajfer, J. 2008. "Discovery of NO in the penis." *International Journal of Impotence Research* 20: 431–36.

Reich, Wilhelm. 1970. *The Mass Psychology of Fascism*. New York: Noonday Press.

Riley, A. 2002. "The Role of the Partner in Erectile Dysfunction and Its Treatment." *International Journal of Impotence Research* 14 (suppl.): 105–9.

Riley, Nancy. 1997. "Gender Equality in China: Two Steps Forward, One Step Back." In *China Briefing: The Contradictions of Change*, edited by William Joseph, 79–108. Armonk, NY: M. E. Sharpe.

Rofel, Lisa. 1999. *Other Modernities*. Berkeley: University of California Press.

Rofel, Lisa. 2007. *Desiring China*. Durham, NC: Duke University Press.

Rofel, Lisa. 2010. "The Traffic in Money Boys." *Positions* 18 (2): 425–58.

Rosaldo, Renato. 1995. Foreword. In *Hybrid Cultures*. Translated by C. Chiappari and S. Lopez, edited by Nestor Garcia Canclini, xi–xviii. Minneapolis: University of Minnesota Press.

Rose, Nikolas. 2006. *The Politics of Life Itself: Biomedicine, Power, and Subjectivity in the Twenty-First Century*. Princeton, NJ: Princeton University Press.

Rosen, Raymond, and Sandra Leiblum, eds. 1992. "Erectile Disorders: An Overview of Historical Trends and Clinical Perspectives." *Erectile Disorders: Assessment and Treatment*, 3–26. New York: Guilford Press.

Rosen, Raymond C., J. C. Cappelleri, and N. Gendrano III. 2002. "The International Index of Erectile Function (IIEF): A State-of-the-Science Review." *International Journal of Impotence Research* 14: 226–44.

Ruan, Fangfu. 1991. *Sex in China: Studies in Sexology in Chinese Culture*. New York: Springer.

Ruan, Fangfu, and Vern L. Bullough. 1989. "Sex Repression in Contemporary China." In *Building a World Community in the 21st Century*, edited by Paul Kurtz, 198–201. Buffalo, NY: Prometheus Books.

Scarry, Elaine. 1985. *The Body in Pain: The Making and Unmaking of the World*. New York: Oxford University Press.

Scheid, Volker. 2001. "Shaping Chinese Medicine: Two Case Studies from Contemporary China." In *Innovations in Chinese Medicine*, edited by Elisabeth Hsu. New York: Cambridge University Press.

Scheid, Volker. 2002. *Chinese Medicine in Contemporary China: Plurality and Synthesis*. Durham, NC: Duke University Press.

Scheid, Volker. 2007. *Currents of Tradition in Chinese Medicine 1626–2006*. Seattle: Eastland Press.

Scheid, Volker. 2013. "The People's Republic of China." In *Chinese Medicine and Healing: An Illustrated History*, edited by T. J. Hinrichs and Linda L. Barnes, 239–83. Cambridge, MA: Harvard University Press.

Schein, Louisa. 1997. "Gender and Internal Orientalism in China." *Modern China* 23 (1): 69–98.

Scheper-Hughes, Nancy. 1992. *Death without Weeping: The Violence of Everyday Life in Brazil*. Berkeley: University of California Press.

Scheper-Hughes, Nancy. 2008. "A Talent for Life: Reflections on Human Vulnerability and Resilience." *Ethnos* 73 (1): 25–56.

Scheper-Hughes, Nancy, and Margaret Lock. 1987. "The Mindful Body: A Prolegomenon to the Future in Medical Anthropology." *Medical Anthropology Quarterly* 1 (1): 6–41.

Sha Yexin. 1986. "Xunzhao nanzihan" [Searching for real men]. *October*, no. 3.

Shapiro, Hugh. 2000. "Neurasthenia and the Assimilation of Nerves into China." Paper presented in "Symposium on the History of Disease" in Academia Sinica, Taipei, Taiwan. June 16–18.

Shapiro, Hugh. 1998. "The Puzzle of Spermatorrhea in Republican China." *Positions* 6 (3): 551–96.

Shen Zhonggui. 1926. "Yijing lun" [On yijing]. *Zhangyi zazhi*, no. 12: 17–18.

Shen Zhonggui. 1927. "Shen zhu lu niao shuo" [On the kidney's function of filtering urine]. *Zhongyi Zazhi*, no. 25: 18–19.

Shi Yonggang and Liu Qiongxiong. 2006. *Lei Feng: 1940–1962*. Beijing: Sanlian shudian.

Shiri, R. 2004. "Effect of Life-style Factors on Incidence of Erectile Dysfunction." *International Journal of Impotence Research* 16: 389–94.

Shusterman, Richard. 2005. "The Silent, Limping Body of Philosophy." In *The Cambridge Companion to Merleay-Ponty*, edited by Taylor Carman and Mark B. N. Hansen, 151–80. New York: Cambridge University Press.

Shusterman, Richard. 2008. *Body Consciousness*. New York: Cambridge University Press.

Simmons, M., and D. K. Montague. 2008. "Penile Prosthesis Implantation: Past, Present and Future." *International Journal of Impotence Research* 20: 437–44.

Sivin, Nathan. 1987. *Traditional Medicine in Contemporary China*. Ann Arbor: Center for Chinese Studies, University of Michigan.

Solinger, Dorothy. 1999. *Contesting Citizenship in Urban China: Peasant Migrants, the State, and the Logic of the Market*. Berkeley: University of California Press.

Song Shugong, ed. 1991. *Zhongguo gudai fangshi yangsheng jiyao* [A selected collection of sexual cultivation in ancient China]. Beijing: Zhongguo yiao keji chubanshe.

Stacey, Judith. 1984. *Patriarchy and Socialist Revolution in China*. Berkeley, CA: University of California Press.

State Administration of TCM of Ministry of Health of PRC. 1993. *Zhongyi xinyao zhiliao yangwei de linchuang yanjiu zhidao yuanzhe* [Guidelines for clinical research on new drugs for treating impotence in Chinese medicine]. Beijing: The Ministry of Health.

Stekel, Wilhelm. 1959 [1927]. *Impotence in the Male: The Psychic Disorders of Sexual Function in the Male*. New York: Liveright Publishing Corporation.

Stoller, Paul. 1995. *Embodying Colonial Memories: Spirit Possession, Power, and the Hauka in West Africa*. New York: Routledge.

Sullivan, Shannon. 1997. "Domination and Dialogue in Merleau-Ponty's Phenomenology of Perception." *Hypatia* 12 (1): 1–19.

Tao Hongjing. 1997. "Yangxing yanming lu" [On nurturing the nature to prolong life]. In *Zhonghua Xingxue Guanzhi* [An ultimate collection of Chinese sexological classics], edited by Fan Youping, Shi Zhichao, Chen Zihua, and Zhao Fengqin, 54–58. Guangzhou: Guangdong renmin chubanse.

Tian Shuliang. 1960. "Niu Huidong shi tan jingyan pangji" [Notes of the discussion by Teacher Niu Huidong of his healing experience]. *Liaoning yixue zazhi*, no. 4: 33.

Tian, Xiaofei. 2011. "The Making of a Hero: Lei Feng and Some Issues of Historiography." In *The People's Republic of China at 60: An International Assessment*, edited by William C. Kirby, 293–305. Cambridge, MA: Harvard University Asia Center.

Tiefer, Leonore. 1986. "In Pursuit of the Perfect Penis." *American Behavioral Scientist* 29: 579–99.

Tiefer, Leonore. 1994. "The Medicalization of Impotence: Normalizing Phallocentrism." *Gender and Society* 8 (3): 363–77.

Tiefer, Leonore. 2006. "The Viagra Phenomenon." *Sexualities* 9 (3): 273–94.

Tierney, Thomas. 1999. "The Preservation and Ownership of the Body." In *Perspectives on Embodiment: The Intersections of Nature and Culture*, edited by Gail Weiss and Honi Fern Haber, 233–61. New York: Routledge.

Treichler, Paula A. 1999. *How to Have Theory in an Epidemic: Cultural Chronicles of AIDS*. Durham, NC: Duke University Press.

Turner, Bryan S. 2008. *Body and Society*. 3rd ed. Los Angeles: Sage.

van Gulik, Robert H. 2003. *Sexual Life in Ancient China: A Preliminary Survey of Chinese Sex and Society from ca. 1500 B.C. till 1644 A.D.* Leiden: E. J. Brill.

Vasavi, A. R. 1994. "'Hybrid Times, Hybrid Peoples': Culture and Agriculture in South India." *Man* 29 (2): 283–300.

Wacquant, Loïc. 2004. *Body and Soul: Notebooks of an Apprentice Boxer*. New York: Oxford University Press.

Walder, Andrew G. 1988. *Communist Neo-Traditionalism: Work and Authority in Chinese Industry*. Berkeley: University of California Press.

Walder, Andrew. 2009. *Fractured Rebellion: The Beijing Red Guard Movement*. Cambridge, MA: Harvard University Press.

Wan Quan. 1997 [1549]. "Guangsi jiyao" [Essential records on multiplying descendants]. In *Zhonghua xingxue guanzhi* [An ultimate collection of Chinese sexological classics], edited by Fan Youping, Shi Zhichao, Chen Zihua, and Zhao Fengqin, 189–227. Guangzhou: Guangdong renmin chubanshe.

Wang Bo. 2011. "Ding Xueliang: Liuxue wei xue zhishi, geng wei zhang jianshi" [Ding Xueliang: Studying abroad more for sharpening vision than for learning knowledge]. *China Youth Daily*, August 23, 10.

Wang Dingyu. 1931. "Wen yijing yu zaoxie zhi zhifa" [Asking for cures for yijing and premature ejaculation]. *Yijie chungqiu* 6 (65): 23.

Wang, Fei-ling. 2005. *Organizing through Division and Exclusion: China's Hukou System*. Palo Alto, CA: Stanford University Press.

Wang Fuzhi. 1981. *Zhuangzi jie* [Exegesis of Zhuangzi]. Beijing: Zhonghua shuju.

Wang Huaiyin. 1980. *Taiping Shenhui Fang*. Taipei: Xinwenfeng chuban gongsi.

Wang Lun. 2007. *Mingyi zazhu*. Beijing: Renmin weisheng chubanshe.

Wang Maohe, ed. 1998. *Zhongguo yangsheng baodian* [Chinese treasured literature of nurturing life]. 2nd ed. Beijing: Zhongguo yiyao keji chubanshe.

Wang Qi. 1985. "Lun yangwei cong gan zhi" [On treating impotence through the liver], recorded by Hong Dehua. *Tianjin Zhongyi*, no. 5: 15.

Wang Qi. 1995. *Zhongyi tishi xue* [A study of traditional Chinese medicine on the bodily quality]. Beijing: Zhongguo yiyao keji chubanshe.

Wang Qi. 1997. *Wang Qi nanke xue* [Wang Qi's study of men's medicine of Chinese medicine]. Zhengzhou: Henan kexuejishu chubanshe.

Wang Qi and Cao Kaiyong. 1988. *Zhongyi nanke xue* [A study of men's medicine of Chinese medicine]. Tianjin: Tianjin kexuejishu chubashe.

Wang Qingjie. 2004. *Jieshixue, Haidegeer he rudao jin shi* [Hermeneutics, Heidegger and contemporary interpretations of Confucianism and Daoism]. Beijing: Zhongguo renmin daxue chubanshe.

Wang Shenxuan, ed. 1932. *Zhongyi xinlun huibian* [A collection of new perspectives of Chinese medicine]. Suzhou: Suzhou guoyi shushe.

Wang Shoukuan. 2004. *Xiaojing yizhu* [Translation and annotation of the book of piety]. Shanghai: Shanghai guji chubanshe.

Wang Wenbin, Zhao Zhiyi, and Tan Mingxun. 1956. *Xing de zhishi* [Knowledge about sex]. Beijing: Renmin weisheng chubanshe.

Wang Zhihua. 1932. "Zhongyi he xiyi zhi yijing de xiangsixing" [My view of the commonality between Chinese medicine and Western medicine on the etiology of spermatorrhea]. In *Zhongyi xinlun huibian* [A collection of new perspectives of Chinese medicine], vol. 9, edited by Wang Shenxuan, 80–82. Suzhou: Suzhou guoyi shushe.

Watson, James L. 2006. "Preface to First Edition." *Golden Arches East: McDonald's in East Asia*. 2nd ed., i–xi. Palo Alto, CA: Stanford University Press.

Watson, James L., and Melissa L. Caldwell, eds. 2005. *The Cultural Politics of Food and Eating*. Malden, MA: Blackwell.

Weber, Max. 1976. *The Protestant Ethic and the Spirit of Capitalism*. New York: Routledge.

Wen, Jung-kwang, and Ching-lun Wang. 1981. "Shen-k'uei Syndrome: A Culture-specific Sexual Neurosis in Taiwan." In *Normal and Abnormal Behavior in Chinese Culture*, edited by Arthur Kleinman and Tsung-yi Lin, 357–69. Boston: D. Reidel.

Whitehead, Stephen E., and Frank Barrett, eds. 2002. *The Masculinities Reader*. New York: Polity.

Wu, Fei. 2010. *Suicide and Justice: A Chinese Perspective*. London: Routledge.

Wu Liande. 1932. "Preface." In *Jiankang shenghuo* [The healthy life] by H. M. Miller. i–iv. Shanghai: Shanghai shizhao baoguan.

Wu, Yi-Li. 2010. *Reproducing Women*. Berkeley: University of California Press.

Wu, Yiching. 2014. *The Cultural Revolution at the Margins: Chinese Socialism in Crisis*. Cambridge, MA: Harvard University Press.

Wu Zhiwang. 1996 [1626]. *Jiyin jiyang gangmu* [To benefit yin and yang: A comprehensive guide]. Beijing: Zhongguo zhongyiyao chubanshe.

Wuzhou Shi Zhongxiyijiehe Lingdaoxiaozu Bangongshi. 1977. *Zhongyixue xuanbian* [A collection of articles of TCM].

Xiao, Suowei. 2011. "The 'Second-Wife' Phenomenon and the Relational Construction of Class-Coded Masculinities in Contemporary China." *Men and Masculinities* 14 (5): 607–27.

Xiaoren. 1998. "Shi shui rang nanren yingbuqilai?" [Who makes men unable to get "hard on"?]. *Shishang* [Trend for gentlemen] 2 (3): 67–69.

Xu Hao. 2007. "Wunian 670 beijing shewai zhishichanquan xingzheng an liucheng waiqi shengsu" [Foreign companies won 60 percent of 670 cases of intellectual property involving international parties over the past 5 years handled in Beijing]. *China Economic Weekly*, January 8. Accessed January 17, 2007. http://www.zgjjzk .cn/more.asp?TN-NID=2007-01-08-10101.

Xu Kun. 2000. "Gouri de zuqiu" [The fucking soccer]. In *Shiji zhi men* [The gate of the century], edited by Dai Jinhua, 330–49. Beijing: Shehuikexue wenxian chubanshe.

Xu Zidong. 2012. "Chong du wenge" [Re-read the Cultural Revolution]. *Southern Weekend*, February 23. http://www.infzm.com/content/71089.

Yan, Yunxiang. 1996. *The Flow of Gifts*. Palo Alto, CA: Stanford University Press.

Yan, Yunxiang. 2003. *Private Life under Socialism: Love, Intimacy, and Family Change in a Chinese Village 1949–1999*. Palo Alto, CA: Stanford University Press.

Yan, Yunxiang. 2010. *The Individualization of Chinese Society*. New York: Berg.

Yan Zhenghua. 1996. "Duanlian, jiankang he changshou" [Physical exercise, health and longevity]. In *Minglao zhongyi tan yangsheng zhi dao* [Renowned and old doctors of Chinese medicine speak of the way of yangsheng], edited by Li Junde, 328. Beijing: Huaxia chubanshe.

Yang Boqin. 1963. "Linchuang yanan er li" [Two clinical cases]. *Jiangxi zhongyi* [The Jiangxi journal of Chinese medicine], no. 5: 27.

Yang, Jie. 2010. "The Crisis of Masculinity: Class, Gender, and Kindly Power in Post-Mao China." *American Ethnologist* 37 (3): 550–62.

Yang, Mayfair, ed. 1999. *Spaces of Their Own*. Minneapolis: University of Minnesota Press.

Yang Xixian. 1962. "Ziwo anmo fangzhi yijing yangwei" [The therapy of self-massage in curing and preventing spermatorrhea and impotence]. *Fujian zhongyi* [Fujian journal of traditional Chinese medicine], February: 25.

Yang Zuomei. 1977. "Yangwei" [Impotence]. *Xin Zhongyi*, February: 10.

Yasuyori, Tamba, ed. 1997 [1984]. *Yixin fang*, vol. 21. In *Zhonghua xingxue guanzhi* [An ultimate collection of Chinese sexological classics], edited by Fan Youping, Shi Zhichao, Chen Zihua, and Zhao Fengqin, 99–154. Guangzhou: Guangdong renmin chubanshe.

Ye Juquan. 1930. "Zhangguo yiyao weisheng changshi" [The common sense of hygiene in Chinese medicine]. *Yijie Chunqiu* 5 (52): 16–19.

Ye Shaogong. 1983. "Zhouzongli guanxin xingjiaoyu" [Premier Zhou is concerned about sex education]. *Fu mu bi du*, no. 4: 3–4.

Young, Robert J. C. 1995. *Colonial Desire: Hybridity in Theory, Culture and Race*. New York: Routledge.

Yuan, J., A. N. Hoang, C. A. Romero, H. Lin, Y. Dai, and R. Wang. 2010. "Vacuum Therapy in Erectile Dysfunction—Science and Clinical Evidence." *International Journal of Impotence Research* 22: 211–19.

Zeng Tianzhi. 1937. "Yijingbing de zhenjiu liaofa" [Acupuncture treatment of yijing]. *Guoyi dizhu yuekan* 1 (January): 42–44.

Zhan, Mei. 2009. *Other-Worldly: Making Chinese Medicine through Transnational Frames*. Durham, NC: Duke University Press.

Zhang, Everett Yuehong. 2001. "Goudui and the State: Constructing Entrepreneurial Masculinity in Two Cosmopolitan Areas of Postsocialist China." In *Gendered Modernities: Ethnographic Perspectives*, edited by Dorothy Hodgson, 235–65. New York: Palgrave.

Zhang, Everett Yuehong. 2003. "Power, Agency, and Medicine in China." *Metascience* 12: 325–29.

Zhang, Everett Yuehong. 2007a. "Switching between Traditional Chinese Medicine and Viagra: Cosmopolitanism and Medical Pluralism Today." *Medical Anthropology* 26 (2): 53–96.

Zhang, Everett Yuehong. 2007b. "The Birth of Nanke (Men's Medicine): The Making of the Subject of Desire." *American Ethnologist* 34 (3): 491–508.

Zhang, Everett Yuehong. 2011a. "Governmentality in China." Introduction to *Governance of Life in Chinese Moral Experience: The Quest for an Adequate Life*, edited by Everett Zhang, Arthur Kleinman, and Weiming Tu, 1–30. London: Routledge.

Zhang, Everett Yuehong. 2011b. "The Truth about the Death Toll in the Great Leap Famine in Sichuan: An Analysis of Maoist Sovereignty." In *Governance of Life in Chinese Moral Experience: The Quest for an Adequate Life*, edited by Everett Zhang, Arthur Kleinman, and Weiming Tu, 62–80. London: Routledge.

Zhang, Everett Yuehong. 2011c. "China's Sexual Revolution." In *Deep China*, co-authored by Arthur Kleinman et al., 106–51. Berkeley: University of California Press.

Zhang, Everett Yuehong. 2013. "Flows between the Media and the Clinic: Desiring Production and Social Production in Urban Beijing." In *Media, Erotics, and Transnational Asia*, edited by Purnima Mankaker and Louisa Schein. Durham, NC: Duke University Press.

Zhang, Heqing. 2006. "Female Sex Sellers and the Public Policy in the People's Republic." In *Sex and Sexuality in China*, edited by Elaine Jeffreys, 139–58. London: Routledge.

Zhang Jiebin. 1991. *Jingyue quanshu* [A complete collection of works by Jingyue]. Beijing: Renmin weisheng chubanshe.

Zhang Jingsheng. 1998. *Zhang Jingsheng wenji* [A collection of articles by Zhang Jingsheng]. Guangzhou: Guangzhou press.

Zhang, Jingyuan. 1992. *Psychoanalysis in China: Literary Transformations 1919–1949*. Ithaca, NY: Cornell University East Asia Program.

Zhang, Li. 2010. *In Search of Paradise: Middle-Class Living in a Chinese Metropolis*. Ithaca, NY: Cornell University Press.

Zhang, Li, and Aihwa Ong, eds. 2008. *Privatizing China: Socialism from Afar*. Ithaca, NY: Cornell University Press.

Zhang Qicheng and Qu Limin. 2005. *Zhonghua yangsheng zhihui* [The Chinese wisdom of nurturing life]. Beijing: Huaxia chubanshe.

Zhang Shusheng. 1995. "Yangwei cong gan lunzhi kaolue" [An examination of the treating of impotence through the liver]. *Beijing Zhongyi*, no. 5: 14–15.

Zhang Xianliang. 1992 [1985]. *Nanren de Yiban shi Nüren* [Half a man is woman]. Beijing: Huayi chubanshe.

Zhang Xianglong. 1996. *Heidegger he zhongguo tiandao* [Heidegger and Chinese heaven's way]. Beijing: Sanlian chubanshe.

Zhang, Xudong. 1998. "Marxism and the Historicity of Theory: An Interview with Fredric Jameson." *New Literary History* 29: 353–83.

Zhang Xuemei. 2004. "150 wan zhang chufang kaichu: Weige jintian jin yaofang" [1.5 million prescriptions have been written: Viagra enters pharmacies today]. *Beijing Evening News*, Sept. 27.

Zhang Zhongjing. 1997. *Jingui yaolue* [Medical treasures of the golden chamber]. Annotated by Yu Zhixian and Zhang Zhiji. Beijing: Zhongyi guji chubanshe.

Zhang, Yanhua. 2007. *Transforming Emotions with Chinese Medicine: An Ethno-*

graphic Account from Contemporary China. Albany, NY: State University of New York Press.

Zhang Yinan. 2002. *Huangdi Neijing Suwen Jizhu* [An annotated exegesis of plain question of Yellow Emperor's Inner Canon]. Beijing: Xueyuan chubanshe.

Zhang Youjun. 1990. *Zhongguo Nanke Yian* [Cases of nanke in Chinese medicine]. Tianjin: Tianjin Keji fanyi chubangongsi.

Zhang Zelin. 1931. "Zhilin yilu biji: Yangwei" [Clinical notes on impotence]. *Yijie chunqiu* 5 (56): 23.

Zhao Hongjun.1989. *Jingdai zhongyi lunzheng shi* [A history of the polemics between Chinese medicine and Western medicine in modern times]. Hefei: Anhui kexue jishu chubanshe.

Zheng, Tiantian. 2009. *Red Lights*. Minneapolis: University of Minnesota Press.

Zhong, Xueping. 2000. *Masculinity Besieged? Issues of Modernity and Male Subjectivity in Chinese Literature of the Late Twentieth Century*. Durham, NC: Duke University Press.

Zhong Youbin, Tan Yuci, and Zhang Jianxue. 1988. "Xingshenghuo bu hexie zai lihun zhong de zuoyong" [The impact of inharmonious sexual life on divorce]. *Journal of Chinese Psychological Hygiene* 2 (2): 76–77.

Zhongguo tongji nianjian 1999 [China Statistics Almanac 1999]. Beijing: Zhongguo tongji chubanshe.

Zhongguo tongji zhaiyao 1999 [China Statistics Digest 1999]. Beijing: Zhongguo tongji chubanshe.

Zhonghua quanguo gongshangye lianhehui. 2006. *Zhongguo minying jingji fazhan baogao 2005–2006* [A report of the development of China's non-state-owned economy 2005–2006]. Beijing: Shehui kexue wenxian chubanshe.

Zhou Chen, ed. 1997. [Qing Dynasty]. *Housheng xunzuan* [The interpretation and compilation of ideas on treating life kindly]. In *Shouyang congshu quanji* [A complete collection of books on longevity and cultivation]. Compiled by Hu Wenhuan, collated by Li Jingwei et al. Beijing: Zhongguo zhongyiyao chubanshe.

Zhou Yihu and Yang Xiaomin. 1999. *Zhongguo de danwei zhidu* [The danwei system in China]. Beijing: Zhongguo jingji chubanshe.

Zhou Zijian. 1936. "Mengyi texiaofang" [An effective formula for curing yijing in dream]. *Zhongyi shijie* 9 (6): 47–48.

Zhu Xi, ed. 1995. *ErCheng yulu* [Teachings of Cheng Yi and Cheng Hao]. Jinan: Qilu shushe.

Zhu Zhenheng. 1982. *Ge zhi yu lun*. In *Nanxi xiansheng yizhu sizhong*. Nanjing: Jiangsu guangling guji keyinshe.

Žižek, Slavoj. 1999. *The Ticklish Subject*. New York: Verso.

Žižek, Slavoj. 2010. "Deleuze and the Lacanian Real." Accessed January 14, 2011. http://www.lacan.com/symptom11/?p=346.

Zou Yunxiang. 1956. *Zhongyi shenbing Liaofa* [Therapies of Chinese medicine for the illnesses of the kidney]. Nanjing: Jingsu renmin chubanshe.

Illustrations are indicated by *f*. Tables are indicated by *t*. Notes are indicated by n.

the body (*continued*)

68–69, 105, 111, 112, 119, 204; sacrifice of, 60–61, 150–54, 237n8; self-castration (*zigong*), 43–46, 235n18; sexual positions, 117, 118–19, 189, 207, 240n6, 241n10; shenti as, 9–10, 229n5, 239n11; somatic awareness, 201–2, 241n11, 249n8; tiyan (experience), 9, 229n4; women's knowledge of, 84–85. *See also* desire, sexual; intercorporeality, sexual; yangsheng (Cultivation of Life)

bodying forth, 202–3, 207, 209

boqi zhangai (erectile dysfunction). *See* ED

Boss, Medard, 202, 250n10

Bourdieu, Pierre, 232n19

The Builders (Ren Yibo), 88, 89f, 92–93

Bullough, Vera, 52

business culture: alcohol consumption, 145–49; debt in, 146–47, 149; entrepreneurial masculinity, 21; impact on marriage, 125–26, 144–45; impotence connected with lifestyle of, 5, 11–12, 51, 92, 121, 130, 147–48

Cao Kaiyong, 36, 91, 141, 175

capitalism, 13, 14, 18, 25, 230n9, 237n8

carnal space, 118, 119, 120, 241n10, 241n11

castration, 43–46, 183, 235n18

Chan, Anita, 67

Chang Che-chia, 233n5

Chen Heliang, 36

Chen Wenbo, 175

Chinese medicine. *See* TCM (traditional Chinese medicine)

Christianity, 5, 46, 164

chushen (family origin), 76–81

circumcision, 103

class discrimination, 75–82, 83, 84, 214–15

Cohen, Lawrence, 44, 232n16

Collcutt, Martin, 230n8

Collection of Perspectives of Chinese Medicine (Wang Shenxuan), 138–39

collectivism: the body, 21, 60–61, 68–70, 150–54; desire and, 9, 42–44, 53, 62–65, 68–70; individualism (gerenzhuyi), 9, 13–14, 60–61, 150–52, 154–55, 237n8; mobility under, 55–56, 57; in post-Mao China, 14; self-sacrifice in, 60–61, 150–52, 237n8; yangsheng (Cultivation of Life), 150–54, 155

Collier, Stephen, 248n22

consumer culture: alcohol consumption, 145–49, 156, 175; choices in, 156–58; illicit sex, 4, 45, 48; impotence connected with, 11–12; loss of jing (seminal essence), 19, 25, 36; pornography, 107, 108, 110–12, 189, 212; sexual desire in, 217, 218–19; xiaojie (sex workers), 48, 108–10, 121, 126, 130, 144, 213, 231n14

cosmopolitanism, 195–97, 223, 247n17

Crossley, Nick, 117

Csordas, Thomas J., 202, 232nn18,19, 250n8

CUHTCM (Hospital of Chengdu University of Traditional Chinese Medicine): commingling of TCM and biomedicine in, 16–17; nanke department of, 17, 31, 36; potency treatments at, 185–86; terminology for impotence, 192–93, 248n20; urology and nanke in, 29; yi-jing treatments at, 36, 37t, 41

Cultural Revolution: blood line theory, 83; chushen (family origin) in, 76–81; food shortages, 93–96, 143–44, 156, 175, 222, 239n14, 244n17; forced relocations during, 84, 87, 99, 235n1; impotence treatments during, 39–40; laosanjie (old three classes), 15, 23, 74–76, 84, 207; naked body in, 68–69, 111, 112, 204; parental status during, 76, 151–52; Red Guards during, 67, 74, 75, 76; sex education during, 204,

ED (erectile dysfunction) (*continued*)
psychotherapy for, 201–2; surgical
procedures for, 209–11; touching and
erectile failure, 119, 241n13; trauma
as cause of, 97–98; treatments for,
7–8, 31, 209–11; yangwei (impotence,
shrinking of yang), 1, 26, 31, 174, 192–
93, 194, 233n3, 246n7
ejaculation: premature ejaculation, 31,
102–3, 108–9, 118, 208; self-regulation
of, 159; spermatorrhea, 31, 139, 141–
45, 233n4, 234n13, 235n17. *See also* yijing (nocturnal emission)
embodiment, 24, 232n18
emotionality (*qingzhi*), 171, 193
employment: *dingti*, 238n3; illegal businesses, 90–91; impotence connected
with, 10, 127; job assignments after
high school graduation (*biye fenpei*),
58, 59–60; moral implications of unemployment, 89–91, 239nn9,10; separation of couples for, 52–55, 57, 58–60,
93; xiagang (laid off), 23–24, 87–92,
99, 127, 182, 231n14, 239nn9,10. *See
also* danwei system; hukou system
Engels, Friedrich, 236n5
erectile dysfunction. *See* ED (erectile dysfunction)
erections: after job layoffs, 88–90, 91,
99, 127, 182; bodying forth, 202–3,
207, 209; of infant males, 198; intracorporeal self-injection, 211; moral
economy of sexuality, 144–45, 183–89;
performance anxiety, 103–4, 108–10;
potency, 8, 33–34, 181–82; sex education for, 204–6; sexual satisfaction,
108–10, 185–87, 189, 204–6; shen (the
kidney), 33–34; *sheng* (strength of
life), 200; somatic awareness, 201–2,
249n8; touching and erectile failure,
119, 241n13
Ermo (movie), 4, 29–30

eroticism, 4–5, 53, 69, 80, 93, 94, 105,
142, 176–77

Farquhar, Judith, 9, 19, 29–30, 64, 136,
149, 195, 249n6
Feng Zhaozhang, 249n5
Ferguson, James, 247n17
fieldwork: biomedicine v. TCM in, 16,
23; geographic locations of, 16, 22;
groups of patients in, 23; motivations
for research, 225–26; site selection,
15–16, 17, 22–23; social networks,
15–16; surveys in/survey cohorts, 16,
17–18, 22–23, 229n6
filial piety, 97–99
film, 4, 29–30, 64, 68, 69, 107
five black categories, 52, 72–73
five inadequacies in a man (*wu bu nan*),
35
food, 93–96, 143–44, 156, 175, 222,
239n14, 244n17
forced relocations, 84, 87, 99, 235n1
Foster, George, 140, 243n13
Foucault, Michel: on biopower, 82,
232n19, 239n5; on books as experience, 225–26; on care of self, 162, 163;
Greeks on sexual moderation, 164; on
modernity, 228; modernity explored
by, 225–26; on phenomenology,
250n15; on the production of labor,
59, 237n8; relationship between ethics
and freedom, 245n22; on repression,
59, 236n7; on sexual pleasure, 162–
64, 227, 241n12; on Western epistemology, 245n22
freedom, 163–64, 245n22
Freud, Sigmund: on impotence, 6–7,
109; on infant sexuality, 198; Oedipus
complex, 7, 13, 45, 96, 230n9; psychic
impotence, 6–7; on sexual repression,
59; on social transformations, 12
frotteurism, 43–44

fuke (gynecology), 30–31, 233n2
Fu Lianzhang, 152–54, 244n18
Furth, Charlotte, 31, 199

Galen, 163, 164
Gilmore, David, 35
Goffman, Erwin, 117, 241n10
Goldstein, Irving, 8
goudui (thicken the relationship), 5,
   125–26, 149
Great Famine, 95–96, 239n14, 244n17
Great Leap Forward, 54–55, 95–96, 99,
   150–51, 239n14, 244n17
Greeks, 19, 160–64
Gregor, Thomas, 35
Guattari, Félix: on desire, 67; lines,
   22–23; production of desire, 13–14,
   18, 25, 219, 230n9; *A Thousand Pla-
   teaus* (Deleuze and Guattari), 74
Gupta, Akhil, 196
Gutmann, Matthew, 34

Hacking, Ian, 176
Half a Man Is Woman (Zhang Xianliang), 4, 51
Haraway, Donna, 212
Hay, John, 68
heart (*xin*), 91, 92, 243n11
Heated Era (*Huohong de niandai*), 64
Heidegger, Martin, 201, 202, 209,
   245n22, 250n10
herbal medicine: kidney-centered perspective, 173, 185, 188, 191; for nocturnal emissions, 218; profits from
   prescribed medication, 192; switching
   between Viagra and herbal therapies,
   183–87, 188, 189–90, 194–97, 248n22,
   248n24; as treatment for impotence,
   16, 38, 91, 136–37, 141, 142, 186, 213;
   in the United States, 248n24; Viagra,
   179, 182–83, 184, 185–86, 223; *zhuangyangyao*, 39, 91, 173, 176–77, 177f

Hershatter, Gail, 14, 50
Honig, Emily, 14, 52–53
hormone therapies, 160–61, 244n21
How the Steel Was Tempered (Ostrovsky), 64
hukou system: employment under,
   55–59; physical separation under,
   52–55, 57, 58–60, 93; quotas in, 56;
   rural-urban divide, 22, 23, 24, 55–57,
   84, 87, 99
hunger, 94–96, 143–44, 175, 239n14
hybridity, 196, 248n22
Hyde, Alan, 237n8

imagined impotence: opening life up
   to the world, 214–17; parental dominance, 103–7; performance anxiety,
   34–35, 106, 108–10, 203, 204–9, 212–
   14; pornography, 107, 108, 110–12,
   189, 212; sexual inexperience, 106,
   108–10, 203, 204–9, 214; social context of, 101–7, 109–10
impotence: advertisements, 1, 2–4, 3f,
   4f, 222f, 234n14; back pain, 166, 167,
   168–69; changing terminology for,
   26, 174, 192–94, 248n20; as death,
   199–200, 249n5; de-moralization
   of, 47–48, 49, 235n20; history of, 5,
   31, 37–39, 46–47, 138, 233n3; media
   coverage of, 1–5, 17, 68, 69, 107, 217,
   222, 231n14, 234n14; in medical literature, 35–36, 235n16; moral symptomatology, 32–33, 35–36, 39, 41–46,
   52, 69–70; political implications of
   treatments, 39, 51–52; psychotherapy
   for, 6–7, 16, 118, 121–22, 171, 245n11;
   reproductive failure, 35–36, 71, 208,
   213–14, 234n9, 234n10, 234n12; as
   shameful, 9–11, 34–35, 39–41, 49;
   vitality, 18, 33–34, 167, 181, 246n7. *See
   also* desire, sexual; ED (erectile dysfunction); herbal medicine; mascu-

rural-urban divide, 22, 23, 24, 55–57, 84, 87, 99

sacrifice, ethos of, 60–61, 150–52, 237n8
Scheper-Hughes, Nancy, 95–96
Schipper, Kristofer, 247n15
Scott-Bradley-Timm inflatable prosthesis, 209–10
Searle, John, 201, 211
self-castration (*zigong*), 43–46, 235n18
self-control, 63–64, 157–60, 162–65, 245n22
self-injection therapy, 210–11, 244n21
semen. *See* jing (Seminal Essence); yijing (nocturnal emission)
seminal essence. *See* jing (Seminal Essence)
sensitization therapy (Masters and Johnson), 7, 109, 114, 115, 193, 241n11
sex education, 43, 203–7, 205f, 213
sex shops, 20f, 42f
sexual inexperience, 106, 108–10, 203, 204–9, 214
sex workers (*xiaojie*), 48, 108–10, 121, 126, 130, 213, 231n14
Sha Yexin, 20
shen (kidney). *See* kidney (shen)
shen (spirit), 92, 181, 239n11
sheng (strength of life), 200, 249n6
shenghuo payment (survival fee, pension), 89, 239n9
shenti, 9–10, 229n5, 239n11
shuaishou liaofa (swinging hands), 155
shugan (smoothing out the liver), 170, 171, 172, 173
Shusterman, Richard, 202, 249n8
sin, historical transformation of, 45–46
Sivin, Nathan, 242n5
smoothing out the liver (*shugan*), 170, 171, 172, 173
social status: access to Viagra, 179–80; biological ties, 81–83; *chushen* (family origin) in, 76–80; employees of state-

owned enterprises, 90, 91, 92; family origin, 76–77, 105, 151–52; five black categories, 52, 72–73; *laosanjie* (old three classes), 15, 23, 74–76, 84, 207; marriage and, 72–74, 76–80, 84–87, 105; reversal of class status in reform period, 74–80; urban-rural relocations, 22–24, 55–57, 84–85, 87, 99; xia-gang (laid off), 89–91, 239nn9,10
somatic awareness, 201–2, 241n11, 249n8
soul, cultivation of, 163
spermatorrhea, 31, 139, 141–45, 233n4, 234n13, 235n17
Stacey, Judith, 238n3
Stallone, Sylvester, 21, 231n14
Stekel, Wilhelm, 7, 96, 109
stepping down (*xiagang* [laid off]), 23–24, 87–92, 99, 127, 182, 231n14, 239nn9,10
surplus repression (Marcuse), 58–59
survival fee, 89, 239n9
Swan Lake, 68, 69
switching between Viagra and herbal therapies, 183–87, 188, 194–97, 248n22, 248n24

Takakura, Ken, 21, 231n14
talk shows, 1–2, 17, 217, 231n14
TCM (traditional Chinese medicine): on alcohol consumption, 148; on back pain, 168–69; biomedicine and, 16–17, 22, 190–93; clinical reasoning in, 171–72; cosmopolitanism, 195–97, 247n17; depression in, 172; efficacy of, 195; five un-malenesses in, 35; kidney defined in, 169, 170–71; *neike* (internal medicine), 34; switching between Viagra and herbal therapies, 183–87, 188, 194–97, 248n22, 248n24; treatments for impotence in, 8–9, 15, 33–34, 172–74, 246n4, 246n6; use of terms in, 192–93, 247n19, 248n20; viability of, 195; Viagra and, 25, 185; yijing in,

37–38, 235n17. *See also* CUHTCM (Hospital of Chengdu University of Traditional Chinese Medicine)

A Thousand Plateaus (Deleuze and Guattari), 74

"Three emphases campaign," 41

Three Gorges Dam Museum (Chongqing), 225

Three Years of Natural Disaster, 99

Throop, C. Jason, 232n18

ti, 9, 229n5

Tianjin Heping Nanke Hospital, 36, 175

tiyan (experience), 9, 229n4

touching, 78, 102–3, 117, 118, 119–23, 238n2, 241nn10,11,12,13

Treichler, Paula, 29

TV call-in shows, 1–2

United States, 5, 193, 248n24

urology: blood dynamics in, 8, 172–73, 194, 210; drug-induced erection, 211; self-injection therapy, 210–11, 244n21; on sexual abstinence, 55; treatment of impotence, 8, 22, 26, 29–30, 34, 191, 244n21. *See also* Viagra

van Gulik, Robert, 114, 247n15

Vasavi, A. R., 248n22

VCD (vacuum constriction device), 250n13

venous ligation, 110

Viagra: affordability of, 179–80; as aphrodisiac, 180–81; Chinese medicine, 167–68, 170; effect on potency, 181–82, 247n14; feared dependency on, 179, 180–81, 184; herbal medicine, 179, 182–83, 184, 185–86, 223; International Index of Erectile Failure (IIEF-5), 71; invention of, 211–12; marital relations/marital fidelity, 188–90; marketing of, 176–78, 177f, 179–80, 230n8; nocturnal emissions,

218; penile rigidity, 185–87, 209–11; Pfizer pharmaceuticals, 1–2, 18, 176, 178, 179, 193, 194f; phallocentrism, 247n14; reception in China, 16, 18, 25, 178–83, 247n14; and the shift to biomedicine, 191–92; switching between Viagra and herbal therapies, 183–87, 188, 189–90, 194–95, 196, 248n22, 248n24; TCM and, 25, 181–83

virginity, 78–79, 80

virility, 39, 86–87, 91, 139–40, 173, 176–77

vitality, 18, 33–34, 167, 181, 246n7

voyeurism, 66–68, 110–11

Walder, Andrew, 56–57

Wang Qi, 141, 171, 174

Wang Shenxuan, 138–39

Watson, James, 96

Weber, Max, 46, 164

Weige, 176–77, 179

wen (cultural attainment), 231n14

white (color), 93, 94

will to impotence (Stekel), 96

women: alternative intercorporeality, 129–30, 129–31, 183, 223, 247n14; athleticism of, 20, 231n13; aunts, 93–94, 96, 100; bodies of, 35, 68–69, 84–85, 105, 111, 112, 119, 122–23, 204, 207; as caregivers, 93–94, 96, 100; class status, 72–73, 76–77, 78–79, 80, 84; death of daughter-in-law, 97–99; experience with impotence, 12, 14, 53, 106, 121, 123–29, 143–45, 188–90, 231n15, 240n6, 247n14, 247n18; fuke (gynecology), 30–31, 233n2; on impotence, 12, 85–86, 121, 231n15; intercorporeal intimacy, 79–80, 111–12, 115–16, 119–20, 241n13; on moral economy of sexuality, 143–45; as partner surrogates, 114–15, 240n6; self-censorship, 63–64; separation of spouses in Maoist era, 52–55, 57, 59–60, 85, 93, 103–4;

women (*continued*)
sexual desire of, 14, 19–20, 84–86, 123–26, 189–90, 207, 231n15, 240n6, 247n14; on Viagra use, 247n14, 247n18; as xiaojie (sex workers), 48, 108–10, 121, 126, 130, 213, 231n14
wu (martial valor), 231n14
Wu Zhiwang, 243n11

xiagang (laid off), 23–24, 87–92, 99, 127, 182, 231n14, 239nn9,10
xiaojie (sex workers), 48, 108–10, 121, 126, 130, 144, 213, 231n14
xin (heart), 91, 92, 243n11
Xing wangguo de yinmi shijie (A Secret World in the Kingdom of Sexuality), 54
xisheng (sacrifice), 60–61, 150–52, 237n8

Yan, Yunxiang, 14, 102
yangsheng (Cultivation of Life): center for, at Mountain of Female Immortals, 113, 114–16; in Daoist literature, 19, 149, 244n16; diet, 156, 157, 158; jing in, 19, 25, 149, 158, 164–65, 223; in the Maoist era, 150–54, 155; qigong, 18, 19, 154, 244n16; as regulation of desire, 19, 25, 136, 154, 159–60, 161, 162, 223; sexual gratification, 156, 160, 161, 244n21; in TCM (traditional Chinese medicine), 149, 156–58; xisheng (sacrifice), 60–61, 150–52, 237n8
yangwei (impotence, shrinking of yang), 1, 26, 31, 174, 192–93, 194, 233n3, 246n7
Yang Wenzhi, 203, 205f, 206, 209
Yellow Emperor, 135, 148, 228
yijing (nocturnal emission): in adolescence, 213; bodily stress causing, 141; historical perceptions of, 37–39, 138;

in Maoist era, 23–24, 42–43; in medical literature, 38–39, 234n14; sexual neurasthenia, 39–41; spermatorrhea, 31, 139, 141–45, 233n4, 234n13, 235n17; treatment of, 31, 36, 37t, 41, 42–43, 47
yikanwan (herbal pill), 185
yindao (yin path, the vagina), 174
yinjing (yin stem, the penis), 174
yinwei (shrinking of the yin), 174, 175, 199, 246n6
yin-yang balance, 20, 34, 138, 199, 231n14, 243n10
Young, Robert J. C., 248n22
Yuanling County Hospital (Hunan Province), 30
Yue Fujia, 233n3
Yu Luoke, 83
Yuquan Hospital, 16–17, 178–79
Yu Zhen, 199

Zai Maozhuxi de jiaodao xia (Fu Lianzhang), 153
Zhan, Mei, 248n24
Zhang, Qicheng, 19, 136, 149, 249n6
Zhang Jie, 63
Zhang Jiebin (Zhang Jingyue), 243n10, 246n7
Zhang Jingsheng, 117, 175, 236n3, 241n8
Zhang Xianliang, 4, 51–52
zhiqing (educated youth), 75, 238n1
Zhishi fenzi (intellectual), 72
Zhong, Xueping, 21
Zhou Enlai, 204, 206–7
zhuangyangyao, 39, 91, 173, 176–77, 177f
Zhuangzi, 136, 245n22
Zhu Zhenheng, 246n7
zigong (self-castration), 43–46, 235n18
Žižek, Slavoj, 183